Consumers
and the
Market

An Introductory Analysis

Consumers and the Market

An Introductory Analysis

SECOND EDITION

Roger M. Swagler

UNIVERSITY OF TENNESSEE
KNOXVILLE

D. C. HEATH AND COMPANY
Lexington, Massachusetts   Toronto

To

Anne Reneé, Tracy, and Karl Andrew

Preface

The late 1970s have been years of significant change for consumers. The basic problems of the market place haven't changed, of course, but the energy crisis, continuing inflation, and a growing concern about the role of government have combined to lend a mood of uncertainty to the entire market structure. The manner in which this uncertainty is resolved may itself be a key to the development of consumer issues during the 1980s. At the present time, consumers are in a passive, private mood. They have less interest in causes or movements than in their personal fulfillment.

The changing consumer mood can be tied to uncertainty about the future, but it can also be traced to a certain disillusionment with the past. Many consumer-oriented efforts turned out to be expensive annoyances. As a result of these unsuccessful efforts, progress toward extending consumer protection has been uneven. The proposed Agency for Consumer Advocacy remains just a proposal, although the Federal Trade Commission has launched significant new initiatives in areas ranging from children's advertising to funerals.

The past few years have also brought some changes to both scholarship and teaching in consumer economics. Consumer-related questions have attracted more serious attention, brightening the prospects for the future. In the classroom, students are being exposed to more sophisticated material. Again, progress is uneven, but it is still progress.

These changes in consumer mood explain the need for a revised edition of *Caveat Emptor*. When it first appeared four years ago, the book represented something of a departure from conventional approaches. Now, however, the approach is more generally accepted, which means there is less need to press for change in this area and more opportunity to get down to the issues. This emphasis on issues explains the more subdued tone of *Consumers and the Market*, Second Edition.

The most obvious change in this edition is the title, which more accurately describes present attitudes toward consumer education. These attitudes call for a closer analysis of the interaction between the consumer and the marketplace. They do not require the admonition of "buyer beware." Each chapter has been revised to accommodate new material and many have been completely rewritten. A new chapter, "Emerging Issues for the 1980s," has been added. The annotated bibliographies have been updated and contain a balance of elementary and more advanced material. The Study Questions and Suggested Projects have also been revised.

For all the changes, however, the basic approach of the book remains the same. Underlying this approach is one of the central concepts of economics—the satisfaction of human wants. From this concept it follows that consumption is a goal of economic activity. Therefore, it is only logical to apply the *basic* principles of economic *analysis* to the *actual* problems consumers face in the *marketplace*. This supposition is the basis of *Consumers and the Market*.

Basic. No elaborate theoretical procedures are needed to investigate consumer problems; fundamental economic principles are sufficient. This means that students who lack a background in economics can still follow the analysis.

Analysis. Describing consumer problems is important, but it is also necessary to place them within an overall framework. Analysis provides students with the means for penetrating the surface and exploring the causes of problems. It also provides cohesion, so that problems are seen as part of an overall pattern instead of random developments.

Actual. Consumers face a variety of problems in their daily lives. These must be covered in any treatment of economics. Abstraction is necessary, but application to real-world problems is equally important.

Marketplace. This is the key to the analysis in the book. Consumers must operate in a large, impersonal marketplace that has the capacity to overpower them. Therefore, understanding the market forces that work on the consumer is the key to understanding consumer problems.

The questions and projects included at the end of the chapters identify important points, suggesting both applications and further lines of inquiry. (No projects are included in Chapters 2 or 11. The material in those chapters does not lend itself to that approach.) Individual instructors can use the projects to whatever degree they see fit. The type of course and the size of the class will determine their appropriateness. My experience has been that the projects are useful in providing students with concrete examples of the topics from the text. They furnish practical laboratory experience for students to develop their understanding of economics. The Appendix contains a detailed discussion of the projects.

The annotated Bibliography and Suggested Readings included with each chapter serve a dual purpose by providing references for the footnotes and a list of additional readings. The annotations identify elementary as well as more difficult readings, thus accommodating students with differing backgrounds and interests. They also give guidance to students who want to read further on a particular question.

I would like to acknowledge my thanks to colleagues around the country who were so supportive of the first edition and whose helpful comments contributed to the changes in this revision. I owe a particular debt to the students who provided suggestions based on their own experience with the book. I should also thank my colleagues at the University of Tennessee for their help in this effort; I am particularly grateful for the support of Judith Kuipers and the help of David Eastwood. Julia Marlowe provided much needed help with research, and Beth Rice proved again that she is a blue-ribbon typist.

As before, I am indebted to my editors at D. C. Heath for their patience and support. My wife Carol Anne deserves special apologies and thanks, for reasons I know are obvious to her. Finally, this edition is dedicated with love and appreciation to our children, who, as I am discovering, are much more capable consumers than I was at their age. If that remains true, then there is hope for future consumers.

R.M.S.

Contents

Consumers and the Market

An Introductory Analysis

-1-

The Genesis of
Consumer Problems

Introduction

A Fact of Life

In 1626 the quiet of the Manhattan Island wilderness was broken by a voice crying, "We've been taken by the Indians!" Had a group of frightened colonists been captured by savage natives? No, it turned out to be a case for Ralph Nader, not John Wayne. The occasion was the Dutch purchase of the island from the Indians, not the first instance of consumer fraud in America, but certainly one of the best remembered.

As schoolchildren learn the story, it was the Dutchman Peter Minuit who bilked the Indians out of the land. But the Indian chief Manhasset knew what he was doing. His Canarsee tribe did not even own the island; they were just passing through when they happened on the Dutch. Manhattan was common hunting ground for *all* the tribes in the area. It is no surprise, then, that Manhasset was only too willing to unload the island on the unsuspecting white men, even if he only got $24 for it.*

Over three and a half centuries have passed since that incident, taking with them the Dutch, the Indians, and the wilderness. Yet cries of "We've been taken!" still ring out, not just over Manhattan, but over the entire United States. They are the cries of dissatisfied con-

---

* There is evidence to support this version of the story, but the details of the incident are still a matter of debate. Perhaps it is best to say, as Winston Churchill did about the legend of King Arthur, "It is all true, or it ought to be."

sumers, their voices blending into a chorus of dissent that marks one of the most significant developments in the American economy in recent years. Should the combination of senseless hunting and residual DDT finally eliminate the bald eagle, as conservationists suggest they might, an angry consumer—fist raised in defiance—would make a fitting replacement as the national symbol.

American consumers are in revolt. That is a fact. Like most revolutions, however, the consumer revolt has gone through several stages. Initially, the consumer's level of consciousness was raised as boycotts, rent strikes, and blasts against do-nothing government agencies became daily features in the news. With the publicity came the recognition that there was a problem, as evidenced by the proliferation of consumer organizations.

Almost immediately, however, there followed a second realization: the problem was more complex than many supposed. Proposed solutions proved inadequate and, in some cases, simply generated more problems. Instead of relief, consumers faced more frustrations. As a result, consumer dissatisfaction continued to grow, extending itself to include many of the efforts that were undertaken in the name of consumer protection.

This is an odd situation, which arises from the fact that the consumer revolt is less a coordinated movement than a spontaneous uprising. It is not being effectively led, let alone controlled, by any individual or group. Individuals continue to think and speak for themselves. The result is a confusing array of crosscurrents, but, despite the contradictions, there is evidence that individuals are rethinking the role of the consumer in a superaffluent society.

As leisure time becomes more important and attitudes toward work change, the word *consumption* itself is being reinterpreted. It is enough to send chills running up and down Madison Avenue—and it has [11]. Such chills, however, are not limited to Madison Avenue. The shock waves that originate with dissatisfied consumers radiate throughout the entire economy. The reason is fairly simple, but critically important. Consumption is such a fundamental part of both our economic and social systems that changes in consumer behavior have implications for the whole society.

The economic importance of consumption is obvious and can be illustrated by considering the impact of consumer expenditures on the economy. Consumption consistently accounts for about two-thirds of the gross national product. This means that consumer spending generates twice as much income as business investments, government expenditures, and expenditures on exports combined. In 1977, consumers spent $1,159 billion out of a gross national product of $1,799 billion [14, p. 4].* Even a small change in consumer spending concerns the experts in Washington and affects everyone from New York stockbrokers to Detroit automobile workers and San Francisco restaurateurs. When consumers buy fewer stocks, cars, meals, or anything else, those businesses will sell less and therefore hire fewer workers. Unemployment goes up and income goes down.

How consumer spending determines income is explained well in most introductory economics books and is not the main concern here [3]. However, while focusing on the consumer per se, you should be aware that what the consumer does has a tremendous impact on economic performance; any radical changes in consumption behavior would revolutionize our thinking on the economy itself. Even that does not tell the whole story, however, for consumption has a social dimension that must be taken into account.

Consumption is an integral part of the American social structure. In other countries the American is stereotyped as a big spender. We often look at ourselves that way, defining success in terms of material well being; indeed, many people equate mass consumption with that cherished abstraction, the American Way of Life. Behind the stereotype, however, there are more significant influences. Consumption patterns reflect the personality of the individual. Fundamental institutions are also involved, because a great deal of consumption is carried out through the family. The dramatic increase of women in the labor force, a development that is closely tied to consumption, illustrates how changing consumption patterns affect the very structure of society.

Consumption and society are related in other ways, too. Consumption is in part culturally determined, and thus can be held up as a mirror of society. Archaeologists can reconstruct the cultures of ancient civilizations through the artifacts they uncover. Similarly, the things we consume—our artifacts—tell a lot about our culture. The earlier reference to the consumer revolt as "one of the most significant developments in the American economy in recent years" is strong language, but hardly an exaggeration. The consumer revolt has the potential for altering the whole structure of American society. Up to now, the changes, while significant, haven't gone very far; however, since both consumption and consumers are normally stable and predictable, *any* variation in their behavior is noteworthy. It is no wonder that consumers are being analyzed with increasing interest and apprehension.

---

* Includes income from unincorporated businesses with consumption.

The Starting Point

Most people would agree, then, that never has there been so much interest in consumer problems. But would there be the same unanimity if that statement were rewritten to read, "Never has there been so much interest in consumer *economics*"? Probably not, and yet the second statement follows directly from the first. In view of that connection, the proper place to look for the content of consumer economics is in the actual problems confronting consumers in the marketplace.

Such an approach requires that we face a whole new set of questions. What are these problems? Where do they originate? How can they be solved? In providing answers to these questions, the study of consumer economics must do more than provide a handy set of tips for shoppers or a how-to guide for buying. Being a good shopper is important, but not enough. The good consumer also understands the present-day marketplace and the consumer's role in it. *The ultimate goal of a study of consumer economics should be to familiarize students with the environment in which they as consumers must operate.* This means not only enabling them to cope with the difficulties of the marketplace as it now exists, but also developing the means to bring about necessary improvement.

That is a lot to ask. When looking into the marketplace, it is not always easy to tell what is happening, let alone why. It is easy for the consumer to get lost among all the complex interrelations of the market. Consumer economics should enable us to make some sense out of it all. That is why we must deal with the everyday problems that confront all consumers, *systematically* analyzing what the problems are and what approaches can lead to their solution. Merely discussing selected consumer problems is not enough. Unless we begin to see how the various problems fit together, we will continue fighting brushfires without getting to the real cause of the blaze.

In fitting the parts together, we will encounter a recurring problem, the division between "big thinkers" and "little thinkers." Big thinkers are prone to talk about the ultimate significance of things, whereas little thinkers are more concerned with the way things work. Economists, as Robert Solow has noted, tend to be little thinkers, concentrating more on the particulars of a question than on its broad implications. He recognizes that there are risks involved in that approach. If we have a "single-minded focus on how the parts of the machine work," we might never think to ask "whether the machine itself is pointed in the right direction" [13, p. 108]. Just as individuals going about their day-to-day tasks as consumers face both big questions and little questions, we must be prepared to deal with a wide range of issues, both big and little. Indeed, the distinction often blurs, because in tracing the impact of some specific development, a little question, we will uncover a problem with broader implications, a big question.

Exploring the Consumer Revolt

Belaboring the Obvious

The consumer revolt is clearly grounded in consumer dissatisfaction and frustration, the immediate sources of which are equally clear. Things seem to cost too much, but the fancy price tags are no guarantee that the product will work when it is out of the store. Even formal guarantees may not help; pity the hapless buyer who returns a silent but supposedly guaranteed radio to find that the guarantee covered only the circuitry and not the faulty tuner.

Services are even more of a problem. A call to a plumber or electrician places the homeowner's bank account in jeopardy, while the only doctors who make housecalls are in television shows (to emphasize that the stories are fictional, no doubt). If something breaks, the frustrations mount even faster. Who hasn't carried a wounded appliance from dealer to repairman to fix-it shop only to conclude that it is cheaper and easier to buy a new one? Even sports fans are not exempt from these frustrations. Star players, and sometimes whole teams, move whenever the grass (or Astro-turf) looks greener elsewhere.*

The consumer has to contend with such problems in day-to-day dealings with legitimate businesses. With the introduction of the all-too-common prospect of consumer fraud, matters get even worse.† The unsuspecting consumer may fall prey to fraud and deception in magazine sales, land deals, auto repairs, and credit practices, to name just a few examples from the seemingly endless array of abuses that lurk around the fringes of the marketplace [6, Chap. 1].

Consumers who are looking for help may be comforted to find that the government has been in the consumer protection business for generations. Less comforting, however, is the realization that consumer protection laws, which seldom even make it to the books without crip-

---

* While no one is predicting any great changes, a consumer group was formed in 1977 to represent fans' interests. It's called Fight to Advance the Nation's Sports or, more appropriately, FANS.

† Communist countries, too, are vulnerable to consumer fraud. *Pravda* reported that a man showed up at a collective farm claiming to be a movie director in need of horses for a battle scene. The farm manager obliged, but never saw the horses again. Shortly thereafter, a nearby meat-packing plant reported record weekly production.

pling amendments, are enforced with a lack of persistence and vigor. The regulatory agencies, which are charged with upholding the "public interest," often act as though they were not the least bit interested in the public. Instead, they become the mouthpieces for the very industries they are supposed to regulate. The tail wags the dog, and while the agency may bark now and then, the bite is usually toothless.

When the government does act, the results are not always encouraging. However well meaning they may be, activities promoted in the name of consumer protection often appear as some distant bureaucrat's idea of what the consumer should want; thus, such plans are greeted by actual consumers with indifference or even hostility. The seat-belt-interlock system, for example, was meant to protect consumers by ensuring that cars could not be started until seat belts were fastened. The mechanism prompted such cries of outrage that Congress acted to rescind the requirement [7, pp. 342–43].

As if all of this weren't bad enough, embattled consumers have come under fire from another quarter. Consumption itself is under attack. The phrase *consumer society* is used in a derisive manner. Radicals see it as the final stages of a sick society. Others simply look on the consumer as shallow and crass, the grandchild of Mencken's *Boobus americanus.** This has come as quite a shock to typical consumers, who have to give up their preoccupation with why the new lawnmower doesn't work to face the charge that they represent a repository of misplaced values.

Environmentalists have taken after the consumer recently also. The drive for ever greater consumption generates pollution as well as products and creates a disposal problem that threatens to reduce the country to a giant trash heap. The billions of bottles and cans that Americans throw away each year are not the country's greatest environmental problem, but the litter they create constitutes a visible reminder of the consumer's role in environmental deterioration [10].

These forces affect the consumer in subtle ways, but there is nothing subtle about the impact of the energy crisis. First came gasoline shortages, then rising power bills, and higher production and operating costs. Mass consumption requires vast amounts of energy, raising the possibility of significant changes in the American lifestyle. That possibility was raised by *The Economic Report of the President,* which warned that the need to conserve energy in the future meant

---

* H. L. Mencken was a journalist and the editor of the *American Mercury,* whose vicious satire ridiculed the American lifestyle of the 1920s. Other writers played on similar themes, as Sinclair Lewis did in *Babbitt.* This sort of characterization was not new, but it is no accident that it became increasingly common during the affluent 1920s.

that "A reduction in standard of living and potential output compared to what we would otherwise enjoy is inevitable" [1, p. 31].

Under this onslaught, it isn't surprising that some consumers have rejected the system. For a few, the commune promised a better life and an escape from the frustrations of the marketplace. Most consumers haven't gone that far, but many have taken "Simplify" as their motto; everything, from food to clothes, is billed as *natural* (including things like makeup, which are intrinsically unnatural). The new asceticism even found a political voice in California's Governor Jerry Brown, who turned around Veblen's phrase and based his political career on *conspicuous nonconsumption.**

The poor consumer who has survived all of this might well ask: "Whatever happened to the American dream?" The scenario was simple enough: Work, save, get ahead; a car, a house, a second car, a better house, and so on. That's the way it was supposed to go. Now consumers find that when they get those things, they do not work, and the consumer is treated like a criminal for having—or even wanting—them. No wonder the consumer is in revolt!

The Paradox of Plenty

While the revolt of the consumer is not surprising, it is in one sense paradoxical. In what seems like a cruel jest, all this frustration is building at a time when American consumers have attained increased affluence. More Americans have more money to buy more things today than at any other time in the nation's history. Yet we can only nod our heads in resignation and mumble agreement when one of columnist Art Buchwald's characters, an economist, says: "I predict it will be a good enough year that people will be able to feel how miserable a healthy economy can be." If we're so rich, why aren't we happy?

This apparent paradox holds the key to the solution of consumer problems. Unraveling it shows that *the very developments that have brought our affluence have also brought us our problems as consumers.* Anyone who has survived an introductory course in economics knows that increased production (or income) follows from increases in specialization and the division of labor. As this process continues, the market becomes more and more important, since individuals become progressively less self-sufficient and more dependent on goods

---

* Thorstein Veblen was an American economist of the early part of this century. He was among the first to analyze the impact of mass consumption and recognize its relation to class and social status. In *The Theory of the Leisure Class* [15] he coined the phrase "conspicuous consumption" in reference to spending for the sake of impressing others. Despite recent changes, such traits are obviously still common.

purchased from others. Adam Smith is credited with first recognizing this point. He devoted the first four chapters of *The Wealth of Nations* to specialization and exchange. He noted:

> It is but a very small part of man's wants which the produce of his own labor can supply. He supplies the far greater part of them by exchanging . . . for parts of the produce of other men's labor . . . Every man thus lives by exchanging. [12, p. 22]

Smith correctly hailed the process as the source of material progress. Since he was writing in 1776, he could not see what a mess it would get us into two centuries later. A retrospective glance should make this point clear.

Americans living on the frontier a century ago endured a bare, subsistence-level existence. They did not, however, share our problems as consumers, because for them consumption equaled production. If the frontier family had food, clothing, and shelter, it was because members of the family had grown or killed the food, made the clothing, and built the cabin. They were self-sufficient, their consumption limited to what they themselves could produce. There were some exceptions, but contact with the outside world of the market economy was limited. It was a harsh life, but the problem was production, not consumption.

As specialization increased and individuals were drawn into the market, living standards increased. The situation changed, but most consumers could manage the changes. Americans of even a couple of generations ago did not face the consumer problems of their grandchildren. In smalltown America, where everyone knew the butcher and the baker, market operations were personalized. The person on the other side of the counter was most likely a friend who could be relied upon. Those who were not reliable, like the butcher with his thumb on the scales, could be sure that the story would be all over town soon and that their competitors would thrive as a result. In short, markets were less complex and individuals could rightly feel that they maintained effective control over them.

This helps to explain an interesting and seemingly anachronistic aspect of the American character—our penchant for making folk heroes out of fast-talking, slightly shady rogues. Examples abound. The medicine-show operator became a fixture in all Westerns. Earlier, no one complained when P. T. Barnum hurried them to the "Egress," and even in the midst of the Great Depression, millions paid to see the antics of that consummate con man W. C. Fields. Ralph Nader would not have had a chance against any of them.

Notice, however, that each of these examples is set in the past, in that simpler, more personal America. Such characters are without modern counterparts. This difference is a very telling illustration of the changes that have taken place. We can laugh at a stubbed toe, but serious illness is not funny; a grimace, not a grin, marks today's consumers. To understand this transformation, this "loss of innocence," as pundits like to call it, we need to understand the changes in the marketplace.

Love and War in the Marketplace

It was specialization that worked these fundamental changes. The virtue became a vice as it was extended throughout the economy. This is the ultimate paradox. The very process that lifted humanity out of centuries of poverty and enabled people to enjoy widespread material benefits has turned on them. The resulting problems are so serious that many people would happily return to a poorer, less complex life.

The specifics of these changes can be identified easily. The development of the economy featured increases in specialization, the application of capital, and the size of establishments. It resulted in lower-cost production, which meant higher incomes and living standards. It also meant, however, that individuals produced fewer and fewer of the things they used; until now it has reached the point where most of us do not directly produce any of the goods we consume.

Frank Knight, an outstanding economist who certainly understood the strengths of the market system, was among the first to see the problem in this regard. He noted:

> Specialization in itself, is an evil measured by generally accepted human ideals. It gives us more products, but in its effects on human beings as such it is certainly bad in some respects and in others questionable.... In this connection, it is especially significant that the most important source of gain also involves the most important human cost. [5, p. 21]

Knight was writing in the 1930s and the "human costs" he had in mind were those associated with the tedium of production. However, he would live to see those costs spread to consumers as individuals become increasingly tied to the marketplace. Consumers are at the mercy of the market, not the personal marketplace of Knight's Iowa boyhood, but a complex mechanism that overshadows the individual.

Consumers no longer know the people with whom they do business. Instead of dealing with a friend when they have a complaint, they find themselves confronting a computer (a literal symbol of dehumanization). Businesses are so large that the patronage of any one individual seems unimportant. The threat "I'll take my business elsewhere" is hollow, because that business doesn't really matter, and elsewhere is probably no better.

The heart of the consumer revolt, indeed, the heart of all consumer problems, is that *consumers operate in a hostile environment.* Too often they are not equipped to protect themselves. Purchasing decisions are complicated, requiring detailed technical information that most people lack. The array of products is confusing, a confusion heightened by the constant bombardment of advertisements. Wesley Clair Mitchell, one of this country's first great economists, identified this problem as early as 1912. Writing in the *American Economic Review,* Mitchell noted that, while production was being revolutionized,

> as a unit for consuming goods, for spending money, the family . . . remained substantially where it was in colonial days. Division of labor in spending has not progressed beyond a rudimentary division between adult men and women of the family. . . . No trade has made less progress than this, the most important of all trades. [8, p. 5]

The years that have passed since Mitchell wrote these words have only underscored his insight. Anyone who doubts this should compare purchasing practices for a business and for a family. Businesses, even relatively small ones, have purchasing agents who specialize in buying for the company. Important purchases involve studying professional literature, setting specifications, and getting bids. Families buy a wider range of products, but no similar pattern of specialization is evident. Whatever changes Mitchell might observe in today's economy, he would find the family, "as a unit for consuming goods," virtually unchanged in the past sixty-five years.

The final frustration, as if one were needed, is that consumers lack the power to control what is happening to them. Consumers lack leverage because their individual purchases are small relative to the size of the market. As a result, they are reduced to a passive role— offered products on a take-it-or-leave-it basis. Their decision is without consequence to anyone else. In some consumers, the feeling of helplessness that comes from these conditions causes despair and may finally lead to bitterness, if not rejection of the whole idea. The alienated consumer can be found in suburbia just as easily as in the commune. In others, this helplessness generates dissatisfaction that can grow into militancy. Thus, those who are fighting back against the system and those who have given up on it are not so different

as they might appear. Both consumer militancy and consumer alienation can be traced to *consumer impotence* in the marketplace.

The consumer revolt emerges as an outgrowth of our supercharged,
superaffluent, postindustrial economy. A number of other recent developments in American life can be traced to the same source. Environmental problems, alienated workers (the "blue-collar blues"),
and our growing uneasiness with the dehumanization of society are
all tied to our high level of development. We have mastered many
of our traditional economic concerns—shelter, food, and clothing—
only to discover that a new set of equally demanding concerns awaits
us.

To illustrate the difference, contrast the type of problems we are
discussing here with the consumer's traditional nemesis, inflation.
Given the way in which prices have spiraled over the past few years,
most consumers would probably list inflation as their major concern.
Economists have shared this concern and, if inflation is not fully
understood, it is not for want of trying. This familiarity hasn't exactly generated affection, but consumers have learned to live with
inflation.

The consumer problems with which we are dealing were not common in earlier generations and therefore did not draw the attention
of economists. Furthermore, these problems have taken consumers
by surprise. Inflation, while unpleasant, is at least familiar. The new
consumer problems are forbidding not just because they are new, but
also because they are tarnishing the vision of the good life. People
feel betrayed by a system that held out the promise of affluence, but
then turned on them once affluence was achieved.

The Analysis of Consumer Problems

Facing the Facts of Life

This feeling of betrayal has produced a number of unhealthy reactions in consumers, the most familiar of which is the what's-the-use
syndrome. It amounts to unconditional surrender, accepting that consumer problems are so overpowering that there is nothing that can
be done about them. The opposite reaction—the angry consumer—
represents a more positive development. Too often, however, such
anger lacks direction and is wasted in outbursts that have no real
impact.

Evidence suggests that within both of these groups there are growing numbers of consumers who simply want to be left alone. They
are more sullen than angry, having been disillusioned by efforts at

consumer protection that result either in more complex and expensive products or what is perceived to be growing interference in the individual's daily life. This reaction is evidence of the need for more systematic analyses of consumer problems. Policies were undertaken without a full understanding of what the real problem was; as a result, the cure was worse than the disease and public reaction was negative.

Consumers here emerge in the familiar role of their own worst enemy. In the words of the comic-strip character Pogo: "We have met the enemy, and he is us." Before anything can be done about consumer problems, they must be squarely faced, for the reality of the situation is that consumer problems exist. Ignoring them will not make them go away any more than trying to escape from consumer protection will produce better public policies. The initial reaction of consumers has been immature, a sort of tantrum. It is now time to abandon such reactions and recognize consumer problems for what they are. No easy solutions may be forthcoming, but if the problems can be analyzed, they can be understood; and if they can be understood, it should be possible to work toward solutions.

The Uses and Abuses of Theory

We have established that consumer problems follow from the inability of consumers to control their environment—consumer impotence. While there is no magic drug to cure this condition, there is a means at hand to deal with it. Since this is fundamentally a question of how the consumer operates in the marketplace, it is logical to use the best available analysis of that process. This suggests using economic theory—what has so far been called the *economics of consumer problems*. To be specific, we need to use the economic theory of consumer equilibrium.

Let's pause to recover from that statement. Anyone who has looked at the chapters on consumer equilibrium and demand in an introductory economics text recalls assumptions, abstractions, and graph upon multicolored graph. But where is specific coverage of consumer problems? These problems simply do not receive textbook treatment. How then can we use economic theory here?

Until quite recently, consumer economics was shunted by economists and treated like a foster child because of a general failure to recognize that consumer economics is the economics of consumer problems. Some economists did identify the relationship, but their work was on an advanced level and was not effectively integrated into either consumer education or introductory economics [2]. There is no reason this integration must be lacking, however, since the analysis follows from elementary principles that do not involve the mystical elements often associated with the higher realms of economic theory.

It is useful to think of theory as a road map. The typical map does not identify every highway, intersection, or cluster of houses. Yet it is tremendously valuable in getting from one place to another because it gives enough information to guide you through unfamiliar territory, without burdening you with unnecessary detail. A road map that contained all possible information would only confuse the driver. Theory serves to abstract key elements and allow us to make sense out of what would otherwise be a bewildering mass of detail. It is to this end that I will use theory in this pursuit.

By so doing, I am running counter to a current fashion that holds economics to be outdated. In an era of affluence, so the argument runs, a science that deals with scarcity has little to say. We will find out that it is those who put forth such arguments who have little to say. Obvious limits exist to applying economic theory, but within those limits it can provide valuable insights. Theory provides us the means to deal with the new problems of affluence just as it helps in analyzing such traditional problems as employment, prices, and output.

Study Questions

1. What does the phrase *consumer economics* mean to you? List topics you would include under that heading. Compare your list to those prepared by other students; are there more similarities or contrasts?

2. Do you live in the same town as your grandparents or other relatives? If you do, how does that affect your life as a consumer (and if you don't, how would it)?

3. Over the past generation many small neighborhood stores have closed and have been replaced by chain stores or regional shopping centers. Explain this process in terms of market development. What do such changes imply for consumers?

4. Given your answer in Question 3, how can you explain the fact that quick-shop stores are reappearing in many neighborhoods?

5. Most people are grateful for the protection they receive from the police and firemen. Why then are people so often hostile toward efforts meant to protect them as consumers?

6. We have said that consumer concerns are an outgrowth of affluence, yet poverty is still a problem in the United States.

What does that imply? Does it mean that the poor do not have to worry about consumer problems?

7. Outline ways in which the environmental problem and consumer problems are related. Show how both are features of a highly developed economy.

8. There has been a widespread revival of interest in arts and crafts in recent years. How can this revival be related to market development and specialization? Can you think of any other reactions to these developments in the market?

9. Look at the styles of dress of the students in your class; is there one predominant style? What does this tell you about changing attitudes toward consumption?

10. What does the word *theory* mean? What is the test of a theory? How can you tell a good theory from a bad one?

Suggested Projects

1. Consult the *Reader's Guide to Periodic Literature* or some similar index and check for articles relating to consumers over the past ten years.
   a. What pattern emerges concerning the frequency of such articles?
   b. Do you notice any changes in the topics covered or the views expressed?

2. Look through a standard introductory economics textbook. What do you find about consumer problems? Comment.

3. Conduct your own survey of problems that bother consumers (see Appendix). Ask the same questions of people in different parts of town and, if possible, in smaller (or larger) towns in the area. What difference would you expect from consumers in different areas? Explain.

4. Do the problems identified under Project 4 follow from the overall problem of consumer isolation in the marketplace? Classify the responses and compare them to your own list of concerns (Study Question 1).

5. Consider again the problems identified. Which of them would have been significant a generation ago? A century ago?

6. Seek out consumer reactions to consumer protection legislation (include such things as flame-retardant sleepwear, fair-credit legislation, nutritional labeling, and other specific legislation

with which consumers are likely to be familiar). Give people a chance to talk about their feelings. Is there a clear pattern to the responses? Explain.

Bibliography and Suggested Readings

1. *Economic Report of the President.* Washington, D.C.: U.S. Government Printing Office, 1975.
   An annual report on the American economy containing basic information and also offering discussions of topical questions (such as energy). A good source of economic data, with more statistics than you will ever need to know.

2. Ferber, Robert. "Consumer Economics, A Survey." *Journal of Economic Literature.* December 1973, pp. 1303–42.
   A thorough review of what economists are saying about consumer economics. Even though some material is more advanced, it remains the best survey available. Contains an especially valuable bibliography.

3. Fusfeld, Daniel R. *Economics.* Lexington, Mass.: D. C. Heath and Co., 1972.
   For an analysis of national income and the role of the consumer, see Parts II–IV.

4. Galbraith, John Kenneth. *The Affluent Society.* Boston: Houghton Mifflin Co., 1958.
   Galbraith was among the first to inquire into the impact of affluence on an economy; his analysis—in Chapters 9–11—of economic organization helps to explain consumer impotence.

5. Knight, Frank H. *The Economic Organization.* New York: Augustus M. Kelley, 1933/1951.
   The serious student will find Knight's reflections upon the price system worth reading. A strong supporter of the market system, Knight offers real insights into the basic functions of markets.

6. Magnuson, Warren, and Carper, Jean. *The Dark Side of the Marketplace.* 2nd ed. Englewood Cliffs, N.J.: Prentice-Hall, 1972.
   A guided tour through the horrors of consumer fraud with a prescription for legislative action. Senator Magnuson has been a leading supporter of consumer protection in Congress.

7. Maynes, E. Scott. *Decision-Making for Consumers.* New York: Macmillan, 1976.
   A good source for information on consumers' operations within markets. Particularly valuable for discussions of price variations. Contains good bibliography.

8. Mitchell, Wesley Clair. "The Backward Art of Spending Money." In *The Backward Art of Spending Money and Other Essays.* New York: McGraw-Hill Book Co., 1937.
   A collection of Mitchell's writings covering the first third of this century. The title essay is a splendid examination of the problems involved in family spending. It is a perceptive analysis; Mitchell deserves special credit for having identified the problem when it was first emerging.

9. North, Douglass C. *The Economic Growth of the United States, 1790–1860.* New York: W. W. Norton, 1966.
   An excellent analysis of the spread of markets and increasingly complex production in United States economic history. Features applications of economic theory to historical developments.

10. *Restoring the Quality of Our Environment.* Report of the Environmental Pollution Panel of the President's Science Committee. Washington, D.C.: U.S. Government Printing Office, 1965.
    An early report on the environment; the issues it identifies remain important, particularly the role of ever-increasing levels of consumption.

11. Silberman, Charles E. " 'Identity Crisis' in the Consumer Markets." *Fortune,* March 1971, pp. 92–95.
    One of the earliest looks at the impact of changing consumer attitudes on marketing and product lines. Predicted trends which have developed in the past five years.

12. Smith, Adam. *The Wealth of Nations.* Modern Library. New York: Random House, 1937.
    Generally accepted as the first economics book in the English language. Chapters 1–4 concern specialization. Students who can absorb the richness of Smith's eighteenth-century style will find him well worth reading.

13. Solow, Robert M. "The New Industrial State, or Son of Affluence." *Public Interest,* no. 9, Fall 1967, pp. 100–108.
    One of America's leading economists comments on Professor Galbraith's approach. His comments are relevant to the types of problems we will face in subsequent chapters.

14. *Survey of Current Business.* U.S. Department of Commerce. Washington, D.C.: July 1977.
    Monthly review of statistics on the economy's performance.

15. Veblen, Thorstein. *The Theory of the Leisure Class.* New York: Mentor Books, 1953.
    Classic social commentary on consumption and consumers by an economist whose own tastes were somewhat unusual. That Veblen is still read indicates the depth of his insight. He fathered, among other things, a whole school of economic thought.

-2-

The Elements of
Consumer Choice

The Economic Problem

In the Beginning

Having argued that economic analysis offers the most fruitful approach to investigating actual consumer problems, it is necessary now to support that argument. How can theory, seemingly so abstract and detached, be applied in this case? The answer can be found at the starting point of economic analysis itself. Identifying that point is easy enough, because all of economics rises, like an inverted cone, from one proposition. There isn't enough of everything for everybody.

In more conventional terms, the problem is scarcity. Scarcity arises from two conditions. The first is that human wants, taken all together, are insatiable. On the other hand, the goods and services available to satisfy these wants are limited. Resources, or factors of production, are required to produce things; because there isn't enough land on which to plant crops or build buildings, labor to put things together, or capital to build factories, things are scarce. Limit*less* wants into limit*ed* resources won't go.

That is the economic problem humans have always faced. The task of any economic system is therefore to satisfy as many of these wants as possible. This establishes consumption—the satisfaction of human wants—as the goal of all economic activity.* In a sense, *consumer*

---

* Note that the satisfaction of human wants is the final goal of economic activity. That becomes important when we broaden the definition of consumption in the next chapter.

17

economics is a redundant expression, like *historical history* or *chemical chemistry,* because all economics is about consumption. Indeed, the word *economics* is derived from the Greek *oikonomikos,* meaning home management or household finance. With this identity established, economists' neglect of consumer economics is difficult to understand. Just think for a moment what things would be like if the basic problem of economics, scarcity, were removed. If there were actually enough things for everyone, there would be no economics and no consumer problems. Individuals could satisfy all of their wants without experiencing any consumer problems. That is obviously not the way things are; consumers are forced to economize, to stretch their incomes as far as possible. The idea of scarcity, then, emerges as the logical beginning of this analysis.

Either/Or

Because it is impossible to produce enough to satisfy everybody's wants, it follows that economics involves *choices* about which goods to produce. Decisions introduce the idea of cost. The fact of scarcity means that the economy cannot have more of everything, assuming that available resources are being fully used. To produce more of one good, say pretzels, it is necessary to produce less of something else, say beer. Since to get additional pretzels, the economy has to give up the opportunity to have the beer, it is correct to measure the cost of the pretzels in terms of the beer given up.

Logically enough, this measure is called *opportunity cost.* If the same resources can be used to produce either a case of pretzels or a case of beer, the real cost—the opportunity cost—of the pretzels is the case of beer that did not get produced and hence is not available for consumption. The point can be further illustrated by the so-called TANSTAAFL principle, or There Ain't No Such Thing As A Free Lunch. Resources used in one pursuit cannot be used in another. The commitment of resources to the lunch means they are unavailable for alternative use. Thus, in order that the lunch be supplied, some other product or service did not get produced.

The problem for the consumer mirrors the problem for the economy as a whole. Think of all the things you would like to have, and you will understand that the individual consumer has limitless wants. Why don't you have all those things? Because your income is limited. The typical individual consumer must also make decisions that involve costs. This means giving up some things to enjoy others. Unfortunately, this point is often confused by the statement "I can't afford ...." Some things are indeed too expensive for most buyers; few of us could afford a villa in the south of France. But very often the statement should be translated as "I don't want to give up what I'd have to in order to get it." If someone who has just purchased a color television set tells you he or she cannot afford a washing machine, that person is really saying that he or she was unwilling to give up the set in order to get the washer.

This illustration clarifies two important points about the theory of consumer demand. First, it is a theory of choice. Consumers must choose what they want from among all the goods and services available. Costs are involved, since consumers cannot have everything they want and therefore must forego some goods. But how do they decide which goods to consume? That is the second point. The consumer always chooses the good valued most highly, which is to say the good that will bring the greatest amount of satisfaction.

The Consumer, Theoretically Speaking

More Bang for the Buck

I have now identified the basic elements involved in the theory. All that remains is to explore the details of the process by which the consumer reaches equilibrium, that happy state of being as well off as possible.* Since the whole question revolves around the satisfaction of wants, assume that the goal of consumers is to maximize satisfaction or utility. This is a commonsense assumption, for it only says that people want to be as well off as possible with the income they have.

It should be clear that if consumers follow the principle of always purchasing the good or service that brings the greatest amount of satisfaction, they will automatically reach this maximization position. If each individual purchase represents the best buy, all such purchases taken together must add up to maximum satisfaction.

You should notice that this is a very personal process. No one tells consumers which good they want most; they make that decision themselves according to their own tastes and preferences. Who knows what you want? You do, and if you make *rational* decisions, meaning purchases designed to fulfill those wants, you're on your way to maximizing your satisfaction. To this I must add that you are *certain* of your preferences; if you were not, you would not know what it was you wanted to satisfy. From this it follows that you would not know what goods to buy.

---

* Students may wish to review the chapters on consumer equilibrium in an introductory economics text. See reference 1 or 3.

So now you are certain of what you want and you are going to make rational decisions accordingly, but you are still not ready to buy. You won't be ready until you know how well each available good will fulfill those wants. You know what you want the goods to do, but you need to know which goods will actually do it. Therefore, you must have perfect *knowledge* of the goods available. Only with this information can you evaluate all possible alternatives in terms of your preference.

The specific manner in which this evaluation takes place can be demonstrated in different ways. However, since they all begin at the same place and end in the same place, we need not be too concerned with these differences. The simplest approach is classical marginal utility analysis, which assumes that since consumers have perfect knowledge and a given set of preferences, they know how many units of satisfaction, called *utiles,* are derived from each good consumed.*

Utility, however, is a sometimes thing, changing as consumption changes. Taken altogether, your wants are limitless, but your desire for a particular good at a particular time is not. This process is given the elegant name *diminishing marginal utility.* All it means is that as you get more and more of something, each extra unit will bring you less satisfaction. Certainly a steak would have different utility for someone who was starving than for a person who had just finished a seven-course meal. Anyone who has ever wondered why he or she took that last drink knows the meaning of diminishing marginal utility.

Diminishing utility helps explain how people end up with a particular mixture of goods and services. The first unit of a good they consume is the one that gives them the most satisfaction, or the most utiles. As they get more of that good, however, additional units of it bring them less satisfaction. A point will soon be reached when more of the first good will bring less satisfaction than some alternative, which means it is time to switch. This illustrates the rule of always making the purchase that gives the most utiles. By repeating the process over and over until income is gone, consumers maximize their satisfaction. A specific example will show the process at work.

Suppose you have a dollar to spend, and you can buy either beer or pretzels, both of which cost a quarter. It isn't necessary that we assume that there are only two goods, but it does make our illustration a lot simpler without changing the results. Further, assume that the marginal utility to be gained from different quantities of the two

---

* Indifference curve analysis is currently a more popular approach. It does not require that a consumer know precisely how much utility is obtained from a good, but only that one good is preferred to another. The conclusions reached from indifference curve analysis, however, support conclusions derived from the classical approach.

goods is represented by the data in Table 2.1. Where did those numbers come from? They are hypothetical, but they are meant to represent the amount of satisfaction you will get from the two goods, based on your relative preferences for them. Now, with an income of $1, you can buy four beers or four bags of pretzels or any combination of the two costing $1. Which combination will you actually buy?

As the arrows indicate, the maximum position is three beers and one unit of pretzels. You prefer the first beer to the first bag of pretzels (10 utiles to 5), and while the second beer gives you less satisfaction than the first, it still gives you more than the first bag of pretzels. So you buy a second beer. You now have 50 cents left to spend and find that the first bag of pretzels and the third beer offer the same utility (5 utiles each). So you buy one of each and you are broke.

You have gained 28 utiles from your dollar; from your preferences, as shown in the table, there is no other way you could have spent your money and been better off. Try some different combinations and you will see that this is true. If you had drunk four beers, you would have gotten only 25 utiles of enjoyment, the same amount you would have received from two beers and two pretzels. By choosing the unit that gave you the most satisfaction each time, you reached equilibrium, a position of maximum satisfaction—consuming three beers and one bag of pretzels.

Note that for the last units purchased the utility was the same. This will always be true, because if it were not the consumer could always improve his or her position by buying more of the good with the greater utility. When prices differ, marginal utility must be divided by price before a comparison can be made; equilibrium is attained when marginal utility divided by price (MU/P) is the same for all goods, or $MU_a/P_a = MU_b/P_b = \cdots = MU_n/P_n$. Thus, when there is no other way that consumers could spend their money and be better off, they have maximized satisfaction.

Table 2.1 Maximizing Satisfaction: Illustration (Income = $1)

Quantity	Utility per Unit	
	Beer @ 25¢	Pretzels @ 25¢
1	10	5
2	8	2
3	5	1
4	2	0

His (Her) Majesty, the Consumer

The analysis of consumer equilibrium is now summarized, with the consumer in the happy position of being as well off as possible. Our theoretical treatment of the consumer is not yet complete, however; one more matter requires investigation. We have been considering the impact of consumer choice on the individual's level of satisfaction. Consumer choices have an impact beyond the consumer, however, reaching to the producer and therefore to the entire economy. In the theoretical development of the market economy, consumers do not exist in a vacuum; they are an integral part of the system.

When you buy a hamburger, your interest in it may go no further than your stomach, but you still have done something more than just buy it. You have voted for the hamburger. In voting for a political candidate, you are saying "I want this person to have the job." Similarly, when you buy the hamburger, you are telling the producer, "I like it; produce more." To vote "no," you simply don't buy. Ford's best efforts could not save the Edsel, nor could *Women's Wear Daily* turn the midi-skirt into a national craze. Both were greeted with "no" votes, which means no buyers.

Consumers, by the pattern of their purchases or the way in which they cast their dollar votes, dictate to producers which goods will be produced. Thus, consumers emerge as the decision makers, using the market system as a communications mechanism. This is called *consumer sovereignty*. It is important from the viewpoint of the whole economy, since it ensures that the goods that are produced will reflect the actual demand of individuals. It is also important to individual consumers, for it means they are not merely passive takers but active participants in production. The lines of causation are clear; consumers direct producers and therefore it is the consumers who have effective power. Instead of being lost in a complex marketplace, consumers emerge as its masters, holding life-and-death power that ensures that their wishes will be respected. We have seen that just as consumption is at the heart of economics, the consumer is at the heart of the economic system.

Coming Back from Wonderland

"Curiouser and Curiouser"

Some students feel light-headed at this picture of the consumer as king. It takes time, after all, to adjust to the rarefied air of unreality. Indeed, the whole analysis needs only a talking rabbit to underscore its Alice-in-Wonderland quality. The Queen of Hearts is as likely a sovereign as the consumer, and the Cheshire cat is no less believable than the marginal utile. Certainly, many economists have come to that conclusion. One such critic, labeling himself a curmudgeon, risked professional disembowelment by dismissing the theory of consumer choice as nothing more than "a set of moderately dull exercises," which have survived only because "several generations of graduate students have been taught to jump through these hoops" [7, p. 410]. Mind you, this is an economist speaking. Since the theoretical treatment is hardly a mirror of reality, there is the strong temptation to dismiss it as unworkable and without value in investigating actual consumer problems.

A more careful examination, however, indicates that such conclusions may be premature. Think about it for a minute. The theory starts from a very realistic position. It assumes that consumers have limited income and that they want to get all they can from it. That is a fairly exact description of most of the flesh-and-blood consumers I know. Yet while the theoretical consumer blissfully maximizes satisfaction, the typical consumer has to muck around in a quagmire of problems where bliss is noticeably lacking. Since they both start from the same place with the same goal, why does one make it and one fall short?

The curmudgeon quoted above gives a hint when he asks of what use is economic theory

> in buying a hi-fi set, or perfume, or a house? Most of my friends . . . are not technical experts on hi-fi sets or automobiles. To a great extent, they are not even always sure of what they want; they are not particularly expert on judging quality; their decisions are made under uncertainty, and they regard the amount of time they spend making their decisions as often being a considerable cost to themselves. [7, p. 410]

Does this curmudgeon have particularly dumb friends? No, they are not much different from the rest of us. They are unsure of themselves, facing an uncertain world in which they lack adequate information to make decisions. The theoretical consumer would not face any of these problems; without doubting, shopping, or making mistakes, the theoretical consumer just maximizes.

That is the point. Economic theory is not much use in buying hi-fi sets, perfume, or houses since all of the problems that real consumers meet are assumed away in theory. The consumer is reduced to the status of a *given*, a known quantity who can be counted on to behave in a predictable way in any given situation. Real consumers, of course, are not givens and must face all the problems that theory assumes away. That these assumptions are not met in real life is the bottleneck that keeps consumers from attaining the blissful state their theoretical counterparts enjoy.

If this is true, we might echo the curmudgeon's question and ask of what use a theory is that does not pertain to real-world situations. This would be missing the point. The theory sets forth the *conditions that must be met if the consumer is to maximize satisfaction.* In setting them forth, theory provides us with a guide to the problems that consumers face. After all, those assumptions are in there for a reason, and that reason should now be clear. Without them, the consumer is going nowhere—which is as far as many consumers get.

It follows that investigating these assumptions should lead to understanding actual consumer problems. More important, investigation should also point the way to their solution. The closer real conditions come to assumed conditions, the closer the consumer comes to the goal of maximum satisfaction. Contrary to appearances, economic theory turns out to be a practical how-to guide for the consumer. By telling us what is necessary for maximizing satisfaction, it provides a focus for our investigation. Now we know where to look in order to come to grips with consumer problems.

Assuming Away the Assumptions

All that remains now is to restate the critical assumption and indicate briefly how each contributes to consumer problems as we know them. The basic rule has been that the consumer maximizes satisfaction by always buying the good that gives the greatest amount of satisfaction. If consumers are to follow that simple principle, a number of other conditions must be met. Specifically, they have to be *rational* about their spending, *certain* of their decisions, and should have knowledge, or *information,* about the products they buy. To enjoy that consumers have leverage in the market, it is necessary to add the assumption of consumer sovereignty—consumers acting to direct production.

The question now becomes "What happens if . . . ?" Suppose, for example, that consumers are irrational, either lacking any clear idea of what they want or buying on impulse. Obviously, they'll be taken. In plainer terms, they are suckers and, to paraphrase W. C. Fields, the market "never gives a sucker an even break." We will become aware that rationality is a slippery concept, but for now we are accepting that consumers need to think through what they want and then buy accordingly.

What happens if we drop the assumption of certainty? Consumers may know what they want now, but what about the future? About all that is certain (never mind death and taxes) is that income, tastes, and prices will change over time. Consumers must therefore take future possibilities into account when making current decisions. This makes what the consumer thinks is going to happen an important consideration; misjudging the future can be very expensive.

The assumption of perfect knowledge is almost comical. Ask anyone who has spent the afternoon shopping. As the curmudgeon's friends would testify, it takes time, effort, and money to gain information, all of which involve costs. Yet ignorance may be even more expensive. Many sad souls have underscored that statement with their own sweat and tears. They're the ones who bought used cars because "the body looked good" or who "didn't have time" to find out about the interest charges on a loan. Therefore, the value of information must be balanced against its costs. How can these costs be cut? Advertising, government standards, word of mouth, and experience can all cut, but not eliminate, information costs. Certainly, inadequate information is a fundamental problem that all consumers face; therefore, reducing information costs is one of the important elements in this analysis.

Finally, there is consumer sovereignty. Most consumers find it difficult enough to be faithful subjects, let alone sovereign. The market is too large and complex for most individuals to affect it directly. This does not necessarily mean they are at its mercy, isolated and powerless; it does mean that consumers must act to adjust the odds. They can accomplish this both by working through the market and by working to change it. These fundamental considerations bear directly on the requirements for being an effective consumer. They define our task for us. We now need to look at each of them more carefully, explore what is involved, and isolate the key elements that affect consumer performance. The analysis begins with the elusive concept of rationality and consumer decisions.

Study Questions

1. Look again at the section on the theory of consumer choice in an introductory economics text. How are the assumptions discussed in this chapter treated? Discuss.

2. Is it common for people to say that the theory of consumer choice is unrealistic? In what sense is that true? In what sense do such comments miss the point?

3. Why would a consumer go on buying a product even after the marginal utility it provided began to decline (that is, the consumer received less satisfaction from the product)?

4. Suppose you are figuring out what a year of college costs, and you add your expenses for tuition, books, room, board, and miscellaneous expenditures. Explain why that figure would *understate* the real cost of your education. Is college more expensive for a senior or a freshman? Why is it even more expensive for an all-American basketball player?

5. You use theory every day, even when you are crossing the street. What assumptions do you make if you are crossing a street in traffic? How do you tell if your assumptions were justified?

6. Look again at the example of utility maximization in Table 2.1. From the preferences shown in the table,
   a. What combination would you consume if you had $1.50?
   b. What combination would you buy if the price of pretzels fell to *two bags for 25 cents* (with income of $1)?

7. Suppose a friend who had just bought a new car told you he or she was dropping out of school for financial reasons. What would you think?

8. There may be no such thing as a free lunch, but what about air? Isn't air free? What about time?

9. We all know people who have trouble making up their minds. How do you think this trait would affect their behavior as consumers?

10. The list that follows contains a variety of topics familiar to most consumers. Categorize them according to the four assumptions we discussed in the text.
    a. Insurance.
    b. *Consumer Reports.*
    c. Buying on credit.
    d. "Child-proof" caps on drugs.
    e. The Food and Drug Administration.
    f. Classified advertisements.
    g. Consumer boycotts.
    h. Product guarantees.
    i. Impulse buying.

11. Look again at your own list of problems from Chapter 1 (or if you conducted a survey, at the problems mentioned by consumers). Categorize them according to the assumptions in this chapter.

Bibliography and Suggested Readings

1. Alchian, Armen A., and Allen, William R. *University Economics.* Belmont, Calif.: Wadsworth Publishing Co., 1964.
   An introductory textbook that develops the theory at a more sophisticated level than most books. Particularly useful in drawing out implications of the theory and in its consideration of information costs.

2. Friedman, Milton. *Essays in Positive Economics.* Chicago: University of Chicago Press, 1953.
   An outstanding collection of essays on theory and its role in economic analysis. Friedman argues that a theory should be judged on how well it predicts, not on how realistic its assumptions appear. One of the most thoughtful discussions of the topic available.

3. Fusfeld, Daniel R. *Economics.* Lexington, Mass.: D. C. Heath and Co., 1972.
   See especially the chapters on choice and consumer equilibrium.

4. Galbraith, John Kenneth. *The Affluent Society.* Boston: Houghton Mifflin Co., 1958.
   Galbraith has modified his position somewhat since this book was written, but Chapters 9–11 are still a good introduction to his view of producer sovereignty as opposed to consumer sovereignty.

5. Katona, George. *The Mass Consumption Society.* New York: McGraw-Hill, 1964.
   Katona was a pioneer in consumer research. During his many years as head of the Survey Research Center, University of Michigan, he emphasized the psychological and behavioral aspects of consumption. This book considers various influences at work on the modern consumer. We will use this and other books by him extensively in the next two chapters.

6. *Selected Aspects of Consumer Behavior.* National Science Foundation, Directorate for Research Applications. Washington, D.C.: U.S. Government Printing Office, 1977.
   A summary of different perspectives on consumer behavior drawn from a variety of disciplines. Some of the material is technical, but the different articles cover a wide range of topics so most students should find something of value. Particularly good for bibliographies.

7. Shubik, Martin. "A Curmudgeon's Guide to Microeconomics." *Journal of Economic Literature* 8 (June 1970):405–34.
   This curmudgeon takes an irreverent look at microeconomics; his view should be particularly appreciated by those students who have been baptized into some of its mysteries.

8. Stigler, George J. *The Theory of Price.* 3rd ed., New York: Macmillan Co., 1966.

An intermediate price theory text that is a good reference for students who want to follow through on some of the implications of the theory of consumer equilibrium. Chapter 1 is particularly good, containing an excellent and entertaining introduction to information costs and a more general consideration of theories.

-3-

Rationality in Consumer Decision-Making

What Does It Mean to Be Rational?

The most basic problem with consumer rationality is trying to decide what it means. Webster's defines *rationality* as "having reason or understanding; intelligent; sensible," which is why dictionaries are not of much value in cases like this. Other sources are not of much help either. Psychologists have wrestled with defining rationality, but have had little success. Even the courts, which are routinely called upon to determine rationality (or sanity), have not produced a common standard of judgment.

In the face of such confusion, it seems a bit presumptuous for economists simply to assume that consumers are rational and let it go at that. In so doing, they are obviously ducking a very complex issue, a move which may be defended by arguing that economists traditionally have been more interested in exploring the conditions necessary for maximizing satisfaction than in investigating consumer behavior per se. However, we cannot sidestep the issue so neatly.

Economists' artful dodging of the issue does give us one bit of help. It tells us something about what rationality is *not*. There is an unfortunate tendency for people to think of any pattern of behavior that is different from their own as irrational. *Irrationality* comes to be equated with *different, strange,* or *unusual.* From the economist's point of view, such contentions are totally unjustified, since they overlook the fact that utility is highly individual. There is no reason to assume that everyone is going to value things in the same way. Quite the contrary, there is every reason to suppose that they will not. Individual valuation, the ranking of priorities according to tastes, is at the heart of the economist's perception of rationality. The rational consumer is one whose purchases are made according to such a ranking.

Thus, a particular behavior observed in the market may be rational for one person, but not for a second. Or, the behavior may be rational in one setting, but not in another. Consider an analogy with clothing: formal attire and blue jeans are different modes of dress, yet each is appropriate in its own setting. You wouldn't wear jeans to a formal dinner, but the problem would be with the situation, not with the jeans themselves. So, it makes no sense to ask: "Are jeans appropriate clothing?" without also asking what the conditions are. Similarly, one cannot ask if a particular behavior is rational without knowing more about the person and the situation.

You should be aware now of the dilemma we are facing. The rational consumer makes purchases according to personal preferences; however, if only the individual knows those preferences, how can anyone be judged irrational? That question, which we'll examine later, should be taken as a warning against making easy judgments about rationality. The possibilities for error in such judgments should be obvious, but, nevertheless, there are those who still haven't grasped the point. As a result, misconceptions about consumer rationality remain all too common.

Misconceptions about Rationality

Some Examples of Misjudgment

Many of the misconceptions that surround rationality stem from the traditional analysis of consumer maximization as I have outlined it. The theoretical consumer carefully attached values to all goods consumed and then purchased according to the number of utiles each offered. It takes nothing more than casual observation to demonstrate that consumers do not behave this way. Thus, there is a temptation to conclude that consumers are not rational, that they are at best creatures of habit, or, more likely, behave in a random, impulsive fashion. Such judgments are superficial. It is our task to discover what behavior is consistent with the theoretical analysis.

As a beginning, take the example of a person buying a bag of frozen french-fried potatoes. The initial urge may be to say "Stop! You can get the same number of french fries for a fraction of the cost if you buy fresh potatoes and prepare them yourself." It is true that the cost would be less, but what of it?

There are alternate ways of explaining the consumer's behavior in this case. One is that he or she is irrational, paying more than is necessary for the french fries. The other is that the consumer is in a hurry and doesn't want to take the time to bother with fresh potatoes—it takes two to three times as long to make the french fries yourself.* Without more information, we cannot tell which explanation is correct. However, whereas one assumes random behavior with no explanations or support, the other explains the consumer's choice within a broader analysis supported by consistent theoretical propositions. It is the difference between saying something happened and explaining why it happened. The theory does not prove we are right, no theory can, but it does support the argument by providing a consistent explanation.

It is hard to tell which is more maligned, the consumer or the economic analysis of the consumer. Both deserve more credit than they typically receive. The analysis of consumer rationality incorporates far-reaching implications and embraces a variety of consumption patterns; such variations, however, aren't accounted for by today's conventional wisdom, which asserts that consumer behavior features a strong current of irrationality. The following statements illustrate the sort of evidence that is offered to support such contentions:

Many consumers buy on impulse.
Most shoppers shop only at one supermarket.
Charge-account customers purchase more than cash customers.
Consumers buy name brands, overlooking lower-cost substitutes.

These statements were gathered at random from the literature on consumers. Assuming that they are true, what do they really show?

Although impulse buying is widely discussed, it is not a very fruitful line of inquiry. It is not at all clear precisely what constitutes an impulse purchase; even if that could be established, it cannot be maintained that such purchases are necessarily bad. It appears that impulse is taken to mean "unplanned," but that cannot be equated with bad; a quick decision may result in a very good buy.† If *impulse* means "random," an element of irrationality may be involved, but there is little evidence to indicate that such behavior is typical of most consumers.

---

* Note that one might say that the person should value money more highly than time, but that kind of judgment of another's preferences is clearly unwarranted. More on the personal valuation of time later.

† The relative importance of the item in the customer's budget is important. If the item is relatively unimportant, it may not be worth the effort to plan the expenditure carefully.

What about grocery shoppers who shop only at one store? It is probably quite efficient. Most shoppers know which grocery stores suit them and which do not. The shopper who becomes familiar with the market and then decides that a particular store is best can hardly be considered irrational for shopping there regularly. Such a decision takes more than price into account; it usually includes quality, service, and location also.

Then there is the statement that credit-card customers buy more than cash customers. That implies that a credit card turns a normal person into an insatiable buyer. The flaw in this argument should be clear. What type of customer is likely to have a credit card? The wealthy, well-established person—the sort of person who would buy a lot anyway. The credit card merely simplifies the process and provides flexibility; its use does not explain why the person buys more.

Finally, there is the matter of buying name brands, even when lower-priced substitutes of comparable quality are available. The key here is information. If consumers have become familiar with a certain brand, by either advertising or experience, they learn to count on it. Other brands may be as good, but costs are involved in finding out. Remember, too, that in some cases the market seems to be organized to keep information from consumers; advertising and conflicting claims may make it more difficult for consumers to obtain the information necessary to make a decision.

Conventionality versus Rationality

There is a common error in the examples cited above. In each case, there is an implied judgment about how people ought to act. One person's (or group's) standards are being applied to others. Since consumer satisfaction is based on *individual* preferences, how can one person tell another how to consume? In economic parlance, the dictum is that one cannot make interpersonal utility comparisons. In commonplace language, "there is no accounting for tastes." While this folk idiom implies a great deal of tolerance for alternative consumption styles, it belies the fact that such tolerance is often very limited.

Each year stories appear in the newspaper about some neighborhood that is disrupted because a homeowner does not conform to the standards of the area; usually it is someone who doesn't mow the lawn or paint the house. Suppose for a minute that this involved some other area of consumption, say food, and the individual in question happened not to like cheese? No one would think it strange that the person did not buy cheese. Shouldn't the same be true of house paint? If the homeowner gets more enjoyment from other types of purchases, buying house paint would only reduce his or her level of satisfaction.

Such cases represent a conflict between community, or social, values and individual tastes, where *community* refers to some group such as a neighborhood, city, nation, or larger unit. The community defines for itself an acceptable range of consumption based on its value structure, traditions, conventions, or religious beliefs. If members of the group all share these values, if the group is culturally homogeneous, things should go smoothly. Societies are commonly pluralistic, however, and everyone does not share the same values. In such cases, it is common for one group to try to impose its standards on others. This problem deserves serious consideration; when treated superficially, it is the source of significant misunderstanding. Community standards, conventionality, become the basis for judgments of rationality for all types of consumption. A second point follows from the first. If these standards are enforced, the level of satisfaction of some individuals will be reduced when they are forced to conform to everyone else's tastes and preferences.

Any law or standard will reduce someone's level of satisfaction. Take the helmet laws that require motorcyclists to buy and wear helmets for their own protection. Unlike other safety legislation (such as requirements for improved braking systems on cars), these laws affect only the driver and do not make the streets any safer for the rest of us. The motorcycle driver might feel that the risk of an injury is not sufficient to warrant the cost of the helmet, but the law overrides such individual preferences.*

If motorcyclists are required to wear helmets, isn't there a certain logic to having pedestrians wear helmets too? They would certainly be safer. That is carrying the argument to an extreme, but it does show the problem. If we can restrict certain types of behavior, should we not try to restrict all types? There have always been people who would answer that question with an emphatic "yes." Efforts, largely unsuccessful, were made to legislate the details of persons' consumption behavior. When legal efforts were unsuccessful, less formal, though not necessarily less effective, social sanctions were applied.

The smaller the unit involved, the greater the likelihood that problems will be intense. Consider the relations between parents and their college-age children. Vacations may become periods of tearful confrontations sparked by the manner in which the "child" behaves, dresses, or spends money. Such confrontations are generally caused

---

* Not all states have helmet laws. Federal efforts to require the passage of helmet laws or face the cutoff of federal highway funds were ruled unconstitutional by the courts.

by the parents' attempts to impose their consumption standards on their children, the parents not realizing that their standards reflect tastes and preferences that their offspring probably do not share. Disagreements are likely to continue until the tastes of the parents and child converge or until the parents awaken to the realities of the situation.

A far more serious example of misjudgment concerns welfare grants in the United States today. It is safe to say that payments are not offered in a spirit of charity and compassion. Welfare recipients are not free to spend their money as they see fit. They can spend it only in designated ways on specified items. This can be justified only if one assumes that those receiving welfare do not know how they should spend their money, but that those giving the money do.

There are no grounds for that assumption. Why should low-income individuals want to spend their money in the same manner as middle-income individuals? Forcing them to do so only reduces the effectiveness of welfare. Furthermore, it is demeaning to deny the recipient the rights enjoyed by others in the economy. Acting as if the low-income family does not know what it wants and needs places a stigma on receiving welfare.* The net result is prejudicial to the welfare system and thus to the client and the country.

This denial of individual preferences is not limited to welfare payments. It shows up repeatedly in laws that restrict certain types of consumption. Probably the best (or worst) example was Prohibition; that "noble experiment" outlawed alcoholic beverages. The results were disastrous, which demonstrates that even if a majority of the population favors something (in this case, a doubtful assumption), it cannot always be forced on the minority.

Unfortunately, that lesson was not well learned. We still have a variety of laws that cover consumption, including controls on alcohol, zoning requirements, blue laws to regulate business operations, and, until recently, limitations on birth-control information and devices. There is obvious disagreement on these restrictions; some readers may feel that all are warranted, others may feel that none are. With such differing attitudes, is it possible to establish any overall guidelines for such cases?

The key here is whether the particular case is purely personal, involving only the individual, or whether it involves (and possibly endangers) the community at large. In the latter case, personal responsibility may be enough to ensure that the interests of the community will be observed. A few irresponsible people, however, can

---

* Low-income groups may have a special need for consumer education and information. That does not mean that they are incapable of making their own decisions; it means they need better information on which to base decisions.

create problems for everyone. If individuals want to drink, that is their business, but if they then attempt to drive a car, that is everybody's concern.

In recent years the courts have tended to adopt a broad view of civil liberties, removing restrictions on purely personal consumption decisions. In areas like censorship, efforts have been made to allow adults as wide a range of personal choice as possible, while restricting the choices of children. This represents an attempt to reconcile personal choice and community responsibility. The movement has been uneven and there are still people who take an inordinate interest in the affairs of others, but progress has been made.

Such topics are not generally included in a discussion of consumer economics, but you can recognize that they are a fundamental part of such considerations. I am talking about nothing less than what you can consume and who decides you can consume it. These questions are going to continue to be important, and intelligent consumers must be able to deal with them in a responsible manner. Public and private responsibility come together here, for each individual is both a citizen and a consumer. If individuals are to carry out their responsibilities in both roles, they must be aware of the issues on both sides.

A Radical Reconstruction

What Constitutes Consumption?

The problems discussed in the previous sections can be traced to an oversimplified view of consumer behavior. As the examples showed, consumer behavior is often different from what it appears to be and any evaluation based on a simple set of rules will fail to account for these complexities. It would be foolish to make a statement about consumer rationality if we don't know what consumers are actually doing. We would be in the position of doctors a century ago who didn't comprehend either bacteria or viruses and thus used treatments that were irrelevant to the patient's actual sickness.

We face, then, the scientist's continuing need to find a better way to describe reality. That better way lies in a broadened definition of consumption that can accommodate the variations in consumer behavior and the complexities of the marketplace. Fortunately, recent extensions of economic analysis provide us with a more general perspective. The discussion can be developed around two questions: "What constitutes consumption?" and "What are individuals really consuming?" The answers to those questions, it turns out, are not as obvious as they might seem.

In the last chapter, I indicated that consumption is the goal of economic activity. That is standard economic thinking, viewing consumption as the process that ultimately results in the satisfaction of human wants. This suggests that only the actual consumption of goods and services provides satisfaction. Although most people recognize that satisfaction can come from activities that are not usually classified as consumption, the implications of that observation have been explored only in recent years [1]. Eating a meal, for example, is obviously consumption, and should provide satisfaction. However, the preparation of the meal might also provide satisfaction, even though it would not be thought of as consumption. More generally, individuals may derive satisfaction from their work, participation in community service, or from their roles as parents, although none of these activities are commonly classified as consumption.

Individuals engage in a variety of activities, all of which are potential sources of satisfaction. Consumption as it is traditionally defined may be the most significant activity in this respect, but it is not the only one. Therefore, if we focus on traditional aspects of consumption behavior, we will likely miss a significant portion of the individual's total behavior as a consumer; that means we will miss important sources of satisfaction.

Consider the role of work again. Individuals who draw large amounts of satisfaction from their work may allocate more time to work. In that case, less time will be left for traditional consumption, but these people will still be better off because they will be spending time where they get the most satisfaction. Or, take the person who chooses a job that doesn't pay as well as others, but is one that he or she enjoys. Because that person is earning less, he or she will have less money with which to buy goods and services, but the total level of satisfaction will be higher because of the satisfaction derived from work. By extension, we can consider the case of the person who decides not to work as much. In this case, the free time provides more satisfaction to the individual than could be derived with the extra money and the things it would buy.*

Extending the definition of consumption allows it to encompass a variety of different behaviors. Consider a family that has risen from poverty; one that is not rich, but judged financially secure. Family members might take some of their consumption in not scrimping. That is, they might splurge a little—behavior that might otherwise be considered inappropriate—and derive great satisfaction since they

---

* Traditional economic analysis distinguishes between work and leisure, although such distinctions aren't always clear. Once we admit that any activity may provide satisfaction, the distinction is no longer necessary. This approach was identified by Gary Becker [1, p. 504].

are experiencing a luxury they had not previously enjoyed. In such cases, the way in which people consume becomes consumption itself.

It is clear from these examples that consumer behavior represents an overall pattern in the allocation of time as well as in the allocation of income. Particular purchases in the market (and the manner in which they are made), reflect a more general decision concerning the allocation of time. The satisfaction derived from the consumption of goods and services should therefore complement satisfaction derived from other activities. It follows that such activities provide the context within which the consumption of goods and services should be considered.

What Are We Consuming?

Having established a broader context for consumption, we must now look more closely at what individuals are doing when they consume actual goods and services. We begin by remembering that although individual preferences dictate consumption patterns, consumption does not take place in a vacuum. On the contrary, consumption must be viewed as a social as well as an economic phenomenon, since one person's consumption may be affected by how or what others consume. An example is the homeowner with the unpainted house. He or she did not care that the building detracted from the overall beauty of the neighborhood. If the neighbors care, however, then their level of satisfaction is reduced.

This illustrates what are called *externalities in consumption;* in the illustration, they are negative, since one person's consumption interferes with others. Externalities may also be positive, as in the case of the person who keeps a parklike yard that others can enjoy. In an increasingly crowded, urban society, such interdependence is becoming increasingly important; individuals must contend with one another's consumption.

The examples above pertain to actual consumption, but consumers' *preferences* may also interrelate. That is, the way one individual feels about a particular item may be influenced by how others feel about it. Suppose you ask a friend whether she likes some product. You can assume that her individual reaction to the product will determine her answer. If you had first told her that this product was very popular, would that have influenced her answer? It would have for many people, since their perception of products and the satisfaction they get from them is influenced by others. Harvey Leibenstein pioneered this line of analysis; he was among the first to specify the different ways in which consumers' tastes can interact.

For the *snob,* interdependence in consumption means that as an item becomes popular, it offers less satisfaction. Snobs will reduce their consumption of a popular item, because they value exclusiveness; if everyone has the product, it loses value and becomes less than the product that was purchased originally [9, p. 201]. The snob effect is particularly important in fashion. Many people attach great importance to being the first with the latest style; producers know this, and you will often see a certain good available in a limited or collector's edition.

The opposite of the snobs are the people who are trying to keep up with the Joneses. Their interest in an item increases as others acquire it. This is the *bandwagon* effect, so common in the world of fad [9, p. 192]. A family might not have been interested in color television until their neighbors bought color sets. Suddenly, that family must have one. Like the snob, these bandwagon climbers are not interested merely in the set itself; they are buying their way into what they see as respectability by being part of the crowd.

Finally, there are the people who think that more is better, especially when applied to price. They buy the expensive good merely because it costs more. They too are buying more than the good itself; they are buying status. This is the classic case of conspicuous consumption that Veblen identified; hence, it is referred to as the *Veblen effect* [9, p. 203; 15, Chap. 4]. Consumption in such cases is meant to impress others, to show that the individual has made it (or has it made). Such types buy liquor for the label, not for the contents of the bottle, and send their children to "all the best schools," not for the quality of the education, but for the name of the institution.

The key element in each of these cases is that consumers are buying more than the goods themselves. The actual goods or services may be relatively unimportant. You may not approve of this type of consumption, and its social value is open to question, but if snobs really get added enjoyment from being snobs, then they are maximizing satisfaction. Behavior that may appear to be irrational or wasteful is actually consistent with their own preferences.

If these cases were merely isolated examples, we could dismiss them as curiosities. If you think about it, however, you should realize that deriving satisfaction from more than the good itself is not limited to cases where social interaction is involved. You may buy a blanket for warmth, but you also consider the way it looks and feels. From a functional point of view, warmth may be the basic property of the blanket, but it still has properties of appearance and texture, and most consumers are going to take these considerations into account.

A more sophisticated view of consumption emerges when we recognize that consumers derive utility from the properties or characteristics of a good. This point of view constitutes a departure from the traditional economic position that goods are valued for their intrinsic or functional qualities only. Increasing numbers of economists, however, are adopting the view that "goods are not goods." In summarizing their approach, a great many misconceptions that surround consumer rationality can be laid to rest. By now you should understand that such misconceptions arise out of confusion over what it is that consumers are actually consuming.

Kelvin Lancaster, who coined the phrase "goods are not goods," has been an innovator in this area. He summarized his approach in three fundamental propositions. Lancaster maintains:

1. The good, *per se*, does not give utility to the consumer; it possesses characteristics, and these characteristics give rise to utility.
2. In general, a good will possess more than one characteristic, and many characteristics will be shared by more than one good.
3. Goods in combination may possess characteristics different from those pertaining to the goods separately. [8, p. 133]

These remarks follow the tenor of our discussion. Indeed, they represent the logical culmination of the argument I have been developing. Consider Lancaster's discussion of why a person buys a meal:

A meal, treated as a single good, possesses nutritional characteristics, but it also possesses aesthetic characteristics and different meals will possess these characteristics in different proportions. Furthermore, a dinner party, a combination of two goods, a meal and a social setting, may possess nutritional, aesthetic and perhaps intellectual characteristics different from the combination obtainable from a meal and a social gathering consumed separately. [8, p. 134]

The point of the argument is simple enough. People who buy meals are not really buying meals at all; they are buying a whole set of qualities or characteristics that satisfy their particular needs. A person who is starving is going to be interested in a meal strictly for its nutritional value. The person who goes to a fast-food carry out, however, is buying a meal plus convenience, while the patron of an elegant restaurant is buying aesthetics in addition to the meal.

While these points have yet to be integrated fully into economic theory, some of them are recognized in everyday speech. Most consumers are aware that they commonly "buy" convenience. Furthermore, you have certainly heard someone say that at a particular restaurant you are "paying for the atmosphere," or that a home in a certain neighborhood costs more "because it's a good address." In such cases, products are perceived to be made up of bundles of characteristics. Consumers' choices, then, depend upon the relative valuation of the different characteristics.

Notice that this view of consumption is tied to a theme already developed—high income and an increasingly sophisticated economy. In a low-income, nonspecialized economy, goods may be valued primarily for their intrinsic qualities. The pioneer family needed shelter and obtained utility directly from the shelter itself. Anything that met that need—log cabin, sod shanty, and so on—was adequate, since it was shelter that counted and the family was in no position to be concerned about anything else.

As incomes rose and the immediate need for shelter was met, the family could afford to broaden its concerns and include such elements as comfort and appearance in its consideration of housing. Today, that process has gone so far that shelter is hardly emphasized as a quality of housing.* Any advertisement for a new apartment complex will tell you more about tennis courts, swimming pools, saunas, and game rooms than about the apartment itself. Similarly, most home buyers take shelter for granted and concentrate on finding the right style, neighborhood, and location.

Thinking about consumption has not kept pace with changing conditions. We still think in terms that may have been appropriate fifty or a hundred years ago, when consumers' incomes were more limited, but these terms do not fit the realities of today's affluence. As a result, we have tended to treat consumption in terms that are far too simple to account for all of its complexities. Investigators have been getting the wrong answers because they have been asking the wrong questions, and they have been asking the wrong questions because they have failed to understand what consumption really is.

Consumption Efficiency

In Lancaster's formulation, consumers face two decisions. The first is determining the combination of characteristics that is preferred. The second is to find how the preferred combination can be obtained as economically or efficiently as possible. The first decision is dependent on personal tastes. The second, however, is independent of tastes, since it simply relates to obtaining the particular characteristics as cheaply as possible. Some people may want characteristic X and others may not (a matter of taste), but *for all of those who want*

---

* Low-income groups are an exception, since they are more likely to be concerned with the need for adequate shelter itself. This, however, only underscores the point. Problems of the poor are considered specifically in Chapter 10.

X, the problem is the same: how to get as much X as possible for their money [7, p. 17].

To take a simple example, suppose you are interested in only one characteristic of housing, floor space. If your choice is between two houses with equal floor space, but one costs more than the other, it would be *inefficient* to buy the more expensive one. You would be paying more than necessary for the characteristic you really want.

Note that there is no judgment about tastes, no consideration of whether the consumer should or should not want floor space. If, however, the consumer wants floor space, then the question of efficiency arises. It is a serious question, because, as I have been stressing, consumption is highly complex. Lancaster notes that the consumption process

> in a society like that of the United States, is very complex. Efficient consumption, even in the presence of adequate information ... involves some managerial skill. ... Conventional consumer theory leads to a presumption that the family which spends its income on an eccentric collection of goods is simply revealing its preferences for that collection. Of course, this might be true, but it may also be that the family is consuming inefficiently. [7, p. 19]

The inefficient consumer, continues Lancaster, "will remain at a lower welfare level than that potentially available. Again, this leads to the presumption that public consumer education would be socially valuable" [7, p. 19].

Those statements resolve the dilemma we have been facing throughout this chapter. Observed consumption patterns depend upon both preferences and efficiency. Without making value judgments about individual preferences, it is possible to raise questions about efficiency. Now you might think it makes little difference whether behavior is called *irrational* or *inefficient*, but in fact the difference is significant. *Irrational* implies that there is something wrong with the individual for behaving that way; *inefficient* merely suggests that the individual could benefit from assistance in executing his or her consumption plan [12, p. 76].

The further consequences of confusing rationality and efficiency can be illustrated by an analogy. A scientist carries out experiments—growing bacteria cultures, for example—under carefully controlled laboratory conditions. If those same experiments were performed outside of the laboratory, would you expect the results to be the same? Of course not. In a nonsterile environment, airborne bacteria and other agents would interfere with the experiment, altering and probably invalidating the result.

The same thing is true of consumer behavior. Most evaluations of consumer performance are undertaken *as though* consumption were carried out in a clinical environment highly favorable to the consumer. Under such conditions, any errors or mistakes can be taken as evidence of the consumer's incompetence. The error in logic should be clear. The consumer's environment is not conducive to careful rational decision making. Suggesting that problems arise out of some fundamental shortcomings of consumers has impeded progress toward more efficient consumption; such progress will come when consumers are better prepared to cope with the market and the market itself is made more hospitable.

Toward More Efficient Consumption

Realities of the Marketplace

It appears that for many individuals efficient consumption is impeded by lack of basic skills. A 1975 study by the National Assessment of Educational Progress found that one adult American in two lacked the basic mathematical skills to function effectively in the marketplace.* [2] The report noted that:

> The consumer-mathematics results should raise some disturbing questions. For example, are we satisfied with American consumer-mathematics ability in light of facts that 45% of the adults did not read a federal income tax form correctly, and under half of the population at ages 17 and adult successfully determined the most economical package size of two cost-comparison exercises? [2, pp. 34–35]

Another recent study surveyed adults' functional literacy, their ability to function in or cope with various day-to-day situations.† The findings were hardly comforting. The report showed that 30 percent of the population lacked basic consumer skills, and that another 33 percent functioned with difficulty as consumers; of all the areas studied, "the greatest area of difficulty appears to be Consumer Economics" [14, p. 6]. In terms of population figures, "some 34.7 million

* The study included a variety of problems on determining costs; household problems, interpreting graphs and tables, and using concepts of averages and percent.

† Areas studied included occupational knowledge, consumer economics, government and law, health, community resources, reading, problem solving, computation, and writing.

adult Americans function with difficulty and an additional 39 million are functional, (but not proficient) in coping with basic requirements that are related to Consumer Economics" [14, p. 6].

If only one-third of all adult consumers can function proficiently in the marketplace, it is hardly surprising that so many consumers encounter difficulties. We might conclude from such studies that most consumers are inefficient; put differently, that means most Americans could improve their standard of living with no increase in income by improving their consumer skills. The obvious need is for more and better consumer education, not just in the schools, but as part of a process of on-going, life-long learning.

Even proficient consumers, however, encounter difficulties in the marketplace. It sometimes seems as if the market is organized to make things difficult for consumers. Take life insurance, for example. Life insurance is important, but how is the consumer to find out about it? Each company's policies are slightly different from those of competitors, so that comparing policies by talking to different agents can be confusing. Under pressure from consumers, insurance advertising has improved, but there is still little information on the real differences among different types of insurance. The different types of insurance policies illustrate what economists call product differentiation. That phrase refers to products that are essentially the same but are made to appear different by superficial changes, packaging, and advertising. All of that is not only very expensive, it is also very confusing. The next time you are in a grocery store, pick out some household item—soaps, for example—and notice how many different kinds line the shelves. You may find over fifty different kinds of soaps and detergents, offered in such a confusing array that it would befuddle the most diligent shopper.

Let's look at another way in which the market is rigged against the consumer. American automobile producers continue to resist safety standards, maintaining that "safety won't sell." They point to evidence indicating more buyer interest in styling, performance, and comfort. The evidence may be valid, but we have to ask why. The answer is simple enough. Detroit has advertised its products almost solely on those terms, so that car buyers naturally view such factors as most important. If fifty years of advertising had stressed safety, quality, and economy, consumers would evaluate automobiles from a different set of standards.

You can go on thinking up your own examples. The market is simply not organized to facilitate careful decisions by consumers. Some observers have made stronger allegations, indicating that it is impossible for consumers to think through alternatives and make choices based on their own judgment. Consumers may think they are making their own decisions, but in truth their judgment is influenced, if not controlled, by producers.

John Kenneth Galbraith has been a champion of this view of the manipulated consumer. The consumer emerges, to modify Galbraith's own analogy, in the position of a squirrel that struggles "to keep abreast of the wheel that is propelled by his own efforts" [4, p. 125]. To Galbraith, understanding the consumer's role in the economic system "means recognizing that wants are dependent upon production." This view "accords the producer the function both of making the goods and of making the desires for them. It recognized that production . . . through advertising and related activities creates the wants it seeks to satisfy" [4, p. 127]. In this context, even efficient consumers have done nothing more than fulfill the role that producers laid out for them. Consumers can do little more than react to the specific direction of advertisers and to the broader pressures of a society that producers dominate.

We need not accept Galbraith's position to appreciate that he is correct about the obstacles that confront the consumer.* Lancaster, in his discussion of efficient consumption, noted that although advertisers will go to great lengths to point out certain characteristics of their products, other, possibly less desirable, characteristics won't even be mentioned [7, p. 18].

Coping With the Market Environment

Given all of the problems that consumers face—lack of skills, bewildering variations among products, and pressure from advertising—it may seem surprising that consumers are able to function at all. Yet consumers obviously function, and some manage to overcome the obstacles and function effectively. George Katona, who was a pioneer in the study of actual consumption behavior, provides considerable insight into how consumers manage.

Not surprisingly, Katona found that no simple formula can explain all the complexities of consumer behavior. He notes that consumers typically do not reach decisions "after careful weighing of alternative courses," although at the same time "consumer behavior is not capricious." Even if consumers do not behave in reality the way they do in economics textbooks, their behavior is not random; it can be understood and explained and, as Katona continues, "in this sense is not conceived as irrational" [5, p. 19].

---

* You should appreciate that there are many other implications of Galbraith's conclusions. I have done little more than introduce the topic here, and will return to it under the discussion of consumer sovereignty in Chapter 7.

You may still ask: Is the consumer rational or irrational? According to Katona:

> This is not the right question to ask. The consumer is a human being influenced by his past experience. . . . He is apt to prefer short cuts, follow rules of thumb and behave in a routine manner. But he is also capable of acting intelligently. *When he feels that it really matters, he will deliberate and choose to the best of his ability.* [6, p. 145, emphasis added]

This view of consumers is very appealing. It pictures them as hurried, hassled, and perhaps a little lazy, but not hopeless. To fully appreciate Katona's conclusion, however, you must recall the earlier discussion of the value of time and its role in consumption.

Consumers must buy such a wide range of products that, if they tried to study each purchase carefully, they would get very little else done. So they do the human thing—they compromise. Small, routine purchases are relegated to habit, a path of least resistance. The shopper becomes familiar with the stores in the area and then shops at the one best fitted to his or her needs. From time to time this may mean passing up good buys elsewhere, but it isn't worth the time and effort to take advantage of them.

New residents in an area typically find that shopping takes them longer than it did before. This is because they have to find out which stores are best for them. Once they have this information, shopping is quicker. They have simplified the process by eliminating decisions. Or perhaps it is more accurate to say that once they have made the decisions, they do not have to keep repeating them. By reserving attention for decisions that really matter, habitual behavior may be a rational reaction to the complexities of the market.

This recognizes that there are costs attached to making decisions. Were it not for these costs, consumers might carefully evaluate all possible alternatives in making decisions. However, in the face of constraints on time and energy, consumers must concentrate on those purchases that take a significant amount of their income. They consider such purchases in terms consistent with those suggested in economic theory. Lowering the cost of consumer decision making should therefore improve the efficiency of consumption.

Cutting decision costs begins with the individual and his or her own structure of preferences. At this moment, for example, you may want a cup of coffee, a new car, and a trip to Europe. Those are quite different commodities, but each of them costs money and takes time. Since the money and time you have are limited, you must decide which of the three you want most. The money and time involved with a cup of coffee is so small that it will not have a great effect on your ability to buy either the car or the trip. Buying a car, on the other hand, would probably put such a dent in your checkbook that you would have to put off any idea of going to Europe. If you really want the car, you should buy it, but you should not turn around and complain about not having enough money to go to Europe.

You should recognize that we have returned to the opportunity-cost argument. Consumers must have an overall idea not only of what things they want, but also how much they want them. With this perception they can order their consumption accordingly. This point can be generalized because it appears that consumers do not always think through what their purchasing implies.

Notice that when we begin to consider the implications of purchases, we reintroduce the idea of consumption efficiency. Knowing what you want is a matter of your own preferences; however, the manner in which obtaining one thing you want affects your ability to obtain other things you want is a matter of efficiency. Thus, even the ranking of individual priorities involves questions of efficiency, since such considerations help define which alternatives will actually be available.

We have taken several different approaches to consumer decision making, but each brings us back to the question of efficiency in consumption. Indeed, the four assumptions listed in Chapter 2—rationality, perfect information, certainty, and consumer sovereignty— might also be thought of as requisites for efficient consumption. Therefore, if we want to pursue the efficiency question further, we need to look more closely at the specific problems that impede efficient consumption.

To be efficient, consumers obviously need information; they also need some power in the market so that they can either protect themselves or ensure that someone else is looking out for their interests. These issues are treated in subsequent chapters. Before dealing with them, however, we must look at another important question relating to consumer decision making. We have discussed the difficulties consumers encounter in carrying out their consumption plans; the very idea of a plan implies a relationship to the future, yet consumers have limited control over it and no real knowledge about it. Thus, if consumers are to be efficient, they must be able to cope with the future as well as the present. By saying that, I have introduced a whole new set of considerations that I will now analyze.

Study Questions

1. Is it irrational to want something because everyone else has it? How would you analyze your desire in this case?

2. The law prohibits some types of consumption (marijuana, for example). Consider the relation between individual choice and social control in this case. Is there any relevance to the fact that many laws against the use of marijuana are not being enforced?

3. Ask some friends what impulse buying means to them. Make sure they define it. Can they answer the questions about it that were raised in the text? Discuss.

4. "I figured that if it was so cheap, it couldn't be any good." Comment.

5. Assuming that consumers are at all rational, how do you explain that fraud and deception are so common?

6. Suppose you quit your job because you didn't enjoy it. Would your friends understand your decision? What about your parents?

7. People always talk about "saving time," even though that's not possible. What does the expression really mean? Why are consumers so concerned about time?

8. Consider housing in terms of Lancaster's analysis. What kind of characteristics might people want? Could different features of the dwelling provide similar characteristics?

9. Distinguish between rationality in consumption and efficiency in consumption? Can either be judged?

10. Why is habitual consumer behavior so important? Does it have anything to do with consumer rationality?

11. Suppose that a particular firm employs two mail clerks. Both are poorly paid, but one buys expensive clothes; the other dresses poorly but is sending his daughter to college. Does this tell you whether or not they are rational? Which of the two is likely to be approved? Is there any real basis for this judgment?

12. If time is so valuable, why is there a revival of interest in gourmet cooking (which is time consuming)?

Suggested Projects

1. Talk with officials at your school's job placement office. What kinds of jobs are students looking for? Has there been a change

in student preferences? What are the most popular kinds of jobs? The least popular?

2. Read the consumer advice columns in a magazine or your local newspaper. What do you think of the quality of the advice? Would the individual be wrong in not following it?

3. Go to a grocery and price five prepared foods. Then get as good an idea as possible of the price if you bought the basic food and prepared it yourself. What is the average price differential? Next, figure the time it would take to prepare the foods yourself. What is the cost of the time you are saving? How much time would it have *cost* you if you had prepared the food yourself?

4. Compare prices in a convenience store with those in a regular grocery store. Do the price differentials vary with different goods? How much are you actually paying for convenience?

5. Look at several advertisements for houses, apartments, and automobiles. Do the ads tend to emphasize the product itself or other qualities it possesses? Is there any relation between the price of the product and the degree to which basic properties are emphasized?

6. Discuss in class or with friends bad purchases that any of you have made. Do these represent irrationality? Can you identify the cause of the mistake in each case? Is there a pattern?

7. Investigate local laws that relate to individual consumption or affect it in some way. You will probably be surprised at the number and extent of them. Do they fall into any pattern. On what basis can they be justified? Discuss.

8. Go to your local bookstore and check the number of *how-to* or *do-it-yourself* books available. Ask the manager which ones sell best? If time is so valuable, how do you account for the popularity of such books?

9. Review the statistics on the number of women working outside the home (see Chapter 11). What do these changes imply for consumer choice? For consumption patterns?

Bibliography and Suggested Readings

1. Becker, Gary S., "A Theory of the Allocation of Time." *The Economic Journal* vol. LXXV, no. 299, (September 1965):492–517.
    The original reformulation of economic theory to focus on time and view consumption as a series of activities. The article is rigorous, but even students with limited backgrounds can benefit from Becker's dis-

cussions. Essential for anyone seriously interested in consumer economics.

2. *Consumer Math.* National Assessment of Educational Progress. Mathematics Report No. 04-MA-02. Washington, D.C.: U.S. Government Printing Office, 1975.
The national survey that indicates that only half of all American consumers have the basic math skills necessary to function in the market. The report provides breakdowns by sex, age, region, and race. Since no test can give a truly accurate picture of how consumers will operate in the market place, the results must be interpreted with care; however, those results are so definitive that it is obvious that problems exist.

3. Davis, Harry L. "Decision Making Within the Household." *The Journal of Consumer Research,* March 1976, pp. 241–60.
A survey of the research on household decision making, including a review of the roles played by different members of the household. Contains an excellent bibliography.
The appearance of The Journal of Consumer Research *in 1975 marked an important step forward for research in consumer affairs. The journal is characterized by an interdisciplinary perspective. Students will find the review articles and extensive bibliographic references especially helpful.*

4. Galbraith, John Kenneth. *The Affluent Society.* Boston: Houghton Mifflin Co., 1958. Chap. 1.
The basic statement about the manipulated consumer. These ideas will figure heavily in our later discussions of consumer power and public consumption.

5. Katona, George. "Consumer Behavior: Theory and Findings on Expectations and Aspirations." *American Economic Review, Paper and Proceedings,* May 1968, pp. 19–30.
An exploration of consumer behavior that I will use extensively in the next chapter.

6. ———. *The Powerful Consumer.* New York: McGraw-Hill Book Co., 1960.
Required reading for anyone interested in consumption behavior. Katona broadens the traditional economic view into a meaningful concept. Chapter 9 on rationality is particularly valuable.

7. Lancaster, Kelvin. "Change and Innovation in the Technology of Consumption." *American Economic Review, Papers and Proceedings,* May 1966, pp. 14–23.
A nontechnical formulation of the ideas presented in the text about goods and consumption. Has especially valuable applications to consumer education.

8. ————. "A New Approach to Consumer Theory." *Journal of Political Economy,* April 1966, pp. 132–57.
The basis for the discussion in the text on why consumers actually consume characteristics that goods possess rather than the goods themselves.

9. Leibenstein, Harvey. "Bandwagon, Snob and Veblen Effects in the Theory of Consumer Demand." *Quarterly Journal of Economics,* May 1950, pp. 189–207.
A classic article on demand theory. You will see in Leibenstein's work a suggestion of the approach that Lancaster later developed. Previously, economists had largely ignored interdependence in consumption, although Leibenstein does review the history of the idea.

10. Maynes, Scott E. *Decision Making for Consumers.* New York: Macmillan, 1976.
A text that covers a range of topics concerning consumer decision making. Focus throughout is on information.

11. McGuire, William J. "Some Internal Psychological Factors Influencing Consumer Choice." *The Journal of Consumer Research,* March 1976, pp. 302–19.
A good review of psychological aspects of consumer choice. Particularly strong on material about how consumers actually use information and the decision-making process itself.

12. Ratchford, Brian T., Taylor, Lester, and Haines, George. "The New Theory of Consumer Behavior: An Interpretive Essay." With "Commentaries." *The Journal of Consumer Research,* September 1975, pp. 65–79.
As the name implies, an interpretation of Lancaster, with additional comments on the interpretation. A useful expansion of Lancaster's ideas. Ranges from technical and nontechnical.

13. Strumpel, Burkhard, et al., eds. *Human Behavior in Economic Affairs.* San Francisco: Jossey-Bass, 1972.
A valuable collection of original essays by leading consumer specialists on different aspects of consumer behavior.

14. *Texas Study of Adult Functional Competency: A Summary.* Division of Extension, The University of Texas at Austin, Austin, Texas, 1975.
Study covering a range of demands that modern life makes on individuals. Suggests that most people are better at other things than they are at consumption.

15. Veblen, Thorstein. *The Theory of the Leisure Class.* New York: Mentor Books, 1953, Chap. 1.
The essential Veblen on conspicuous consumption. A primer for anyone interested in the topic.

-4-

The Role of Expectations
and Uncertainty

Living in a World of Ifs

How many times have you heard someone say "If I had only known!" or "If I had known then what I know now. . . ."? Such laments are common and are usually followed by a shrug of the shoulders and the observation "Hindsight is 20–20." Foresight, of course, is something less than 20–20; in fact, we are all myopic as far as the future is concerned. We may have an understanding of the past and some grasp of the present, but the future is conjecture.

We do make statements of fact about the future, but we know they are subject to limitations. You may say to a friend, "I'll meet you for dinner at eight," when what you really mean is "If nothing unforeseen happens to either of us, we'll have dinner at eight." Simply stated, it is impossible to make an unconditional statement about the future; we do not even know whether or not we have a future. In order to cope with the situation, we pretend nothing too drastic is going to happen. We try to plan our lives in an orderly fashion based on the idea that the future will be pretty much like the past. This makes sense as far as day-to-day living is concerned, because it would be impossible, and certainly depressing, to ponder all of life's unknowns.

Still, we have a pervasive, some would say perverse, interest in the future, and it seems to be growing. Soothsayers, seers, and fortune-tellers of all kinds do a booming business from people who want a glimpse of what is to come. The revival of interest in astrology reflects this same phenomenon and is a rejection of the rational, scientific approach to coping with change. Perhaps it is a matter of daring fate, of the individual's standing up to the unknown. In this respect, people haven't changed much over the years. For all our technological advances and increased understanding, we still face the future alone.

The considerations just mentioned may seem esoteric, and they would be if it were not for one fact. *The future is now.* I am not talking here, as it has become fashionable to do, about the pace of change being so rapid that it overcomes us. No, I am saying that present actions have an impact beyond the present; they extend into the future. Therefore, future developments must be considered in current decisions. The catch is that no one can be sure about what those future developments are going to be. Yet since such developments must be taken into account, it is individuals' perceptions of the future—what they think is going to happen—that becomes important. Things that have not happened yet, and indeed may not happen, have a direct bearing on the way we behave.

From the consumer's perspective, this means that possible future developments affect present consumption. We can see this in different ways. There is the young married couple who puts off buying furniture because they aren't sure that they will still like Danish modern five years from now. Or the construction workers who decide not to buy that color television, even though they have the money, out of fear of being laid off. Consider, too, the college students who would like to major in English and be writers, but who take business courses instead because they are worried about job opportunities after graduation. And finally, there are the insurance representatives, selling security and reducing life to a set of probabilities.

In each case, we can see that the future influences present actions. Even though no one knows what the future holds, we form expectations about what we think is going to happen and these expectations influence our current behavior. The future may be an abstraction, but it significantly affects the way we behave in the present. As in the examples above, people make consumption decisions according to what they think is going to happen. This clearly makes such expectations very important ingredients in consumer behavior.

Evaluating Future Developments

Discounting

There are three points to keep in mind throughout our evaluation: (1) the future hasn't happened yet, (2) some of it will not happen for a long time, and (3) some of it may never happen. If the future is un-known—our first point—then even if you have an idea about what is going to happen, you can't be sure about it. As a result, that future event cannot be weighed as heavily in your decision-making process as some event that is known with certainty. If you get up in the morning and it is raining, you won't leave home without your um-brella or raincoat. However, if skies are clear in the morning, the fore-cast of rain in the afternoon would not have the same impact on your behavior.

Reducing the weight (or importance) of future developments is known as *discounting*. The question then becomes: "If you do not take future events at face value, how much weight should they be given?" Our second and third points provide the key to that question. In deciding how much importance to give a possible future develop-ment, you must consider the length of time until the expected event and the likelihood of its happening. Depending on the answers to those questions, a future event may be given nearly as much weight as current happenings, or it may be disregarded altogether.

Time is one factor. Human nature puts things off. We may be wor-ried about tomorrow, next week, or next month, but our concerns generally do not extend much further than that. We may, in our more contemplative moments, wonder where we'll be ten years from now, but such reflections always seem to be pushed aside by the pressures and demands of the present. This suggests that the further an event is in the future, the smaller its impact on present decisions. You wouldn't wear a raincoat just because rain is in the long-range fore-cast. We can apply these ideas to planning about future income and summarize their impact by the statement: A dollar now is worth more than a dollar a year from now. It is true that if you put your dollar in savings, it will earn interest so that in a year you will have, say, $1.05. But have you ever thought why you are paid interest? It is to induce you to give up the use of that dollar for a year. If you have a dollar now, you can spend it and get the enjoyment from whatever you buy; you cannot do anything with next year's dollar until next year. There-fore, if someone offered you the promise of a dollar a year from now in exchange for a dollar now, you would not make the trade because you would lose the use of your money for a year. So, you have to reduce the value, or discount, next year's dollar to obtain its present value, meaning its value to you now.*

For the same idea in less abstract terms, suppose that a rich uncle

---

* Accounting students will recall that in a mechanical sense, present value is given by the formula $PV = C/(1 + r)^n$, where C is the income flow, r is the in-terest rate, and n is the number of years. If the interest rate is 5 percent, the present value of $1 in a year is $1/1.05, or about $0.95. The present value of $1 in two years is $1/(1.05)^2 = $1/1.1025, or a bit less than $0.91.

dies when you are twenty and stipulates in his will that you are to receive $1 million on your twenty-first birthday. You would probably increase your spending immediately, going on a buying binge even though it meant using credit and going into debt. After all, that money from your uncle will be yours in a few months and you will have more than enough to cover your accounts. Suppose, however, that your uncle mistrusted foolish youth, and while he left you the million, he said you could not have it until you were sixty-five. Forty-five years is a long time to wait, even for a million dollars. The present value of $1 million in 45 years is only $31,327.88, with an interest rate of 8 percent.* It might influence you in terms of buying insurance or retirement benefits, but would probably have no impact on your current consumption levels. The money is simply too far away to have very much value. As you grow older and there is less time left for you to wait, its value would increase, but that is small comfort when you are twenty.

From these examples, you can see that even when future events are virtually assured, they must be adjusted because they are in the future. The further in the future their potential occurrence, the greater the adjustment. If you are thinking of buying a car, you might buy a more expensive model if you think you are going to get a raise next year. On the other hand, if that raise is two or three years off, you probably would not take it into account in buying the car. Suppose, though, that you thought you were going to get a raise and therefore bought the more expensive car. Then, the boss does not come through with the extra money. You would be in a fix. That further illustrates the point we have been making: You can't be certain about the future. We used the phrase *virtually assured* above, but future events are rarely virtually assured. Therefore, they must be adjusted further, according to the probability that they will happen.

If an event is unlikely, it will not have much impact on current actions, even if its potential impact is very great. A 10 percent chance of rain won't send you looking for cover. A sweepstakes ticket that gives you a one-in-a-million chance of winning a million dollars wouldn't affect your consumption much either, because the odds against you are so great. If you happen to win, you could invite all your friends and have a tremendous bash, but it would not be wise to make the arrangements in advance.

Taking these two factors together, you can see that the greater

---

* Higher interest rates are commonly used in such calculations, since future interest rates are themselves unknown. Whatever rate is used, it is clear that the value of the money will be significantly reduced.

the probability of the event and the sooner it occurs, the greater its influence on your current actions. The range of possible future developments must be evaluated in these terms. A one-in-a-million chance for a million dollars at age sixty-five would not rate even a second thought from most college seniors. But those same seniors will be out buying cars, clothes, and maybe even furniture because in a few months they will have jobs. The jobs will not pay a million dollars, but the job market entrants can be relatively sure of getting their money, and soon. Thus, the high probability of getting even a small amount of money in the near future will affect consumers more than the remote chance for a large sum in the distant future.

The Range of Expectations

Consumer expectations about development in areas other than income are important in determining current consumption behavior. Expectations may apply to any of the factors that affect consumer behavior. In particular, expectations about tastes and prices are significant. The time and probability rule also applies in these cases. For the consumer who is buying something that will last a long time, there is a chance that tastes will change over the lifetime of the product. Therefore, when he or she is making the purchase, the possibility of changing tastes must be taken into account. This applies particularly to housing and consumer durables (automobiles, home furnishings, and appliances) [12]. If the item will be used up rather quickly, such considerations are not going to be very important. The nature of the item is important too. If it is purely functional, like a garden hose, then it is unlikely that tastes are going to change.

The expense of the item and its relative importance in the consumer's budget must also be considered. Tastes in clothing, for example, change annually—some fashion fads do not even make it through one season. Yet if the item is relatively inexpensive, the consumer may go ahead and buy anyway. Thus, if a particular type of wild tie is currently the rage, a man might buy one, knowing that even if the fad doesn't last he is not out very much money. That same man, however, might buy a more conservative suit that is likely to be in style for a number of years. The greater expense of the suit makes him cautious and forces him to consider changing tastes.

Our general time-probability rule suggests that the more uncertain consumers are about changing tastes, the less likely they will be to buy. The time element is important in the example of the newly married couple who put off buying furniture because they are not sure what they are going to like in five years. No one can be certain that tastes will not change over time; probably most people expect that they will. The key question is: "Is there any reason to suspect that tastes will be changing soon?" If the answer is "no," the tendency would be to go ahead and buy. Possible changes of taste in the distant future are too remote to have an impact on the present.

We can analyze consumer expectations about changing prices in a more straightforward manner. In a period of inflation, and most of the years since World War II can be categorized under that heading, consumers form expectations about continued inflation. Any feeling they have that prices are going to continue to rise is built into their consumption behavior. This may be shown in many ways. It appears in union contracts, for example, where there is added pressure to include a cost-of-living adjustment. Short of such an agreement, the negotiator may ask for a 10 percent increase, 5 percent to cover inflation and 5 percent as an actual increase. In individual decisions, expectations of higher prices tend to encourage current consumption. Why wait if things are going to cost more later? Such an attitude tends to discourage savings, especially if consumers feel that even with interest the purchasing power of their savings will decline [14, chap. 14].

If, on the other hand, consumers feel that prices are going to fall in the future, they would tend to postpone consumption. While this has not been the case with the overall price level in recent years, it has been true for particular products. Electronic calculators are one obvious example. Price trends in color television sets have been downward also, although the decline has been less spectacular. That pattern is typical of most new products.

Confrontations with the Future

The Future in Retrospect

The future may be thought of as both a *challenge* and a *resource* to the consumer. It is a challenge because it is unknown, and the consumer must therefore be prepared for various eventualities. This preparation commonly takes the form of savings or insurance, both of which offer the consumer a hedge against adverse developments in the future: *they represent the application of current resources against the future.* Since money used for savings or insurance cannot be spent on current consumption goods, the level of current consumption is depressed.

The future is also a good resource, however, in that it represents potential earnings. All but the oldest consumers can look forward to earning money in the future and *the possibility exists of transferring that money from the future to the present.* That is a fancy way of saying that consumers use credit or go into debt. If you think about it, debt means spending money you have not yet received, and then paying it back as you earn it. I hinted at this when I talked about college seniors spending the earnings expected from jobs they had not yet begun.

You can now see that there are two elements involved here. Consumers' perceptions of the future determine how they will spend their current and future income. *They may either transfer current income into the future (savings, insurance) or transfer future income to the present (debt).* This offers flexibility—consumers are not limited to present resources, but can draw on future resources also.

Transferring income forward or backward raises abstractions and complexities. Some abstraction is necessary to summarize the argument, but it is easy enough to translate these ideas into everyday terms. The complexities are more difficult to handle. In essence we are investigating how the consumer balances the demands of the present against the demands of the future. To understand the process and cut through some of the complexities, let's look first at the general pattern; once we have done that, we can admit individual variations. In this way, we can use the general case as a reference against which to measure the effect of individual variations. This should bring us closer to an explanation of observed consumer behavior.

Tomorrow's Dollars Today

In establishing a general pattern for the transfer of income, we begin by looking at the consumer's entire lifetime, considering both income and needs. Not surprisingly, this approach, which has become a common feature of economic analysis, is called the life-cycle or permanent-income hypothesis [9 and 10]. By taking this view there is an immediate difficulty. Individuals' incomes come in unevenly over their lifetimes. Typically, income is lower in the early working years and then follows an upward trend until individuals reach their maximum earning years in their forties and fifties. Income then tends to level off or fall slightly before dropping sharply with retirement. Unfortunately, this pattern does not match the individual's need for money.

Expenses are high for a newly married couple. Even the most frugal find that it is expensive to set up housekeeping. There are appliances to purchase, clothes for work, and a car. Soon the couple wants a home, and if they have children costs increase even more. Older citizens do not face the same problems, but they too find that costs are high relative to income. Medical bills in particular are likely to increase; even if health is not a factor, simply enjoying retirement is expensive.*

Thus, the bulge in income comes during the middle of an individual's working years, while the bulge in expenditures comes at the beginning and the end. The obvious solution is to transfer income from the peak earning years around middle age to the periods when needs are greater. Income and expenditures are then matched and evened out. This recalls the earlier reference to diminishing marginal utility. Diminishing marginal utility applies to money too. Thus, we can buttress our commonsense argument with the more elegant contention that individuals' total level of satisfaction over their lifetimes will be greater if they transfer money from periods when its marginal utility is low to times when it has a higher marginal utility.

Transferring income is relatively simple. It means going into debt or taking money out of savings when expenditures are greater than income and saving or paying off debts when income is greater than expenditures. Note that we are not talking about a net increase in purchasing power, but merely transferring purchasing power from one period to another. Once money is spent, it is spent, so consumption can be increased during one period only at the expense of consumption in another period. The consumer's level of satisfaction is increased, however, because money is available when it is needed most.

Thus the young couple borrows money and goes into debt. Then, as income rises, they pay off their debts, accumulate savings, and buy life insurance. The key is that during this period their income has grown not only in absolute terms, but also relative to their expenditures; otherwise, they would not have money to live on. Later, when income declines relative to expenditures, the couple draws on savings and collects on insurance.

This formulation has much to recommend it. Young couples do go into debt for cars, appliances, and housing. If most of us waited until we could pay cash for a house, we should all be living in apartments. Once these fixed costs are taken care of, there is more money left over. With incomes rising, families can pay off debts and begin more significant savings. These savings will be important in later years when income again declines. There are simplifications involved here, of course. People buy many cars, appliances, and even houses over their lifetimes. Similarly, costs may be high during middle age, too, particularly if there are children to educate.

---

* The pattern here is also affected by the availability of comprehensive medical insurance. If such a program is available for the elderly, medical costs may actually decline.

The general pattern laid out here may not be representative of every case, so we need to ask about the influences that would either keep consumers from following this pattern or prompt them to conform to it. In other words, we are analyzing the forces at work on consumers when they distribute their lifetime income. To understand how the individual operates within the general framework, we must look closely at individuals' expectations about their futures.

Formulating Consumer Expectations

Impact of a Changing Environment

Individuals base their expectations of the future on their experience in the past. Consumers become familiar with their environment and come to know that certain things remain constant over time; these fixed points are used in forming expectations about the future in the same way that ancient sailors used the stars to navigate uncharted waters. There is nothing mystical about these consumer guideposts. They are nothing more than lessons learned from experience passed along from person to person, from generation to generation. Recent college graduates, for example, can look forward to increasing incomes based on the experience of friends or relatives. A person with 50,000 miles on his or her car knows to expect higher repair bills. People moving from the country to the city should expect higher living costs.

The people in these examples may have no personal experience to go on, yet, because of the experience of others, they have a reasonably sound basis for formulating expectations and planning for the future. They cannot be certain, of course—some college graduates don't make it and some cars run forever (I'm told) without needing repairs—but enough people have faced similar experiences to pass along a fund of useful knowledge.

The individual develops a sense of probabilities, what is likely to happen and what isn't. Suppose your car has 50,000 miles on it; should you replace it? You know cars typically need more repairs with that much mileage. You also know your car's own repair record. You might ask a mechanic what he or she thinks. While you will not be able to get a definitive answer, you will be able to get a reasonable idea of what you should do. Consumers base their expectations on a certain perception of order and structure that allows them to project into the future and thus reduce uncertainty. That works fine as long as the situation is stable, but when this structure is disturbed, and the signposts to the future are changed, consumers naturally become confused.

Recall the earlier comment that if consumers expect prices to continue rising, they will tend to buy now. However, if consumers have come to view a particular price level as *normal* (their signpost from experience), they may cut back consumption in anticipation that prices will return to the norm. That seems to be what happened recently with interest rates. After years at lower levels, interest rates rose in the late 1960s. That trend continued, somewhat unevenly, into the 1970s. Consumers, who were used to thinking of interest rates in the neighborhood of 4 or 5 percent, had a hard time accepting rates of 7, 8, and even 9 percent as "normal." Thus, many consumers waited for the rates to go back down, even though the best evidence was that they would remain high (which they did). Such changes in established patterns disorient consumers because their experiences no longer hold.

The same sort of change is evident with vocational choices. For years we have heard of a teacher shortage in this country, so that any student enrolling in a college of education could be sure to find a job on graduation. Suddenly we hear of a teacher glut, and many graduates with teaching degrees are being forced into other lines of work. To a prospective teacher, this sort of change is difficult to accommodate. If you had planned to be a teacher and were conditioned to thinking of a bright employment picture, the change in outlook required would be considerable.

In an even more fundamental sense, the same thing is true of the value of a college education. The idea that a college education means a better job and higher earnings is an article of faith for most Americans. Many high school students grow up with the idea of continuing their education; it is not something they think about, it is just accepted. Now, however, we find that in many areas there is a surplus of college graduates. The best jobs seem to be available to those with vocational training, many of whom do not have traditional four-year degrees.

It is not yet clear whether or not this educational development represents a long-run change. If it does, it means that the whole society will have to reorient its thinking about the importance of higher education. The basis on which expectations have been formed in the past will have to be changed. During the period of flux, when the signals about the future are confused, there may be no good basis for forming expectations. Such a catch-as-catch-can situation tends to be not only confusing but also nerve wracking.

If the general rule established earlier is correct, periods of great uncertainty should cause consumers to postpone purchases. When people are not sure what is going to happen, there is a tendency to wait and see. Instead of going right ahead with higher education, more and more high school graduates work for a year or two after getting out of school. They may plan to go on to college, and a few years ago they might have gone on directly, but now they are temporizing, and seeking a better picture of what lies ahead before making a decision.

The onset of the recession in late 1974 provides another example. Consumers were experiencing double-digit inflation, which should have promoted current consumption; yet, with the first hint of a recession, purchases were postponed. The signals about the future were mixed and consumers retrenched. The situation resolved itself in the worst possible way, with both recession and inflation. Consumers, however, had already reacted to that possibility by hedging their financial positions.*

We can see, then, that while consumers are not necessarily creatures of habit, they do come to depend on certain features of their environment in judging the future. In a setting that either is static or features controlled change, expectations can be formed with some confidence. More significant change not only disorients the consumer, making it difficult to read signals about the future, it also affects the consumer's own attitudes and outlook. Turning from the consumers' environment leads us to the consumers themselves.

The Role of Consumer Attitudes

Consumers are individuals. If we cannot expect everyone to have the same tastes and preferences, we certainly cannot expect everyone to have the same expectations about the future. Different people react to uncertainty in different ways, just as they react to good differently. It is like that old saying about the difference between an optimist and a pessimist looking at half a glass of water—one says that it is half full, while the other maintains that it is half empty. Two individuals can confront the same situation with the same amount of information and draw radically different conclusions. When the conclusions have to do with future possibilities—about which no one can be certain— the range of variation becomes even greater.

The difference becomes clear when we observe how people confront the future. Some people have an aversion to risk; they will try to hedge against future developments by saving, buying insurance, or generally following a conservative strategy. Others, like gamblers,

---

* During the final quarter of 1974, consumer spending on durables fell, as did the overall level of consumer debt; savings rose and, during 1975, reached their highest rate since the end of World War II [8, pp. 202, 212, 262].

adventurers, or speculators, seem to seek out risk. Most of us are somewhat in the middle or move from one group to the other depending on the circumstances. No single strategy fits everyone.

These differences may be reflected in individuals' consumption patterns. An aversion to risk will promote the consumption of safer products. A risky product *may* cause you injury at some time in the *future.* Safer products, on the other hand, generally are more expensive. So, the question becomes: "Do you pay more now to ensure against possible damage later?" You should recognize that the question involves a discounting problem [3]. The time-probability rule suggests that the lower the probability of injury and the longer the time involved, the less extra you would be willing to pay for a safer product.* We don't change the answer if we rephrase the question and ask: "How much risk are you willing to assume?" Putting the question that way, however, focuses on individual variations. The level of risk acceptable to one person may be too high for another.

Expectations, like so many other factors that affect consumption, reflect deep-seated personal attitudes. These are evolved from cultural, ethical, and religious beliefs. If an individual's religion places a high value on thrift, this is going to be reflected not only in the way that person consumes, but also in savings patterns and attitudes toward debt. Thrift, which somehow ends up being the antithesis of debt, is highly valued in the American tradition. Everyone is familiar with homey little admonitions like "Waste not, want not," and "A penny saved is a penny earned." Those, it seems, are always followed by a recitation of Polonius's advice, "Neither a borrower nor a lender be." If a society's collective wisdom is summarized by such statements, it is a pretty good clue to prevailing attitudes.

This means that while individuals may form expectations according to their own personal judgments, these judgments are influenced by social pressures. This fact suggests that there should be a degree of continuity and stability in such judgments. That is particularly true when members of a society share common goals and aspirations. Any change in attitudes, then, has far-reaching implications that are likely to be disquieting. This is not just a passing observation; it is a highly relevant comment on recent developments in the United States. Everyone is aware that we are witnessing important attitude changes in this country. To appreciate what has been happening, it is neces-

---

* Problems arise when long periods of time are involved or when the probabilities aren't known. Birth-control pills, for example, may be hazardous, but until recently the true extent of the danger wasn't known; furthermore, a teenager may not fully appreciate the impact of health hazards that won't make themselves felt for another twenty years. Thus, there may be a tendency to undervalue the risk. See Chapter 8.

sary to realize that these changes are closely tied to changes in expectations. To understand these developments fully, then, requires an explanation of the change in expectations. For that, we must roll back the calendar some forty years and look at the bleak decade of the 1930s.

A Digression on Depression

Probably no event in America's recent experience has had as great an impact on the nation's psyche than the Great Depression of the 1930s. The Depression was nothing less than a national trauma. It shaped the thinking of the people who lived through it to such a degree that neither they, nor the country, would ever be the same again. Readers who are younger than forty may not remember the Depression or any direct impact it had on them; nevertheless, it has considerably affected their lives because of the tremendous impact it had on the lives of others. The statistics are startling enough. Income in 1932 was only half of what it had been in 1928.* Today we worry if unemployment goes above 4 percent, but during the Depression it was as high as 33 percent, that is, one worker out of three without a job. Average unemployment for the decade was 17 percent.

The true meaning of the Depression cannot be measured with statistics. Its impact was much greater than even these data would suggest. The society seemed lost in a sea of despair as old landmarks were swept away and cherished assumptions were questioned. Economists and policymakers alike groped for new solutions, and although some of their efforts were salutary, in retrospect most never really came to grips with the problems.

The years of unparalleled prosperity that lie between us and the Great Depression have brought many changes. Social welfare programs have been expanded and a policy of full employment has come to be taken for granted. Most people feel that the experience of the 1930s will not be repeated; there is an *apparent* psychology of prosperity [15, pp. 174–76]. Yet the Depression did leave a scar; it is less ugly now that years have passed, but it is still visible.

This residual Depression psychology contributes to differences in attitudes and motivation between older and younger Americans. Installment credit is one example. Those who endured the Depression may fear the worst about the future and are less likely to use credit freely. Younger people, who have no such fears, are more willing to use credit [1, p. 150]. In a slightly different vein, labor leaders find

---

* In money terms. Real income only fell by one-third because of the decline in prices.

that the Depression, which served to force American labor into a solid unit, means little to younger workers. They are unmoved by the stories of how bad things used to be or of the labor victories of the 1930s. The increasingly restive and critical stance of many young workers reflects their changed concerns.

Similar forces are at work in the changing character of consumer demand. Until recently, home appliances were available only in white, reflecting the fact that demand was primarily functional; consumers were more interested in how things worked than how they looked. Now appliances come in a wide range of colors with optional "decorator accessories." If you are interested primarily in what the appliance does, this additional play to appeal is frivolous. The net effect is certainly to make consumer durables less durable, since if you redecorate your kitchen, you may find that your flaming red refrigerator does not go with your new avocado color scheme. This move into the realm of aesthetics would have been unthinkable even a generation ago. It clearly reflects both greater affluence and the numerous young buyers in the market.

Having noted these differences, I must hasten to add that in some cases the changes may not have been as great as appearance might suggest. Consider again the reaction to the recession of 1974–1975. Consumers reacted very strongly to the recession's early warning signs. Then, as the recession deepened into the worst economic downturn since the Great Depression, rising unemployment threatened job security and forced individuals to look at basic economic concerns. The demonstration of just how frail our affluence is was a chilling experience for those who had grown used to continued economic expansion. The public reaction showed that, for all our variety of concerns, it is security that still matters most.

The recession had a distinct impact on vocational interests among college students. The previous college generation had been characterized by apparent commitment to causes and personal growth. Students who followed them came with more sharply focused vocational and professional interests. One of the first questions asked about any course was: "Will that help me get a job?" The security that a college education was supposed to grant was no longer taken for granted.

It is too soon to evaluate these changes fully. It is clear that individuals are more concerned about security than they appeared to be. Therefore, the Depression psychology will remain even after the Depression generation passes from the scene. That generation feared economic hardship and dreamed of a better life. Today's consumers have similar fears but must recognize that some aspects of the better life are decidedly undreamlike. Facing the worst of both worlds, consumers must now construct their own dreams; as they do, we can expect more questions about the system, material gains, and consumption itself.

Time and Change

We have seen that expectations of higher income should increase current consumption; similarly, expectations of higher interest rates will affect saving and borrowing patterns. What about the expectation of change itself? We might argue that if consumers expect change to be built into their lives, other expectations become less important. Consider the contrasts between a couple buying a home today and a similar couple buying a home a generation or two ago. The latter lived in a less mobile society; when they looked at a home, it was probably in lifetime terms. Thus, they had to find one that fitted them exactly, giving careful consideration to the future related to family size, tastes, income, and taxes. Today's couple is most likely thinking about a much shorter time frame. They may be planning to be in the house no more than two or three years. Therefore, they need only be sure that the house meets their current needs and the immediately foreseeable developments.

If consumers see every move as temporary, then long-run elements are not going to figure very heavily in their decisions. Lack of permanence is a function of change within the society. We have become conditioned to change, expecting it and accepting it. In such a transient setting, expectations remain important; the couple probably would not even be buying the house if they didn't expect a favorable income trend in the future. However, long-run expectations are not going to be very important, for in a sense there is no long run. Instead, consumers see only a sequence of short runs. That may sound like double talk, but it means simply that if consumers do not see their decisions as final, they will be influenced mostly by immediate considerations.

This, then, is the meaning of my earlier statement that the key expectation may be that of change itself. Change has become such a part of our lives that we take it for granted. It is hard to imagine that the situation was ever otherwise. Yet a static environment characterized most of human history. Even in this country, which has always been relatively dynamic and mobile, the real impact of change was not felt until recently, when technological breakthroughs in organization, transportation, and communications made greater mobility possible.

It is easy to overemphasize this point. Evidence can be brought to refute it. Many people still live in the same town, even in the same house, in which they were born. Many consumers still think of large purchases in long-run terms, so they expect to have their refrigerator or automobile more than just a few years. It is also possible to argue that beneath all the apparent change, attitudes and lifestyles remain surprisingly constant. This evidence can be accepted and is worth remembering, particularly by those who say that our's is a "plastic" or "throwaway" society. At the same time, it is impossible to understand what is happening to today's consumer without recognizing that for a significant proportion of the population there has been a fundamental shift in perspective. For these people, long-run considerations are less important; it follows that long-run expectations are less important too.

It is difficult to know precisely how to evaluate this shift in emphasis. Our present condition is relatively new, so we really have not had the time to evaluate it. We do not even know whether it is just a passing phase or represents a lasting condition. Until these determinations are made, we must reserve judgment. We can see, however, that today's consumers differ from their counterparts of earlier generations, and the contention of a shift from a long-range focus is supported by the fact that there are characteristics peculiar to present-day consumer problems that reflect a highly developed economy.

On Measuring Expectations

We have examined different aspects of consumer expectations and seen how they are linked with consumer behavior, but have yet to specify the mechanism by which expectations are formed and translated into action through current purchases. It is logical to begin by looking at past experience. When things are going well, individuals have a tendency to think they will continue that way. Conversely, a series of reversals will make consumers more cautious about the future. Such experiences establish a trend, a pattern by which to measure the future. These are subject to change, but the overall tendency is consistent. Success establishes a favorable psychological climate and encourages optimism about the future, and failure does just the opposite.

Individuals basing their interpretation of the future on their past experience reflect differences that are observable and measurable. Individual variations will occur, because, as George Katona notes, "Only in certain lower-order responses do we find a one-to-one correspondence between the stimulus and the response" [14, p. 34]. Human response is complex, influenced by different influences (*intervening variables,* in psychological parlance). Nevertheless, a pattern should be discernible that allows us to explain consumer behavior from expectations.

I have indicated that this pattern derives from past experience, which Katona identified as "molding our habits, motives and attitudes." He continued by noting, "Expectations are a subclass of attitudes that point to the future, since our time perspective extends both backward and forward in a highly selective manner. There is no place for a sharp distinction between attitudes toward the past and the future..." [14, p. 34]. What emerges is a complex picture in which attitudes are bound closely to individuals' past experiences, future aspirations, and the environment in which they live. Various studies have been undertaken to test this point, and, despite mechanical problems and the complexities of measurement, they have shown that expectations affect consumers significantly. As you may suspect, this is clearest with durable-goods purchases, since in most cases these purchases can be postponed if necessary. By asking questions like: "Are you making as much (or more, or less) as you were a year ago?" and, "Do you think prices will go up in the next year or so?" consumer attitudes can be categorized [7, p. 365]. When these attitudes are measured against actual purchasing behavior, they clearly show a link between expectations and consumption.

This is not a complete answer to how such expectations are formed. Evidence in this case supports the idea that attitudes are in a continual state of flux, changing as the consumer's environment changes. Again, in Katona's words:

> Wants are not static. Levels of aspiration are not given once for all time. They are *raised with success and lowered with failure.* Success and failure are subjective concepts indicating the individual's perception of his accomplishments as well as disappointments. They are group determined by being viewed in relation to the success and failures of others in one's group. [13, p. 21, emphasis added]

To test his hypothesis, Katona classified people according to what had happened to their income in the four-year period just past, and what they expected was going to happen during the next period. Thus, two values were involved for each individual, one actual and one expectational. All individuals whose income had gone up were classified with a plus (+). If they expected income to continue to rise, they rated a second plus for expectations (++). If, however, they felt income would now level off, they would be classified as equal (+=). Those who felt income would now fall were designated with a minus (+−) [13, pp. 24–25].

Thus, there are nine different possibilities. People start off with actual income increasing (as above, +), stable (=), or decreasing (−), and then form expectations about future changes. They may, therefore, be classed as (++), (+=), (==), (−=), and so on. The (++) group is the most optimistic; they are individuals whose incomes have gone up and who consider that they will continue to rise. Those whose incomes have not changed and who expect no change are (==), representing a static situation. Individuals who have met with failure and foresee continued disappointments are the most pessimistic, or (−−). Using these categories, Katona collected information on individuals in different groups, seeking first to find out about purchasing intentions and then checking those against actual purchases. Significant results emerged.* The (++) group emerged clearly as the most avid consumers. Despite past purchases, they expressed buying intentions more frequently than other groups. They proved to buy 50 percent more durables than groups with no (+), and were three times as prone to use credit [12, p. 27].

Thus we can conclude that consumer expectations are important in current consumption and that these expectations are a function of experiences in the recent past. While this example concerned income expectations, similar studies have shown similar results for expected changes in prices and other variables [7 and 12]. The approach to consumption that emphasizes expectations as a factor seems justified.

Toward a Strategy for Tomorrow

The Elements of Time Preference

Expectations help determine how consumers divide present and future income. Economists call this division time preference, which for us simply means the value attached to consuming now as opposed to consuming later. We already know that, with all else equal, consumers would rather spend now and enjoy their consumption directly. But what about when all else is not equal? To illustrate, suppose it is April and you are thinking of buying a $1200 sailboat, but you only have $600. If you save $45.50 a month for the next year, you will have enough to buy the boat for the following summer. If you want the boat for the coming summer, however, you would have

---

* The results were adjusted to take into account other variables like age, sex, and family size.

to borrow the $600; paying that back over the next year would cost you $54.50 a month.*

Either way, you will have the boat paid for next spring. Either way, you will have to cut back your spending over the next year so that you have money to save or make your payments. Which should you do? It is clearly cheaper to save and buy the boat next spring; borrowing will cost you $108 more. If you wait, though, you will not have the boat to enjoy for the coming summer. The question can only be answered in those terms. If this summer's sailing is worth $108 to you, then you should go ahead and buy now; if the things you could buy with the extra $9 a month over the next year are worth more to you, however, then you should wait.

If time preference were the only consideration, a decision would not be hard. Suppose two people confronted that situation and one bought the boat now while the other waited; we would say that they were merely demonstrating a different time preference. If we reintroduce uncertainty, however, the situation changes. Maybe one person is unsure about next year's tuition money. In that case, he or she probably would not want to go into debt. Savings, on the other hand, would make a lot of sense; that person could draw on it for tuition if need be, and, if it were not needed, could then go ahead and buy the sailboat. These are the kinds of considerations that enter into analyzing time preference.

Notice that I did not say that saving is good and debt is bad. There are no grounds for making such an arbitrary statement. Rather, we perceive a series of conditions, and, depending on those conditions, either saving or borrowing may emerge as the better choice. Both have their advantages, but neither one is going to be right for all situations. The distinct features and implications of both savings and borrowing indicate how consumers may use them to advantage. A definition of savings will focus our thoughts. Economists define *savings* simply as "money not spent"; consumers accumulate wealth by postponing consumption. Consumers can do several things with this money. They can hold it as cash, put it in checking or savings accounts, buy bonds, or put it in the stock market, housing, art, or land. That is quite a variety of choices, some of which are commonly thought of as investment, or even consumption, rather than savings.

A commonsense definition of savings will satisfy our purposes. To arrive at it, we will apply a *liquidity* criterion. An asset is liquid if it

---

* This assumes you can earn 6 percent interest on both the $600 you start with and the savings you accumulate over the year, and that, if you borrow, you will have to pay a 9 percent interest charge.

can be easily and safely converted into spendable form. Cash is clearly the most liquid asset, since it is immediately spendable. However, since it earns no return, it is not a very good form of saving; the same is true of checking accounts. Savings accounts are highly liquid, as certain government bonds are. These are the classic forms of savings, offering both earnings and security.

Common stock is less liquid, because, although it is generally easy to sell, there is more risk involved and it may be necessary to sell at a loss. Other assets are even less liquid. Housing, for example, may be an excellent hedge against inflation, providing a service at the same time, but it cannot be sold on short notice and selling carries both costs and a risk of loss. The same is true of art and land, because it is very easy for the amateur to make a bad purchasing decision in these areas.

You may have noticed as we have gone through this list that earnings potential increases as liquidity decreases. This suggests that an individual's savings should be varied or balanced (*diversified* is the word brokers use). It makes sense to have a mix of assets, some of which are liquid and some of which have large earning potential. The consumer with even modest savings will want to strike some balance between the two.

Striking a balance may not be easy—*there are information costs attached to savings.* Consumers need information about the general types of savings and specific information about the particular types selected. That is, consumers must first choose among stocks, bonds, or banks, and then decide which bank or which bond would be best. The information costs may be relatively small, amounting to nothing more than shopping around to see which savings institution (bank, savings and loan, credit union, and so on) offers the best interest. For assets of high yield and low liquidity, however, information costs can be significant. To make a good buy in land, one must know the market, which requires an awareness of population trends, growth rates, and other factors affecting demand. Collecting and analyzing such information requires time and effort beyond the means of most individuals.

The same thing is true of the stock market, although help is generally available through brokers. In that case, the broker assumes the information costs and charges the client a fee. People may set a few dollars aside each week to "play the market" because they enjoy it, but for them it is a hobby, essentially consumption. Those who are seriously interested in the stock market, however, would do well to seek professional advice. Brokers cannot tell you what the market is going to do, but, because of their specialization, they are equipped to deal with information costs.

Cornelius Vanderbilt offered sage advice about buying a yacht: "If you have to ask how much it costs, you shouldn't be buying it." The same advice holds true for the type of assets we are discussing here. If you can afford to lose money, well and good, but if not, be cautious. It may make good sense to buy land for a summer place or just to have room to get away from it all, but don't expect it to make you independently wealthy.

The careful reader will recall that this whole discussion was the first of two points; happily, the second point is closely related. It is merely that the structure of the economy hinders, rather than helps, consumers in making these decisions. That is not a new point, but it is worth reemphasizing.

Consumers are expected, indeed required, to master the ins and outs of saving and borrowing in the same way they are expected to learn how to ride a bicycle. No one can teach you how to ride a bicycle; either it comes naturally or it doesn't. If it doesn't, you keep trying until you succeed. The worst you can pick up is a few bumps and scratches along the way. Unfortunately, if you try to master money management that way, you can pick up a lot more than bumps and scratches. However, most people are forced into this hit-or-miss approach for lack of an alternative. This is doubly unfortunate because, although the problems are real enough, they are not overpowering. In short, good alternatives are not an impossible dream; they can be realized. What is needed is an increased educational effort incorporating a wide range of approaches. In addition to formal classroom training, this effort should include such things as short courses for adults, public-service broadcasting, enforced informational broadcasting by financial institutions, and other means that will distribute information cheaply and easily.

It may seem strange that in considering uncertainty we should be so concerned with information costs. At the same time, however, you can see that determining how best to hedge against the future is intimately bound up with information. While consumers must accept that the future is unknown, they can prepare themselves to deal with it. To do so, they need a consistent strategy, which in turn requires a knowledge of the particular mechanisms involved in hedging against uncertainty. Thus, information about these mechanisms emerges as a proxy for information about the future itself.

That Proverbial Rainy Day

In American folklore, savings or frugality runs a close third to the flag and apple pie. That would be all well and good if the folklore reflected reality. In fact it doesn't. Debt is actually the American way, whether you are talking about the modern suburbanite, the colonial plantation owner, the early capitalist, or the nineteenth-century homesteader. Virtue, of course, is often promoted and then forgotten, but the issue runs deeper than that. Savings is promoted as a virtue, but the reasons why it is a virtue are seldom made clear. That's actually not quite correct, for there is usually some notion of a rainy day associated with the need to save. At a time when weather forecasters give the chances of rain in terms of probabilities, you would think that we could do better than that.

There are different reasons for saving, all of which fall into two broad categories: saving for some particular goal and saving as a hedge against the future. The sailboat goes into the first category, the rainy day into the second. There is really not much more that we can say about the first type of saving. People do save for houses, vacations, college education, or many other things (a few people may save just to save, but they are in the minority). Saving is specific; the consumer has a particular target or goal in mind, and saves for it [18].

The rainy day presents more problems, mainly because no one is sure precisely when it is going to rain or how hard or how long. The question then becomes: "How much should I save?" One savings and loan advertises that "saving 10 percent of gross income means financial security," which means that few Americans are financially secure. On the average, savings in 1976 were less than 7 percent of personal income (income before taxes), and the figure for earlier years was significantly lower [8, p. 212]. The answer to how much— one is tempted to say "the obvious answer"—is that there is no set figure that is the *right* amount of savings for all individuals. That should hardly be surprising, since we have been continually emphasizing the importance of individual variations. The right amount for the individual depends on many factors like age, amount and type of insurance, private pension plans, and debt level, as well as on less tangible things like lifestyle and aspirations.

The function of savings has changed significantly over the past generation. In earlier years, the elderly were the responsibility of their children, but that arrangement does not work well in an urban society. Thus, the need for savings rose; but, to relieve the need for large savings, new private and public insurance plans emerged. The best known are social security and Medicare, which do not assure older citizens a financially secure life, but do affect the need for cash savings. Another form of insurance is given by the pension plans in business. Because of improved fringe benefits, many workers earn retirement benefits to supplement social security and personal savings. In a sense, this is a form of forced savings, augmented by employer contributions.

Not all contingency saving is for old age. Again, however, the amount of savings varies. If the individual has adequate medical coverage, including provisions for long-term illness and disability, the need for personal savings will be reduced. Similarly, a single person will need smaller savings than a married couple with children and a mortgaged home.

There are two points to be made here. The first is that savings takes different forms in modern society. In a sense, some insurance premiums, social security contributions, and payments to pension funds are savings. As a result, most people really save more than they think. Simultaneously, with these other forms, the need for personal cash savings is reduced. The second point is that it is probably counterproductive to name a percentage of income and say that individuals should save that much. Personal variation is simply too great for that to make much sense. This variation pertains to both reaction to risk and the financial position of the person. The only sound way to make a savings plan is to sit down and take a good look at both your lifestyle and your finances. Out of this should come some picture of your savings needs.

Here is a place where professional advice would be helpful. Happily, it is available to at least part of the population. Your bank is a good source for such help, even though it has, in a literal sense, a vested interest in your savings. But capable professional advice is not as readily available as it ought to be. Poor people are at a particular disadvantage; they may not be aware of where to go for help, and even if they knew, that help might not be forthcoming. There is a tremendous need for improvement here, at both the public and private levels.

We must admit, then, that while it makes sense for most people to save some money, it is difficult to say much more than that. Individuals need to work out their own savings plans for themselves. Notice that I have not said that savings are unimportant; on the contrary, they offer needed security against possible adverse future developments. It is merely that different individuals have different needs and hence different savings requirements. Consumers should not save out of either fear or vague social pressures. They should be aware of what they are saving for and why. That knowledge is the basis for an intelligent personal savings program.

Insurance: A Policy Statement

Thus far, when mentioning insurance, the primary concern was with savings. Now I am reintroducing insurance as the classic hedge against the future; it therefore relates directly to how consumers divide income between the future and the present. If you want to insure yourself against future developments, current income must be used, which means that present consumption levels must be reduced. In this respect, insurance has a lot in common with rainy-day savings. However, insurance has a unique feature that distinguishes it from other types of hedging. The amount you collect from insurance is not necessarily limited to a certain sum, while the amount available from savings is limited to the amount you have saved plus interest.

There is another side to the coin. If you do not need the insurance, you get nothing back (with some exceptions), but with savings the money is always yours to use as you wish. The return from insurance is consistent with the principle of insurance. If you knew that you were not going to have any serious illnesses, it would not pay you to buy health insurance. Similarly, if you knew that you were going to be alive at age seventy, it probably would not pay to buy life insurance. You cannot know these things, and most people do not want to take the risks involved in the absence of accurate knowledge. This is where insurance comes in; insurance companies can cover risks that would be impossible for the individual to bear. They can assume risks because they operate under the fundamental law of large numbers. If you have a red marble and put it in a bowl, you certainly would not bet that anyone reaching into the bowl would come up with anything but a red marble. Even if you add a white marble, the odds are only fifty–fifty. Suppose, though, that you add 999 white marbles to the one red one and mix them all thoroughly. You would probably be willing to make a fairly large wager that the person would not draw the red marble. It is not a sure thing, but the odds of 999:1 in your favor make it as good a bet as you are likely to get.

Insurance companies make that kind of bet all the time, although they would probably not appreciate the analogy. When you buy health insurance, you are saying "I bet I get sick," and the company is saying "I bet you won't." Just in case you do, however, the company is making the same bet with thousands of other people. You may get sick, along with several others, but the odds are against everyone's getting sick. Thus, while you may collect, the company still comes out the winner because it is receiving payments from thousands of policyholders and paying out to only a few.

Probability is the essence of insurance. By studying records of sickness, accidents, and mortality, the companies can determine the probability of occurrence of any of those events. They know, for example, that the odds against a forty-five year-old male's dropping dead are 30:1 (hypothetical figures). They then know how many men they must insure and how much they must charge in order to come out ahead. The company, then, is covering its bets, and in so doing providing a service to the individual that he could not provide for himself. The odds may be 30:1 that he will not die, but if he happens to be the one, that's it. Thus, his premiums are an insurance against that chance.

Now that all sounds simple enough, and it is; in the administration and sale of insurance, however, many very difficult questions emerge. Insurance is not always available to all people, and it sometimes seems that the choice of who is insurable is made on very unsound grounds. Then there are questions about the earnings of insurance companies. The companies invest premium payments, earning a further return on their investments. The role of the public interest is not always clear in this instance. I am mentioning these problems because it would be improper to imply that all issues on insurance are covered here. These questions are vitally important to the consumer and are subsequently considered as aspects of consumer power and government protection. Our interest here is with how the consumer can hedge against the future.

Insurance can perform many functions. It may be more than insurance; it may also be savings. Straight-life and endowment policies carry a savings feature. You pay more for such insurance but, if you live, you receive the cash value of the policy when it matures. The companies therefore are selling you insurance and collecting your savings. These are in turn invested and the money is paid back to you at the end of a specified period or to beneficiaries on your death.

How well does the insurance company do in managing your savings? Most do fairly well. There is something to be said for this approach, especially when information costs are considered, since it is the company that assumes these costs. Furthermore, individuals who lack the discipline to save may find that such a program of forced savings enables them to save more than they could on their own. Individuals who can manage their own savings, however, will find their efforts well rewarded. With effort, individuals can better the performance of insurance companies on their own. Here is how it works. The cheapest kind of life insurance is called term insurance because it is purchased for a particular period, or term. It is pure protection, with no savings features. However, term insurance is cheap, so you can buy it and then put the difference between what it costs and the cost of a straight life policy into some form of savings.

If you did that, how would you come out? The magazine *Changing Times* asked that question [5]. The magazine's staff compared a $10,000 straight-life policy with a $10,000, thirty-year decreasing-term policy, both purchased at age thirty-five. The study assumed that the difference between the premiums on the cheaper decreasing-term insurance and the straight-life insurance would be invested in a mutual fund; brokerage fees were included.* For age 65, the cash value of the mutual-fund holdings was figured at *more than three times* the cash value of the straight-life policy. This approach therefore enables you to cover your risks with term insurance and accumulate savings far in excess of what the combined savings-insurance program would have provided.

There are several facets involved in this sequence. Mutual-fund performance varies over time and among different funds. Furthermore, there may be tax advantages to the individual who saves through insurance. The key considerations, however, are information and convenience. Managing your own savings, even through a broker, takes time, effort, and discipline. Once such a program is well established, information costs can be minimized, but they still remain a consideration.

The potential advantages of the independent approach may still be sufficient to convince many individuals that the extra effort is warranted. Again, it is impossible to say that one approach is the right way. That determination can only be made relative to the individual's own situation. If consumers know the alternatives, they can make their individual decisions in full understanding of what is involved in each case.

Life insurance furnishes the bulk of insurance savings. Most people obtain health and accident insurance through their jobs.† As far as other types of insurance are concerned, there is a simple rule: It pays to shop. Policies do differ from company to company, but that is not the only point to consider. Service is important, and it is also necessary to find an agent whom you can trust. You may have to read or otherwise inform yourself on insurance so that you will have a better idea of what is going on. Such an investment of time and effort will most likely pay handsome dividends in providing you with improved service and coverage at reasonable rates.

The consumer must contend with the fact that the industry is not organized in such a way as to facilitate comparisons. Happily, though, some improvements can be noted. An important step was taken toward better information flow when the Pennsylvania Insurance Department published its *Shoppers' Guide to Insurance* [17]. This publication ranks companies in terms of the costs of their policies and

---

* With decreasing term insurance, the value of the policy declines over time; a policy worth $10,000 at the age of thirty-five might offer only $5,000 coverage at age fifty. It was assumed in this example that the earnings from the mutual fund were reinvested.

† Health insurance is dealt with specifically in Chapter 11.

the benefits they provide, offering one of the most comprehensive evaluations yet made available to consumers. While it created quite a stir when it was issued, at least one company included the report in its advertising, encouraging people to write for it.

A Dollar Down and a Dollar a Week

Anything that can be said about the need for improved information and life insurance can be redoubled and applied to credit and debt. It is often maintained that people do not care about interest charges, but only about how much they have to pay and for how long. The extent to which this is true measures public misunderstanding. It would be premature to issue a blanket condemnation of the public because they are uninformed. Although credit and debt are very complicated, individuals get very little help in figuring them out.

Like life insurance companies, lending institutions often advertise, but they provide little information. You may learn that Bank X is giving away china (if you deposit *just* $1,000), but more substantive information is hard to come by. Finance companies hold out the hope of "solving your money worries," but seldom mention interest charges or even hint at improving household management. The possibility that the number of nagging little bills being consolidated will constitute one back-breaking load is not broached.

The lack of information is not much different for insurance and for credit and borrowing. The ads give barely a hint of the real issues involved. There are two differences, however, which make the lack of knowledge about credit more serious. The first is the very nature of debt. After all, you cannot be taken to court for not saving or be repossessed for buying the wrong insurance. Mistakes in those areas can be devastating enough, but mishandling debt means financial disaster.

The nature of debt, spending future income, leads to the second difference, reduced future consumption levels. Future income is already encumbered or marked for repayment of debts. While consumers have some flexibility about future consumption levels, the adjustments that can be made are limited. Some costs are fixed, like food and shelter, and cannot be escaped. In the extreme case, consumers may find that they are unable to meet current demands on their income because of the prior demands made by debt service or installment payments.

We have been undergoing a credit explosion in recent years. Credit has become readily available to more people than ever before. This is most obvious in the ubiquitous consumer credit cards, which have become the symbol of the modern consumer. Beyond that, bank loans of all types are more available. Banks even advertise their loans, which must come as a shock to traditionalists who remember banks as the staunch defenders of financial conservatism and personal frugality. Financing is also available from other institutions, often from businesses themselves. They may cater to people who are high credit risks and therefore had difficulty getting credit elsewhere. Not surprisingly, such credit charges are typically very high, though they are buried in such complex language that individuals do not really know what they are. They may not find out even after the truck pulls up to their door to take back their furniture [4].

There are a variety of horror stories commonly told about such cases, stories mustered to show that consumers are foolish and indifferent. They do not demonstrate that at all; rather, they underscore the need for better information flow and more consumer education. Public awareness simply has not kept pace with expanding credit availability. Many people have access to credit today, but too many of them do not know how to use it. The public has had difficulty in coping with the change.

If that is the problem, what are the issues involved in using credit or debt? The basic one is that you do not get something for nothing. If you use credit, you pay for it through interest charges.* Moreover, these interest charges are compounded. That means you pay interest on the interest, and if you carry that very far, the expense mounts. The variations and complexities are almost endless. While all the possibilities cannot be covered, the most common problems can be discussed and a few basic rules set out.

The most obvious need is for consumers to find out what interest charges they are actually paying. Some progress was made in this area with the federal truth-in-lending law, which requires that lenders state interest rates in annual terms. Thus, a seemingly minute 1⅓ percent monthly charge emerges in its true form as an 18 percent annual interest rate. Even that does not complete the picture, however, for that is a simple rate that doesn't take compounding into account. If you pay off a $100 debt at $10 a month, for example (usually the minimum payment), and the interest charge is 1½ percent a month, your effective annual interest rate is over 21 percent. This means that whatever you bought cost over one-fifth more than the price tag indicated. All this is very confusing, even if you sit down with a pencil and paper (or better yet, a calculator) and try to figure it out.

One basic principle should be clear. The smaller your monthly pay-

---

* This does not apply to 30-day accounts or charges paid within the month.

ments and the longer they are drawn out, the greater the amount of interest you pay. That should make sense, because the interest rate is applied against the principal, and the more slowly the principal is reduced, the larger the interest charges are going to be. Notice that I have not said this is necessarily bad. It would be quite sensible for the person who values current consumption highly, or in other terms, who applies a very high discount rate to future income. It may be argued that people do not actually discount future income; this is true in the sense that they do not carry out formal calculations. Most people, however, are well aware of what they want now and what they want later. Further, they know how much it is worth to them. In that sense, they do discount the future. Those who place a relatively low value (a high discount rate) on future income would find small payments and high interest rates quite to their liking.

There are limits to the strategy of using credit. Some people find that they can only make payments to cover interest charges and they never reduce the principal. Theoretically, they could go on paying for ever. If the amounts involved are large, this will place a serious drain on the individual's financial resources. Very few people would be able to carry on for very long under such conditions.

While these problems confront all consumers, they bear most heavily on certain groups. Lower-income consumers face an obvious problem. The very poor may not be able to obtain any credit, while those who are just a little better off are typically forced to more expensive credit sources; thus, the poor are more likely than other income groups to use credit provided by the seller [2]. This creates a special burden, since those least able to pay are forced to bear the heaviest interest charges.

Women also face special problems. It was, and is, common for women to have difficulty in obtaining credit on their own. The impact of such discrimination should be clear when you recall our discussions on shifting present and future income; to deny women the opportunity to shift income in this way robs them of a significant degree of financial flexibility. The Equal Credit Opportunity Act bans discrimination against women in granting credit, but the full effect of the law has yet to be felt. The credit problems of women and the poor are treated in greater detail in later chapters.

The difficulties we have been considering should recall the discussion of efficient consumption in the previous chapter. Not only must consumers know how they value consumption now as opposed to consumption in the future, but they must know the implications of the various alternatives open to them. Without this knowledge, they are in no position to consume efficiently. Improved educational pro-

grams and better information flow can only improve performance.
Wesley Clair Mitchell, in 1912, felt there was reason for optimism.
He observed:

> With greater confidence we may rely upon progress in physiology
> and psychology to make wider and more secure the scientific foun-
> dations of housekeeping. But such progress will have little practical
> effect unless the results of research are made available to far larger
> circles. This work of popularizing scientific knowledge, however,
> promises to become increasingly effective [16, p. 18].

We can only wonder what Mitchell's reaction would be if he realized
that over half a century later most of these promises were still unfulfilled. The need for "popularizing scientific knowledge" still exists.
The means are at hand to do it; it is possible to give consumers the
information, training, and assistance they need to operate effectively
in the marketplace. Carrying out such a program is something else
again, but it is clear that until the importance of the problem is recognized, nothing substantial will even be attempted.

Study Questions

1. Suppose you had your choice between two refrigerators, both
   of which can be expected to last for ten years. Brand A costs
   $400 to buy and $50 a year to operate; Brand B costs $500 to
   buy, but only $40 a year to operate. Assuming the two are
   identical in all other respects:
   a. Assuming no change in the cost of electricity, explain why
   Brand A is the better buy;
   b. If the cost of electricity rises, what would you have to know
   to decide which is better?
2. Discuss the impact of uncertainty about future energy supplies
   on consumers' current consumption.
3. If the interest rate is 5 percent, would a bond worth $5,000 in
   five years be a good buy at $3,750 now? Suppose the interest
   rate were 7 percent? Would it be a good buy at 5 percent if it
   did not mature for eight years?
4. Suppose you are asked to observe the consumption behavior of
   two couples, each earning $9000 a year. One is made up of
   recent college graduates, while the other is made up of grandparents in their late sixties. How would their consumption patterns differ? Would you expect any similarities between the
   two?

5. Briefly explain how expectations might affect current consumption behavior in each of the following cases:

   a. A teacher who expects both income and prices to go up in the future.

   b. A construction worker whose wages have been going up steadily, although he has been laid off several times in recent years.

   c. A person who is now 25 and will inherit $500,000 when her 55-year-old aunt dies.

   d. A farmer who expects his income to go down in the future.

   e. A worker who expects her income to fall, but thinks prices will rise.

6. A university administration announces an increase in retirement benefits that requires an increase in payroll deductions. Younger faculty members oppose the move, while older ones support it. Should the administration have expected this reaction? Explain.

7. Why does inflation favor current consumption? Does it also favor going into debt? Explain.

8. Suppose you have your savings in an account earning 5½ percent and your neighbor tells you that you could be earning 6 or 7 percent. Assuming all savings are insured, should you switch your savings? What do you need to know before you answer?

9. Art of good quality appreciates tremendously over time. Why, then, don't more people put their money in art, for which a high return is practically assured?

10. People typically save and go into debt at the same time (that is, they have both a mortgage and a savings account). Others gamble and buy life insurance. Are these combinations of behavior consistent? What do they tell you about the individuals' attitudes towards risk and uncertainty?

11. Under what conditions might it be wise for a person to

    a. Have no savings.

    b. Have no life insurance.

    c. Have neither savings nor life insurance and go deeply into debt.

Suggested Projects

1. We are all familiar with homey little sayings like "A penny saved is a penny earned"; "A bird in the hand is worth two in

the bush"; and "Eat, drink and be merry, because tomorrow we die." Write up a more comprehensive list of such sayings. What do they tell you about reactions to the future? Can they be used to gauge society's attitudes?

2. We have suggested that since the expansion of credit is a fairly recent development, younger people should be more prone to use credit than older ones. You can test this hypothesis by developing a set of questions that reflect people's attitudes towards debt. You might ask questions like:

   a. Is going into debt wrong?

   b. Should debt be used only for purchasing homes?

   c. Should debt be used for buying cars but not appliances?

   d. Should debt be used only in emergencies?

   e. Should you ever carry a credit balance over 30 days?

   Allow people to agree, give no opinion, or disagree (or add strongly agree or strongly disagree, see Appendix). Sample different populations such as students, parents, urban, rural, random groups, and so on. Do any differences emerge? Do these follow the pattern you expected? What factors beside their classification might influence people's reactions?

3. If your community has a Consumer Credit Council Service of some kind, meet with the counselors and discuss the most common problems they encounter. What do they feel causes consumers to get into serious debt problems?

4. Survey consumers' knowledge about managing future resources. First, check at different:

   a. Banks, loan companies, and insurance companies for information on interest rates (for both saving and borrowing) and the cost of different insurance policies. Once you have this information;

   b. Survey consumers' knowledge in these areas. Do consumers know how rates and charges vary? Do they know where to go for the best buy?

5. Look up figures on total consumer (or private) debt? What has been happening to the level of debt? How is the level of debt affected by changes in the performance of the economy?

6. Price expectations have had a major impact on home buyers. Discuss this question with realtors. Do they use the rising price of houses to get people to buy now? Do prospective buyers mention it? If you can find people who have bought a house recently, discuss the question with them.

7. Do people really discount the future and take this into account

when they consider future income, debt, and savings? Discuss how you might devise a means of testing that question.

8. Analyze the advertising of various financial institutions (banks, savings and loans, finance companies, and financing offered by the retailer). Do these ads offer significant information to the consumer? Would any of them confuse the consumer? (See Chapter 6 for more detailed consideration of this question.)

Bibliography and Suggested Readings

1. Axel, Helen, ed. *A Guide to Consumer Markets, 1973/1974*. New York: The Conference Board, 1973.
A statistical review of consumers and their purchasing patterns. Material is well presented and covers a variety of useful topics.

2. Brandt, W., and Day, G. "Information Disclosure and Consumer Behavior: An Empirical Evaluation of Truth in Lending." University of Michigan, *Journal of Law Reform*, vol. 7, no. 2 (Winter 1974): 297–328.
A valuable article on consumer credit behavior. Offers particular insights into problems faced by low-income consumers, and suggests something about the limitations of policies to provide more information.

3. Calabresi, Guido. *The Costs of Accidents*. New Haven: Yale University Press, 1970. Chapters 4–6.
Approaches the question from a legal perspective, but provides a readable discussion of the risks of hazardous products. Suggests alternative strategies for dealing with the risks.

4. Caplovitz, David. *Consumers in Trouble*. New York: The Free Press, 1974.
Subtitled "A Study of Debtors in Default," this book reviews over 1,300 court cases of default drawn from four large cities. The study is more descriptive than analytical and draws particular attention to the role that fraud and deception played in the consumers' problems. An interesting introduction for those interested in social aspects of debt issues.

5. *Changing Times*. Kiplinger publication, October 1962.
Worth checking for information on insurance and related questions. As indicated in the text, this magazine has produced some good comparative studies, providing information that is typically difficult to obtain elsewhere.

6. Duncan, Greg J., and Morgan, James N. *Five Thousand American Families* (Four Volumes). Ann Arbor, Mich.: Survey Research Center, In-

stitute for Social Research, University of Michigan. Annually from 1973.

As the title indicates, a report on a large-scale research study that has followed the economic progress of five thousand selected American families. A wealth of data on income dynamics and how the families adapt to changing conditions. Data currently cover a seven-year period. Anyone with a serious interest in families' financial patterns should look at this set.

7. Dunkelberg, William C. "The Impact of Consumer Attitudes on Behavior: A Cross-Section Study." In *Human Behavior in Economic Affairs,* ed. Burkhard Strumpel, et al. San Francisco: Jossey-Bass, 1972, pp. 347–71.

Another study relating attitudes to consumer buying patterns and intentions to buy. Valuable for practical illustrations of problems involved, including actual questions asked.

8. *Economic Report of the President, 1977.* Washington, D.C.: U.S. Government Printing Office, 1977.

Data, current and historical, on income, savings, and consumption patterns.

9. Ferber, Robert. "Consumer Economics, A Survey." *Journal of Economic Literature.* December 1973, pp. 1303–42.

A particularly good reference for summary of alternative theories on consumer expenditures and the factors influencing them.

10. Friedman, Milton. *The Theory of the Consumption Function.* Chicago: University of Chicago Press, 1957.

Imaginative and thorough study of the relations between income and consumption; basis for development of the permanent income hypothesis. Also contains interesting material on uncertainty and how it affects economic analysis.

11. Halter, Albert N., and Dean, Gerald W. *Decisions Under Uncertainty.* Cincinnati: South-Western Publishing Co., 1971.

Illustrates problems of decision making under uncertainty. Latter parts are less analytical and give practical applications. Good for students seriously interested in these subjects.

12. Juster, R. Thomas, and Wachtel, Paul. "Uncertainty, Expectations and Durable Goods Demand Models." In *Human Behavior in Economic Affairs,* ed. Burkhard Strumpel, et al. San Francisco: Jossey-Bass, 1972, pp. 321–45.

A study of the impact of consumer expectations on the critical area of consumer durables. Another good illustration of statistical techniques applied to real problems.

13. Katona, George. "Consumer Behavior: Theory and Findings on Expectations and Aspirations." *American Economic Review, Papers and Proceedings,* May 1968, pp. 19–30.

Important and understandable study on the formulation and impact of expectations. For all its (++) and (−−), this paper offers a straightforward approach.

14. ———. *The Mass Consumption Society.* New York: McGraw-Hill Book Co., 1964.

15. ———. *The Powerful Consumer.* New York: McGraw-Hill Book Co., 1960.
    Anyone who reads nothing else on uncertainty and expectations should read these two books. Students will find them understandable and interesting. They are particularly valuable because they apply to actual developments and assume a broad, interdisciplinary approach to the problems.

16. Mitchell, Wesley Clair. "The Backward Art of Spending Money." In *The Backward Art of Spending Money and Other Essays.* New York: McGraw-Hill Book Co., 1937.

17. *Shopper's Guide to Insurance.* Harrisburg, Pa.: Pennsylvania Insurance Department.
    The best available comparison of insurance policies. Makes dollar-for-dollar comparisons so that consumers can evaluate policies. An excellent comparison of costs and benefits. Pennsylvania plans to offer similar studies in other areas, a good illustration of a service that state regulatory agencies can, but commonly do not, offer.

18. Troelstrup, Arch W. *The Consumer in American Society.* 5th ed., New York: McGraw-Hill Book Co., 1977.
    A personal finance textbook offering a broader perspective than most. Contains some good material on the mechanics of savings and insurance.

19. Youmans, K. C., Hendricks, G., and Keller, J. *Consumer Durables and Installment Debt.* Survey Research Center, Institute for Social Research, University of Michigan, 1973.
    Another publication from the Survey Research Center on consumer spending patterns. Contains extensive discussion and complete statistical review of families' actual expenditure patterns on durables and the role of installment credit.

-5-

The Flow of
Consumer Information

The Problem of Being Informed

The Informed Consumer—A Fable

It was sad that night several years ago when I went to the refrigerator to get a beer. I reached in and took out the can, but my heart sank when I opened it. The happy "snap" was followed by an unfamiliar "glurg." Tearfully, I screamed to my wife, "The refrigerator is freezing my beer!" "So," she replied, "it's been freezing the lettuce for six months." Even in my disoriented state I understood that there was no use in pursuing the topic with someone who did not understand the difference between freezing beer and lettuce. Sadly I concluded that the time had come to buy a new refrigerator.

That sounded simple enough, but one problem became clear as soon as we began our search for a new box (that is what a refrigerator is called in the trade, a "box"). I knew nothing about boxes, or refrigerators either. How many cubic feet did we need? Where did we want the freezer? What were the advantages of a side-by-side model? Did we really need the model with an automatic icemaker that served drinks through the door? I have always thought of refrigerators as things that keep food cold, but I soon discovered a whole set of confusing specifications and features.

As I wandered through the multicolored world of no-frost refrigerators, I could have consoled myself with the thought that I was not alone. Most people do not know much about refrigerators, or about most of the other things they buy. Economic theory admits no such problems. It assumes that consumers have perfect information about all the products they want. If I had known one of these theoretical consumers, I should not have had to search at all; I should merely have had to ask my perfectly informed companion.

The impossibility of such an encounter emphasizes both the importance of information and the distance between theory and reality in this case. It is obvious why the assumption of perfect knowledge is necessary; without it the consumer could never reach equilibrium. The same thing is true of the real-world consumers. Information is required for efficient consumption, but in this case we are not in a position to assume the problem away. We have to deal with it. In doing so, we must shift our focus slightly. The main emphasis thus far has been on consumers themselves and their evaluations of their wants and needs; although these matters have external aspects, they are essentially internal and personal. The products that satisfy consumer wants, however, are external, and to judge them the consumer needs to know what the product will do. The performance of a particular product is definite; it does not depend on any subjective evaluation. Either a refrigerator will hold 17 cubic feet of food or it will not; that is all there is to it.

Efficient consumption therefore requires that consumers match their tastes and preferences to the products in the market, a process that obviously requires information. In this context, consumers' ignorance about the things they buy looms even larger. Yet we cannot place all the blame on the consumer. Things are so complex that it is impossible to know everything about everything. Even if the market were static this would be a problem, but it isn't; products are always changing. The stereo buff might find that with the advent of quadrasonic sound he or she has to relearn everything about the field. Pity, too, the poor car buyer who has spent a lifetime understanding all about cam shafts, pistons, rods and points, who suddenly confronts the rotary engine.

The High Cost of Ignorance

It is hardly an exaggeration to conclude that information is the most important element in the whole range of consumer issues. If there were no information problem, not all consumer problems would go away; they would, however, be significantly reduced. Furthermore, the solutions to the remaining problems would be greatly simplified. If you doubt that, consider the fact that the alternative to information is ignorance.

Ignorance means that consumers lack adequate information on which to base their decisions. It follows that *ignorant consumers are also defenseless consumers.* Unless they have information, consumers cannot be sure that the product they are buying is the right one for them. They cannot even be sure that the product or service is what it claims to be. If you pick your car up after having it in the garage, for instance, how can you be sure the mechanic took care of its difficulty if you know nothing about automobiles?

In short, *knowledge is power.* The consumer who has it can make intelligent decisions; or, in other words, consumers who have information can look after their own interests. *Improved consumer information is actually a form of consumer protection.* That is why there is no mention of consumer protection laws in economic theory; they are not needed because (theoretically) consumers can protect themselves. In reality, consumer protection laws remain important because, although information flow can be improved, perfect information is impossible. The market is simply too complex for everyone to understand about all the products in it.

Nevertheless, the case for improved information remains strong. It is impossible to legislate against every possible type of consumer fraud. Furthermore, once enacted, a law must be enforced, and that takes time and money. Thus, in addition, it makes sense to give consumers the power to protect themselves. The more the consumers are so equipped, the less the government will have to look after them. Consumers *can* look after themselves; they are not stupid and irrational, as they are so often portrayed, but merely ill equipped to do the job they are supposed to be doing.

There is one additional advantage to improved information over legislation; it can protect consumers from themselves. No law can do that.* Everyone makes mistakes, but with better information, such mistakes should be minimized. This marks the consumer as the first line of defense against abuses in the market. If individual choice is to have any meaning, individuals must have the information to make those choices. Given that information, consumers can emerge as a powerful force within the marketplace. Without it, they are no better

---

* Some laws can help though. One example is legislation that gives consumers three days to change their minds after signing a contract. This so-called cooling-off period helps offset high-pressure sales techniques. Consumers who were pressured into signing might, on reflection, think better of it. See Chapter 8.

than sheep, and the best they can hope for is that some benevolent shepherd will look after them.

The High Cost of Information

There is no doubt that ignorance is expensive, but so is information. Consumers must be prepared to absorb these costs. This point is too often overlooked. It is easy to come out against ignorance, but that begs the question. Everybody is against ignorance. The costs of reducing ignorance have to be weighed. There is nothing mysterious about these costs; they include the time, effort, and money expended to obtain enough information to make an intelligent choice. In plain terms, a consumer has to shop around in one way or another before making a purchase. In a sense, you don't really shop for products, you shop for information about the product, and that involves costs.

Consider again my quandary with the refrigerator. It would hardly have been wise for me simply to go out and just buy one. I first had to become familiar with refrigerators, their features and prices, before I could know what to do. Such activities took time—time I could not spend on other things. They also took gasoline and operating time on the car. And remember the babysitting money—nothing makes shopping more painful than dragging two preschoolers from store to store. All of these costs have to be taken into account and added to the cost of the refrigerator.

Information costs may vary considerably from person to person. If an appliance dealer's refrigerator had started freezing his beer, he would have had less trouble than I did in picking a new one; he would have been familiar with the elements involved in the decision. We pick up bits of information as we go along. Some comes from experience, while some we pick up randomly. It may seem useless at the time, but, at some later date, it may come in handy. The more information accumulated in this way, the shorter the search will be for a given purchase. I knew almost nothing about the particulars of refrigerators when I started out, but I did carry along some information. I knew, for example, that the compressor is the heart of the refrigeration mechanism, which means that the guarantee on the compressor is most important. I also knew that frost-free varieties use more electricity. So there were some things I didn't have to learn; or perhaps it is better to say that I knew enough to know where to start finding out more.

The most important basic information is knowing that the product exists. That may seem so obvious that it hardly deserves mention, but under certain circumstances it can be a significant factor. While most everyone knows about refrigerators, at least part of the population is unaware of many other available goods and services. If you are confounded by a wet basement, for example, knowing about a new waterproof paint will take care of your difficulty quickly and inexpensively.

A more significant example is the family that does not know basic nutritional requirements. The shortcomings of the family's diet may be contributing to ill health, and the family does not know what is wrong. Most people are informed about nutrition and take the information for granted. However, given the tremendous variation in information levels, one cannot assume the existence of universal information. Too often, an information gap forms the basis for serious biases. It may be said, for example, that a certain group of consumers does not shop wisely, when the problem really stems from a lack of information rather than irresponsibility.

This situation serves to complicate the information-cost question. It means that we need to be concerned not only about information on certain products or services, but also basic information on market operations and product types. It also means that we must be concerned with getting this information cheaply and easily to the people who need it; the information itself is usually available. The problem lies in the transferral mechanism, meaning that although the information is there, it is not well distributed.

As the marketplace has become more complex, information costs have risen and the consumer's position has deteriorated. This recalls the low level of specialization within the family. Families purchase a wide range of products and the complex structure of the market makes it difficult for either families or individual consumers to cope with many products. There is, moreover, little opportunity for greater specialization. The only alternative is to develop mechanisms to disseminate information cheaply and easily to all consumers. We need to analyze the nature of information costs as well as available sources of information and how they can be improved. To do that, we must be more specific about precisely how information costs affect the consumer.

The Optimal Quantity of Information

The obvious implication of the discussion thus far is that although the consumer needs information to make purchasing decisions, *the consumer must weigh the cost of the information against the benefits obtained from it.* This suggests the rather surprising conclusion that it will not always pay the consumer to seek additional information. The conclusion is surprising because it means that the optimal amount of information—the amount that is right for each consumer—

will be less than the maximum amount of information available. Such a contention seems to run counter to the discussion of the theoretical consumer and popular notions of the responsible, well-informed consumer. Cost is clearly at the heart of the matter. In theory consumers are perfectly informed, but theoretical consumers do not face information costs. If knowledge is free, it makes sense to get as much of it as you can; since it isn't, that rule no longer holds.

This point seems to be missed all too often in popular discussions. The virtues of information are extolled and the well-informed consumer is held up as the ideal. Such exercises are certainly counterproductive; when we mere mortals set out to emulate the ideal type, we find the process not only expensive, but nearly impossible. Having come up short, we appear to be failures. It is quite likely that the myth of the stupid consumer is founded in such unrealistic prototypes that not only discourage individual consumers, but also mask the real issues involved and thus inhibit the movement toward a workable solution to the problem.

Realistically, then, how can we expect the consumer to cope with information costs? To answer that, let's go back to my experience with the refrigerator. As I continued my shopping, I began to feel that I had heard it all before. I found as I visited additional dealers, they didn't tell anything about refrigerators that I didn't already know. Furthermore, the price variations I was quoted by successive dealers got smaller and smaller. I could be fairly sure that the price quoted by the next dealer would be somewhere between the highest and lowest prices I had already received. In short, it appeared that there was not much to be gained by shopping further. I could have gone on, visited more shops, made more phone calls, and read more reports, but would it have paid? I might have found a tremendously good buy that would have made it all worth while, but that was highly unlikely. Even if I had found a slightly lower price or uncovered some desirable feature that I had not been aware of, it probably would not have been enough to warrant the extra effort. Thus, I can offer this rule about the optimal quantity of information: *The consumer should search until the expected savings from additional search is equal to the cost of that search* [16, pp. 216–19].

Suppose you are just beginning to search; you can reasonably expect that the information you gain will be more than enough to compensate you for your time, effort, and money. Certainly, then, you should continue searching. There comes a time, however, as in the refrigerator example, that the cost of the extra search is higher than the expected savings. When that point is reached, it does not pay to seek additional information.

There is nothing mysterious about this process. It merely reflects the probabilities. When political pollsters take their polls, they do not talk to every voter; they select a sample that reflects the character of the population as a whole. If their techniques are correct, they can feel reasonably safe in attributing the ideas expressed in their sample to the entire population. When you go shopping, you may not think of it in terms of taking a sample, but that is what you are doing. You visit a few stores—say, five out of fifty—and obtain information about price and performance. This sample should give you a pretty good profile of the market, including price dispersion and available features. If you feel that your sample is a good approximation of the rest of the market, there is no sense in searching further. You make your decision based on the information you have, assuming that the rest of the market is similar to the portion you have canvassed. You may be wrong, but if the cost of finding out is greater than the potential savings, it would not be worthwhile to make the effort.

The optimal amount of search will vary with the individual and the amount of information already possessed. The character of the market also plays a role. The individual who finds that prices at the first five stores visited are all very similar might stop searching, concluding that the odds are against finding any significant variation. On the other hand, one who finds significant variation with no clear pattern would feel that additional search is warranted; since extreme variations exist, even greater variations are possible. The geography of the market has something to do with this. If stores are grouped so that it is easy and cheap to visit several, search costs will be lower than if the stores are spread out.* You might have to drive all over town to visit three junkyards, while you could visit three clothing stores in a single shopping center [16, pp. 218–19].

Finally, the product in question must be considered. Our rule says that the consumers will shop more when expected savings are greater. The higher the cost of the item, the greater the potential or expected savings. We can predict, therefore, that consumers will shop more for expensive items than for cheap ones. For the latter it may not even pay to shop at all. Suppose you are looking for a ballpoint pen, the kind you can pick up for 20 cents. Sometimes you see them on special for a dime, but it would not pay to shop around for a special. You would not save enough to make the search worthwhile. On the other hand, if additional search would save you 50 percent on a car or an appliance, you would continue to search; the expected savings would

---

* This is primarily why stores tend to cluster. Their proximity helps all of them, since customers will be attracted by the fact that they can shop easily at many stores. All the stores benefit from the fact that customers' information costs are reduced. Students interested in location theory will find considerable literature on this topic.

clearly make the effort worthwhile [16, pp. 218–19; and 17, pp. 1–4].

Search sometimes has consumption value; the act of shopping may provide satisfaction (recalling the discussion in Chapter 3). In such cases, the individual may search beyond the point where expected savings equals cost. This activity is efficient as long as the individual derives sufficient enjoyment from shopping to cover the additional cost. The buff or enthusiast represents this type of behavior. The camera buff will read magazines, reports, and so on about cameras, obtaining information quite in excess of that needed to buy a camera. The same is true of other hobbyists. For them, obtaining the information is recreation.

The consumption value of search will vary among individuals and types of searches. Some people simply do not enjoy shopping. Others may enjoy only particular types of shopping; the automobile expert might be a virtual encyclopedia of information about cars, but hate to shop for furniture. Finally, the situation is important. You may enjoy leisurely shopping, but if you have to replace something in an emergency, search will be purely functional, valued only for the information it uncovers.

Differing Types of Information

The information strategy discussed thus far is appropriate whenever *search* is involved prior to the purchase of the product. There are certain types of information, however, that cannot be obtained before you buy the good. There are things you can find out about coffee before you buy (such as grind and price), but what you are really interested in is how the coffee will taste, which you cannot evaluate until you actually drink the coffee. Such products cannot be evaluated until they are consumed; information comes from *experience* [13, pp. 315–18].

In the case of such goods, then, consumers cannot seek out relevant information prior to purchase. Instead, consumers gain information by purchasing the product, using it, and then deciding whether or not to buy that brand again. This process continues until the consumer decides that he or she is unlikely to find a brand superior to one already tried. Suppose you buy Brand X and it is adequate; then you buy Brand Y, which you don't like. Should you go back to Brand X (which is at least acceptable) or buy Brand Z?

Note that information costs are involved in this case, too; the costs involve the satisfaction you lose by trying an inferior product to the best one previously tried [13, p. 318]. Expectations are also involved, since your final decision will be made according to whether or not you expect a different product to provide more satisfaction. Thus, the elements involved in the experience case are similar to those involved for search, but the process is different.

The characteristics of experience products help explain several common occurrences. It is common, for example, for firms to offer free samples when a new experience good is introduced. By offering you a free sample, the firm gets you to try (that is, to experience) the product. Your information costs are cut and there is at least a chance that you will switch to the new product. The same thinking explains why new products are often offered at special prices.

Some products have both search and experience characteristics. A mattress, for example, is a search good in that you can seek out information on construction, materials, degree of firmness, and the like. The final evaluation, however, can only be made after you have slept on it for some time. Similarly, you may seek out information on a movie (Who is in it? Is it in color?), but you won't know whether or not you like it until you have seen it.

In some cases, however, you cannot evaluate a product or service even *after* you have consumed it. You may take your car to a mechanic, but can you be sure that everything that was done actually needed to be done or that everything that needed doing was done correctly? If you are like most other people, you probably can't tell. Similarly, most consumers can't determine for themselves the precise quality of the medical or legal services they receive.

In such cases, the consumer cannot evaluate the product even after it is consumed without incurring prohibitively high information costs. Such products are therefore called *credence* goods [7, pp. 68–69]. Extra information is helpful in the credence case—you might ask a friend to recommend a doctor, for example—but definitive information is not available. It follows that consumers are particularly vulnerable, since they cannot obtain the information needed to protect themselves.

As a result, government intervention is common in the credence case. The licensing of doctors and lawyers and the inspection of drugs are examples of government intervention to protect consumers in situations where individuals cannot gain the information necessary to protect themselves.* Protection takes the form of efforts to ensure that practitioners meet minimum standards of competence, meaning that consumers cannot make a really bad choice. Such protection is not always comprehensive, and it has its drawbacks (see Chapter 8),

---

* Although I indicated that information is a form of consumer protection, there is an important difference between information policies and protection policies. The former give the consumer a better base for making his or her independent decision. The latter generally limit the range of the consumer's choice.

but the need remains. The tragedy of women seeking illegal (or "backroom") abortions illustrates the problems that accompany consumers' efforts to deal with credence qualities on their own.

It is common for information from search and experience to be used as a substitute for (unobtainable) information on credence qualities. The extent and source of your doctor's training is search information and may be used in lieu of definitive information on his or her competence (note that doctors usually display their diplomas). Similarly, universities with large libraries usually play up that fact; the size of the library (which can be measured directly) is taken as a proxy for the quality of the education provided (which cannot be measured directly).

Such tendencies indicate that the information available to consumers may not in itself be particularly useful. You can find out the number of threads per square inch in fabric, but you are not buying threads per square inch; you are buying warmth or durability or some other characteristic. Information on the weave of the fabric is useful only to the extent that it tells you something about such characteristics.

Summarizing Information Needs

It should be useful at this point to summarize what I have said about information in order to understand better how the various points fit together and to appreciate their relevance more fully. By restructuring the discussions, we can develop a measure to judge the effectiveness of policies intended to increase information flow. For our purposes, it is most efficient to reconsider the question of information under the headings of cost, learning, relevance, and limits.

Cost. The two key elements that emerged from our discussion as the determinants of the amount of search are *expected savings* and *cost*. To improve the flow of information it is necessary, therefore, to either *increase expected savings or to reduce the cost*. At equilibrium, the two are equal $(C = ES)$, but if expected savings increase so that $ES > C$, it will be worthwhile to seek out more information. Reducing information costs has the same effect. For a given level of expected savings, it would pay to obtain more (of the now less expensive) information. In either case, additional search is required to restore the equality, and this increases the flow of information.

To a degree, these two alternatives are merely different aspects of the same process. Information costs are actually involved on both sides of the equation, since information is an important element in forming expectations. Individuals must have some idea of expected savings and that idea must be based on information; better information will lead to more realistic expectations. Individuals who feel that all dealers charge the same price, for example, might not search at all, thus passing up the likelihood of significant savings. Providing the consumer with high-quality, low-cost information should therefore improve both the individual's position in the market and the overall operation of the marketplace. This fact has been demonstrated [10].

Learning. The consumer's level of information is not static, it rises as the individual learns new information and falls as old information is forgotten or rendered obsolete. This is clearest in the case of experience goods, where gaining information is essentially a learning process. However, information from search may be internalized in a similar fashion; information from experience (or using the product) complements information originally gained from search. If, for example, you are buying children's clothing, you are probably interested in durability. You shop to gain information on fabric and construction. Once the clothes are purchased and worn, you can observe how durable they are. You will use that information to complement your original search information in making your next purchase. If the clothes didn't wear well, that experience will cause you to reinterpret search information.

These considerations establish the relationship between information and the broader question of learning, which in turn links the individual's development as a consumer to the overall pattern of human development. The dynamics of these processes are not fully understood, but we can at least admit the possibility that mature, experienced consumers may not engage in extended search; having assimilated information over the years, they do not feel the need for additional information. At the very least we know that individuals' patterns of information gathering will be affected by their prior level of knowledge.

Relevance. A related point concerns the relevance or usefulness of the information. Highly detailed information (such as construction specifications) might be useful for an engineer, but won't be of much help to most consumers. Information must be provided in a form that is readily assimilated and easy to use. Nutritional labeling laws, for example, have been criticized on the grounds that most consumers don't have enough background in nutrition to utilize the information. Part of the problem is simply an extension of information costs. Given the value of time, consumers are not going to utilize information that must be pondered and interpreted (the shopper who double parks and dashes into the grocery store for a couple of items isn't going to scrutinize labels for nutritional information).

There are other, more complex questions involved that concern the manner in which consumers process and finally utilize information; again, there is much we don't know about these functions, but we do know that the manner in which information is organized is very important [13]. We also know that there is such a thing as information overload, a situation in which the individual has too much poorly organized information and therefore becomes confused (just as a driver may be confused if several passengers are giving directions at the same time).

Limits. It follows that although we know most consumers need more information, we cannot be sure that simply making that information available will have a significant impact on consumer behavior. We need to know more about how consumers learn and how they use information to ensure that a dollar spent on information will result in a commensurate decline in the individual's cost of information. We know that in certain cases the potential is limited; when credence qualities are involved, additional information may be hard to provide. Furthermore, there are individual situations when information will not help much. Information can help consumers define their alternatives more clearly, but it cannot produce alternatives. If the consumer's problem is a lack of mobility that limits him or her to one store or set of stores, then information about possibilities elsewhere would be of limited value.

In a related point, we should note that information policies tend to provide the greatest benefit to middle- and upper-income consumers. The federal government's Consumer Information Center, for example, makes an effort to distribute its materials as widely as possible; the center's studies, however, indicate that most of its information goes to families with incomes well above the national median [5 and 18, p. 18].

This isn't surprising when you consider that middle- and upper-income consumers, on the average, have more education and are in a better position to use the information. However, the situation raises serious questions about how well policies to expand information flows would serve the entire population. There is an obvious need not only to make information understandable, but to provide more general programs that enable consumers to benefit from existing information.

Strategies for Cutting Information Costs

Government and Information Flow

Consumers face a gigantic task in their quest for information, but fortunately they do not have to bear the entire burden themselves.

Government, recognizing the importance of these matters to the consumer, has assumed some of the weight. This recognition has been uneven, however, and government has proved to be an uncertain ally; thus consumers may look to government for help, but should not expect a total solution. For analytical purposes, the various public policies that affect information flow can be classified under three main headings: legal limitations, standards, and direct information.

Legal Limitations. This category covers a broad range of government activities. Consumer protection laws may not in themselves provide information, but they can free the consumer from certain concerns.* The government in this case is acting like an umpire, setting and enforcing the rules of the game. Consumers can then operate within the rules, free from the need to investigate such questions on their own and able to concentrate on obtaining supplemental information.

Historically, this is the oldest form of government protection and involves such basic matters as contract rights. If the consumer signs a valid contract, he or she can be sure that it will be enforced. In this sense, the extensive legal framework that has grown up around the marketplace can be considered as a part of the information flow mechanism. It takes information, of course, to make the legal mechanisms effective, since they can work only if they are enforced and if consumers are aware of their rights.

Some consumer protection laws apply directly to consumer information. If a business advertises a special sale, merchandise has to be marked down after having been previously offered for sale at the higher price. Similarly, if firms advertise merchandise at special prices, adequate stocks must be available. The "bait-and-switch" technique, advertising an item at an extremely low price but then selling it out quickly so that buyers can be switched to a higher priced item, is now illegal. Such regulations can be evaded, but they do offer consumers some protection by cutting information costs; if something is advertised as on sale, consumers will know that it really is on sale and that it will be available.

Despite remarkable progress in recent years, serious problems still remain. New deceptions are practiced and old ploys remain. Many important areas of consumer protection that relate to improved information have not been adequately covered. Even when the laws are passed, however, enforcement is spotty. In such cases, consumers will be forced to seek out additional information themselves, and, in so doing, lose the benefits of lower information costs. The result is

---

* I will discuss the particulars of consumer protection legislation in Chapter 8.

similar when people do not know what protection is available to them or what their rights are. This is especially apparent among low-income consumers, but it is by no means limited to that group. If knowledge is power, then such people are powerless.

Standards. The second way that the government supports the consumer and directly affects information costs is the imposition of standards. Standards take many forms, but compose two main categories: (1) product or personnel standards, and (2) disclosure standards that specify how much information producers and sellers must provide to the public. The first type is illustrated by the way in which health departments license establishments that serve food, attesting that they need minimal health standards.

Meat inspection and grading offers a good example of the differing impact of protection and information policies. Meat is inspected to ensure that it is free from contamination; the consumer's alternatives are limited to meat that is fit for consumption and choices are made accordingly. However, meat offered for sale is also graded, providing the consumer with additional information. Grading itself does not limit the consumer's choice, but instead gives the consumer additional information on which to base an individual decision.

A wide range of governmental regulations are imposed in areas where market operations alone are judged insufficient to protect the public interest. The need is clearest in the case of complex and highly technical products. To evaluate the safety and effectiveness of drugs, for example, requires technical information beyond the means of all but a very few consumers. Since consumers cannot get necessary information on their own, they cannot effectively check the operations of firms in the drug industry. For this reason, government takes on the responsibility of ensuring that drugs meet specified standards of safety and effectiveness and that they are sold at reasonable prices.

You should recognize that such cases fall into the credence category. Because of the complexity of the market and the products it contains, consumers cannot be provided with the information necessary to protect themselves. My central thesis, that consumer problems are an outgrowth of a highly developed economy, is again confirmed. Two centuries ago, modern drugs were unknown; thus information costs were minimal and consumers could rightly expect to get whatever information they needed on their own. The Industrial Revolution and the technological changes that accompanied it have changed the situation, creating the need for agencies to assume the burden of information costs from the consumer in these areas.

Again, the quality of enforcement is tremendously important. If enforcement is lax, consumers may be lulled into a false sense of security. Consumers, in effect, are provided with inaccurate information; individuals are worse off because they think they are protected and hence aren't on the lookout for problems. Meat inspection is again a good example. There are periodic scandals about unsanitary conditions in the industry that can only undermine consumer confidence. This increases information costs as consumers conclude that they cannot trust the standards to be a true representation of quality.

The other area of government involvement in standards has developed more recently; that is to set standards of information disclosure for producers and sellers. Truth-in-lending laws are one example; by forcing disclosure of effective interest rates, these laws provide consumers with better information on which to base decisions.

A similar argument can be made for truth-in-packaging laws, which require that the package accurately represents what is inside. Packages are often misleading about both the quality of the contents and the quantity; large packages are used to make it appear that the contents are comparable, but, when you open the box, it is only three-quarters full. Unit pricing is aimed at this problem. With family sizes, giant economy sizes and personal sizes, it is almost impossible to figure out which is the best buy. Unit pricing requires that cost per unit (3¢ an ounce, $1.35 a pound, 50¢ a quart, and so on) be clearly marked on the package. This would facilitate comparisons by the consumer both among brands and among various sizes of the same brand.

As an alternative, the government could require standardized packaging. Note, however, that if unit pricing were required, there would be less incentive for companies to promote so many different-sized packages, since consumers would already have the information the packages were meant to conceal. Thus, there would be a tendency for sellers to move to more standardized packages on their own. The result is the same, but in the second instance market forces are the effective agent; the point is that consumers need information in order for such forces to work.

It may therefore seem surprising that, although a variety of new disclosure requirements have been adopted in recent years, their impact has been mixed. Unit pricing (while it isn't required in most cases) has met with indifferent results. Care labels in clothing sometimes annoy consumers and have generated disputes between industry and government. Nutritional labeling is considered too complex for consumers to understand.

Truth in lending, which represents one of the most far-reaching disclosure efforts, has not produced any dramatic changes in credit markets. In this case, disclosure seems to have produced more awareness of interest charges, but that awareness hasn't changed behavior [2]. Among lower-income consumers, the reason appears to be their lack of access to more attractive sources of credit. If credit cannot be obtained from less expensive sources, then knowing about them isn't very helpful.

It would be wrong, however, to conclude that disclosure has been a failure. Despite recent changes, disclosure is still the exception rather than the rule; furthermore, the practice has not been incorporated into any coordinated policy effort. Little attention has been given to the long-run aspects of disclosure. I have indicated that consumers gather information over long periods and that such information helps establish purchasing patterns. An added bit of information, therefore, must be interpreted in terms of existing information and established behavior patterns. In many cases, one bit of information is not critical enough to affect any drastic change in such patterns.

Direct Information. The third area of government involvement with information costs lies with the actual provision of information. Government at all levels, particularly the federal, collects and distributes vast amounts of information. Government publications are available on nearly every type of consumer interest. There is even a publication indexing other publications for the consumer [9]. Some of the same services are also available at the local level. County extension services are most valuable in this regard.

The government collects information for its own use that could be valuable to the consumer. The General Services Administration (and other agencies) sets specifications for the products that the government buys. If this information were released on a systematic basis, consumers would benefit from the prior evaluation that the government carried out. While some of this information is released, much of it is jealously guarded (even though it involves only mundane products) and has even been the cause of lawsuits.

However, the federal government has adopted a more aggressive strategy toward providing information in recent years. The Consumer Information Service (CIS) is responsible for distributing government consumer publications; the CIS advertises on television and through other media in an effort to ensure as wide a distribution as possible. Activity has increased at the state level also. Pennsylvania's *Shoppers' Guides* were mentioned in the last chapter, while in Maine the state's Bureau of Consumer Protection has aroused public interest with a series of publications on credit, complaints, and real estate [3].

The federal Environmental Protection Agency's (EPA) mileage ratings on new cars represent one of the best known public efforts to provide information. Unfortunately, the EPA ratings also illustrate some of the difficulties involved with the information approach. The EPA ratings have gained wide distribution and must be incorporated by auto makers in their advertising (of course, the cars with the best ratings don't need to be forced to use the figures). The problem is that while the EPA figures give a good sense of the ranking of cars, the actual figures do not reflect the mileage that the driver can expect.

The reason is that the EPA does not conduct road tests (which would be too expensive); rather, the figures are based on laboratory tests. If your car is well tuned, you might come close to the EPA figures on a windless summer day in Kansas, but otherwise you won't because the figures are based on warm engine tests with no wind or grade. The average driver, then, becomes upset when his new Baas-mobile, which has an EPA rating of 40 mpg, can do no better than 34 mpg. The result is distrust of the EPA ratings and disillusionment with the entire process.

This confusion arose because the public did not understand the EPA figures (the agency does plan to change its testing procedures to bring results closer to actual highway figures). However, despite the need for improvement, the ratings have had several good effects. A common standard was imposed, which, although it may contain in-accuracies, is at least consistent; auto makers could no longer make mileage claims based on their own (often questionable) tests. Further-more, the manner in which the EPA ratings were featured in the advertising of cars with good mileage shows how the private sector can distribute public information.

The government's experience with the EPA ratings should help to improve future information programs. Despite the problems, the value of a more aggressive strategy has been demonstrated; such approaches need to be refined and extended. Other experiments are being tried, such as county extension services that are being offered in store-front offices in some low-income areas. This brings informa-tion and expertise to the people and, as the workers become an ac-cepted part of the community, they can work with the people more effectively.

Private Information Sources

Although public agencies may help consumers cut information costs, the final burden of collecting information still rests with individuals themselves. Either individually or collectively, they must obtain the information they need to operate day after day in the marketplace. Given the current state of affairs, they often do this in a hit-or-miss fashion, but they still have to do it. We need to look, then, at how individuals or groups can cut information costs.

As noted earlier, a consumer's accumulated knowledge is tremen-dously important. Buyers learn about the features of the most im-portant products they buy, the brands they like, and the dealers they can trust. The last point should be underscored. Since it is impossible to learn everything about every possible product, finding the right dealer can be a big help. You may not know much about meat, but if you can trust your butcher, you will eat well. Confidence is the key word, and that takes time to build, but it is worth the effort. Most good consumers are good consumers because they deal with sellers they can trust.

Unfortunately, the pattern of American life over the past few decades has worked against the development of such arrangements. Increased urbanization and mobility are two of the most important factors involved. True, the consumer has more options in an urban area, but it is often more difficult to find the right store and, since businesses tend to be larger, it may be more difficult to develop a good working arrangement. Technological change also plays a role; new techniques for cutting and packaging meat, for example, have already eliminated the butcher's role in some instances.

Even if a pattern of trust is developed, the consumer may move to a new area and have to start all over again. For many, if not most, Americans, the day is gone when they can expect to trade with the same merchants they knew as children and whom they had grown to trust. Even the small town, which we have tended to romanticize in this analysis, is changing. Many stores are closing and, if they are replaced, it is by national chain stores, which have no particular attachment to the local population.

Increased mobility works against consumers in other ways, too. It is quite likely, for example, that they will be removed from family and friends. This cuts them off from potentially valuable sources of information. In the past there was a sort of internship associated with becoming a consumer. When children went out in the world on their own, they did not go very far; members of the family were available if help was needed, including help about purchasing decisions. Very useful information could be passed along in this way. Now, it is common for families to be spread across the country (or even the world), so that this learning process cannot be continued.

Sharing information is called *pooling* and may be as simple as asking a neighbor for advice on finding a good mechanic. Some arrangements, however, are more formal; consumers have joined together to share information in an organized manner. These efforts, like so many other recent developments in consumer affairs, have taken different forms. In some cases they are nothing more than clubs or interest groups, gatherings of friends from either the neighborhood or work. At the other extreme, there are formal organizations with legal status and businesslike organizations. Some are set up as cooperatives, others on a profit basis.

While this sort of business operation to provide information to consumers is relatively new, the idea of business organizing to provide specific information to consumers is not. Some businesses have recognized that a better-informed consumer is in their own interest, and thus they provide informational services to the consumer. Although there may be certain biases built into such offerings, they are still of potential value to the consumer.

Varying amounts of product information are available to the consumer at the point of sale. Smaller, neighborhood stores, while they may have higher prices, also provide more information. In such cases, you are paying for the information directly as part of the product price; if you already had the information, you might do better buying at a large discount store.

In certain cases, individuals specialize in the provision of certain types of information. Stock brokers and real estate agents are familiar examples. It is often more economical for the consumer to go to such brokers for information than to try to obtain the informtion on their own. Such services can work to the advantage of the alert consumer who uses them wisely. Problems may arise, however, particularly concerning fees; federal regulators have forced brokerage firms to be more competitive in their fees, and real estate agents are under similar pressure in some areas.

Businesses, particularly at the local level, have an interest in promoting consumer satisfaction. The individual consumer has more leverage at this level, so a dissatisfied consumer represents at least potential harm to business. For this reason, business in most areas has organized Better Business Bureaus, which keep files on local businesses and distribute such information to consumers. There are two main ways in which the BBB can be helpful. It can provide information before the sale or transaction, and help the consumer afterward if he or she is not satisfied [1].

Better Business Bureaus are financed by businesses, and they naturally have a business perspective. Their goal is "promoting consumer satisfaction," but that may mean nothing more than soothing words and efforts to defuse the consumer's wrath. They may make you feel better without really solving your problem. Opinion is divided on the overall effectiveness of BBBs, partly because their effectiveness varies from area to area. Some are apologists for business, and others work hard to bring business and consumer together. The rise of consumer concern has revitalized lagging operations in some areas, forcing them to be more responsive [4].

Consumers may also receive information through guarantees and warranties. In the past, such information was likely to mislead, as phrases like "unconditional guarantee" and "fully guaranteed" were widely misused. Recent legislation and administrative decisions, however, have curbed the worst of these abuses; warranties must now state explicitly what is and what is not covered, as well as set out terms of the coverage [8]. The consumer must still look carefully at the word *guarantee*. Conditions must be spelled out, but these may include such things as requiring the consumer to package the product and return it to a central service area; most consumers find these procedures bothersome. All of this applies to written guarantees; verbal agreements have no validity beyond the integrity of the individual. This means that everything should be in writing. An offhand "Oh, we'll take care of that" is easily forgotten or denied.

No discussion of private efforts to distribute information would be complete without including product testing organizations, the two most important being Consumers' Research and Consumers Union. The former is the oldest product-testing service in the United States; while its growth has not kept pace with Consumers Union in recent years, the basic idea of the two groups is similar. Consumers' Research has also been important in exposing consumer fraud.

Consumers Union currently represents the most significant private effort in the United States to evaluate products and pass this information on to consumers. Its monthly publication, *Consumer Reports,* provides the results of tests on literally thousands of items, in many cases representing the only available source of such information. There is also an annual *Buyers Guide* that summarizes information on different products. For many years, CU stood alone as the only group calling attention to consumer problems. There is no question that during that time it served the consumer well.

Nevertheless, CU has come under criticism. One complaint, which may grow out of the nature of private testing services, has to do with audience. Product testing is expensive, and since, to maintain its integrity, CU has never accepted advertising, it must depend on membership fees to support its activities. That means the information goes to those in middle-income groups and above; again, those with the greatest need don't get the information. Consumers Union has also been criticized for the products tested, which represent the whole range of consumer goods. This means that some of their tests cover products that, while not necessarily frivolous, are at least not of pressing importance to consumers.

At the heart of the question is the attitude of the organization itself. CU confines itself to providing information. Some observers feel it should take a more active role; they would like to see it become more of an active agent on behalf of consumers, pressing consumers' interests through investigation, legislation, and the courts. The organization has become more active in these areas, but its main thrust is still information. Were it to change its focus, it would be taking on a much more difficult job and in the process could become a much different organization [21].

It is almost a requirement of examinations like this that they conclude by referring to the need for more education. So as not to disappoint anyone, we shall follow that tradition. Education has the potential for improving the efficiency of the individual's consumption. I have stressed that additional information is worthless to consumers unless it can be utilized. Thus, consumers must know what to do with the information they receive. This suggests the need for a broadly based consumer education program that incorporates not only formal educational training, but community programs and media exposure as well. The media, particularly television, offer tremendous potential for consumer education and, although the past record may not encourage optimism, the possibilities still exist.

Developing Information Potential

A National Information Policy?

You may have already been struck by the thought that although there are numerous sources of information available to consumers, there is a distinct lack of coordination and organization among them. Despite the fact that government has moved to reduce information costs, it has failed to develop an overall policy for either its own efforts or those from the private sector. The need for such a policy should be clear. The goals I have outlined suggest that the policy should aim at providing high-quality, low-cost information to all consumers. In order to suggest how that might be done, it is useful to look at what other countries have done in trying to provide information to the consumer.

Sweden has moved further than most other countries in developing a comprehensive consumer information policy. Responsibility was recently centralized under the State Consumer Board, representing a shift from an earlier reliance on independent, quasi-public agencies [20, p. 285]. The two key elements in the Swedish approach are product testing and labeling; the former was carried out by the State Institute for Consumer Information, the latter by the Institute for Informative Labeling.

The Institute for Consumer Information functioned as a public version of the Consumers Union. Its board was made up of both public and private members, including members of Parliament and labor and business representatives [18, pp. 362–75]. The Institute for Informative Labeling was a private group, although it had a tradition of public support. Its goals were to standardize labels and increase consumer awareness of them. The institute specified format, set product specifications and issued licenses for labels that conformed to its standards [18, pp. 37–52].

It is still too soon to tell how the centralization of power under the State Consumer Board will affect the operations of these agencies. However, by establishing themselves as important parts of the Swedish marketplace, they demonstrated the possibilities of coordinated action on consumer information. One of the appealing, and sensible, features of the Swedish program was the pattern of public and private cooperation; some fear that this may be lost under more centralized control [20, p. 285].

Another Swedish effort that deserves mention is a remarkable publication called *Weak Points of Cars* [22]. It is published annually by the Swedish Motor Vehicle Inspection Company, which itself is supported by public and private groups. Each year, every car in Sweden over three years old must undergo a safety inspection. Like similar programs in the United States, it is geared to keeping unsafe cars off the road. However, all the information collected in these inspections is tabulated and published in *Weak Points of Cars,* providing consumers with a clear, understandable profile of every make of car on Swedish roads. The service is also valuable to manufacturers, because it allows them to identify problems and correct them on subsequent models.

In the rest of Europe, there is also extensive public support for private groups and private cooperation with public efforts. The countries making up the European Economic Community (or Common Market) maintain their own national consumer agencies. The Common Market itself has tried to move toward a common consumer policy, but progress has been uneven. The Consumers Liaison Committee, founded in 1962, was never financed adequately and finally languished. Efforts have been made to increase cooperation with national consumer groups [11, pp. 20–22]. The Common Market currently maintains an office of Special Services for Questions of Consumer Interest, but it operates with minimal budget and staff [18, p. 499]. These patterns are worth noting, because they say something about priorities (the Common Market was founded in 1957) and because they reflect the difficulties in developing policies that cross national boundaries.

From our perspective, it is also difficult to make comparisons among countries. Sweden, for example, is a much more homogeneous country than the United States, with fewer ethnic differences and a more even distribution of income. Thus, what works in Sweden might not necessarily work here. At the same time, you may have observed that none of the elements in the Swedish program are really new. In most cases, similar programs are being carried out in this country. A parallel effort, though it would require some changes, would not represent the wholesale importation of alien ideas or entirely new concepts.

Indeed, we should not want simply to import the apparatus from Sweden or some other country. While most of the procedures are relatively advanced, they still have their shortcomings (including the problem of getting the information to those who need it most). Perhaps the most important lesson Americans can learn from the European experience has to do with the benefits of public-private cooperation. Americans have a tendency to think that public and private groups will never meet, that there is an innate antagonism between them that marks them as distinct entities incapable of acting in concert. Such notions simply do not reflect reality. Although there are numerous examples of conflict, government and the private sector cooperate in many ways. Public groups encourage private business development through research activities and through cooperation with private groups in developing new markets. This process is most obvious in agricultural development. Through extension services and land-grant universities, the Department of Agriculture has acted as partner in American agriculture. Indeed, it is often impossible to differentiate between private and public undertakings.

Active collaboration between public and private groups on providing information would therefore represent no significant departure from established procedures. This collaboration could take different forms. It might mean public funding for private groups, or it could mean a joint public-private venture. What is needed is the recognition of common interests between the public and private sectors and active coordination of their respective efforts. This could be done through a product testing institute, which could occupy a position similar to the United States Bureau of Standards. It should be responsible, however, not just for product testing, but also for coordinating information gathered by other groups.

The basic question, remember, is one of getting information to the people. No country has really come to grips with this issue; some are more active than others, but none have really tried to merchandise information. What Americans could bring to this approach is a talent for merchandising and marketing. We have developed these skills far beyond most other countries. All that remains is to apply them to information. For a country that takes justifiable pride in its sales techniques, there should be no problem. If we can sell soap, cars, and political candidates, we can sell information. If there is a broadly based recognition of both the importance of information and the possibilities for improvement, that improvement can be realized.

An effective program of this sort would undoubtedly be expensive. Consumers would pay through both higher taxes and higher product prices. The real question, however, is whether the individual's private search costs would be cut by more than the program cost. If that were the case, there would be a net saving to the individual and to society. Given that individual search is rather inefficient and that the costs of a bad decision can be high, there is reason to believe that a large-scale program of information distribution would more than pay its own way. There are certainly enough arguments in its favor to warrant giving it a try.

Some Daydreams About Tomorrow

Most of what has been said thus far is quite conventional. Some of the proposals are innovative, but they are within the framework that is familiar to us all. Looking forward, however, calls for considering some new possibilities. The technology of consumption has not changed very much over the years. It is still in the horse-and-buggy era compared with technology for other parts of the economy. Consumer problems, on the other hand, are of the space-age variety. It would be impossible to think of sending rockets into space using the technology of the 1880s. Why then should our thinking about consumption be limited to techniques that are even older?

One proposal for a new approach calls for the establishment of a local consumer information system. The idea is based on the observation that while local markets are important to consumers, variations exist among markets and consumers lack the information they need about those variations. As we have noted, information is often available in the sense that someone has it, but the typical consumer has difficulty obtaining the information. The local system would therefore provide:

Local price information; the cheapest places to buy products which show little quality variation.

Local excessibility to quality-rated products; implies a rating (such as Consumers Union's) and information on where such products can be found and at what prices.

Experience rating of vendor services: dealing with credence qualities of services.

Consumer ratings of retailers [12, p. 295–96].

There are a variety of ways that such a system could operate. The key is that it should collect available information and channel it to consumers. One possibility in this regard was long the province of popularized science magazines, but is now a reality: the home computer. Electronic calculators have already made a difference in terms of families' shopping and bookkeeping practices. The potential for the computer is even greater. A wide range of information on consumer goods—the kind of information system discussed above—could be stored in the memory of a large computer. From their home terminals, consumers could tie into the central unit whenever they wished. Similarly, information on the complexities of family financial management (including credit) could be made available.

Such devices are now becoming available to consumers. Computer terminals in the home are increasingly common and a growing market for home computers (especially kits) is developing.* The technology for interfacing or linking units together has also grown rapidly. Thus, it is now possible to think realistically about a system that would provide a week's worth of nutritionally balanced menus on command; these menus could be developed in light of family size, income, and tastes. Family financial management programs are already available.

It may seem that there are big-brother overtones to having a computer in the home and feeding it personal data. The danger need not materialize, however; the individual's integrity and privacy could be maintained. The scope of individual action could be expanded because of the expanded amount of information. We need not be preoccupied with the precise form the technology is taking; rather, we need to consider the range of possibilities and be sure that we are not hind-bound in our thinking.

As the pace of market development accelerates, consumers are falling further behind. In making up for past mistakes, we must be aware of future possibilities. We now have at hand (or in development) the technology to make consumption truly efficient. Much technological development in the past worked against that goal; we are now in a position to redress the balance. The prospect should be exciting to those who feel it is time that technology serve the consumer directly.

While the computer has fascinating possibilities, it is not the only avenue available. The media, particularly the electronic media, offer opportunities that are nearly as great. Furthermore, they are already

---

* The first edition of this book predicted that "reasonably priced units for the home should be available within five years." That prediction proved conservative.

established, so the technological limitations would not be significant. The mere mention of the media should suggest advertising; while the information potential of advertising has hardly been tapped, that potential is so great that we need to look at the possibilities more closely.

Study Questions

1. Explain why information costs are higher on less frequently purchased goods.
2. Would information costs be higher on a new appliance or a used one? Would they be higher on a used stove or a used refrigerator? Explain carefully, identifying the various kinds of information involved.
3. We mentioned in Chapter 4 that newcomers to an area find that shopping takes them longer than before. Explain the reasons, judged from the context of this chapter.
4. Why would information costs—the amount of shopping or search required—increase during periods of rising prices?
5. In some markets (like the automobile market), price is not set but is determined by bargaining. Do such procedures affect information costs? Explain.
6. Does the information necessary to select a spouse fall into the search, experience, or credence category?
7. A major grocery chain recently came out with a Brand X (generic, unbranded products) line of products; these are sold at a considerably lower price. What are consumers' information costs in this case?
8. The government sets standards on many different products, including peanut butter. Peanut butter must contain a given percentage of peanuts. Could the same result be achieved by replacing the standard with a requirement that the label clearly indicate the percentage of peanuts in the product? Are there any advantages to this approach? What do you think would be necessary for it to be successful?
9. What is the chief shortcoming of publications like *Consumer Research* and *Consumer Reports* as sources of information?
10. Explain why information policies are of limited value:
    a. When credence qualities are concerned.
    b. In dealing with the problems of the poor.
    c. In helping consumers with little education.
    Is there any way these problems can be overcome? Discuss.

Suggested Projects

1. Become an expert consumer on some item, some appliance would likely be best. Find out *everything* you can about it (don't limit yourself to consumer publications; check trade journals, too). Now that you have the information, go out and shop. Evaluate the information sellers provide. You know about the product, so ask questions. Do the sellers have the answers? Try different kinds of stores. What kind of information do you think consumers get at point of purchase?

2. Again, pick a specific product (a durable) and select two groups of students from the class:

   a. The first should study available literature on the product, including government publications, test results, material from extension services, and any other relevant information.

   b. The second group should go out and shop for the product, visiting different stores and collecting information on special features and price.

   Both groups should keep careful records of how much time all of this takes as well as listing any other costs incurred (gasoline, and so on). Your purpose is to get as much information as possible. When it is all collected, decide how much you would have searched if you had really been buying the product. Include in your considerations the number of stores that had to be visited before a price range was defined and the number of publications studied before information became repetitious. Did these follow the pattern suggested in the text? What kinds of informational aids would have made the job easier?

3. Conduct a survey of information sources available in your area. In addition to those suggested under Project 1, include local consumer groups (public and private), Better Business Bureaus, and any other potential source of significant information to the consumer. Is adequate information available on most products? Does this information get to the people who need it?

4. Conduct a survey to find out what sources of information consumers actually use. You have to be careful here, because most people do not think in terms of information costs. Thus, you might ask something like: "When you go out to buy a product, how do you find out which one is best for you?" or more simply, "How do you get your information on which you base your decision?" You might ask them to rank a series of alternatives (past experience, suggestions of friends, shopping around, test results, and so on) or merely let them suggest answers (see Ap-

pendix). What seems to be the most common source of information? Do the results suggest any possible ways to improve information flow?

5. Gather a few samples of warranties or guarantees on different products. Did you find any that were actually misleading? Check the FTC guidelines on warranties; are the guidelines met? Do you think they actually would affect your decision if you were buying?

6. Pick a product like detergent or toothpaste that is available in many different-sized containers. Is there any relation between the sizes offered by one producer and another? How does the price per unit (per ounce, per pound, and so forth) vary among brands and among various sizes of the same brand? Be sure to check and see what company makes each brand; how many different companies did you find? What does this suggest? How can you evaluate all of this in terms of its impact on the consumer?

7. You are probably aware that your local government (or state government) sets standards in many areas, including barber shops and restaurants. Make a comprehensive search for areas in which standards are imposed. Were you aware of all of them? How effective for the consumer, do you think, are these standards?

8. Examine the information provided on labels for food products. Do you think the product is represented fairly?
   a. Do you think the information is presented in a useful form?
   b. Talk with shoppers (ask the manager's permission) to see if they use the information.
   c. If the products are experience goods, what is the use of the information?

9. We noted that auto repair falls into the credence category. Does your state or community have any certification requirements for mechanics? Make a survey of friends to see how they chose a mechanic.

Bibliography and Suggested Readings

1. Better Business Bureau. *Editorial Reports.*
   These pamphlets are available through your local BBB and cover a whole range of consumer topics from buying meat to finding a mechanic. They are brief, to the point, and well worth picking up.

2. Brant, W., and Day, G. "Information Disclosure and Consumer Behavior: An Empirical Evaluation of Truth in Lending." University of Michigan *Journal of Law Reform*, vol. 7, no. 2 (Winter 1974): 297–328.
A good study on disclosure, both its successes and shortcomings, in the area of credit. Suggests that shortcomings are most obvious in the case of lower-income consumers.

3. Bureau of Consumer Protection, State of Maine. Augusta, Maine.
An example of imagination in a state consumer protection agency. The Bureau publishes a series of "Down Easter Guides," which have been well received by the state's citizens (though not by all business interests). The Bureau's publication on what to do with a faulty product (or lemon) drew the attention of federal authorities who wanted to distribute it.

4. "Consumer's Fighting Back via Better Business Bureaus," *U.S. News & World Report,* December 18, 1972, p. 58.
A review of activities of the BBB and their relation to consumerism.

5. *Consumer Information Catalog.* Consumer Information Service, General Services Administration. Pueblo, Colorado.
A quarterly catalog of timely government publications available and of interest to the consumer. A wealth of information for those who are interested. The Consumer Information Center represents an increased effort on the part of the federal government to make its publications more readily available.

6. *Consumer Reports.* Consumers Union, Mt. Vernon, N.Y.
CU's monthly publication containing testing information and consumer tid-bits. A bible to some, a bore to others, *CR* is still the primary source of product-testing information in the United States.

7. Darby, M. R., and Karni, E. "Free Competition and the Optimal Amount of Fraud." *Journal of Law and Economics,* vol. XVI, no. 1 (April 1973): 67–87.
The basis of our discussion of credence goods. Somewhat technical, but worth looking at for a discussion of the credence case and how private efforts might work to protect consumers.

8. Federal Trade Commission. *Warranties.* Washington, D.C.: U.S. Government Printing Office, 1975.
Consideration of the new requirements for warranties contained in the Magnuson-Moss Warranty Act. Senator Magnuson is a long-time supporter of consumer causes in Congress.

9. *Guide to Consumer Services.* Washington, D.C.: U.S. Government Printing Office.
An index of federal agencies dealing with consumer affairs, including the organization's name, purposes, and legal duties. A good summary of where to find what.

10. Hawkins, M. H., and Devine, D. G. "Implications of Improved Information on Market Performance." *Journal of Consumer Affairs,* Winter 1972, pp. 184–97.
    Documentation showing that improved information improves the manner in which markets function and the efficiency with which consumers function in those markets.
    The Journal of Consumer Affairs *is a must for anyone interested in consumer affairs. It was the first publication of its kind and carries articles over the whole range of consumer issues. American Council on Consumer Interests publishes the journal.*

11. Kemezis, Paul. "The Consumer and the Common Market." *European Community* 159, October 1972, pp. 18–23.
    A report on consumer-related developments in the Common Market countries, with special emphasis on background of information policies.

12. Maynes, Scott E. "Informational Imperfections in Local Consumer Markets: Assessment and Implications." *Advances in Consumer Research IV.* Association for Consumer Research, 1977, pp. 288–96.

13. McGuire, William J. "Some Internal Psychological Factors Influencing Consumer Choice." *The Journal of Consumer Research,* March 1976, pp. 302–19.
    A good review of information processing and recall. Good bibliography.

14. Nelson, Phillip. "Information and Consumer Behavior." *Journal of Political Economy,* March-April 1970, pp. 311–29.
    The analysis of search and experience goods and the differing strategies they require from consumers. Contains valuable insights into consumer behavior. *The Journal of Political Economy* is a good source of articles on information and consumer behavior for the serious student.

15. Scherhorn, Gerhard, and Wieken, Klaus. "On the Effect of Counter-Information on Consumers." In *Human Behavior in Economic Affairs,* ed. Burkhard Strumpel, et al. San Francisco: Jossey-Bass, 1972.
    A report on a West German experiment to provide consumers with additional information on gasoline prices and detergents. Indicates positive reaction of consumers to information that the marketplace would have denied them.

16. Stigler, George. "The Economics of Information." *Journal of Political Economy,* June 1961, pp. 213–25.
    The classic article on information costs. Despite analytics, most students will find it readable and useful. It forms the basis for the basic approach to cost in this chapter.

17. ———. *The Theory of Price.* 3rd ed., New York: Macmillan, 1966. A very brief, but highly instructive introduction to information costs in Chapter 1.

18. Thorelli, Hans B., and Thorelli, Sarah V. *Consumer Information Handbook: Europe and North America.* New York: Praeger, 1974.
As the name implies, a handbook on information policies and programs in Europe and North America. The best source of comparative data available. Details on programs in each country. Judgmental at points, but still the essential source for those interested in comparative policies.

19. Thorelli, Hans B., Becker, Helmut, and Engledow, Jack. *The Information Seekers.* Cambridge, Mass.: Ballinger Publishers, 1975.
A comparative study of consumers in Europe and North America who actively seek out information. Sheds valuable light on behavior.

20. Thorelli, Hans B. "Philosophies of Consumer Information Programs." *Advances in Consumer Research, IV.* Association for Consumer Research, 1977, pp. 282–87.
A review of recent developments in national consumer policies, with emphasis on the distinction between state control and private cooperation. This list of references does not exhaust Thorelli's work; he is obviously a leader in the area of information programs.

21. *Washington Post.* Series on Consumers Union, April 22–25, 1973.
Four articles by *Post* staff writers on CU's problems at a time when the organization was making decisions about its directions. Looks at the power plays within the organization as well as differing views on its goals.

22. *Weak Points of Cars.* A. B. Svensk Bilprovning, Swedish Vehicle Inspection Company, Vällingby 1, Stockholm, Sweden.
The Swedish publication that tabulates the results of annual inspection. It illustrates some of the possibilities for distributing information. Of interest to car buyers in this country, but experiences may differ because of the availability of service. Issued annually.

-6-

Advertising and Information

Toward A Consumer Perspective

A Consumer Viewpoint

Regardless of who you are or where you happen to be as you read this, you have almost certainly been exposed to some kind of advertising today. In the last chapter I spoke of ways in which the consumer can seek out information, but with advertising, the situation is reversed; it seeks you out, coming into your home over the television and radio and in newspapers and magazines. Advertising is an integral part of American life, and billions of dollars are spent each year to ensure that it stays that way. However, despite such massive expenditures, it isn't at all clear what advertising does *for* or *to* consumers. It is clear that all those dollars spent on advertising haven't fulfilled the consumer's need to know about products. There is evidence, in fact, that the opposite is sometimes true; advertising may confuse consumers and in some cases even mislead them.

The irony of this situation can be traced to basic differences in how advertising's function is perceived. Thus far we haven't spoken of information in terms of telling consumers what they ought to do. We have treated information as impartial evidence that consumers evaluate as they make independent judgments. The intended outcome is a purchase that will promote greater satisfaction; presumably, informative advertising would embody these same elements.

At this point, a conflict arises because advertising intends to sell a particular product. It follows that the function of the ad must be

117

to persuade the individual to buy the product. Thus, persuasion replaces impartial evaluation and any persuasive technique that works will be employed. Success is measured in terms of increased sales, and any ad that boosts sales is by definition good. If an ad for Scrubbo Cleanser shows a celebrity extolling its virtues and that gimmick happens to sell Scrubbo, that's all that matters.

There's the rub, the difference in perception mentioned above. Information is meant to provide consumers with a better basis for making independent decisions; advertising is meant to persuade consumers to buy a product. Advertisers are interested in informing the public only if that information will help sell the product. That is why most of what is written about the subject is of little or no value to the student inquiring about advertising from the consumer's point of view. Advertising has been analyzed mainly from the seller's perspective, which views the consumer as someone to be attracted (some would say *manipulated*) rather than someone to be given information.

Dollars and Sense

This raises an obvious question: Should advertising be asked to perform an information function? In answering that question, remember that while information can be gotten to consumers more cheaply than it is now, someone still has to pay the cost of getting it there. Two possibilities suggest themselves: government and business. The government reduces information costs to consumers by forcing businesses to disclose key facts, establishing standards, or providing information directly. The costs are then either forced back on business or paid out of tax monies. If government bears the costs directly, it is ultimately the consumer as taxpayer who shoulders the burden. This may be a more efficient approach, but information costs have only been reduced, not escaped.

If business is forced to bear the cost of providing information to the consumer, this cost, like any other cost of production, would be reflected in the final price of the product. The degree to which this price increase would be passed along to the consumer depends on the degree of competition in the market.* In most cases, however, the consumer will end up paying some, if not all, of the added costs through higher product prices. Again it is the consumer who ultimately pays the costs of information. If it has occurred to you that you are *already* paying higher prices to cover advertising and promo-

---

* The less competition there is, the easier it is for firms to pass higher costs along to consumers. In more competitive markets, there are more firms, so consumers have more choices, and it is harder for a single firm to manipulate price.

tional costs, then you see the point. Look carefully at the data in Table 6.1. The dollar amounts are impressive (nearly one-half *billion* dollars for Procter & Gamble), but the percentages may be more significant. The percentages can be read as the number of cents out of each dollar spent that go to pay for advertising.* Among the top 100 national advertisers, advertising expenditures run as high as one-fourth of sales [6, p. 30]. Few are that high, but it remains clear that a significant portion of the consumer's dollar goes directly to advertising.

This is precisely why information is so important. If advertising efforts were channeled into providing information, there would be a *net gain* to consumers, who would then be receiving something for the costs they are already paying. In that sense, informative advertising would be relatively cheap in that it would be available *at little or no extra cost.* Remember, too, that the potential for advertising as

Table 6.1   Advertising Expenditures: In Dollar Amount and as a Percent of Sales for the 15 Leading National Advertisers: 1976

	Company	Ad Expenditures[a] (in millions)	Ad Expenditures As Percent of Sales
1.	Procter & Gamble Co.	$445.0	8.4
2.	General Motors Corp.	287.0	0.6
3.	General Foods Corp.	275.0	7.6
4.	Sears, Roebuck & Co.	245.0	2.0
5.	Warner-Lambert Co.	199.0	15.3
6.	Bristol-Myers Co.	189.0	9.5
7.	Ford Motor Co.	162.0	0.5
8.	American Home Products Corp.	158.0	8.8
9.	Philip Morris Inc.	149.0	3.5
10.	Mobil Corp.	146.5	0.5
11.	R. J. Reynolds Industries	140.3	2.4
12.	Unilever	135.0	10.7
13.	General Mills Inc.	131.6	4.5
14.	Heublein Inc.	129.1	8.3
15.	Colgate-Palmolive Co.	118.0	3.4

Reprinted with permission from the August 29, 1977 issue of *Advertising Age.* Copyright 1977 by Crain Communications, Inc.

[a] National advertising, measured media only (includes newspapers, magazines, television, radio and outdoor).

* These figures actually *understate* the cost of advertising to the consumer because they do not include local advertising (Sears, Roebuck & Co., for example, spends more on local ads than on national) [6, p. 30]. The figures also omit the closely related costs of packaging and promotion.

a mechanism for providing readily available information is difficult to overestimate. The beauty of advertising, as we've noted, is that it reaches everyone; at present, that may be a mixed blessing, but the potential benefits are tremendous. There is no better way for consumers to obtain so much information so effortlessly.

Advertising and Information Content

An Overview of the Media

Thus far we have talked about advertisements as a single group, when in fact there are important variations among them. The most obvious differences are among the media. Television, radio, magazine, and newspaper advertisements come to mind, but they don't cover all the possibilities; there are also specialty or trade publications, billboards, and other outdoor advertisements, flyers, loudspeakers, and other forms that attest to the ingenuity of individual advertisers. If, as Marshall McLuhan says, the medium is the massage, then it is important to understand something about the characteristics of advertising on the various media.

We begin by looking at the distribution of advertising expenditures among the media. A glance at Table 6.2 shows that the top ten advertisers rely heavily upon television (except for cigarette companies, which cannot advertise on television). As a group, these advertisers spent over $1.2 billion on television advertising. Smaller companies spend less on television, but it is the largest firms that represent the bulk of advertising expenditures. Thus, advertising expenditures are highly concentrated in a relatively small number of firms and those firms concentrate on television. The high cost of national television advertising, up to $150,000 for 30 seconds, indicates why television advertising looms so large in the overall expenditure picture [4, p. 74].

Television (particularly national television) is geared to a mass audience; thus, it is less likely that specialized information can be provided. The very nature of television also encourages less informative advertising. Because of its versatility, television can represent a variety of aspects of a product, and there is a natural temptation to use picture and sound to create a mood or an image rather than providing information. In short, television gives the advertiser a means to do a variety of things that don't provide much information.

Radio advertisements present a slightly different situation. These differences follow from the differences in the media, which in turn affect the pattern of radio broadcasting and advertising. This is reflected in the degree to which radio has become specialized; some

Table 6.2 Distribution of Advertising Expenditures by Medium: Top 10 National Advertisers: 1976

Ad Rank[a]	Company	Total Expenditures (in millions)	News-paper	Genl. Mags.	Farm Pub.	% of Total Dollars Spot TV	Network TV	Spot Radio	Net-work Radio	Out-door
1.	Procter & Gamble Co.	362,345.5	1.8	4.5	—	40.2	53.4	0.1	—	—
2.	General Foods Corp.	225,156.6	3.6	9.1	—	29.5	57.3	0.4	0.1	—
3.	General Motors Corp.	203,784.3	19.1	18.2	0.9	13.3	35.3	10.0	0.8	2.4
4.	Bristol-Myers Co.	152,632.7	0.9	16.9	—	11.6	67.3	3.3	—	—
5.	American Home Products	145,189.3	1.5	4.4	0.3	23.1	67.1	2.5	1.0	—
6.	R. J. Reynolds Industries	138,612.6	40.1	30.2	—	4.6	4.2	—	—	20.8
7.	Philip Morris Inc.	134,316.5	33.2	28.9	—	4.7	18.2	1.3	—	13.6
8.	Ford Motor Co.	131,919.7	11.3	16.1	1.7	21.4	37.9	8.5	1.6	1.5
9.	General Mills Inc.	117,934.6	3.3	9.3	—	33.9	49.5	4.0	0.1	—
10.	Unilever	105,586.2	2.7	4.5	—	35.2	57.1	0.5	—	—

Reprinted by permission from the August 29, 1977 issue of Advertising Age. Copyright 1977 by Crain Communications, Inc.
[a] Includes only major media categories for national advertising.

stations broadcast only music—rock, country and western, or classical—while others specialize in ńews. In metropolitan centers, there
are stations that serve particular ethnic groups, while in rural areas,
there are farm-oriented stations. Some churches have their own stations, and so do some colleges and universities. With this diversity,
it is difficult to generalize about radio advertising. Yet the nature of
the medium itself forces certain constraints on radio advertising that
limit all stations, regardless of orientation.

It is harder to talk about something than to show a picture of it.
If advertisers are going to talk about the product anyway, there is a
chance that they will say something informative (although it is possible to talk without saying anything substantive). Most companies
have a multimedia advertising package, so that their radio ads complement their television efforts; some companies even run the sound
tracks from their television ads.

The printed page is the oldest form of modern communication. It
was through the printed media that advertising got its start and took
on its present form. Many newspapers and magazines lost advertising
revenues to such an extent that some well-known ones have ceased
publication. At the same time, others are prospering because they fill
a special need of advertisers. There are implications in this situation
that directly affect the information that the ads pass along to the
consumers.

Newspapers contain a type of advertising that is purely informative—classified ads. These serve the consumer directly by locating
items and in effect creating a market. These ads perform the classic
function of bringing buyer and seller together. If you were interested
in buying a used lawnmower, you might reasonably assume that
someone in the area had one for sale; your problem would be finding
that someone. It would be very difficult without classified advertising.
In its early form, most advertising was of the classified type. Other
examples survive, such as the announcements on bulletin boards in
neighborhood supermarkets. For the most part, however, advertising
has gone beyond these elementary functions and now concerns itself
with persuasion and advocacy.

For day-to-day operations in the marketplace, newspapers remain
one of the consumer's greatest assets. This is hardly surprising, because newspapers are an important means of local advertising. They
afford local advertisers the chance to let consumers know what they
have, what specials they are offering, and other information concerning hours and location. In terms of price information, newspaper advertising is probably more useful to consumers than any other type.

Magazine advertising includes a wide variety of approaches. Where
color is involved, there is a tendency toward showy, but not neces-

sarily informative, ads. However, like radio and newspapers, magazines have become more specialized, a trend that has hurt mass-circulation magazines. This is significant for consumers, because the general circulation publications contain more general, less informative ads. The specialty magazines, on the other hand, are aimed at a particular audience. It can be assumed that persons reading one of these publications have an interest in the particular topic and perhaps some information about it. During the late 1970s, however, the rising costs of television advertising have renewed advertisers' interest in magazines. At this time, it is impossible to tell how this trend will develop, but to date it has meant more magazine advertising, with the largest increases going to more general, less informative national ads.

A Standard of Judgment

To this point I have discussed advertisements in the rather general terms as being more or less informative. Such judgments obviously require some kind of standard or measure of information content. Various standards have been suggested, but the most common is the content analysis approach used by the Federal Trade Commission (FTC). The FTC is the agency within the federal government that is charged with monitoring advertising; its efforts are gaining more attention, and from time to time you will see that the agency has charged that a certain ad is misleading and must be removed. Such judgments are based on standards that the FTC has developed to classify advertisements into three categories: *informative,* ads that provide significant information; *puffing,* ads that ballyhoo the product without really saying anything about it; and *misleading,* ads that either directly or implicitly misrepresent the product.* These are not necessarily mutually exclusive categories, but they do provide a structure for analyzing information content [13 and 15].

According to the FTC, informative ads provide information on price or relative price, functions of the product, construction specifications, and performance standards. I recall an ad for a chain saw that meets these criteria almost to the letter. The ad shows the saw in use, gives the price ("under $100"), details its features (metal body, self-oiling chain, automatic-recoil start, and so on), and tells something about what the saw will do ("cut logs up to 20 inches in diameter"). If you were in the market for a chain saw, that ad would be helpful; it tells you enough about the saw for you to evaluate it.

Puffing ads, on the other hand, do not provide the consumer with

---

* The FTC uses *deceptive* instead of *misleading.*

that type of service. They substitute superlatives, endorsements by leading personalities, or claims of uniqueness for hard facts on price and performance. They are fluff (rhymes with puff) and while they may be entertaining, they are not very informative. Soft-drink commercials, which show happy, beautiful people downing gallons of a particular brand, fit into the puffing category. Magazine ads for liquor, which typically feature a close-up of the bottle, are another example. Puffing ads do not mislead, but they do not inform either; as their middle position suggests, they represent a sort of neutral territory.

That may be damning with faint praise, but it is more than can be said for misleading advertisements. Such ads feature unsupported—and often unsupportable—claims and rigged or irrelevant tests, and they portray the product in unnatural situations. These are typical traits of misleading advertisements, but since the range of possibilities is so broad, it is difficult to limit them. Ads may be misleading without resorting to outright lies, though that it not unknown. An advertisement is misleading if it portrays the product as something it is not. There are many examples of misleading advertisements in the history of television, including plastic placed over floors to show a "true wax shine" and shots apparently taken through an automobile window to demonstrate that the glass is distortion-free, when in fact the window had been wound down.

The FTC guidelines sound straightforward enough, but you should appreciate that there are a variety of problems involved in their implementation. First of all, the advertisement may not fit neatly into a single category. An ad may contain features of two or more types. Reliability also deserves mention: One can read, or view, between the lines of advertisements, but it is necessary ultimately either to accept or to reject what the advertisement says. An ad may appear to be quite informative, providing details about the product and demonstrating its effectiveness through different tests. *Appear* is the key word, for it is not always possible to trust what is being said. The track record of advertisers hardly inspires confidence.

Even with standards and a set of criteria for making evaluations, there is bound to be an element of personal judgment in their application. If the price of a product is $99.95, is it misleading to advertise it as "under $100"? Is it misleading to advertise soft drinks with those happy people and their beautiful smiles without mentioning that the drink promotes tooth decay? Most people would probably feel that to call these examples misleading would represent an overly strict application of the standards, but others might not agree.*

---

* As a check, students are urged to repeat the evaluations reported in the following section. See suggested projects.

Given that judgments are involved, no absolute standard can be imposed. The real question is whether the FTC's system of content analysis is a workable approach. To test that question, the FTC guidelines were applied to a sample of actual national television advertisements. The results are enlightening in terms of both the approach and the advertisements.

Information in National Television Advertising

For several reasons, television is the logical place to apply the FTC guidelines. As noted above, television accounts for the greatest portion of advertising expenditures, so it is necessary to look to television to see where advertisers spend their money. National ads were selected not only because of their predominant position in advertising budgets (see Table 6.2), but also because they have a greater impact and are not subject to variation from one area to another. Finally, we should note that television advertising is important because the medium is such an integral part of the American lifestyle. Television affects the way we perceive the world and absorb its images. Thus, television not only reflects modern life, it is part of that life.

The results reported here are based on a sample of 321 thirty-second ads videotaped from the three national commercial networks during February 1977. In implementing the FTC guidelines, two intermediate categories were introduced: informative puffing and puffing misleading. This provides a place for ads that are largely puffing but do give some information, or ads that puff away to the point of becoming misleading. The sample was drawn from four designated time segments: weekday afternoon, prime time, news programming, and sports advertising.* Thus it is possible to compare information content for different time segments.

Two raters were trained in the use of the FTC guidelines and each rated the ads independently. The two agreed on their ratings for 84 percent of the ads, and in only 3 percent of the cases did their ratings disagree by more than one category. This suggests that despite variations among individuals, the FTC scale can be applied in a uniform fashion.

The results of the survey are summarized in Table 6.3. A glance at the "total" column shows that half of the ads fell into the puffing category. Puffery, then, is the norm for national television advertis-

---

* Time segments were defined as follows (all times EST): weekday afternoon, 1–3 P.M.; prime time, 8–11 P.M.; sports programming, weekend afternoons; news, weeknight network evening news programming. Note that no children's programming was included in the survey.

ing, which means no substantive information is provided. About 10 percent of the ads were judged to be informative. That is not very impressive when you consider that the sample is drawn from about 20 hours of viewing time. So, if you watched 20 hours of television, you would have 17 minutes 30 seconds of informative national ads.

It might be heartening to note that there were so few ads judged to be actually misleading. It is possible, however, to argue that there should not be *any* misleading ads. When the misleading and puffing-misleading categories are pooled, nearly 10 percent of the sample contained ads with some misleading elements. The puffing-misleading ads generally earned that designation by exaggeration, gross over-statement, or implications that misrepresented the product. These may be only venial sins, but they still have a negative impact on the viewer consumer.

An interesting pattern emerges when we look at information content by time segment. No striking differences are apparent. Puffing ads predominate in all time segments, although afternoon programming features slightly more puffery and slightly less information than other segments. The most significant feature of the time-segment breakdown is the concentration of misleading ads during the afternoon. Afternoon programming features game shows and soap operas that are commonly oriented toward women; the significance of that relationship will be discussed in the following section. The overall conclusion from the time-segment breakdown is that, in terms of the information content the ads provide, it doesn't matter a great deal when you watch television.

By way of summary, we must say that national television adver-

Table 6.3 Information Content in Designated Time Segments: Numbers of 30-Second Ads

Level of Information Content	Time Segment				
	Daytime Afternoon	Prime	Sports	News	Total
Misleading	7	0	0	1	8
Puffing Misleading	9	7	3	2	21
Puffing	68	30	33	30	161
Informative Puffing	33	15	30	18	96
Informative	12	11	8	4	35
	129	63	74	55	321

Source: "The Relationships Among Information Characteristics and Sex-Role Portrayal in Network Television Advertisements." [24]

tising provides very little information; it is difficult to reach any other conclusion. There are some bright spots—nearly 40 percent of the ads contained some information. Some information, however, isn't a very good showing when you consider the amount of money spent on television advertising and the degree to which it saturates the country. Had local ads been included, the percentage of informative ads would probably have been higher; local ads can provide specific price and product information more easily. However, a higher percentage of informative ads would *not* mean that the percentage of advertising expenditures going to information would be correspondingly higher. A local tire company may advertise a sale and provide the consumer with a great deal of useful information (price, size, and so on). However, that ad will cost only a tiny fraction of the price paid for prime national advertisements. From the consumer's point of view, the local ad is probably a better "buy," but that also means that the bulk of advertising expenditures are going to less informative national ads.

The Problem of Experience Goods

Thus far we have discussed ads in terms of their information content, without reference to the products being advertised. If, however, we are to address the problem of improving information content, we must now broaden our investigation to include consideration of the products in the ads. The basis for that need goes back to our discussion of *search* and *experience* products in the last chapter. Search products, you will remember, are those goods that the consumer can evaluate prior to purchase (the horsepower of an engine or the color of a suit); by contrast, information on experience goods can only be obtained by actually using the product (the taste of a cup of coffee or the effectiveness of a deodorant) [20, p. 315].

You should recognize that experience products are heavily advertised, particularly on television. Foods, toiletries, soft drinks and beer, patent medicines, and many other personal consumption items fall into the experience category.* Furthermore, other products, such as automobiles, combine search qualities with significant numbers of experience qualities. In the sample discussed in the previous section, 223, or nearly 70 percent, of the 321 ads surveyed were judged to be for experience goods [24].

By now you should see the problem. If the only way a consumer can obtain information about a product is to use it, how can any real

---

* The third category discussed in the previous chapter was *credence* goods. These products and services are not heavily advertised at this time. Some products, such as patent medicines, may have credence qualities, but these can be analyzed in experience terms.

information about the product be provided in an ad? No ad can tell you how a soft drink will taste, how a hair spray will work, or how you will feel in a particular article of clothing, and yet hundreds of products in these categories are advertised regularly. Since it is the experience that counts, the advertiser must try to convey a feeling for the product through the ad; the experience may be second hand, but if you see all those happy people drinking cola, you might remember the brand name and try the product yourself.

The result, of course, is puffery, which helps explain why that category dominates advertising. The advertiser has little choice but to puff, because there is little that can be said about the product.* Nelson, who developed the distinction between search and experience goods, was the first to make this point [19]. His hypotheses were supported by the sample of television ads discussed earlier; the search goods in the sample showed a significantly higher level of information content than did experience goods [24]. Other researchers have found similar results [23].

In some cases, advertisers choose to use puffery when they don't have to. Advertisements for automobiles, for example, can give precise information on price, engine specifications, and construction. Often, however, that opportunity is neglected in favor of showing the car in luxurious settings, where the emphasis in on mood and style and superlatives replace substance ("the most glamorous Baasmobile ever").

Even though some discretion is involved, it remains true that many ads simply cannot be made more informative. It follows that it would be impossible to dictate that advertisements must provide information without forcing significant changes in current advertising patterns. Puffery may be toned down, but it cannot be eliminated because of the very nature of the products being advertised. This presents a serious obstacle to any program designed to improve the overall level of information content in advertising.

An Alternative Approach

The difficulty with experience goods is not the only problem with the content analysis approach of the FTC guidelines. A potentially more serious concern is stated in the question: At what point does a statement become misleading or deceptive? Suppose, for example, that a gasoline ad claims to "Put a tiger in your tank!" That statement is

---

* Price is always a search quality, but these products tend to be relatively inexpensive and price differentials may not weigh heavily in the consumer's decision.

false, and yet hardly anyone would consider the ad misleading. The reason is that everyone knows the statement is false and was not meant to be taken literally.

That is clear enough in the case of the tiger, but what about other ads in which phrases like "lowest price ever," "best buy yet," or "runs forever" are thrown around? At what point can the consumer reasonably be expected to differentiate between intended puffery and intended fact? The Federal Trade Commission's answer to the problem is the *average man concept.** An ad is not considered deceptive if the average man can be expected to recognize the intent of the message [1, p. 571].

Given the manner in which the term *average* is abused, that approach doesn't really solve the problem. Are we speaking of the average man in terms of intelligence, education, or experience in the marketplace? If we're talking about the average man on an average day, we must remember that the average man makes mistakes and take that into account. Not surprisingly, there have been a large number of court cases on this point.

The concept makes sense only when some kind of rule of reason is applied and the whole question is viewed in a behavioral context. The question revolves around what individuals are going to believe and how those beliefs affect behavior. Thus, in order to make the content analysis approach work, human behavior has to be taken into account. This fact has prompted some experts in the area to suggest an alternative approach to the deception problem. An ad should be considered deceptive, they argue, only if it affects the consumer's beliefs and she or he then acts on those beliefs in a harmful way [17].

Briefly put, there would be no deception if no one is deceived. An ad might misrepresent a product and thus be termed misleading under the FTC's system, but if no one believes the ad, then there would be no real deception. This *behavioral* definition of deception focuses on the impact of the ad on the consumer's behavior. In order to be put into effect, the behavioral approach would require extensive screening of ads before groups of consumers representing a cross section of the population. The technical aspects of that process would be complex and would quite probably generate disputes.

The behavioral approach doesn't really address the question of improving the overall level of information in ads and is therefore of limited value in that regard. However, it is valuable as a reminder that the ultimate significance of an advertisement lies in its impact on the individual. It is the interpretation of the ad that finally matters,

---

* Presumably, the average man could be a woman.

which means some attention should be given to the manner in which individuals treat information from advertising.

There is some evidence to show that most consumers approach advertising with a critical eye. Most people assume that advertisers exaggerate; therefore, individuals tend to discount much of what they hear or see in ads. Under such circumstances, it is difficult to deceive a person; the individual's reluctance to accept advertising claims at face value turns out to be the first line of defense against deception. Given that situation, there is a possible danger in efforts to promote truth in advertising. If individuals come to believe that ads must be truthful, they will be more vulnerable to deception. Unless the law is perfectly enforced, advertisers would have more incentive to try and mislead consumers because there would be a greater chance that their efforts would pay off [19]. Things would not have to turn out that way, but they could; the possibility emphasizes the need to take consumer behavior into account when considering advertising. Unless the situation is analyzed fully, well-intentioned efforts could end up having harmful effects.

Current Trends and Developments

Combating Negative Information

The preceding sections dealt with information and deception in advertising in general terms. Before we proceed with the question of the information potential of advertising, we should look at some specific cases and see how these issues are actually working themselves out in the marketplace and the courts. To a considerable extent, that story centers around the Federal Trade Commission. The responsibility for monitoring advertising has been part of the FTC charge since it was founded in 1914; however, it was not until 1938 that the commission was given specific authority to prosecute for misleading advertising when only the consumer interest was involved (see Chapter 8).* It would be wrong, however, to assume that the FTC has acted alone. The following examples show that private consumer groups have been active, and, in some cases, have been responsible for forcing the Federal Trade Commission to act.

One example that shows the impact of private initiative is the

---

* *Monitor* is the key word here; except in rare cases when litigation is involved, the FTC does not regulate or give prior approval to ads. The agency only reacts to existing ads, often in response to consumer complaints.

advertising campaign run by the Shell Oil Company several years ago. You may recall the ads that billed Shell's *Platformate* as an additive that added significantly to mileage. It showed car after car crashing through a paper barrier, having gone farther than cars using gasoline without Platformate. Unfortunately, the campaign was as flimsy as the paper barrier. True, the cars using gasoline with Platformate did go farther, but as *Consumer Bulletin* was the first to point out, Platformate (or something like it) is found in nearly all gasoline meant for use in automobiles [21]. You could not buy the kind of gasoline Shell was using in the test. Any gasoline purchased from any pump would have Platformate in it and would go as far as Shell's.

Shell maintained that since the ad merely said that cars go farther on Platformate, there was no deception involved. No one bought that argument, however. *Advertising Age,* the trade journal for advertisers, sounded an "Amen" to a letter written by an agency executive that said: "This is the kind of deception that gives all of advertising a black eye and makes the task of the honest practitioner of the craft just that much harder. It's also great fuel for those who promulgate government control of advertising . . ." [3].

Pain relievers represent another area of apparent deception and certain confusion. Aspirin is the main ingredient in such products, and aspirin, it turns out, is aspirin. A 1962 study published in the *Journal of the American Medical Association* indicated that statistically there is no difference in the performance of the five leading brands of pain relievers [12]. That was over fifteen years ago, yet producers still turn out advertisements that claim that their brand is superior, supporting their arguments with supposed *scientific tests.* Students who are familiar with statisical testing techniques know that such claims must be taken with a grain of salt (or perhaps aspirin). There is no evidence that if they were repeated on a larger population the results would be the same.

Nevertheless, the claims continued unabated until finally, in 1973, the FTC entered the case. The FTC filed suit against the major pharmaceutical companies, maintaining they must either provide acceptable scientific evidence to support the claims made for their pain relievers or take the ads off the air. Five years of litigation have not resolved the case and there appears to be no prospect of an impending settlement.

If the Geritol case is any precedent, the question of pain relievers could be in the courts for years to come. Geritol claimed to "strengthen iron-poor, tired blood" or "iron deficiency anemia." No one was quite sure what tired blood was, but experts agreed that iron deficiency anemia is rare in the United States and, in any event, is not usually associated with a lack of iron in the diet [9]. The FTC brought suit, but the case was in the courts for over a decade before the questionable ads were removed.

Protracted litigation is also underway in the Listerine case. For most of this century, Listerine has been advertised as an effective agent against colds. In fact, it is simply a mouthwash, and as Listerine ads now state, it does nothing to kill germs or fight colds. Even so, it took a series of court battles before the claim was removed from Listerine's advertising, and, even now, the notion that the product is something more than a mouthwash may linger on [5]. Because of that possibility, the FTC asked Listerine to do more than simply remove the ads; the company was asked to pay for *corrective advertisements*. Corrective ads, as the name implies, are meant to correct previous misinformation provided to consumers, and are also involved in the Geritol and pain reliever cases (in the latter, the FTC is asking that 25 percent of the companies' future advertising expenditures go to corrective ads).

The FTC had earlier required corrective advertising of a fruit juice company (for false nutritional claims about its drink) and of a diet bread (which claimed to have fewer calories, but in fact was only sliced thinner). In these cases, however, the corrective ads had limited impact because they were so mild. It wasn't really clear to consumers that the companies were admitting any wrongdoing. If corrective advertisements are to be effective in making up for deception, they must be clear and straightforward.

The problems with corrective advertisements are further illustrated in the STP case. As was true with Platformate, it was a consumer organization that originally raised questions about the product (an oil additive). In 1971, *Consumer Reports* indicated that STP was at best unnecessary, and at worst a possible danger to the car's engine [11, p. 422]. The issue was unresolved and STP continued to expand its operations; in so doing, it included performance claims in its advertising, claims that were supported by a series of tests conducted by independent laboratories.

Those tests, however, proved questionable and the FTC brought suit. The case was settled in early 1978 when STP agreed to pay a $700,000 fine and pay for a series of corrective advertisements. The ads were labeled "FTC Notice" and referred to "certain allegedly inaccurate past advertisements." Included in the ad was the statement "Agreement to this settlement does not constitute an admission by STP that the law has been violated" [26, p. 14]. Not only were the ads confusing and seemingly contradictory, but they were run mainly in business publications. The idea was to get the message across to other businesses that the FTC itself meant business; however, the campaign did little to clear up misconceptions that individual consumers might have had about STP.

It is evident that the Federal Trade Commission has become more active in dealing with possible deception in advertising, but the impact of that activity is not yet clear. Advertisers have at least taken notice, but whether future ads will be any different is unknown. If enforcement is sustained, gradual change could take place. If, however, the FTC's activities are seen as isolated events, change seems unlikely.

Children's Advertising

The Federal Trade Commission's activities with respect to advertising have not been limited to the prosecution of individual cases. In an effort to deal with more general concerns, the commission has employed a broader approach in certain problem areas. Children's advertising offers a notable and well-publicized example. The implicit assumption in the *average man* concept is that individuals can make critical judgments about advertising content. In the case of children, that assumption may not be warranted, which marks children's advertising as a topic of special concern.

That concern, however, is a fairly recent development. A decade ago, no special attention was given to children's advertising. Then, in 1968, a group of Boston-area women formed Action for Children's Television (ACT) in an effort to improve the quality of children's programming; advertising was among their first concerns. ACT called for a ban on children's advertising, basing its request on four problem areas:

1. Developmental—young children have not yet developed the cognitive skills to evaluate material presented in advertisements. Thus, children are particularly vulnerable and impressionable [16].
2. Family life—pressure from children to buy advertised products could have a negative effect on the parent-child relationship.
3. Nutritional—concern was expressed with both the dubious nutritional information contained in ads and the poor nutritional content on many heavily advertised snacks and cereals.
4. Content—it was maintained that products (particularly toys) were oversold, leaving a misleading impression of the product's capabilities [18].

The FTC called hearings on these matters, but no further action was taken. However, pressure from ACT brought about a degree of self-regulation by the industry. The number of minutes of commercials per hour of children's programming was cut from 16 to 9½ and performers on children's shows no longer were to promote products. Also, a clear distinction had to be made between the programming and advertising (usually by a fade out or graphic design) [18]. Pressure from consumer groups also induced three vitamin manufacturers to withdraw their advertisements from children's programming.

Through all of this, the FTC's position remained vague; the commission seemed to support the reform efforts, but resisted efforts to force change on the industry [2]. The FTC's period of inactivity stretched into 1977, but then increasing concern with nutrition prompted staff investigations. As a result of the investigations, the following proposals were approved by the commissioners in early 1978. The FTC proposes that:

1. All advertising aimed at children under six be banned.
2. The advertising of candy and highly sweetened cereals be banned from all children's programming.
3. Companies that advertise lightly sweetened cereals be required to spend an equal amount on purely informative nutritional advertising [7].

At this writing, hearings are being held on the FTC proposals. It appears that at least some of the recommendations will be implemented; it is also probable that court challenges await any action the FTC takes. Recent court decisions extend First Amendment rights (freedom of speech) to advertisers, and it appears that litigation will be based on that argument. Whatever happens, the FTC's action (after a decade of indifference) illustrates the power that public opinion can have when it is organized and directed.

The controversy over children's advertising deserves a final comment. The entire argument is built around the idea that advertising, particularly on television, is more than just a way to sell products; it affects the whole pattern of living. That point is particularly relevant to children, but it can be applied more broadly. I've suggested throughout this chapter that advertising is a part of what we commonly call lifestyle; any effort to discuss the issue in narrower terms runs the risk of dangerous oversimplification.

Advertising by Professionals

While the FTC is attempting to limit advertising geared to children, the commission is seeking to promote advertising by professionals— medical doctors, lawyers, pharmacists, and so on. Few professionals of this type have advertised in the past, in part because tradition held that advertising was unprofessional and in part because professional associations banned advertising. The FTC began its efforts to promote advertising by professionals in 1975; a ruling by the Supreme Court in 1977 upheld the right of professionals to advertise and accelerated the rate of change [10, p. 70].

In the last chapter, I indicated that information about professional services falls into the *credence category,* goods or services that cannot be fully evaluated even after they are consumed [20, p. 315]. Professional competence, not advertising, seems to be the key issue. Furthermore, it would be difficult to advertise prices in many cases until diagnosis and treatment were complete. To confound the issue, it is impossible to repress the image of a doctor doing a television commercial in the manner of a used car dealer ("Special, Today Only . . .").

Surely such jokes have circulated around the FTC, but that is not what the commission had in mind. The ban on professional advertising, the commission maintained, denied information to consumers and thus represented a restraint of trade. The logic of the argument is based on the fact that although many professional services are complex and involved, others are routine. A will for a middle-income family, for example, is a rather straightforward document and is relatively inexpensive. However, if there is secrecy about prices, the client-consumer won't know if he or she is actually paying a reasonable price.

The same logic holds for the advertising of prescription drug prices. Once the drug has been prescribed by the doctor, the patient-consumer ought to know where it can be filled most economically [2, p. 1632]. Such drugs must meet federal standards, so there is little risk to the individual. Even in more complicated situations, comparative price information should be helpful. If you find out, for example, that your family doctor is the most expensive in town, it hardly seems unreasonable that he or she be able to justify the expense. The doctor might be worth the price, but if patient-consumers aren't aware of relative prices, they won't be able to inquire.

One of the problems with the pricing of professional services has to do with price discrimination, which means charging different individuals different prices for the same service. In the marketplace, most products are sold at a single price to all consumers, which means that those who would be willing to pay more for the product are getting a bargain; it is easy to see that if each individual is charged the maximum that he or she would be willing to pay, the seller would benefit.*

---

* Price discrimination is legal in such cases and may be justified on the grounds that the poor thus receive treatment more cheaply.

Because of the nature of their services, professionals are able to practice price discrimination, but disclosure of fees makes the practice more difficult. Advertising should reduce the range of prices for similar services. Some professionals may resist advertising for that reason.

It is difficult to provide an overall evaluation of the impact of advertising by professionals. Contrary to the expectations of those on both sides of the controversy, it is unlikely that advertising will bring about any great changes. For example, allowing doctors to advertise isn't the answer to rising medical costs. However, in a small way the consumer should benefit. The change isn't momentous, but it is reasonable, and, as in the examples mentioned above, it should help the consumer. There may also be a more subtle, long-range benefit to consumers; more candid information about professional services should promote a more objective approach to the subject, and that should serve the consumer's interest.

Problems and Possibilities

Catching Up to the Present

Our discussion of advertising and information has ranged over a variety of issues; it is hoped that as you covered the material, your thinking about advertising has changed somewhat. The various problems addressed above cannot be dealt with until consumers begin to perceive the possibilities that advertising affords. There are limitations, to be sure, but advertising still has a potential educational and informational value beyond the capabilities of most alternatives. *It is nothing less than a resource,* a badly abused and misused one, but a resource nevertheless.

Putting advertising in that context serves another purpose: It helps us break out of the mental rut we are in when it comes to thinking about the question. Advertising is such a part of our lives that it is difficult to think of it except as it currently exists. Our thinking about advertising is badly out of date. Even when advertising has the potential to reach into every American home instantly, we still think of it in terms of the medicine show or the weekly newspaper. During the last century, advertising was unregulated and often outrageous, but that hardly mattered. If the medicine show advertised a cure for fallen arches, heart attacks, and sore backs, it did so to a small group that could evaluate the product and the advertising. Even if someone was suckered into buying the product, the amounts involved were probably small.

Technological change, however, has altered the situation radically. Faster presses, the introduction of color, and widespread distribution improved the traditional media. Radio and television have spread the reach and potential effectiveness of advertising still further. Frederick Lewis Allen chronicled these changes during the 1920s. The ads of fifty years ago make today's look like the picture of responsibility. For example, Allen tells of the unhappy people who had

> ... succumbed to pyorrhea, each of them with a white mask mercifully concealing his unhappy mouth. ... The woman who would undoubtedly do something about B.O. if people only said to her what they really thought. ... These men and women of the advertising pages, suffering or triumphant, *became part of the folklore of the day.* [8, p. 73, emphasis added]

Those people, or their grandchildren, have become part of American culture and they are treated with a degree of nonchalance that masks their real importance. Consumers continue to treat advertising lightly even though increasing complexities in the market and technological change have reduced consumers' abilities to counter the forces of advertising. You should recognize this argument as an aspect of the more general consumer problem—the consumer's inability to work in a changed environment. Consumers do not seem to have caught on to the fact that the environment has changed, which has permitted the freewheeling and largely unchallenged development of the advertising establishment. The implications of advertising for consumers and its potential usefulness have not really been grasped.

Notice that I have come out in favor of advertising, not against it. My criticism has to do with certain aspects of the way products are advertised, not with advertising itself. Unfortunately, even the mildest criticism of advertising tends to polarize opinions. Some groups seem to feel that there is something sacred about the current content and structure of advertising; they equate the status quo with what they call "our free enterprise system." Whatever that is, it is not a very good description of advertising and the American economy in the 1970s. Advertising expenditures are highly concentrated among a small number of firms. This concentrates a tremendous amount of power in a few hands. It can be argued that, rather than support free enterprise, massive advertising expenditures actually promote monopoly elements by giving an extra advantage to certain firms. Advertising becomes a way of maintaining control of a market and forestalling competition. Thus, a doctrinaire approach only masks the real issues and confuses the question.

Some New Directions

Any change in advertising must begin by educating the public to what advertising *could* be. The success of Action for Children's Television shows that if it is properly organized and directed, public pressure can bring about changes in advertising. Most changes thus far have emphasized limitations, but change can also be cast in positive terms, with the emphasis on realizing advertising's informational and educational potential.

However, it should be clear that it isn't enough to simply say to advertisers: "Thou shalt be informative." As noted, some ads (for experience goods) cannot be really informative. We can reasonably assume that most consumers recognize this fact; the emphasis in such cases should then be placed on preventing distortions and deception. In areas where more informative ads are possible, however, higher levels of information content should be encouraged (and in some cases required).

We can assume that businesses act in their own self-interest, which means that more informative ads will be forthcoming when such ads are in the company's self-interest. That will only happen when consumers begin to demand more information. This is a realistic possibility if consumers are aware that information is available; public service broadcasting might encourage this trend by stressing the kinds of information consumers can expect.

A significant problem with this proposal is validating the information provided in advertisements. Here is where a national information policy comes into the picture. Information provided through advertising would be an integral part of that overall policy. The Environmental Protection Agency has been criticized for its mileage ratings, but at least they have put an end to the gross exaggerations that formerly characterized mileage claims.

EPA ratings must be included in automobile ads, but other public information could be used voluntarily. If tests showed that the Clomp-Clomp lawnmower was the safest, most economical, and most dependable mower on the market, then Clomp-Clomp should be able to use those findings in their ads. The public would know that the company was not just making wild claims, since the information would have been validated. Thus, advertisements would be a way of getting quality information to the public.

Where does that leave companies whose products do not measure up well in such tests? They would not be forced to say that in their ads, but they would not be able to make any claims of performance of quality either. That would provide a powerful incentive to improve their product. Better information flow would therefore bring pressure on producers to offer quality products, which is precisely the way markets are supposed to work. Now producers can hide behind the consumer's lack of information and pass off inferior products.

I have treated advertising at great length simply because it has the potential to provide high-quality, low-cost information to all segments of the population. *Information* needs to be interpreted very broadly in this context. That is, it includes not only information about products per se but also about types of products and services. In short, advertising could perform a genuinely educational function. Insurance advertisements, for example, could include detailed information about types of insurance, strengths of each type, and the best insurance package under different circumstances. Similarly, advertisements for banks or other financial institutions could include sound financial advice. By the ingenuity of advertisers, this information could be put across in an easily understandable fashion. It is difficult to think of a more effective way to get information to a broad cross section of the public. As people were continually exposed to this sort of advertising, they would gradually develop a more sophisticated understanding of these complex issues. Citizens might decide that some percentage of total advertising time should be given over to such educational efforts. In this case, I am not talking about advertising a product, but rather providing information on a class of products or services.* Because ads of this type would be different from product advertising, public trust should be greater.

A program of this sort is based on the idea that advertisers have a responsibility to provide information to consumers. If that information is not contained in ads for particular products, it would be presented in the more general, educational ads.† Some people may feel that advertisers should not be forced to assume a social responsibility, but the proposal only assumes that those who benefit from a system should in turn work toward improving it. Companies have a right to advertise; they also have a responsibility to the public. This is not a very radical idea.

If you think the changes suggested here sound like pipe dreams, remember that changes have already taken place in advertising. It

---

* Advertisers could be required to set aside a percentage of their total advertising budgets to fund such efforts. These costs would be passed along to the consumer, but considering the potential value of such a program, the expense should be well worth it in terms of individual consumer's savings.

† Some hint of this idea is contained in the FTC proposals for children's advertising. Companies that advertise certain types of cereals would be required to pay for ads about nutrition. By extending the idea, advertisers of medicines could fund ads on health, and so on.

was not too long ago that cigarette advertisements, now banned from television, were making health claims about their products. Similarly, the very idea of corrective advertising would have seemed radical a few years ago. Thus, it is not unrealistic to suppose that advertising over time can be made to convey information. The changes will not take place overnight and the program will not come in a single package. Progress generally comes in small steps. In this case, the ultimate goal makes the journey worthwhile.

Study Questions

1. It is often argued that without advertising the economy would stagnate, since it is advertising that sells products. Evaluate that contention. Differentiate between a single firm's increasing its sales and increased sales of all products. That is, if one tire company advertises, will it necessarily increase the total number of tires sold throughout the economy?

2. In the case of new products, the argument presented in Question 1 has some validity. Is it, however, necessarily inconsistent with informative advertising? Why or why not?

3. Why is it that so little information is provided in advertisements? Evaluate the following explanations:
   a. Companies do not want consumers to know about their products.
   b. There is really nothing substantive to say about the products.
   c. Puffing sells better than information.
   d. Consumers do not care about information and perhaps do not even want it.

4. You may have noted that for compact cars, particularly imports, price is usually given in the ads. For larger models, such information is much less common. What does that show about the approach used to sell different types of cars? If price information is given in some ads, is there any reason it cannot be in others?

5. In the United States, the air waves are public property that radio and television stations are licensed to use. What is the significance of this fact in relation to federal regulation of advertising?

6. Television networks have departments that screen ads before they are aired. Remembering where networks get their money, how effective do you think this process is? Would it be reason-

able to institute a policy that makes the networks (or local stations) responsible for any misleading advertisements they carry?

7. Certain types of advertising, cigarettes and liquor, for example, are banned from television. What is the rationale for this policy? Could the same rationale support limitations on children's advertising?

8. Review the rationale for allowing professionals to advertise. Do you think ads of this type require either special rules or closer monitoring?

9. Corrective ads appear to have great potential, yet most observers agree that the ads have had limited impact. Give several reasons why this should be true. Does this tell you anything about how consumers perceive advertising?

10. An Olympic star who was endorsing a breakfast cereal was forced by the California Attorney General to swear in court that he had actually eaten the cereal as a child. Does that sort of enforcement help consumers? Could it hurt consumers? Even if he did eat the cereal, what does that prove?

Suggested Projects

1. Repeat the evaluation of the information content of television advertising reported in the text; use the same categories, standards, and guidelines.
   a. Assign several students to time and classify national ads. How do their results compare with those in the text? Do they agree with each other?
   b. Assign several students to do the same thing for *local* ads. How do their results compare with the evaluation of national advertising?
   As a rule of thumb, ask this question about each ad: "Does it tell me anything that would really help me if I were buying the product?" Make notes on ads that illustrate the various categories and discuss the ads.

2. A similar evaluation can be carried out for radio and printed media. In doing the evaluation for:
   a. Radio, be sure to get samples from different types of stations at different times of day.
   b. Magazines and newspapers, review different types of publications. You may count either the number of ads or (for a

more precise measure) the amount of space taken by different types of ads.

Compare your results in a and b. Then compare with the results from the evaluation of television advertising in Project 1. Do any patterns emerge?

c. For printed media, be sure to review different types of publications. As a rule of thumb, ask this question about each ad: "Does it tell me anything that would really help me if I were buying the product?" How do the findings compare with those reported in the text? Make notes on ads that illustrate the various categories and discuss the ads.

3. Prepare a report on the Federal Trade Commission's activities with respect to advertising. Explore the commission's legal status and authority. Has there been any change in the FTC's approach in recent years?

4. If your local paper carries weekly grocery ads, calculate potential savings through the information they provide. Is the savings sufficient to cover the cost of the paper, the investment of time, and possible extra trips to different stores?

5. Your library probably has microfilm copies of leading (and local) newspapers and magazines that go back several years. Beginning with the earliest copies available, compare advertisements from different periods. What changes are evident? Do you think these represent improvement?

6. Find examples of ads that you consider to be misleading (in printed media). Show the ads to a sample of consumers and record their reactions. Do the consumers think the ads are deceptive? Discuss.

7. Review the FTC's activities with respect to corrective ads to identify specific cases where corrective ads have been involved. See if you can find examples of these ads (again, in the printed media).

a. Do you think that the *corrective* nature of the ads comes through?

b. As in Project 6, show the ads to selected consumers and record their reaction.

Bibliography and Suggested Readings

Questions concerning information and advertising are part of the larger problem of information costs. Students should therefore refer to the citations in the previous chapter for additional references. Many of them treat material which is covered in this chapter, even though they do not deal with advertising directly.

1. Aaker, David A., and Myers, John G. *Advertising Management.* Englewood Cliffs, N.J.: Prentice-Hall, 1975.
   A good review of issues surrounding advertising; deals with more than just the technical aspects of advertising.

2. Action for Children's Television *News,* Spring 1976.
   The ACT newsletter is the best way to keep up with the group's activities, providing current information on ACT programs and organizational efforts.

3. *Advertising Age.* February 29, 1969.
   Because this is a trade journal for advertisers, its perspective is pretty well defined. Nevertheless, it remains a good source for thoughtful consideration of advertising, regulation, and, particularly, for statistical information on advertising expenditures.

4. ———. January, 31, 1977.

5. ———. August 8, 1977.

6. ———. August 29, 1977.
   Each August, *AA* prints its annual report on the nation's top 100 national advertisers.

7. ———. October 24, 1977.
   A report on preliminary reaction to the FTC's proposals on children's advertising.

8. Allen, Frederick Lewis. *Only Yesterday.* New York: Harper & Row, 1931.
   An informal social history of the 1920s, full of vignettes about life during America's first great flirtation with mass consumption. Enjoyable reading and valuable in understanding present attitudes. Good section on advertising.

9. Buxton, Edward. *Promise Them Anything.* New York: Stein & Day, 1972.
   An alternative to the advertiser's perspective. The book casts a critical eye at advertising and advertising practices.

10. Clark, M., and Lord, M. "Dr. Huckster." *Newsweek,* January 9, 1978.
    A news report on the FTC's battle with the American Medical Association over doctor's advertising.

11. *Consumer Reports.* July 1971, pp. 422 ff.
    A report that questioned the value and safety of STP oil additive. The advertising campaign that ultimately resulted in the Federal Trade Commission's suit against STP followed this article.

12. DeKornfeld, Thomas. "A Comparative Study of Five Proprietary

Analgesic Compounds." *Journal of the American Medical Association,* December 29, 1962.
A landmark study showing that there is no significant difference in the effectiveness of leading pain relievers.

13. Federal Trade Commission. *Hearings on Advertising.* Hearings before the 92nd Congress, 1st session, 1971. S.1461 and S.1763. Washington, D.C.: U.S. Government Printing Office.
Hearings on the FTC's role in regulating advertising. They offer a comprehensive review of the subject.

14. ———. *News Summary.* Washington, D.C.: U.S. Government Printing Office.
A weekly summary of FTC activities. An excellent and painless way to keep up with what is going on about the commission and advertising.

15. ———. *Trade Practice and Rules.* Washington, D.C.: U.S. Government Printing Office.
A guide to FTC regulations and rules on advertising standards.

16. Galst, Jann, and White, Mary. "The Unhealthy Persuader: The Reinforcing Value of Television and Children's Purchasing Influencing Attempts at the Supermarket," *Child Development,* December 1976, pp. 1089–96.

17. Gardner, D. M. "Deception in Advertising: A Receiver Oriented Approach to Understanding." *Journal of Advertising,* 1976, *30,* pp. 5–19.
A very useful discussion of the behavioral approach to deception in advertising. Students will also find Gardner's other works on the topic to be useful.

18. Melody, William. *Children's Television: The Economics of Exploitation,* New Haven: Yale University Press, 1973.
Required reading for those interested in questions of advertising directed at children. The title defines the book's perspective, but it offers a useful review of the issues and early development in the dispute.

19. Nelson, P. "Advertising and Information." *Journal of Political Economy,* 1974, *31,* pp. 375–80.

20. ———. "Information and Consumer Behavior." *Journal of Political Economy,* 1970, *15,* pp. 308–35.

21. "The Platformate Illusion." *Consumer Bulletin,* January 1968.
The original tip-off on Platformate, which remains a classic case. Provides another example of how a private consumer group can make itself felt in these matters.

22. Preston, Ivan L. *The Great American Blow-Up.* Madison, Wis.: University of Wisconsin Press, 1975.
A freewheeling look at advertising, with the emphasis on the problems

associated with puffery. Students should enjoy the tone of the book and will find it a useful review of the question.

23. Resnick, A., and Stern, B. "Information Content in Television Advertising." *Journal of Marketing*, 1977, *41*, pp. 50–53.
    A study that generally confirms the results reported in this chapter. The authors found that over half of the ads contained no information at all.

24. Scott, Nan E. "The Relationships Among Information Characteristics and Sex-Role Portrayal in Network Television Advertising." Unpublished Ph.D. dissertation, The University of Tennessee, Knoxville.
    The study that provided the data used in this chapter. We'll make use of the research on sex-role portrayal in Chapter 11.

25. Singer, James. "Attack Launched on Rules Prohibiting Price Advertising." *National Journal*, November 29, 1975, pp. 1632–33.
    A report on efforts to permit and promote advertising of prescription drug prices.

26. *Wall Street Journal.* February 10, 1978, p. 14.
    STP's "corrective ad." The advertisement was carried in similar publications about the same time.

-7-

Consumer Power
in the Marketplace

The Attack on Consumer Sovereignty

On "Monarchizing"

When Shakespeare's sovereign Richard II sat upon the ground "to tell sad stories of the death of kings," he might well have been speaking for today's American consumer. True, the textbooks say the consumer is sovereign, but the real power seems to lie elsewhere. While the marketplace may allow the consumer "to monarchize" from time to time, it is all a sham, merely "infusing him with self and vain conceit." Many are the consumers who might have asked the question with which Richard ends his lamentation: "How can you say to me, I am a king?" [*Richard II*, III, ii]

No such doubts are admitted into the secure world of economic theory. In that world, sovereign consumers direct the allocation of resources, and hence the productive process, by the pattern of their expenditures. The dollar vote emerges as a means of rewarding favored producers and punishing others. Outside of the textbooks, however, few observers see things working that way; most would argue that the consumer shares the gruesome fate that awaited Richard II. The reduction in consumer power can be linked to increased specialization, which while increasing efficiency, also broke the direct link between production and consumption. Once that link was broken, the individual's influence was further diluted by growth in market size, so that now the individual consumer is only a small cog

146

in the giant market mechanism. The result is consumer impotence—a chief source of consumer complaints.

The transition of consumers from active agents in the economic system to passive bystanders has also placed consumption in a new perspective. Consumption becomes an end in itself, based on nothing more than the gratification of passing whims and fancies. It is in this context that the word *consumer* has become a pejorative term, meaning "one who takes but never gives." If that is all consumption is and if consumers do not exercise control, then pretending that they do only serves the interests of producers. It gives them license, as John Kenneth Galbraith has argued, to manipulate the system to their own ends. "The fox," Galbraith noted, "is powerful in the management of the coop" [8, p. 10]. Under those conditions, consumers cannot operate effectively and neither can the market system. Thus, the question of who has what kind of power may be the central question in all of consumer economics.

The Nature of Consumer Power

In dealing with the question of consumer power, we must recognize that traditional economic analysis is of limited value. A perfectly competitive economy is characterized by the diffusion of power, under which neither individual producers nor consumers can influence the market. Economists' treatment of power as a nonconcept can be traced to Adam Smith's famous "invisible hand." He used that phrase to refer to the mechanism that ensured that the public good would be served if each individual sought only his or her personal goals. Thus, power made its debut in modern economics as an unseen, mystical force. Smith's invisible hand was not subject to individual direction; the individual's role, in fact, was unconscious.

A closer look at the modern analysis of consumer sovereignty reveals a similar line of thought. Sovereignty implies power, but in this case it is a strange sort of power, held by consumers as a group rather than by the individual. Power is diffused and collective, expressed through the market as a collection of individual choices. The system works because no one has any real power. That last sentence might be rewritten to read "The system works *as long as* no one has any real power." From the consumer's point of view, that is why the system does not work very well. Consumers have upheld their end of the bargain, making decisions as individuals and thus diffusing their power. Producers, however, have accumulated sufficient power to influence the market, and consumers have no effective counterweight.

The restoration of the consumer's position requires that consumers have the power to protect themselves and influence events. This statement, however, covers a great deal of ground. It is one thing for consumers to protect their positions by insulating themselves against the vagaries of the marketplace. Influencing events is something else again, for it requires that consumers have an impact on the market. The consumer may have the power to attain one goal, but not the other. Thus, the phrase "consumer power" itself means very little as a general statement; such power exists at different levels. This realization holds the key to sorting out the confusion commonly associated with this topic. *It is not sufficient merely to speak of consumer power; to make any such statement meaningful, it is necessary to specify the degree and extent of such power.*

To cope with the day-to-day problems of the marketplace, consumers need some leverage simply to ensure that they are treated fairly. This is the first level of consumer power—the individual's ability to look after his or her own interests in the marketplace. However, while individuals may wring fair treatment for themselves from the system, there is nothing to ensure that these benefits will be universally shared. The assurance of the extension of fair treatment to all consumers in the marketplace is the second level of consumer power. Note the emphasis on all consumers and the fact that such benefits are enjoyed as a matter of course.

Although such a change would represent a significant accomplishment, it should not be confused with consumer sovereignty. Sovereignty implies more than being treated well in a paternalistic system; it means that consumers actually direct the system. The consumer must not only have choices among goods and services, but also choices among choices. Thus, consumer power, which seems like such a harmless little phrase, actually covers a complexity of topics. To appreciate all the subtleties and interrelationships, it is therefore necessary to analyze each of the three levels of consumer power separately.

The Individual in the Marketplace

Sources of Consumer Leverage

It is clear that consumers are seriously disadvantaged in their individual confrontations with the market. It is necessary to distinguish, however, between a difficult situation and a hopeless one. Even though the marketplace is a hostile environment, the knowledgeable —or perhaps it is better to say *crafty*—consumer can still survive in it.* *Survive* is the key word. This discussion deals with the lowest level of consumer power. It is hardly a very sweeping assertion to say that consumers have some power that they can use to improve their positions in the market.

It is certain that if consumers do not seek such improvement, no one else will. For all the changes in the market, consumer satisfaction still hinges on individual transactions. The market, which we have been talking about in such abstract terms, ultimately comes down to a buyer and a seller. To balance the odds between the two, it is necessary for consumers to assert themselves. That may sound simplistic, but there is no way around the fact that if consumers are to receive better treatment in the marketplace, they must demand it. The consumer who makes the effort and follows an aggressive strategy will be well served. On the other hand, consumers who act like sheep will be treated like sheep.

An aggressive strategy begins before the consumer actually enters the market. Consumers who know what they want and know something about the products and services involved are in a strong position. Once in the market, the consumer must demand explicit information. Being satisfied with ambiguities increases the probability of dissatisfaction later. When the consumer is dissatisfied, however, the need for an activist approach is the greatest. If a product is not performing adequately or a service is not rendered properly, then it is necessary to complain and to keep complaining until the deficiency is corrected [4].

Businesses are interested in profits, not consumers, but there is an obvious relation between the two. If businesses recognize that to secure their profit position consumer demands must be accommodated, they will respond to consumer pressure. Furthermore, businesses are notoriously squeamish about bad publicity, particularly now that the consumer movement has exposed the raw nerve of business to probing. Armed with a critical strategy that is liberally reinforced with persistence and imagination, the consumer should sooner or later be able to obtain satisfaction.

There certainly are limitations to this approach, the most obvious being the scope of its effectiveness. An individual cannot remake the market or rebuild the institutions of the economy. But, particularly at the local level, where businesses are small and the individual's patronage is likely to be important, this action can strengthen the consumer's position. Drugstores are a good example. It is likely that

---

* Low-income groups must be exempted from this analysis. Because they typically lack even minimal leverage, they do not have many of the options outlined here. Still, this discussion applies to something over 80 percent of the population. See Chapter 10.

you buy drugs and sundries at a fairly small store. Such an environment is not overpowering, and it is possible to get answers to questions and consideration of special problems. Finding a good drugstore will not allow you to do much about the pricing policies of drug companies (such problems represent a different level of power). Individuals can, however, minimize the impact of problems on themselves and make their environment as congenial as possible.

Unfortunately, these benefits are in no way guaranteed by the workings of the market. Consumers must work for whatever they get. In general, businesses will not do a great deal more than is required of them. If consumers demand very little, then that is what businesses will provide. The implication here is that consumers have themselves to blame for many of their day-to-day problems. It is a sort of vacuum theory. It would be a rare case indeed for a salesperson to berate a consumer for not demanding more specific information about a product. If the consumer is willing to accept vague generalities, the businessperson is not going to offer more. Businesses will lower their sights accordingly, moving into the vacuum created by the consumer's abdication of rights. In this way, the minimum level of service or performance that the consumer can reasonably expect is systematically lowered.

It is tempting to characterize the consumer as one who has fought the good fight and lost, but too often the consumer seems unwilling even to open hostilities. It appears, therefore, that consumers have contributed to the deterioration of their own position by being satisfied with too little. This is consistent with the well-known image of the apathetic consumer. It hardly fits, however, with either the portrait of the consumer developed throughout this book or the observed increase in consumer activism. A more consistent and explicit picture of the forces working up the consumer is therefore required.

The Changing Face of Affluence

It should come as no surprise that the explanation of these divergent tendencies rests on the impact of affluence upon the consumer. Our theme has stressed that affluence is intimately bound up with consumer problems in general. It may be true that the consumer is exploited, but it must be admitted that never have people been exploited in such comfort and style. While the fact of affluence is obvious enough, its consequences are much more difficult to trace. Notice the use of the plural—*consequences;* instead of a single line of causation, there are many forces at work, which may be pulling the consumer in different directions. Affluence has both an immediate impact and a more subtle effect that materializes over time. The latter may be ultimately more important and yet masked by more obvious short-run changes.

As consumer incomes rise, the composition of consumption changes. The difference relates to the concept of income elasticity—the rate at which the demand for a particular product changes as income changes.* The demand for foods prepared at home, for example, tends to have a fairly low income elasticity. Once people are adequately fed, additional increases in income will result in increased spending on things other than food or in a switch to prepared foods and restaurant meals.

Economists have understood the nature of this process for some time, but only recently have they begun to appreciate how it is affected by widespread affluence. The key element is a broad definition of cost, which includes not just money outlay, but time and effort components as well. As incomes rise, the latter become increasingly important, meaning that those goods with a higher time-effort component will decline in relative importance in the consumer's budget. The consumer can now *afford* to express a preference for goods that save time and effort. It is easy to see this tendency at work in the growth of demand for such things as automatic dishwashers, self-defrosting refrigerators, and garbage disposals. In such cases, the dollar cost may be higher, but that increase is more than offset by savings in time and effort.

However, that is only part of the story. We have used the word "consumption" to mean the use of a product, but in the case of durable goods, the definition can be extended to include the operation and maintenance of the product [15, pp. 38–46]. A riding mower that won't start doesn't make mowing the lawn any easier; no product that requires a great deal of maintenance can be thought of as contributing to the conservation of time and effort. Undependable products are expensive not only in terms of money, but also in terms of the consumer's increasingly valuable time.

These tendencies have shown themselves in different ways. More and more companies are stressing quality and dependability in their advertising and others are stressing service. Individual consumers are turning away from more complex items to simpler products; you have probably heard someone comment on some gadget by saying "That's just another thing to go wrong." Consumers aren't turning

---

* For our purposes, income elasticity can be defined as the percentage change in demand divided by the percentage change in income. Let Q_x stand for the quantity of good x and Y for income and we have $\%\Delta Q_x/\%\Delta Y$. Thus, if income goes up by 10 percent and the demand for x goes up 5 percent, the income elasticity would be 0.5; hence, the good is income-inelastic, for the increase in demand did not keep pace with the increase in income.

their backs on convenience, but they are defining *convenience* more broadly, and time lost to maintenance is *not* convenient. In the case of automobiles, part of the attractiveness of compacts is that they are easier to maintain (and auto producers underscore that fact by stressing do-it-yourself tune ups).

Most of what has been said thus far refers to essential items, especially consumer durables. Affluence is also making itself felt in other areas. Because of the nature of the items involved, the consumer is in a position to pick and choose, to be discriminating. This trend is evident in the fashion industry, particularly men's clothing; the fate of the white shirt is a good example. As a writer for *Fortune* noted, the once homogeneous middle class "has become increasingly fragmented in recent years ... by an increasing insistence by the customers on using consumption to express themselves, to help in the fashioning of their own identities" [19, p. 19].

The net result of these changes is an increasingly demanding consumer. In essentials, consumers demand products that function dependably, minimizing total costs. With nonessentials, consumers demand individuality.* It is not inconsistent for both elements to come together in the same product. The consumer may want a refrigerator with decorator panels that can be changed with the decor in the kitchen, but only if the machine itself is mechanically sound.

At this point you should be bothered by the inconsistency between this portrait of the increasingly demanding consumer and the earlier contention that consumers have weakened their own positions by not being sufficiently demanding. This inconsistency indicates the difference between the short- and long-run effects of affluence. The process just described clearly belongs in the latter category. It has been countered, however, by short-run tendencies, which until recently have been more obvious. Resolving the dilemma calls for unraveling these various elements.

Timing is critical. While the mass consumption society has been emerging for most of this century, it has reached maturity only recently. Because affluence was a new experience for most people, they felt they should be grateful for the range of goods available to them. Consumers were in fact appreciative, and remained preoccupied with their new-found affluence. It was not until the 1960s—the longest continuous economic expansion in the nation's history—that the situation began to change. As it did, however, a new set of forces came into play.

When consumers began to look at their purchases with more criti-

---

* Total cost considerations may enter here, too. Consumers want fashion, but they want it in easy-to-care-for styles.

cal eyes, they discovered that there are costs attached to an activist strategy. If you have a complaint, you must confront the seller, explain what is wrong, and justify your case. That is usually sufficient, but even if you meet with such early success, you have still invested a considerable amount of time, effort, and money. Time and effort costs become more important to consumers as incomes rise, but those are precisely the costs involved in this case. Consumers' costs of complaining increase with time and effort spent.

Costs are further increased by the fact that all of this is likely to be unpleasant. Only the most combative find this sort of undertaking enjoyable, which contrasts with what we said about searching for information. In this case, the disutility of complaining must be added onto the other costs. If only a small purchase is involved, it may not be worthwhile to put yourself through a disagreeable experience. The costs involved would be more than the possible gain. With the many goods and services the typical consumer buys, pursuing all possible complaints would be an overwhelming task. It follows that the consumer is likely to follow through only on those complaints where significant amounts of money are involved.

The difference between the short-run and the long-run impact of affluence on the consumer should be clear. Short-run influences combined to promote the image of the passive, indifferent consumer, which to a degree is still with us. At the same time, however, the more subtle and ultimately more important long-run forces began to make themselves felt. It is not mere chance that consumerism first emerged as a significant force in the 1960s. It took that long for the process that was creating a more demanding consumer to make itself felt. That process also expressed itself through market forces. Previously, a consumer who had found a particular product unsatisfactory might not have complained, merely resolving not to buy it again. Several consumers complaining together could cause demand for a product ultimately to decline. Complaints became more common. Costs remained an inhibiting factor, but consumers developed a clearer perception of their own self-interest as their level of dissatisfaction rose. What has often been mistaken for militancy is nothing more than consumers reasserting themselves and demanding from the market the sort of performance they have a right to expect. As more consumers assumed this posture, it became socially acceptable, sanctioned as correct behavior. People who even a few years ago would have thought it bad form to complain now expertly follow up on their grievances. By its very nature, this process is slow and unspectacular. However, the ultimate impact of more discriminating consumers is of fundamental importance in the marketplace.

It would certainly facilitate this analysis if all of these developments had unfolded in a neat, sequential fashion. Unfortunately, that is not the case. Elements of consumer indifference coexist with consumer activism. Change has proceeded unevenly. The result is a confusing patchwork full of seeming inconsistencies and paradoxes. Despite the confusion, it is clear that consumerism is not a fad; it will not pass quietly away. Rather, it has become a permanent feature of society. The full impact of consumer activism has yet to be felt. Not only is the consumer reawakening as yet incomplete, but most activity to date has been directed at reclaiming lost ground. Consumers are paying for their earlier indifference. When this remedial action is complete, they will be able to direct their energies toward reshaping the system itself.

The Imperatives of Consumer Organization

Collective Security

The second level of consumer power consists of assuring all consumers not only fair treatment in the marketplace, but a voice in its operation as well. Those goals lie beyond the capabilities of the individual consumer. Both the size and complexity of the marketplace are important, the former because it dilutes the individual's influence, and the latter because it makes figuring out the market's operation difficult.

Therein lies the rationale for consumer organization. It is blissfully simple. While the marketplace may overwhelm the individual, like-minded consumers should be able to organize themselves into groups of sufficient strength to assert their influence. In reaching that conclusion, consumers are following a well-worn path. Large corporations dominate the marketplace; their size gives them a degree of power well beyond that of a small firm. Similarly, giant unions can win concessions from management that would be impossible for individual workers.

You may recognize this as the idea of *countervailing power,* first articulated by John Kenneth Galbraith over twenty-five years ago [7]. In a competitive situation, power is diffused. However, as one group accumulates power, it assumes a dominant position. This naturally disadvantages others, who are thus encouraged to organize themselves to protect their own interests. They acquire power as a counterweight—hence, countervailing—to offset the original power center. This can be seen in the progression from big business to big government to big labor, each developing in response to earlier concentrations of power elsewhere. Consumer organization therefore follows as a logical step in the sequence.

A very useful analogy can be made here with the experience of workers. In the simple, preindustrial economy, labor-management relations were on a personal or even neighborly basis. The individual worker probably had a skill, and, in the typical firm of small size, there was easy access to the employer in case of a complaint. All of that was changed with industrialization. The worker's position was weakened as skills became less important. Only basic skills were required and low-paid workers quickly replaced the more expensive artisans. With the advent of big business, the worker's position deteriorated still further. Management became more and more remote and the individual's influence was diluted as the number of workers grew. Those who objected quickly discovered that they were very small, and easily replaceable, parts of the operation.

The response of the workers was organization. Progress was slow and uneven at best, but despite numerous false starts, hostile public opinion, and an unsympathetic government, the rights of labor to organize and bargain collectively were finally recognized. Thus, workers as a group were able to assert themselves to a degree that would be impossible for the individual. Despite the obvious differences between the worker in the firm and the consumer in the marketplace, the principle of strength through organization applies in both cases.

Types of Consumer Organization

In one way or another, all consumer organizations are geared to helping the consumer come to grips with the problems of the marketplace. Under that general heading, however, it is possible to delineate four main types of organization. The first is direct market action, a pooling of dollar votes to give the real-world consumer the same sort of leverage his counterpart in theory enjoys. The second type provides information, as discussed in Chapter 5. Thirdly, there are organizations that focus on legal, administrative, and legislative goals. Finally, there are efforts toward cooperative purchases among consumers, offering the opportunity for greater specialization.

Direct market action applies to those groups that use purchasing power to affect the market; as such, it represents a logical extension of the theoretical apparatus discussed earlier. Boycotts are the best illustration of this process. If consumers feel that a particular store is unfair, they may direct their business elsewhere. If the boycott is effective, the store will be forced to come to terms. The punishment is administered through the market, using the conventional technique of the dollar vote.

In theory, the individual's dollar votes direct production. In the real-world marketplace, however, the individual's purchasing power is such an insignificant fraction of the total that, except in localized circumstances, its influence is insignificant. It is therefore logical for individuals to unite and direct their purchases as a group. With blocs of dollar votes to shift around, the group has leverage that its individual members lack. The amounts of money involved are large enough to have an impact. Such groups are merely doing collectively what economic theory says the individual should do. The use of the market mechanism marks such efforts as an extension of traditional techniques, not a departure from them.

Direct market action is therefore a very conservative response. This point is often missed in analyzing consumer organizations. Too often, the public image of consumer activists is one of militancy, suggesting a radical stance and vaguely subversive possibilities. This distortion is significant, because, while such groups use classic market techniques, they are damned as threats to the market system. The truth is that such groups are working within the existing market system, using its mechanism to attain their goals. By creating new power centers to balance existing ones, consumer groups are merely equalizing the odds. The status quo clearly favors business interests; those who complain against consumer organization are simply bemoaning their loss of leverage against the consumer. What they are really saying is that it is unfair to deprive them of the unfair advantage they hold over the consumer.

Part of the hostility toward direct market action may be explained by the fact that such techniques are often used to attain noneconomic goals. Boycotts are commonly directed toward social or political ends. There is a rich tradition for such activities in the United States. Indeed, they lie at the very foundation of the American state. Recall that our colonial forefathers forced the repeal of the Stamp Acts by boycotting British goods and that the celebrated Tea Party in Boston was part of a boycott of British tea.*

This is by no means an isolated example. Farmers in the nineteenth century attempted repeated boycotts of groups that they thought were unfair, just as their descendants may now withhold products from the market in protest of the low prices they receive. Boycotts also played an important part in the civil rights movement. The

---

* Although the word had not been invented yet. *Boycott* was the name of a 19th-century Irish landlord who was cruel, even by the standards of the time. His tenants refused to pay their rents, and soon any withholding action aimed at the redress of grievances came to be known as a *boycott*.

Reverend Martin Luther King, Jr., first gained national recognition with his Montgomery bus boycott. More recently, boycotts have been used to help other disadvantaged groups; witness the national boycotts of grapes and lettuce in support of unionization efforts among California farm workers.

It may seem strange to think that consumer groups have borrowed this technique from others, since what is involved is nothing less than consumption itself. Nevertheless, it is clear that the tactical use of consumer buying power was well developed before consumerism became a significant force. While consumers' efforts to reclaim this approach have encountered certain difficulties, it remains a logical and potentially effective means for consumers to reassert themselves.

Direct market action has been most successful at the local level, where it has been used against merchants who had previously taken advantage of their customers. Boycotts in ghetto areas have received the most attention, for it is there that the problems are usually most conspicuous. However, they are increasingly being used over a broader range of establishments. In a more positive vein, some organizations—church groups, for example—are using their purchasing power to reward businesses they feel are particularly worthy of support.

At the national level, boycotts have not been so effective. The long-run impact of recent coffee and beef boycotts was minimal (although they may have been important as a gesture). Boycotts may serve, however, to reinforce tendencies already established. At a time when individual parents were becoming concerned with dangerous toys, small but vocal consumers' groups helped crystallize feeling and forced producers to face the problem. The boycotts may have lacked formal organization, but by making individuals more aware of the problem, they promoted a widespread consumer response.

As consumer awareness grows, it is certain that the collective use of dollar votes will become more common. Consumer organization, however, is by no means limited to that approach. The older, established organizations in the United States have concentrated their efforts elsewhere, trying to lower information costs to consumers. The best known of these organizations are Consumers' Research, founded in the 1920s, and Consumers Union, which followed a decade later. The operations of these groups were discussed in Chapter 5, so the whole analysis need not be repeated here. However, it is worth noting where they fit in the overall pattern of consumer organization. These groups, with their specialized facilities and larger resources, can undertake testing programs that individuals can not. Thus, they provide another example of how consumers, by pooling their resources, can improve their position in the marketplace.

It is interesting to note that both of these groups have broadened their perspective in recent years, interpreting information more liberally. Instead of just providing information about products, they have increasingly become clearinghouses for consumer information in a broad sense. Both groups keep a watchful eye on advertising and keep their readers posted about legal and institutional developments that affect the consumer. While it is still up to the consumer to make use of this information, the technique has been successful.

Even with information, however, consumers are still at a disadvantage. Legislation is complex, and a sustained lobbying effort is required to influence it. Lawsuits require specialized legal services and large amounts of money. The requirements in both cases are likely to be beyond the means of the individual. An aroused public can indeed have an impact, but there are so many things to get aroused about that public opinion alone cannot protect the consumer.

As a result, a different type of consumer organization has come to the fore in recent years. This type concentrates on protecting consumer interests through legal, legislative, and administrative actions. The legal and institutional framework within which consumption takes place is growing more and more complicated. Thousands of laws affect the consumer and a seemingly unlimited array of administrative agencies directly affect the consumer's day-to-day activities. It takes a professional merely to understand all of this, and to translate understanding into action requires a well-trained staff. In that simple marketplace I have referred to so often, the consumer could master the legal framework, but, without effective organization, today's consumer finds that difficult.

It should be useful at this point to subdivide the category by making a distinction between individual's rights and the rights of consumers as a group. To illustrate the former, consider a tenant who has been illegally evicted. The landlord may get away with breaking the law if the tenant is either unaware of his or her rights or cannot obtain legal help. Thus, the imbalance of power in the marketplace works against the rights of the individual. A number of promising developments have taken place in this regard. Despite uncertain and usually inadequate funding, legal aid societies have brought legal services to large numbers of people who might otherwise have been without them. Conventional law firms now allow their members a certain amount of free time to work on public-service cases, and a growing number of public-interest law firms devote their total energies toward such problems [10].

The question of the consumer interest, in a collective sense, is somewhat more difficult. Rather than merely protecting the individual, the goal in this case is extending consumers' rights by changing existing legal or administrative practices. With all its test cases and appeals to higher courts, this is an expensive and time-consuming process. The potential benefits, however, are great because the outcome affects not just the individual but all consumers. At the risk of sounding overblown, it can be said that eternal vigilance is needed in this area. Both legal and administrative decisions must be continually scrutinized. Indeed, the task amounts very nearly to being a watchdog on the system. The need for organization is clear, since individuals, with their own affairs to watch, cannot be expected to fulfill this function.

The final type of consumer organization constitutes a more direct attack on consumer problems. Consumers, rather than try to change the marketplace, may create an alternative to it by forming jointly owned and operated cooperatives. Cooperatives are owned by their members, who are also customers; since profits are not involved, member-owners can enjoy improved service or lower prices. On many campuses, students have used this approach and formed cooperative student bookstores. Instead of trying to change existing campus or commercial bookstores—and the complaints against them are legion—students have devoted their energies to providing an alternative. Similarly, employee groups who feel that financial institutions are not serving their interests have joined to form credit unions. These are probably the most successful examples of cooperative efforts.

While cooperatives hold forth bright promise, their actual performance has been disappointing. The trouble is that if cooperatives are to operate on a large scale, they need not only formal organization but skilled management also. That requirement has been the bane of the cooperative movement since its beginnings over a century ago. Most cooperatives are short-lived because they suffer from inadequate capital and a lack of managerial talent. If a cooperative is to be successful, it requires the same sort of financial and managerial resources as any business venture. These are not likely to be forthcoming, particularly in so-called bootstrap operations. Unless the effort is backed by a sufficiently large organization that can command the necessary resources, its effectiveness will be limited. This suggests that cooperative developments might be more successful after viable consumer organizations have been formed.

Obstacles to Consumer Organization

It is now time to face an obvious question: If consumer organization is such a logical response to consumer problems, why haven't consumers organized more effectively? To provide an answer, let's return to our earlier analogy with the union movement. Workers were able to assert their influence through organization, which suggests that consumers should follow a similar course. The analogy, however, is imperfect; the differences between workers and consumers place the latter in a more difficult position and illustrate the problems associated with consumer organization. These difficulties arise from the differences in the common interests among workers and consumers. Workers had a most immediate issue to unite them: the prospect of economic betterment. Nevertheless, the triumph of the union movement took over three generations from its beginnings in the 1870s to the victories of the 1930s. During that time, the movement was so beset with factionalism that union solidarity was little more than a slogan.

Consumers can hardly be encouraged by this record. Unlike the workers, consumers have only weak common bonds. Everyone is a consumer, and therein lies the problem. Consumers may be united by the fact that they all buy things, but this is insufficient to offset the many forces that divide them. Since consumers represent the population as a whole, they reflect all the divisions common to the entire population. This lack of cohesion makes organization difficult. Common goals, specific and immediate, are needed to sustain an effective organization. In this case, there are so many issues, so many goals, and so many consumers that it is hard to imagine them all coalescing into a single movement, let alone a single organization. The very strength of consumers—their numbers—turns out to be their weakness. Common policies and common goals are difficult if not impossible to achieve. It may be possible to put together an alliance to fight for a particular goal, but once that goal is met, it is difficult to keep the group together. This helps explain the erratic performance of many consumer groups. An immediate goal can help overcome the diversity of interests by providing the group with a central focus, but the image becomes blurred by the demands of day-to-day business [2].

A second complication follows from the first. Organization is a means, not an end in itself. Even if a group organizes successfully, the broad range of consumer problems still creates serious difficulties. Again, the contrast with the labor movement is striking. While early union leaders had to work under adverse conditions, it was clear to them what they had to do. They could concentrate their efforts on improving pay and working conditions, focusing on individual firms or on legislative action.

Consumer groups enjoy no such luxury. Anthony Downs, who pioneered this type of analysis, illustrated the point using the tariff laws. A tariff is simply a tax on imports, and citizens continue to demonstrate that they have no love for taxes. With higher tariffs, consumers are forced to pay higher prices, which means that tariff legislation regularly favors a few producers at the expense of millions of consumers. How can this imbalance be maintained? The answer lies in the consumer's old adversary, information costs. Downs notes that producers can afford to bring pressure on the parts of the tariff legislation that affect them. By contrast,

> Few consumers can afford to bring any influence to bear on any parts of the law, since each consumer's interests are spread over so many products. In fact, most consumers cannot even afford to find out whether tariffs are raising the prices they pay for any given product. [5, p. 257]

Everything affects the consumer, so consumer groups must be concerned with everything. The wide range of interests means that resources will be spread impossibly thin.

Now it may not be too difficult to inform people about any particular issue, but when all of the other things about which people need to be informed are taken into account, the true proportions of the problem become apparent. The word *informed* here must be taken to mean more than just "know about." Knowledge per se is only the first step; effective action requires a familiarity with the legal and administrative structure and the ability to use it to bring about change. It should be clear then that merely asserting that consumers' problems will be solved through organization is naïve. The potential for improvement comes with organization, but forbidding problems must be overcome before that potential can be realized. Understanding the problems is the first step. The next step involves devising a strategy that accounts for these difficulties and can work around them.

Toward More Effective Organization

The wide range of consumer problems and the consequent plurality of consumers' interests are the main obstacles to consumer organization. From this it follows that *an organization with limited, specific goals will have the best chance for success.* Individuals attracted to the group can be expected to share a common interest. Information costs will also be reduced, for such a group can concentrate on collecting information about the particular problem it has selected. This approach is no guarantee of success, but by withstanding the temptation to take on all comers, and by concentrating instead on specific problems, chances of success should be improved.

Given the importance of specific goals, organization at the local level is usually the most effective. Problems in such cases are more immediate and individuals' perceptions of their self-interest is clearer. Furthermore, the problem is more likely to be of manageable proportions. If, for example, a local store has been taking advantage of its customers, they might organize a boycott; the profit margins of most small stores are small enough so that even a 10 percent change in sales can have an impact. In larger markets, the problems are magnified. It is one thing to boycott a local grocery, but a boycott of General Motors is something else again. It would be difficult to find sufficient numbers of consumers with the motivation to take on the challenge; beyond that, organizational and managerial problems would be compounded.

The rent-strike movement represents one of the most successful examples of local consumer organization. Rent strikes constitute a kind of boycott, because tenants withhold rent until conditions in their buildings are improved. Organization is required (a single tenant would have simply been evicted), but the groups are localized and administrative problems are therefore minimized. Groups of tenants around the country have won victories that individuals could never have achieved [14, Ch. 4 and 5].

Rent strikes also show how specific, local consumer efforts may benefit large numbers of consumers. Victories in the rent strike cases usually meant changing the basis for landlord-tenant relationships. Until recently, these relations (and the laws governing them) were based on antique notions of feudal responsibilities left over from the Middle Ages. The landlord survived as the lord of the manor, leaving the tenant in the position of a serf. The revised laws are based on a contract relationship between tenant and landlord, specifying the rights and reponsibilities of each.* This means that *all* tenants now have a sounder basis for pursuing complaints with landlords [21].

Consumer groups can be successful beyond the local level if they focus on a specific issue. The accomplishments of Action for Children's Television (ACT) were discussed in the previous chapter. Other groups, such as environmentalists, have successful national organizations. Not all consumers support the efforts of such groups (after all, advertisers and land developers are consumers, too), but the various organizations show that consumer organizations can have an impact.

Some consumer organizations, like Consumers Union, could not

---

* It is the landlord's responsibility to ensure that the property is fit for human habitation; if it isn't, tenants need not pay rent until improvements are made. Revised laws are in effect in most, but not all, states [21].

function effectively at the local level. CU specializes in providing detailed product information, and that can be done most effectively on a large scale. While there has been increasing debate over the aims of CU, its policy of limiting itself to a particular—though still very broad—area has enabled it to survive and to serve consumers over the years.

There are enough examples of successful consumer groups to show that organization can be effective, but it remains true that consumer organizations generally lack the clout of business and professional groups. The latter tend to be better financed, reflecting the greater resources that businesses can draw on for issues that affect them. In a head-to-head confrontation, the odds are against the consumer group. This suggests that consumer groups should either avoid confrontations or look around for help.

The second alternative seems logical enough, but it hasn't always come naturally to consumer advocates. Consumer groups have had a tendency to be long on virtue and short on strategy, which means they have been reluctant to form temporary alliances with those who might share a common view on a certain issue. Anyone who has ever been in a fight knows that it is nice to have others on your side; you may not have much else in common with these "friends," you may not even like them, but as long as they are fighting with you, you are not going to ask too many questions.

Consumer organizations have been in enough fights now to recognize the value of such a practical approach. Joining up with another group—say a business organization—on some specific issue doesn't mean the consumer is being sold out; neither does it mean that the two groups' long-run interests are the same. It is simply a matter of having the most punch on a particular issue and that may call for cooperation with other groups who (for whatever reasons) share common views on that issue.

The saccharin case (perhaps "incident" is a better word) offers a concrete example of such developments. Saccharin was banned by the Food and Drug Administration (FDA) after the sugar substitute was linked to the development of cancer in laboratory animals [18]. The announcement generated a great deal of controversy and, among some consumers, particularly dieters and diabetics, prompted angry responses. Pharmaceutical companies also opposed the ban and joined with consumer groups to successfully delay (and perhaps eventually rescind) the implementation of the FDA's order. We are not offering any judgments about who was right in this case; it is simply offered as an example of how cooperation can be effective.

The FDA's action on saccharin illustrates another, more general, problem. What precisely is *the consumer interest* in this instance?

After all, the action was taken by a federal agency that presumably was seeking to protect consumers. It was clear that many consumers didn't share the FDA's view of what their interests were; no single view of the consumer interest emerged. That's hardly surprising when you consider the earlier emphasis on plural interests among consumers. It may well be that in most cases there is no such thing as *the* consumer interest; it would be more proper to speak of consumer *interests*, acknowledging that consumers represent diverse points of view.

The difficulty in defining interest dramatizes the problems facing general-interest consumer groups. So-called public-interest lobbies face a difficult task in determining whether or not they really represent the public interest. That is one reason such groups have a hard time holding together. These groups can be effective, as in the case of Common Cause, but only if they are careful to build a solid base of support with some segment of the public and then avoid the temptation to take on all comers. Success lies in representing part of the public on a few issues rather than trying to speak for everyone on everything [20].

You may have noticed that neither the word *consumerism* nor the phrase *consumer movement* have appeared in this discussion. Consumerism is something that all consumers practice and is therefore hardly very useful; the phrase consumer movement is actually misleading, because it suggests some well-organized, carefully directed effort. That's wrong. The semantics might not be very important if they hadn't generated misconceptions that are proving counterproductive. Speaking of a movement implies common interests, and assuming that such common interests exist leads to tactical and strategic mistakes (see Chapter 8).

Instead of aspiring to the status of a mass movement, consumer groups need to build a solid organizational base around specific issues. Individuals who are concerned about those issues can provide the necessary base of support. The success of groups that have followed such a strategy is evidence that it works. Those who have a taste for crusading may find such an approach unexciting, but those who recognize the realities of the situation should see that it holds the prospect of eventual success.

In Search of the Sovereign Consumer

Who Pulls the Strings?

Thus far consumer power has been examined in terms of giving the consumer more leverage in the marketplace. That leverage is obviously necessary if the marketplace is to become a more congenial place for consumers. Congeniality, however, should not be confused with sovereignty. Consumers could obtain the power to ensure that they would be treated fairly and yet still not be sovereign. Sovereignty means that consumers decide how the society is going to use its resources.

That fact suggests the distinction between consumer choice and consumer sovereignty. The consumer today has choices, but the question is: Who decides what those choices are? Consumer choice means that the consumer is presented with a series of options. Sovereignty implies that consumers themselves determine what those options are [17].

The phrase "directing production" therefore means that the sovereign consumer has choices among choices. To illustrate this point, Abba Lerner harkens back to a simple economy organized around family production. He says:

> Every family had its own house and garden where it produced everything it needed. It alone decided what to grow or to make and how to divide its time between work and play. No other family was concerned with how it made its choices, and it was not concerned with how other families made their choices. [13, p. 258]

Such families were sovereign because they had direct control over their resources, made their own decisions on how those resources were to be used, and hence determined what goods would be available. Poverty, however, went along with sovereignty, for the range of possible production (and therefore consumption) was extremely limited. Today's consumers, while they are not sovereign in the earlier sense, enjoy a level of affluence undreamed of by the frontier family.

If consumers do not determine what their choices will be, who does? The answer is producers. The real world emerges as a mirror-image of the textbook; in the real world, producers are sovereign and consumers respond to them. John Kenneth Galbraith has championed this view for nearly a quarter of a century. Whereas at first he was a voice crying in the Massachusetts wilderness, he has become the spokesman for a significant body of thought. The outlines of the Galbraithian position have already been suggested. Galbraith's view is based on an observation that John Maynard Keynes originally made that human wants may be classified as either absolute or relative. Absolute wants are independent of other's consumption, while relative wants are not. Thus, Keynes felt that while relative wants might be limitless, he believed it should be possible to satisfy all absolute wants [6, p. 122]. Galbraith concludes that if relative wants do not originate with the individual, they cannot be very urgent. Rather, they are contrived by producers who convince consumers of what they want. Thus, in Galbraith's words: "One cannot defend production as satisfying wants if that production creates the wants" [6, p. 124]. Therefore, to understand how the system works requires the recognition

> that wants are dependent upon production. It accords to the producer the function both of making the goods and of making the desires for them . . . [production] . . . through advertising and related activities, creates the wants it seeks to satisfy. [6, p. 127]

The implications of this argument are far-reaching. Our concern here is with what it does to the consumer's position. Certainly, the idea of consumer sovereignty has gone out the window; the consumer is less than ineffectual in this schema. In Galbraith's revised sequence, it is the producer who is sovereign, dictating responses to the consumer who has no real voice in the system. If this picture is drawn correctly, consumers are merely puppets dangling on corporate strings. That is hardly a very flattering characterization but it isn't an impossible position either. Consumers still have their affluence to enjoy, and there remains the possibility that they may obtain some lower level of market power. If it could be assumed that producers were benign, consumers could settle back in comfortable resignation and accept the inevitable reduction in their status.

A Closer Look

Presented with an either/or choice between the Galbraithian position and the classical doctrine of consumer sovereignty, most would admit that the former is closer to the reality of the modern marketplace. Yet casting the question in such terms is itself unrealistic, for the consumer's position does not submit to such easy categorization. The truth is most likely to be found in the murky gray area that lies between the bits of clarity provided by well-formulated positions.

The logical place to begin sorting all of this out is Galbraith's analysis of relative, or culturally determined, wants. This point has raised a great deal of controversy. The outstanding conservative thinker Friedrich Hayek seized on it in identifying what he saw as the *non sequitur* of Galbraith's position. The fact that wants may be culturally determined did not, to Hayek, prove that they are unimportant. He maintained that in the arts, for example,

> Professor Galbraith's argument could be easily employed without any change of the essential terms to demonstrate the worthlessness of

literature or any other form of art. Surely, an individual's want for literature is not original with himself in the sense that he would experience it if literature were not produced. [11, p. 347]

Hayek was arguing against what he saw as the collectivist tendencies in Galbraith's argument; one need not agree with his overall view to see that he has a point. To amplify it, let us go back once more to our frontier family living in their newly constructed log cabin. Since the cabin meets the family's immediate need for shelter, it could be classified as an absolute want. It is likely, however, that the cabin is also cold, drafty, and dreary. Isn't it logical to assume that the family, of its own accord, would think of improving the quality of its shelter as soon as possible?

Most people wouldn't classify improved insulation, a better fireplace, and a few coats of whitewash as relative wants. Such desires could originate with the individuals involved. If that is true, then what about adding a recreation room or installing central air conditioning? In the latter case, the desire to avoid summer heat is a natural tendency. The differences here are in degree rather than kind; as a result, the level of comfort at which wants become secondary is not at all clear.

Since it is obvious that many wants are culturally determined, the distinction itself is almost superfluous. With affluence, people seldom buy goods for the intrinsic value anyway; they buy a whole series of characteristics that the good has. Since the valuation of those characteristics is highly individual, it would not be very productive to try to distinguish among them, even if it were possible.

Let us accept that most wants are culturally determined, then, and try a slightly different approach. The question should not be what determines wants, but rather, what determines the culture? Consumers are conditioned by their social setting; thus, the determination of that setting directly influences consumer wants and consumption. If this premise is accepted, it appears that many of those who object to culturally determined wants are in reality objecting to the culture itself. Their real complaint is with the value system that produces a particular set of wants. Were consumers to express more of a preference for better social services and improved educational and health facilities, those too would be culturally determined wants. The difference between wanting such things and wanting a second car lies in the character of the culture.

A number of radical writers have clearly identified this point. Paul Baran, the Marxist theoretician, makes it quite clear. He indicates that he, like other Marxists, has never "advocated the abolition of

consumer sovereignty and its replacement by the orders of a commis-
sar" [1, p. xvii]. Baran maintains that the real point is:

> whether an economic and social order should be tolerated in which
> the individual, from the very cradle on, is so shaped, molded, and
> "adjusted" as to become an easy prey of profit-greedy capitalist en-
> terprise and a smoothly functioning object of capitalist exploitation
> and degradation. The Marxian socialist ... believes that a society can
> be developed in which the individual would be formed, influenced
> and educated not by the "values" of corporate presidents and the
> outpourings of their hired scribes, but by a system of rationally
> planned production for use, by a universe of human relations deter-
> mined by and oriented toward solidarity, cooperation and freedom.
> [1, p. xvii]

Even if you don't think that consumers are merely "objects of capitalist exploitation," you should appreciate that the passage was
worth quoting at length. Baran makes it clear that he feels that the
present system works to the advantage of the capitalist and that
consequently the consumer is abused. Whether that is true or not,
the individual certainly responds to the system and its values.

The subject of consumer sovereignty has become even broader.
With affluence, consumption becomes intimately bound up with the
culture itself; sovereignty in one requires sovereignty in the other. If
it is true that consumers have lost their ability to direct production,
it is also true that consumers have lost control over their culture. To
understand that statement, it is necessary to inquire into how the
present system evolved.

A Process of Evolution

While affluence has profoundly affected consumers, the changes it
brought about were gradual. We have been speaking in terms of
quantum leaps, comparing how things began with how they are now.
It is a long way, after all, from the frontier cabin to central air conditioning, but it is the events of in-between that are important. Those
things were tied together and represented only small changes. Instead
of thinking of a movement from the horse and buggy to the modern
automobile, we should think of the change from the horse to a Model
T, from there to a Model A, from crank to electric starters, and so
on. Taken alone, none of these changes are particularly startling;
their cumulative effect, however, has been monumental. The point is
that there were no clear breaks with the past. To be sure, there was
much talk of new eras and bright tomorrows, but most of it was

verbiage and things were never much different from what they had been immediately before.

That helps explain why the fundamental changes that took place *over time* were not perceived as such; they crept up on people. Since there was continuity to the pattern of change, there appeared to be no reason to change basic ways of thinking. Methods from the past were merely extended into the future. If it was logical for the frontier family to want to improve its cabin, is it not equally logical for a family today to want to improve its house?

In short, the consumer continued to think in terms of gradual change, perceived as improvement. The economic system obliged by turning out more and apparently better things. The system was responding to the basic desires of consumers. Particulars are not especially important. Few consumers yearned for electric can openers before they were available, but saying that such gadgets were therefore passed off on the public misses the point. Consumers were conditioned to think in terms of continued improvements, so there was nothing surprising about electric can openers. It was a natural development, even if that specific prcduct was not developed in response to a particular need. What consumers did, in effect, was to indicate to producers that they wanted more of the same. That meant continued refinement and more convenience. Since the system seemed capable of turning out an endless supply of goods and services, there was no real need to specify what form these changes would take. The particulars would take care of themselves. With more of everything, whatever one wanted would turn up sooner or later.

This raises a rather disturbing possibility: *consumers may be much more sovereign than most people think.* That point is easily missed because sovereignty applies not to particular goods and services, but to the general form and direction of the system. Consumer sovereignty, which seems so unrealistic when presented as an abstraction, actually emerges as a workable concept. The form that consumer sovereignty takes may not follow the textbook version, but the process is indeed similar. Were that the whole story, we might be able to leave the question at this point. While one might not like the results that consumer sovereignty has produced, it would have to be admitted that at least the consumer has had a hand in shaping the marketplace.

To end the discussion here, however, would be to leave before the story is complete. The overall process has been identified, but its ramifications have not been considered. Affluence has influenced both producers and consumers so that neither group is the same as it was before. Yet, until recently, the consumer's approach to the market was fundamentally unchanged. That is the crux of the matter. On the producers' side, the changes are obvious. Small firms grew into giant corporations, competition was' reduced, and the surviving giants acquired not only market power, but enormous advertising and merchandising capabilities. This concentration is particularly significant because consumers had given producers carte blanche as far as the specifics of increased production and new products were concerned. It meant that a few firms had a lot of power in deciding what goods would be available to consumers. However, as long as producers were fulfilling the general requirements that consumers set down, the problem did not appear to be serious. Producers were thus able to consolidate their positions; they behaved more and more as if they directed the system, which in effect they did. What developed was a sort of uneasy truce, broken only when consumers became concerned about the basic direction of the market system. That concern was itself a product of affluence.

Consumers finally awoke to the fact that conditions had changed. Affluence made consumers more demanding; they expected products to perform better and to fit their personal preferences exactly. The idea that consumers should be grateful or that producers are somehow doing them a favor has gone forever. While these changes have been uneven, they have combined to break down the consensus that had previously existed about the form and direction of the system.

This time it was producers who were caught unawares. Accustomed as they were to directing the market, they chose to ignore the increasingly assertive spirit the consumers showed. Thus, when the flood of foreign cars inundated the American market in the late 1950s, automobile makers chose to treat it as a fad rather than as an expression of a preference for smaller, less expensive, and more economical cars. As a result, despite Detroit's belated response, the share of the American market taken up by imports grew from an insignificant 4 percent to over 30 percent. In some cases the changes were subtle, as in fashion, where individualization gradually replaced standardization. In other instances the changes were dramatic. Consumer complaints began to make the headlines, and company after company felt the wrath of hostile consumers. These changes can be interpreted as an effort by consumers to reassert their control over the marketplace.

That is about where things now stand. The picture is confused by the complexity of the changes under way and the interaction of forces in the marketplace. It is therefore not easy to tell exactly what is going to happen. Consumers themselves are not sure; they reflect different motivations. Some still do not care, while others are demanding radical changes. Some of those in between merely want higher-quality products, while others are not sure whether products inherently warrant the fuss. At the same time, consumers are finding that reasserting their influence over the total operation of the marketplace is not very easy. Producers are entrenched in their positions and not easily dislodged. They are not about to give up the privileges they have accumulated, and their power enables them to resist effectively. This is true both in the marketplace—where large firms are invulnerable in the short run—and in the political arena. Producers have political as well as economic power and are adept at using it.

It is possible to make several observations. Evidence to date suggests that fundamental change is under way. The word *fundamental* is critical, for nothing short of control of the system is at stake. Given America's demonstrated pragmatism and willingness to experiment, it is unlikely that any radical change will emerge. Some accommodation will be reached so that both producers and consumers can claim a measure of victory. The best guess about the future is that present trends will continue, giving consumers more of a voice in operating the marketplace. Producers will have to become more carefully attuned to consumers' wishes and more responsive to them. George Katona feels that this process is already well along. In a comparative study of consumption in the United States and Europe, he observed that there is

> a two-way process of influence, from consumers to business as well as from business to consumers. . . . Interaction prevails in this respect as in all forms of learning. Both the traditional doctrine of consumer sovereignty and the thesis of Galbraith that large producers control and manage their customers' presume a unidirectional process of influence, which in fact represents the exception rather than the rule. [12, pp. 115–16]

Judged from past experience, Katona's scenario represents the most likely pattern of development. It is possible, however, that past experience may not be a very good guide. If producers have become so inflexible that they cannot adapt, if consumers demand truly radical change, if the society's value system is undergoing a profound alteration, then the outcome could be quite different. At this point, it is possible only to speculate.

There is another term in the equation that will surely be involved in the solution. Political power is an important element in the confrontation between producer and consumer. Both sides are anxious to enlist the support of government to their respective causes. The success of one or the other in doing so may determine the outcome. Thus, the question of consumer power leads ultimately to the relation between the consumer and government.

Study Questions

1. Improvements in communications and transportation have tended to produce big market areas. This is particularly noticeable with large suburban shopping centers, which draw customers from a wide area. Explain how these developments have weakened the consumer's position. What effect have they had on the cost of complaining?

2. Self-service discount stores are now common throughout the country. Is the consumer's position in such stores stronger or weaker than it would be in a conventional department store? In a neighborhood store?

3. Apply the concept of income elasticity in the following cases:
   a. While food generally has a low income elasticity, why is this less true in ghetto areas?
   b. Potatoes are a classic example of a good with a low—or even negative—income elasticity. Explain why.
   c. Food has a low income elasticity, but what about food outside the home?

4. What are the total costs to consumers of products which are undependable? Why are these costs increasing?

5. During the summer of 1978, a wealthy socialite in Newport, R.I. attracted attention when she joined in a rent protest movement. Comment in terms of our discussion in the text.

6. Inflation has been a continuing problem in recent years. Do you feel that it has helped promote consumer activism? Explain.

7. Labor unions were used in the text as an example of effective organization. In fact, most groups within the economy are organized, including medical doctors, teachers, farmers, and nearly all business and industrial groups. What advantages do these groups have that consumers lack? Can consumers learn anything from them?

8. Because of product differentiation, you can walk into any grocery and find a stunning array of different brands of many products. Explain how this illustrates the difference between consumer choice and consumer sovereignty.

9. Is consumer sovereignty, as it is presented in textbooks, possible in a modern, technological economy? If not, does that mean that the consumer has no hope of reasserting control over the economic system?

10. If consumers were actually sovereign, would that mean that every consumer would be able to find the products he or she wanted in the market? Discuss.

Suggested Projects

1. Are there any tenant's organizations in your area? If so, find out who they serve and what they do.

2. Find out about the details of your state's law governing landlords and tenants. Develop a survey about the law and administer it to renters in your area. Do they know what their rights are? You might also ask them what their main concerns are and see if these are covered under the law. (See also Project 1, Chapter 8.)

3. Make a survey of other consumer organizations in your area. How would you classify them according to the four types examined in the text? Do you feel that they have developed to the point that they are viable organizations that contribute to the consumer's welfare? Do you see a need for developing a new type of organization in your area? Discuss.

4. Beyond private law firms, what sort of legal services are available to consumers in your area? Is there a legal aid society or a law firm that specializes in consumer problems? Do you feel that consumers in need of legal advice are adequately served?

5. Try to estimate the cost of pursuing a complaint about a product or service. Consider the costs of gasoline, time, and the like as in Project 2, Chapter 5. Do you feel it is these costs that limit consumer complaints, or is it that many people find complaining distasteful?

6. Are there any consumer cooperatives in your area? If there are, meet with their managers and find out about their activities. What are the main problems these organizations face?

7. Review the operation over the past year of some large public interest organization, like Common Cause; you can use the *Reader's Guide* or some other index for this purpose. Is any pattern evident? How well do you think such groups have come to grips with the problems outlined in the text?

8. It was argued in the text that consumers are demanding higher quality and more dependable products. If that is true, producers should be aware of it; this awareness should in turn be reflected in their advertising. Make a spot check of advertising to find out to what degree these qualities are stressed.

Bibliography and Suggested Readings

1. Baran, Paul. "A Marxist View of Consumer Sovereignty." In *The Political Economy of Growth*. New York: Monthly Review Press, 1957.

A noted Marxist examines capitalist production, providing a penetrating and often disquieting analysis of the consumer.

2. Brill, Harry. *Why Organizers Fail.* Berkeley, Calif.: The University of California Press, 1971.
   An inside account of efforts to organize a rent strike. A good study in the politics of poverty and the difficulties of dealing with both local and federal bureaucracies. As the title suggests, not all efforts were successful.

3. Dickinson, Ernest. "New Jersey, A Testing Place for Tenant Power," *New York Times,* March 7, 1976.
   A report on tenants' organizing efforts. As in other states, efforts in New Jersey included affluent consumers in expensive apartments; the rich could afford to organize.

4. Dorfman, John. *Consumer Survival Kit.* New York: Praeger, 1975.
   A readable and valuable book of survival tactics in the marketplace. This book is an adaptation of the highly acclaimed series from public television.

5. Downs, Anthony. *An Economic Theory of Democracy.* New York: Harper & Row, 1957.
   The classic analysis of political activity in a democracy using the outline of economic theory. We have already seen how Downs's conclusions help explain the difficulties involved in consumer organization. We shall make further use of his work over the next two chapters.

6. Galbraith, John Kenneth. *The Affluent Society.* Boston: Houghton Mifflin Co., 1958.
   Especially Chapters 9–11. Though modified somewhat by Galbraith's later writings, this remains a complete statement of his *revised sequence* and producer's sovereignty.

7. ———. *American Capitalism.* Boston: Houghton Mifflin Co., 1952.
   Galbraith's first big work. It contains his statement of countervailing power and identifies the main themes that dominate his later books.

8. ———. "Power and the Useful Economist." *American Economic Review* 63 (March 1973): 1–11.
   Professor Galbraith's presidential address to the American Economics Association. It represents something of a break with his earlier work by dwelling on the possibility of conflicting power relationships. In doing so, it foreshadows his most recent work.

9. Gintis, Herbert. "Consumer Behavior and the Concept of Sovereignty: Explanations of Social Decay." *American Economic Review, Papers and Proceedings* 62 (May 1972): 267–78.
   A radical critique contrasting classical, Galbraithian, and radical views on consumer sovereignty. In the last of these, the author stresses the consumer's alienation.

10. Handler, Joseph. "Public Interest Law: Problems and Prospects." In *Law and the American Future*, ed. M. Schwartz. Englewood Cliffs, N.J.: Prentice-Hall, 1976.
A review of public service law, including discussions of potentials and limitations. A good introduction to the topic.

11. Hayek, Frederick. "The Non Sequitur of the Dependence Effect." *Southern Economic Journal*, April 1961, pp. 346–48.
A famous assault on Galbraith's contention about the urgency of different levels of wants.

12. Katona, George, Strumpel, B., and Zahn, D. *Aspirations and Affluence*. New York: McGraw-Hill Book Co., 1971.
A comparative study of consumption patterns and consumer attitudes in Western Europe and the United States. An important effort to study consumer behavior across national and cultural boundaries. We shall use this work further in Chapter 11.

13. Lerner, Abba. "The Economics and Politics of Consumer Sovereignty." *American Economic Review, Papers and Proceedings* 62 (May 1972): 258–66.

14. Lipsky, Michael. *Protest in City Politics*. Chicago: Rand McNally, 1970.
Subtitled "Rent Strikes, Housing and the Power of the Poor," this well-documented study offers another account of the rent strike movement. Particularly good in terms of analysis of the impact of the movement.

15. Linder, Staffen B. *The Harried Leisure Class*. New York: Columbia University Press, 1970.
A rare gem of a book. Readable and insightful, Linder's analysis will have you wondering why you hadn't thought of that. He was among the first to identify a fact that economists had previously succeeded in overlooking: consumption takes time. The implications of that fact are far reaching.

16. Maynes, E. Scott. *Decision Making for Consumers*. New York: Macmillan, 1976.
Chapters 9–11 offer an in-depth look at consumer sovereignty. A well documented, yet largely nontechnical account that is worth reading by anyone wishing to pursue the topic.

17. Rothenberg, Jerome. "Consumers' Sovereignty Revisited and the Hospitality of Freedom of Choice." *American Economic Review, Papers and Proceedings* 52 (May 1962) pp. 260–68.
The author contrasts consumer sovereignty with consumer choice and concludes that the latter may be preferable. A thoughtful consideration of the complexities involved.

18. "Saccharin and Cancer: Another Look." *Science News*, February 11, 1978. See also "Reappraising Saccharin—and the FDA," *Time*, April 25, 1977, pp. 75–76.

Two accounts of the on-again, off-again ban on saccharin. Illustrates why the issue tended to confuse and annoy the public.

19. Silberman, Charles E. "Identity Crisis in the Consumer Markets." *Fortune,* March 1971, pp. 92–95.
A look at how changing consumer demands affected traditional production and marketing techniques.

20. Tolley, H. "Common Cause and Campaign Financing." *Intellect,* October 1977, pp. 122–25. See also Bode, K. "Money for Campaigns." *New Republic,* February 1977.
Two stories on Common Cause, the public interest lobby. As titles suggest, the group has focused on campaign financing issues. While Common Cause hasn't changed the world, it has had more of an impact and a longer life than many predicted.

21. "Your Rights as a Tenant." Housing Unit, University of Tennessee Legal Clinic, Knoxville, Tennessee.
This pamphlet summarizes the Landlord-Tenant law in Tennessee, a statute that is patterned after national model legislation (and is therefore similar to laws in other states). Similar publications should be available in most areas.

-8-

Government and Consumer Protection

The Setting for Government Protection

The New Fatalism

To a growing number of American consumers, the phrase consumer *protection* is synonymous with government *interference.* That's a rather pessimistic note on which to begin a discussion of consumer protection, but there is no escaping the fact that many Americans feel that government is meddling in their lives and that so-called protection is more a bother than a blessing. The public seems to be losing patience with the weekly revelations of new health hazards or dangerous products. Having been fed a diet of automobile recalls, cancer scares, and warning labels, consumers seem to be saying, "We'll take our chances, just leave us alone!"

It is impossible to tell whether this backlash is merely the response of a small (but vocal) minority or whether it represents a rising tide of opinion. In either case, the new skepticism about governments' consumer protection efforts marks a change in thinking. As mentioned in Chapter 1, the majority view for nearly two generations has been that government should intervene to protect the consumer. Now that basic assumption is being questioned.

To some observers, these trends signal the decline of the consumer movement. As noted in the last chapter, however, it is questionable whether any such movement ever existed; therefore, it could hardly decline. There is, in fact, no evidence to show that consumers have suddenly become more content or that their individual problems are any less pressing. It is in the manner in which those problems are being addressed that difficulties arise. Discontent with government protection illustrates both the difficulty of developing a comprehensive protection program and certain critical weaknesses in the present structure. The backlash may be a kind of cop out, representing an unwillingness to face up to some very complex questions. However, ignoring the problems isn't going to make them go away and postponing action is dangerous. Therefore, we must ask: What happened? Why is consumer protection being questioned by the very people it is supposed to benefit? I laid the groundwork for dealing with those questions in the last chapter; I will develop the answers further as we proceed with our analysis of the particulars of consumer protection.

Toward a Balanced Perspective

The question of relations between the government and the consumer would be easier to deal with if some historical norm or typical relationship existed. In fact, however, the opposite is true. Over a relatively short period of history, the relation between government and consumer has been subject to repeated changes. The weight of opinion has swung from active government policies to a more passive approach and back again.

Consumption is as old as humanity, but the characteristics we associate with present-day consumers are a much more recent development. It was not until about 200 years ago, when *laissez-faire* began to dominate public thinking, that consumers emerged as independent agents in the economic system. Prior to that, consumers had been restricted by the weight of tradition, religious beliefs, and government control. Furthermore, the typical person lived at the subsistence level and therefore didn't really function as a consumer in our sense of the word.

With rising standards of living and the development of markets, consumers gained their independence. They were on their own, making their own decisions according to their own preferences. This meant that consumers had to look after themselves, but they were equipped to do so. Markets were small and products were relatively simple. If a product was overpriced, unsafe, or otherwise undesirable, consumers merely rejected it in favor of one that was more suitable. Until early in this century, consumers could look after themselves and there was little need for protection from government.

You should recognize this theme and thus know why the situation has changed. As markets grew progressively larger and more specialized, the consumer's position grew correspondingly weaker. The odds against the consumer worsened and it was only logical that individuals should look to government as a means of offsetting the power of sellers in the marketplace. The logic here is the same as that employed in our earlier discussion of consumer organization; the idea of countervailing power is implicit in both. Therefore, while it is useful to distinguish between government protection and consumer organization, they are really alternative responses to the same problem. Both represent efforts to come to grips with the realities of the modern marketplace.

Remember that in a political sense, the words *consumer, citizen* and *voter* can be used interchangeably. Political power in a democracy rests with the people, and the government exists as their instrument. Thus when consumers seek protection from government, they are in effect seeking it from themselves. Effective consumer protection should follow from the fact that consumers are citizens and citizens elect the government.

However, things haven't worked out that neatly. The same obstacles that hinder consumer organization, particularly the *pluralism of consumer interests,* also make effective political action difficult. As a result of consumers' inability to focus their efforts, government has been less responsive to attempts to promote consumer protection. However, even when government does respond, the lack of consensus among consumers means that many individuals may disagree with the action taken. For example, when the federal government mandated that children's sleepwear be flame retardant, it did so in response to pressure from concerned parents. However, the vast majority of children are not involved in burns from sleepwear; thus, parents focused on the impaired performance characteristics of the sleepwear—flame retardant sleepwear isn't as soft and doesn't wear as well—rather than on the potential gain from reduced risk of fire.* It is that kind of situation which promotes the backlash discussed earlier.

Finally, we should note that consumer protection isn't determined simply by give and take between consumers and government. Business interests are also involved. Business and other special interest groups have a considerable advantage, which is implicit in the term *special* interest. Because they have specific interests, these groups are able to focus their efforts and bring more effective pressure on government. The result is that businesses are often able to get their point

---

* The situation became more complicated when it was discovered that *tris,* which is used to make the garments flame retardant, may cause cancer. This illustrates how complex these questions can become.

across when consumers cannot. I will discuss the implications of this fact later.

Defining Consumer Protection

Government intervention in the economy is so widespread that it cannot be fit into a single category. The problem is to decide which sorts of government actions should be counted as consumer protection. Because everyone is a consumer, anything the government does affects consumers. Even if we limit ourselves to policies that affect consumers as consumers—that is, actions that directly affect consumption—the possibilities are still extensive. Tax policies clearly affect consumers, and so do agricultural, energy, and banking policies. Foreign policy is no exception. The sale of wheat to the Soviet Union in 1972–73 was primarily motivated by international political considerations. Yet it was so massive that it helped create rising prices and actual shortages in the United States. In the case of energy, it is obvious that any policy changes will have an effect on consumers.

It should be clear, then, that the field of consumer affairs, policies that directly affect consumers and consumption, is much broader than consumer protection.* Can any limits be set for investigating these questions? The easiest way is to reemploy the concept of countervailing power. We only need ask this question: Does a particular policy tend to sustain consumers in the marketplace by helping them to cope with its size and complexity? The policies that qualify under this rule are those that bring to the consumer the advantages that other groups in the economy enjoy.

In this regard, there is no question about the recent development of specific consumer protection legislation. Such things as safety standards, turth-in-lending laws, and prohibition of misleading advertising clearly meet this requirement. Similarly, the activities of independent regulatory agencies qualify as consumer protection. These agencies are specifically charged with maintaining the public interest in the operation of particular industries, and, in historical terms, are among the most important forms of consumer protection.

Consumer protection takes other, less obvious forms too. Antitrust legislation is one notable example. Here the effect on the consumer is less direct, but no less important. The government, by curbing monopoly elements in business, attempts to promote competition.

---

* Even this does not exhaust all possibilities. Governments also supply goods and services to consumers—police protection, roads, education, and the like. The next chapter analyzes these problems.

This in turn should benefit the consumer through lower prices and increased business responsiveness to consumer needs.

In the United States, these responsibilities are divided among various governmental units. Under the structure of the American government, which in lofty prose is described as the American federal system, citizens are affected by various levels of government. There is a tendency to think of the federal government as *the* government, but from the consumer's point of view, developments at the state or local level may be equally important.

The Regulatory Complex

Independent Regulatory Agencies

Any discussion of consumer protection in the United States must focus on the various independent regulatory agencies within the federal government. These agencies represent a uniquely American response to the problems of the consumer in a modern economy (there are no comparable agencies in other Western democracies). As the name implies, the *regulatory* agencies are charged with regulating various aspects of economic activity. They are given responsibility in areas where it is felt that market forces would be inadequate to ensure competition and protect the consumer. It is the word *independent*, however, that is the most distinctive feature of the regulatory agencies. Commissioners on the various agencies are appointed by the president and must be approved by the Senate, but, once they are in office, they serve terms of from five to seven years and cannot be removed unless they are guilty of an impeachable offense.* Thus, while the agencies are a part of the executive branch, they are not under the president's direct control. The idea was to remove the agencies from politics and insulate them from routine political pressures.

The first independent regulatory agency (the Interstate Commerce Commission, ICC) was created about a century ago (1879); most of the other agencies were created as an outgrowth of the reform movement that swept government early in this century [35, Chaps. 12 and 14]. The agencies fall into either of two general categories. The first

---

* This means that if the president doesn't like the course an agency is taking, there isn't much he can do except to wait until a vacancy occurs and appoint a new commissioner. It also means that when a new president takes office, he must live for a time (perhaps his entire term) with appointees from the previous administration.

deals with public utilities in the broad sense, such as transportation (the ICC or the Federal Aviation Authority, FAA) and communications (Federal Communications Commission, FCC).* Firms in these areas are granted what amounts to limited monopolies under the condition that they accept regulation. The second type operates within the private sector, overseeing general business practices or specific aspects of operations in key industries. These agencies, like the Federal Trade Commission (FTC), Consumer Product Safety Commission (CPSC) and the Food and Drug Administration (FDA), are more closely associated with consumer protection.

You should recognize that the logic for regulation recalls our earlier discussion of credence goods [33, pp. 90–93]. The individual consumer cannot be expected to judge the safety or value of a drug or an airplane. Thus, the government, through the regulatory agencies, assumes the information cost for the consumer. If a drug is approved by the FDA, the consumer can buy it with the knowledge that tests have shown the product to be both safe and effective.† In such cases, the agencies function in areas where consumers cannot be given the information they need to protect themselves.

Historians disagree in their interpretation of the regulatory agencies. Some feel that the agencies represent an ingenious method for dealing with the problems of a complex economy [19]. Others maintain that the agencies are (and were created to be) agents of the very industries they supposedly regulate, promoting stability in the industry and generally serving the interests of business [22]. Whichever view is correct, the agencies are a fact of American life and all consumers have (literally) a life-and-death interest in the manner in which the agencies perform.

Evaluating Regulation I: Performance

While it is often said that people are known by the company they keep, the company they do not keep may be a better basis for judgment. If you know who a person's enemies are, you know a lot about the person. If regulatory agencies are judged on that basis, their list of enemies is impressive indeed. They have succeeded in bringing together in opposition individuals who otherwise have very little in common. They have, for example, provoked hostility from Ralph Nader, the action-interventionist, and Milton Friedman, the leading

---

* In 1978, a bill was introduced in Congress that would in essence abolish the FCC and transform the present licensing system for broadcasters.

† Similar functions (such as meat grading by the Department of Agriculture) are carried out by other executive departments; they are not independent regulatory agencies.

advocate of free markets. The prescriptions differ in that Mr. Nader would strengthen and regenerate the agencies, while Dr. Friedman would abolish them, but both agree that such agencies are not now serving the public as they should. Groups like the American Bar Association and Consumers Union have expressed similar reservations.

Detailing all the complaints against all the agencies would require volumes in itself. There is a common pattern to such complaints, however, so problems may be identified by looking at selected agencies. While the specifics may differ, the overall situation does not change much from agency to agency. Indeed, only a cursory review is needed to conclude that there is a consensus among observers that the regulatory agencies simply are not doing their job. The American Bar Association, for example, concluded after an investigation of the Federal Trade Commission that it suffered from a "serious misallocation of resources and a confusion of priorities." To solve this problem, the report suggested that the FTC should

> set up its own apparatus to define and to keep current a unified plan in the consumer area. Past efforts to do this have produced no effective results. The primary requisite for planning is adequate information about what consumer problems are. . . . [2, p. 54]

To appreciate those comments, you have to remember that the FTC has been in operation for well over 50 years.

The same picture emerges if we look at the Food and Drug Administration, which, because of its broad powers in the inspection of food and the regulation of drugs, is among the most important of all the agencies to the consumer. It is a very telling commentary that when the FDA forces a drug off the market—because it is either unsafe or worthless—the news makes the front pages. If firemen do *not* put out fires or postmen do *not* deliver the mail, it makes news; with the FDA, it is the other way around. The agency is merely doing its job, but that fact alone is newsworthy. The problem is typical of many other agencies; that is, its performance is uneven. The typical pattern has been for an agency to get an energetic new director and to vigorously carry out its responsibilities. This burst of activity is seldom sustained. Because of personnel changes, lack of resources, or political pressure, the agency lapses again into inactivity.

Part of the problem can be traced to the institutional framework of regulation. While the various commissions have professional staffs, commissioners themselves are usually not professionals; they are lawyers, politicians, or industry experts who are appointed for a specific term. Since reappointment is uncertain, a short-run perspective is encouraged. This in turn leads to what one analyst calls a "minimum squawk" strategy, in which various interests are balanced in an effort to avoid upsetting anyone. The particular strategy that any commission follows depends on how it perceives its responsibilities and who it thinks its clients are. That point is particularly important because agencies often behave as if their first responsibility were to the industries they are supposed to regulate instead of to the public. In what seems to be a switch of roles, the commissions become spokespersons for the industries.

Some would argue that the agencies have simply been bought off, and there have been instances when that has happened. Out-and-out graft, however, is an inadequate explanation; the situation is more complex. It arises from the complex and technical job that the agencies must perform. Suppose the telephone company requests an increase in rates; the request will be accompanied by a battery of supporting documents covering technical and financial questions. Since the telephone company has an obvious interest in the case, it will be able to focus all of its considerable resources on seeing that the request is approved. The regulatory commissions are rather small, after all, so that the commission members are the focal point of intense lobbying. Even if the commissioners are fair minded and honest, most of the information they receive will come from the company.

The complexity, and the consequences, of these issues are illustrated by the crash of a DC-10 near Paris in 1974. The crash, which remains the worst single plane disaster in the history of commercial aviation, killed 346 people. The disaster was caused by a faulty cargo door. Those familiar with the DC-10, including the Federal Aviation Authority, had known of the problem with the door for at least two years, when a similar incident had happened near Detroit, but a crash was averted [32, p. 1]. The FAA had ordered all DC-10s grounded until the necessary improvements were made, but carriers and producers protested that such a procedure would be too expensive. The FAA then revised its directive and allowed the airlines to correct the defect as a part of routine maintenance, but required that explicit instructions for fastening the door be printed on the inside of the door* [32, pp. 7–10].

That seemed like a reasonable compromise, but DC-10s were used worldwide. The plane that crashed outside of Paris was leased to a Turkish airline and the attendant could not read English (rendering the warning and instructions on the door useless). The result was disaster. To date, over $65 million in claims have been paid by McDonnell-Douglas, General Dynamics (which supplied the door), Turkish Airlines, and the U.S. Government [16, p. 1].

---

* The door itself was not defective and was safe when closed properly.

Did the FAA succumb to industry pressure? In retrospect, it is easy to say that the planes should have been grounded. However, if there had been no crash, the agency's interim solution might have been hailed as a reasonable means to accommodate conflicting interests. In fact, if there had been no crash, the public would never have known about the cargo-door problem; it would have been filed away along with numerous other routine decisions.

Evidence from investigations after the crash suggests that the FAA went out of its way to be accommodating to the industry [32]. However, the point of this example is not to berate the FAA; rather it is to point out the complexities of the problem. The case illustrates the difficulties regulatory agencies have in balancing consumer and business interests. In the DC 10 case, it took a disaster to bring those difficulties to light; consumers must be concerned about the many daily cases that aren't publicized but involve potentially important issues.

Outright conflict of interest may not be involved, but there are natural ties between the regulatory agencies and industry. Staff members of each are likely to have similar backgrounds, read similar trade publications, and deal with similar problems. In short, they speak the same language, and this is bound to carry over even when they are in adversary positions. This is all the more true because movement between the agencies and industry is common, so each is likely to be, or have been, in the other's position.* This is something of a problem. Promising staff members of a regulatory agency may be hired away by the industry to a job with a much more attractive salary. Thus, it is difficult for the agency to keep its most qualified people. This practice may also affect the direction the agency takes. One expert noted:

> Since employment in the regulated industry is one of the most obvious opportunities after a regulator's term in office, alienating members of the regulated industry may prove very costly.... Some regulators may behave without regard to this consideration.... Most regulators in ordinary consideration of self-interest, however, must be expected to weigh this calculation heavily. [18, p. 48]

The problem of inadequate resources was dramatically demonstrated a few years ago when the Federal Communications Com-

---

* This movement between industry and government is sometimes called the "revolving door." President Carter attempted to deal with the problem by asking high-ranking appointees not to take jobs in industries they regulated for two years after their government service. Such restraints, however, might make it difficult for government to attract highly qualified individuals.

mission announced that it was dropping its investigation of the American Telephone and Telegraph Company. The company was so big that the commission simply did not have the resources to carry off such an investigation. There was a touch of pathos in the Department of Defense's offer (eventually rejected), to lend the FCC some cost accountants so that they might continue the probe.

This discussion has centered on the consumer interest, with little to say about the consumer. Suppose now that consumers are moved to action by the proposed increase in telephone rates. That in itself is quite a supposition, for while consumers may be annoyed by the increase, it will still amount to only a small fraction of their total budgets. Thus, while the telephone company has a clear view of its own self-interest, it is much less likely that the consumer will. If consumers pursue the case, they are immediately confronted by the complex legal and administrative structure of the regulatory system. Next, they must master a tangle of administrative decisions and court rulings full of unfamiliar phrases like *rate base* and *fair rate of return*. All of this requires time, money, and effort beyond the capabilities of most individuals. It is beyond the capabilities of most consumer groups too. If the FCC could not take on AT&T, it is unlikely that a consumer group can. As a result, the consumer's influence is likely to be small. The combination of plural interests and information costs is difficult to overcome. Traditionally this has meant that the *public interest* is whatever the regulators say it is. They may keep the faith, but every pressure on them is pushing in the other direction.

Most of what has been said thus far applies to federal regulation. Regulation, however, goes on at the state and local level also, where the problems are even more severe. Regulation must be carried out with even fewer resources than at the federal level. This is a genuine concern to consumers because many key industries are regulated at the state level.* Public utilities, for example, are generally regulated within the states they serve. The same is true of insurance companies, resulting in particularly weak regulation of that industry. When the Pennsylvania Insurance Department assumed a more activist position, an uproar resulted. In Iowa, the Commerce Commission has recently been revitalized and despite minimal resources, works actively in support of the public. Over its first five years, however, the commission prosecuted just one case.

Regulation at the local level is even more of a problem. There is often no professional body to carry on the regulatory function, so it

* At the state level, members of regulatory bodies are sometimes elected.

falls to the city council. That such groups are not equipped to deal with the problem goes without saying. Yet local transportation companies (like taxis) are usually regulated in this way. At present, cable television is also regulated at the local level. Given the potential for growth in that industry, the consumer interest could be endangered.

At this point, it is logical to ask: How does the uneven performance of regulators affect the public confidence in the regulatory system? It is probable that the typical consumer is unaware of the activities of most regulatory agencies. However, the periodic controversies that do make the news can hardly inspire confidence. A decline in public confidence certainly would contribute to the overall reaction against consumer protection. If existing regulation is perceived as ineffective, consumers are bound to question the value of additional protection.

Evaluating Regulation II: Issues

The performance of regulatory agencies raises serious questions, but there are other issues relating to regulation that are equally important and possibly more disturbing. The most significant of these is the possibility that problems arise even when the agencies do what they're supposed to. The problems in this case are less with the agencies themselves than with the basic structure of the regulations they administer. There is evidence that regulations that have been enacted to protect consumers actually have a negative effect on consumers' interests. This possibility has been recognized for some time. In the case of transportation, for example, there have been lingering doubts about the impact of regulations setting freight rates and passenger fares.

Regulation spares the carriers the dangers of possibly harmful competition. Anyone who remembers gasoline price wars knows what competitive price cutting can do. Rate regulation makes that nearly impossible in transportation.* Furthermore, by guaranteeing the carrier its routes and limiting the number of competitors, regulation secures the fiefdom of each firm. Similarly, the government defines what constitutes unfair business practices (through the FTC). A limit on business practices can easily be extended into a limit on competition. If a few firms dominate an industry, there is always a

---

* During the Ford administration, the president proposed a degree of deregulation of freight rates for interstate trucking. Allowing more competition among carriers was intended to lift some of the burden of regulation from the industry. The proposals were rejected by the industry.

tension between the good of the industry as a whole and the good of the individual firms. The latter is likely to win out, even if there is a gentlemen's agreement among producers. Thus, regulation serves to keep potentially maverick firms in line.

The mavericks, however, have a way of breaking out, as recent developments in the airline industry illustrate. Laker Airlines' (a British firm) no frills trans-Atlantic service cut the cost of the London-New York flight by one-half [26]. Public pressure forced acceptance of the lower fare in this country. The lower fare then set off a round of rate reductions among regularly scheduled lines. Note that it was a relatively small firm that chose to buck the system; the major carriers had more to gain by the status quo and thus opposed change. The lower rates represent a significant savings to consumers; put differently, one could say that regulation resulted in significant overpayments by consumers.

Recent developments in other areas have raised additional questions about the impact of regulation. One of the most important cases involves the Food and Drug Administration. Since 1962, all new prescription drugs have had to undergo extensive testing to ensure that they were effective before they could be sold. The 1962 amendments complemented earlier FDA regulations that required drugs to be tested for safety; efficacy testing is intended to keep ineffective (as opposed to unsafe) drugs off the market and was greeted as a major victory for consumer interests [34, pp. 574–77]. Efficacy testing, however, is expensive and time consuming. After 1962, the average time involved in introducing a new drug rose to over four years and the number of new drugs introduced dropped sharply [30, Chap. 1]. To some this suggested that ineffective drugs were in fact being kept off the market (or weren't being developed). Others, however, felt that the development of potentially beneficial drugs was being impeded and that the public suffered because the introduction of such drugs was delayed [30]. Evidence was provided that supported the latter argument, but the procedures involved were complex and the issue remained unresolved.

In 1977, however, the issue attracted widespread attention when Abbott Laboratories applied for a license to market Valproate (valproic acid), a drug for the treatment of epilepsy. The drug, which was being sold in Great Britain, represented the only known treatment for certain types of epilepsy. However, the FDA ruled that the formal requirements for efficacy testing had not been met and the drug could not be introduced. This produced an outcry from epileptics, the affluent of whom were already going abroad for treatment.

Public reaction forced the FDA to reconsider, or rather to seek new evidence. Such evidence was found, and in early 1978 the drug was made available on an interim basis [10, p. 23]. A spokesperson for the FDA indicated that "new drugs are not approved by referendum—even medical referendum," but it is clear that public pressure forced the agency to reevaluate its procedures [10, p. 23]. The thought that individuals were suffering needlessly turned opinion against the agency. The paradox, of course, is that the agency was merely enforcing regulations that were enacted to protect consumers.

The Valproate case illustrates the complexities of such situations. The alternatives are equally unappealing; are we to support needless suffering or ineffective drugs? A rule of reason suggests that both be rejected in favor of some middle ground. However, that middle ground may be difficult to find, especially when the issue becomes emotionally charged. That is what happened in the case of Laetrile, a reputed cancer remedy.

At this time, there is no scientific evidence to support the effectiveness of Laetrile (although there is evidence that it can be dangerous) [23]. Therefore, the FDA has not approved the drug and has attempted to stop its (illegal) production and distribution. An objective reading of the facts in this case supports the FDA, but objectivity isn't a characteristic of the debate. Patients suffering from cancer are understandably anxious to find a cure; their pressure has forced several state legislatures to legalize Laetrile, actions that raise questions of jurisdiction between federal and state authorities. In 1978, the FDA agreed to initiate more extensive tests of the drug. There was no new medical evidence to suggest that Laetrile was effective, but there was an obvious need to defuse the issue. That is where the issue stands at this writing. *Consumer Reports* maintained that approval of Laetrile would "open the door to the legitimization of quackery" by devastating "the carefully structured consumer-protection drug laws enacted in modern times" [23]. Approval would raise the possibility that any group with enough political clout could force the acceptance of a remedy.

However, when the Valproate and Laetrile cases are considered together, certain questions are raised about those "carefully structured" regulations. The effectiveness of regulation finally hinges on public trust. Anything which undermines that trust will make it more difficult for the agency to function. If an agency's credibility suffers because of what are perceived as overly restrictive regulations, consumers suffer a double loss; they lose because of the restrictiveness of the rules (as with Valproate), but they also lose because effective protection will be more difficult to provide when it is really needed (as appears to be the case with Laetrile).

The Question of Standards

Before we can draw further implications from these discussions, we need to consider the questions raised in the preceding section in terms of the broader issue of product standards. When the Food and Drug Administration tests for safety, it is setting a standard; by defining the word *safe,* the FDA decides which drugs are sold. The question: How safe is *safe?* in essence asks how demanding the standard should be. Standards are so widespread in the economy that they qualify as one of the most common forms of consumer protection.

A standard is simply a minimum level of acceptable quality, which is meant to guarantee the consumer that the product meets specific requirements for safety, performance, or cleanliness. Licensing represents a closely allied concept; in that case, individuals who practice a particular trade are certified as meeting minimal levels of competence.* Both standards and licensing may be encountered at all levels of government (licensing is most common at the state level); the regulatory agencies have the responsibility for implementing many federal standards. In some cases, private groups are involved, as in the licensing of medical doctors, lawyers, and, to a lesser extent, teachers. In these instances, private professional bodies and state licensing agencies cooperate in certifying members of the profession.

Within the federal government, most regulatory agencies and many executive departments set standards. Examples include standards for meat grading (Department of Agriculture), pollution standards (Environmental Protection Agency) and safety standards for nuclear energy (Department of Energy). However, the Consumer Product Safety Commission—as its name implies—has the primary responsibility for setting standards on consumer products. The CPSC is also charged with enforcement of existing safety programs (such as toy safety) [12, pp. 73–75].

The central problem in establishing standards (or licensing requirements) is the level at which the standard is to be set. That is essentially a problem of determining the *level of acceptable risk.* If the standard is set higher, the product will be safer and the risk to the consumer will be lowered. Most people are not going to come out in favor of risky products, which means that the natural tendency is to say that the higher the standard the better. There are, however, some drawbacks associated with that stance; the benefits of standards to consumers must be weighed against the costs.

---

* The most common example being a driver's license. If you are a licensed driver, it means you have met minimal requirements of knowledge and skill. Note that there are still a lot of bad drivers.

The costs of standards to consumers take a variety of forms, the most obvious of which is dollar cost. Standards are expensive to develop and implement and thus tend to raise product prices. Less expensive varieties of the product may be driven from the market.* The price increase will hit lower-income groups the hardest because the less expensive products they might otherwise buy will not be available.

Standards also may tend to limit competition or promote monopoly elements in industry. That fact may not be obvious, but remember, standards cost money to implement. Smaller firms may not be able to meet the cost of equipment required. In that case, the larger firms benefit and secure a stronger hold on the industry; in the long run, that works against the consumer's interests. There is evidence that standards have been used in this way [22]. Costs to consumers are very similar in the case of occupational licensure.

So many different kinds of standards are in force today, that it is difficult to prove an overall evaluation. In the case of local building codes, standards may stifle innovation. On-site inspection of wiring is one example. On-site inspection makes sense if the wiring itself is done on the site, but with new developments in preconstructed, modular housing, the wiring is done in the factory. If the wiring has to be torn out and inspected again, the cost savings of factory production are lost. Yet that is what has happened in many places, contributing to spiraling housing costs.

At the federal level, results are mixed, although it is only recently that efforts have been made to determine the impact of standards in cost-benefit terms.† In those terms, the children's sleepwear flammability standard mentioned earlier proves cost efficient, in that the savings from injuries averted are greater than the costs of the standard to the consumer (but the possibility of cancer from the flame retardant was not included in the analysis) [7]. In the case of automobile safety, however, Sam Peltzman maintains that standards have been ineffective. He questions whether standards have been responsible for lowering fatalities and suggests that vehicle-related safety efforts may have contributed to rising numbers of pedestrian accidents [29].

* A new federal standard for power lawnmowers, for example, requires that a clutch be used to engage the blade (so the blade won't be moving when the mower is stopped). This feature is available on most brands now, but only on the most expensive models. When the blade clutch is mandated, the less expensive, simpler models won't be available and the price of power mowers will rise.

† Cost-benefit analysis attempts to put a dollar value on both the cost of a program and the benefits which should result. The two figures are then compared to see if the benefits of the program outweigh the cost. See [6].

In the case of occupational licensure, the problems are similar. The critical question in this case is: Who does the licensing? If the profession licenses its own members, there will be a natural tendency to try and limit entry, which gives a degree of monopoly power to those in the profession and secures their control over price and output. Even if a state board is responsible for licensing, there will still be a problem because such boards are filled with appointees from the profession. The American Medical Association has come under repeated attack for limiting entry into the profession [13, pp. 137–60].

As malpractice suits indicate, licensing is no final guarantee of quality. However, consumer's interests may be damaged even if quality is maintained. Despite problem areas, the average level of medical care in the United States is high; this does not mean that Americans necessarily receive high quality care. Medical services are so expensive, that many individuals either don't seek help or resort to dangerous self-care. New evidence in other professions suggests that higher standards for licensing may reduce the quality of services actually received (because consumers can't afford the service). In states with higher standards for electricians, for example, the number of injuries from electrical accidents is higher; consumers try to do it themselves rather than pay a high-priced electrician and the result is injury [20, p. 127].

In what seems to be a paradox, it appears that in these cases *lower quality* services would benefit consumers. It is not a matter of advocating inferior quality, but rather of *ensuring that quality matches the needs of the consumer.* You don't need a highly trained surgeon to give you a good physical any more than you need an electrical engineer to rewire the circuit breakers in your home. To take a more specific case, midwives can handle most of the problems associated with routine pregnancies; midwives are trained professionals, but are less expensive than medical doctors. In many states, however, midwives are prohibited from practicing unless supervised by a doctor.

Licensure, then, may result in overqualified practitioners; put differently, this means that lower-priced alternatives are not available. If you were buying a pair of slacks, you wouldn't necessarily buy the most expensive ones available. In some cases (such as yard work), the expensive slacks might not fit your needs at all; a cheap, but serviceable pair would be much better. In the case of licensed services, however, you don't have that choice. You are forced to buy the most expensive variety.

In the case of both licensure and standards, the heart of the question is the *level of risk the consumer should be allowed to accept.*

As discussed in Chapter 4, some consumers are willing to assume more risks than others. However, giving individuals a choice about how much risk to accept requires that the persons know what the true risk is and understand the implications. In the case of consumer products, individuals may not even be aware of the risks involved. Furthermore, many risks fall into the low-probability, high-injury category. That is, the chance of the event happening is slight, but if it happens, the damage will be great (burns involving children's sleepwear fall into this category).

These circumstances help explain why consumers so often resist actions that are supposedly taken for their own good. They simply don't see it that way. To consumers, the benefits seem remote, but the costs are real; therefore it is the costs that attract attention and generate discontent. The "leave-me-alone" syndrome reflects this discontent. Many consumers feel that standards have become intrusive. These individuals are expressing a desire to make their own choices. If those desires are taken lightly and criticisms are not dealt with, the entire structure of consumer protection could be threatened.

The obvious need is to reevaluate the present structure. Given the credence qualities involved in most of these cases, it would be impossible to do away with standards and licensure. Providing more information would not itself be a viable alternative. However, additional information in conjunction with a more flexible system of standards does hold some promise. In the case of professional services, less expensive alternatives can be fostered. I noted the example of midwives, but possibilities for paramedical services exist in other areas of medicine as well. In such cases, more information would be needed to ensure that consumers know which level of service is appropriate for them.

Where products are concerned, the range of choice could be expanded in a similar fashion. Dangerous products could still be banned, while other products could be graded according to the level of risk. A simple, uniform grading system would be easy for consumers to learn. High-risk products could be in category III, intermediate risk in II, and low risk in I (with color coding to match: red, yellow, and green). These distinctions may seem arbitrary, but they would expand the range of consumer choice over the present system, which divides all products and services into only two categories: safe and unsafe. Whether this approach or some alternative is used, the important point is that the present system be reassessed. It is hardly an exaggeration to say that one of the most pressing problems in consumer protection is the consumer protection system itself.

Other Federal Protection

The "Agency for Consumer Protection"

The federal government is involved in such a range of consumer protection activities that there are obvious difficulties in coordinating them all. Remember too that the information programs discussed in Chapter 5 should be considered as part of consumer protection. Given this diversity, it's not surprising that problems arise. One agency may seek new safety standards on automobiles, for example, while another tries to promote energy savings through better gasoline mileage. If the safer car is heavier, the two goals conflict.

The need for coordination and the need to ensure that existing agencies are actually looking out for consumers' interests suggests that some agency should have specific responsibility for consumer protection at the federal level. If responsibility is scattered, it is hard to know who is accountable. At present, there is a Consumers Affairs Office within the president's staff and a consumer office in the Department of Health, Education and Welfare. To bring the various functions together, there have been various suggestions for either a cabinet-level Department of Consumer Affairs or an independent agency with that title. The former was first suggested by the late Senator Estes Kefauver over twenty years ago. Many states have departments of consumer affairs, and at that level they have proven their effectiveness. At the federal level, however, consumer protection responsibilities are so spread out that to bring the functions together in one agency would require a major governmental reorganization.

Because of these difficulties, recent efforts to promote an Agency for Consumer Protection within the federal government have taken a slightly different approach. Rather than create a superagency or add yet another department to the bureaucracy, the idea was to create a sort of watch-dog agency that would have the responsibility of ensuring that other agencies were carrying out their responsibilities to the consumer. In the words of the 1975 bill proposing such an agency, the agency would "represent the interests of consumers before Federal agencies and courts . . ." [9, Sec. 5(b)1]. The idea is similar to the ombudsman concept (see Chapter 9); the office would represent consumers rather than protecting consumers directly.

To date, the story of the Agency for Consumer Protection can be summarized as a series of near misses. In 1972, Congress was on the verge of passing such legislation, but ran out of time. Later, the bill was actually passed by both houses of Congress, but was vetoed by then President Nixon. A threatened veto by President Ford killed a later bill when supporters felt there were not enough votes to override the veto. References to *the bill* are somewhat misleading; there were actually a series of bills.* Each time the issue was brought up, it took a slightly different form. The earlier versions were generally stronger than the later ones. President Carter's support for a consumer protection agency encouraged proponents of the measure, but that support was not enough to get the bill through Congress; Congressional support for the idea had eroded and, in early 1978, the bill failed to clear the Congress. The future of the proposal is unclear now, but no further action seems likely for some time [1].

When President Ford vetoed the consumer protection bill, he offered an alternative approach. Instead of having a single office responsible for looking after consumers' interests, he proposed that each department have its own consumer representation plan [5]. Each department or agency would have an internal unit to look out for the consumer. The proposal was enacted, although it didn't excite particular interest. Having a consumer unit within each department seemed wasteful (and in some cases—such as the State Department —of limited value). Furthermore, overall coordination was still lacking.

To some observers, the erosion of Congressional support for the Agency for Consumer Protection showed a diminished interest in consumer issues. Others attributed the bill's defeat to the watered-down state of the bill and the effectiveness of the business lobby against it. In terms of what has been said in the previous sections, the lack of support for the proposal shows the need for reevaluation of the entire federal approach to consumer protection. If there weren't doubts about what is being done now, there would be less reluctance about doing more. Reform of the existing structure and the creation of an effective agency for consumer protection would seem to be logical, and perhaps even necessary, complements.

Antitrust as Consumer Protection

As I have noted several times, consumers are better able to look after their own interests in a more competitive marketplace. Thus, to the extent that competition can be strengthened, the consumer's position should be correspondingly stronger. At about the same time that America developed its penchant for creating independent regulatory agencies, it also began to face the problem of concentrated

---

* The name of the proposed agency also changed. It was sometimes known as the Agency for Consumer Advocacy or the Consumer Protection Agency [12, pp. 272–75].

economic power. The development of monopolies or trusts concentrated vast amounts of power in the hands of a few firms. It is natural that reformers should have focused on combating these developments. From the consumer's point of view, the problems involved in antitrust are similar to those related to regulation. Like regulation, antitrust is complex and, if anything, even more legalistic. Plural interests and information costs again combine to reduce the consumer's effectiveness. Thus, if the consumer's interests are to be safeguarded, political pressure is required to ensure that the law is vigorously enforced.

Since consumers' strategies are essentially the same in both cases, the analysis of antitrust can be developed quite briefly. Every introductory economics textbook contains a section on the evils of monopoly. Given the firm's goals and cost structure, it can be demonstrated that monopoly results in higher prices and lower output, hardly a solution that consumers are likely to favor. This provides the basic rationale for antitrust activities. If monopoly is bad, then fighting it is good. The situation is not really quite that simple, however. Pure monopoly—one firm in an industry—is relatively rare in industry. Thus, it is necessary to speak of monopoly elements or actions in restraint of trade. The courts decided rather early that bigness was not the same as badness, so that a firm could not be considered a monopoly just because it was large. Thus, General Motors survives with over half of American automobile production despite repeated antitrust threats.

Antitrust efforts begin with the Sherman Antitrust Act of 1890. The act makes "contract, combination, or conspiracy in restraint of trade" illegal, and further stipulates that efforts to monopolize trade are also illegal [36, pp. 54–55]. A law is useless unless it is enforced, and the Sherman Act was not vigorously enforced for over a decade. Even then it proved inadequate, and monopoly power continued to accumulate. In response to public pressure, the Clayton Act was passed in 1914; it forbade unfair pricing practices, restrictive contracts, and noncompetitive mergers. Along with the Federal Trade Commission, which is charged with enforcement, these acts remain the foundation for American antitrust activities.

A distinction is necessary between the general effect of monopoly and specific instances of monopolistic behavior. The latter is much more clear-cut. If two firms in an industry get together and set prices or rig contract bids, that is clearly "in restraint of trade," and the consumer suffers. Such was the case when General Electric and Westinghouse conspired to set prices on electrical goods in the 1960s and when big oil companies later rigged asphalt bids on public contracts.

The general effect of monopoly cannot be dealt with in simple terms. The automobile industry is an example. That industry is obviously concentrated; there are four domestic producers, one of which (American Motors) is very small. General Motors clearly dominates the industry. Its Chevrolet Division, for example, typically accounts for more sales than any of the other three companies. Is the consumer hurt by this concentration? To answer that, it is necessary to remember that the companies, because of their size, not only control price but also can dictate to the consumer (in the short run) what sorts of automobiles will be produced. Detroit at first failed to respond to pressures for smaller cars. Significantly, only American Motors made serious moves in that direction, a policy that paid off as demand for small cars continued to rise. Furthermore, the industry's record of innovation is much better with frills than with substantive improvements. Safety features were not incorporated until federal pressure was applied. Similarly, foreign producers took the lead in such innovations as safer body construction, dual braking systems, cleaner engines, and other minor yet very helpful touches like rear-window defrosters.

This, remember, is only one example. Others might be drawn from any other big manufacturing industry. The problem is that the policy implications of all of this are not clear. Bringing about increased competition in the automobile industry is easier said then done. Because of capital requirements and economies of scale, it is impossible to return to the large number of small companies that characterized the industry in its earlier days. Furthermore, the courts have tended to make good conduct the most important criterion in antitrust deliberations.* The structure of the industry and the number and size of the firms have received much less attention. The conduct of an industry is obviously important to consumers, but so too is structure. It is structure that finally relates to consumer power, for with a larger number of smaller firms, consumer leverage will be increased. Thus, antitrust is not always enforced in the manner best calculated to serve consumer interests.†

There is a final point that should be made about the underlying assumptions of antitrust. It is assumed that competition is healthful and should therefore be encouraged. Some observers feel that such efforts run counter to the realities of the situation. They maintain

---

* Except under Section 7 of the Clayton Act. I am indebted to David H. Ciscel for these points.

† A major antitrust suit was launched recently against AT&T. A number of issues are involved, the most prominent being AT&T's control of long-distance hookups. If the government wins its case, consumers might benefit from lower rates, but their leverage with the phone company won't be increased.

that economic concentration is a fact of modern economic life and that efforts to restore competition are likely to be ineffective. Facing large corporations realistically means accepting them for what they are. Galbraith and others who advocate this point of view would not, however, suggest that the economic giants be given free rein. They argue that the public should come to grips with the large companies and control them. The word *control* is used here in a more general sense than it has hitherto been used. It means that the public should be represented in the operation of these firms, which is a more active concept than regulation.

Those who feel that this violates the principles of the market system should take a close look at how things work now. It is argued that large parts of the economy are characterized by a private planning system rather than markets. Since firms plan their own output, profits, and so on, the system obviously works to their advantage. Dealing with this reality requires bringing this planning system under public control and directing it in the public interest [15]. Such efforts might require developing new economic forms. This development would be consistent with the continual evolution of economic organization, which never fits easily into static categories. It is necessary for consumers to acknowledge this evolution; indeed, their self-interest demands it. With that recognition goes the ability to treat problems in a straightforward way, seeking the best solution possible. Again, consumer awareness emerges as the prerequisite for effective action. As we have suggested, consumers can mobilize support for their position, but only if they are aware of what is involved and organized to press their point of view. They may want to search for new solutions or to increase pressure on the Antitrust Division of the Justice Department for more vigorous prosecution under existing laws. Neither alternative is viable in the absence of awareness.

Patterns of Consumer Protection

An Overview of Protection

The modern history of government efforts to protect consumers began after the Civil War. The federal government passed the first specific consumer protection legislation over a century ago with the Mail Fraud Act of 1872. That ought to suggest the effectiveness of such legislation, since mail fraud remains a serious problem today. Early consumer protection can be summarized quickly; there wasn't much. In the sixty-five years that followed the enactment of the first legislation, only two new federal laws were passed. Both were important and remain the cornerstones of an effective consumer policy; they are the Pure Food and Drug Act of 1906 and the Federal Trade Commission Act of 1914. In their initial forms, however, both suffered critical weaknesses. It was not until 1938 that the FTC was provided the authority to prosecute deceptive advertising in the consumer interest. In that same year, the power of the Food and Drug Administration was extended to cover cosmetics and to require that drugs be proved safe before they could be sold.

Since 1960, a variety of new consumer protection bills has been enacted (see below). Thus, despite its long history, wide-ranging consumer protection is a relatively recent development. This fits well with the general analytical pattern we have laid down, which maintains that consumer problems are a function of the sophistication and development of the economy. It was not until the economy reached this relatively high level that the problems could or would emerge as significant concerns.

The accelerated pace of consumer protection legislation did not represent a clean breakthrough. The legislative pattern is full of cutbacks and changes. The ultimate goal seems vague and only dimly understood. Legislation covers the safety of children, boats, toys, automobiles, and pipelines. Additional legislation ranges over problems in food quality (an effort begun six decades earlier), lending controls, packaging and labeling and drug quality, to touch on only the less esoteric efforts. These are, by and large, significant issues, though some are less pressing than others.* It is their very diversity, however, that is significant, for it underscores the *lack of a coordinated policy.* Recent consumer protection legislation has been specific instead of attacking the problem as a whole. While this has brought about some genuine improvements in the consumer's position, the effort has been a hit-or-miss affair.

There are so many problems that Congress could spend all of its time passing laws to cover them and still not keep up. Dealing with specifics is a never-ending process. What is needed is a systematic program that would deal with fundamentals. The random approach means not only that important problems may be missed but that it will be more difficult to maintain momentum and direction. This failure to develop a systematic approach can be explained by our earlier analysis. Effective protection will be forthcoming only when public pressure is organized and directed. Pressure has not been lacking, but, until very recently, it has not been sustained. Issues crop up, often in response to some disaster, that attract attention and

---

* Boat safety, for example, is important, but how many consumers does it affect? Ghetto residents are hardly likely to give it very high priority.

result in pressure for legislative action. Thus, much legislation is the result of short-run influences and chance developments. When these pressures have passed, they leave their legislative remains much as a seashell is left after the animal inhabiting it dies.

This problem is complicated by the fact that something is not always better than nothing. The laws passed to deal with these problems are often less than adequate and sometimes even harmful themselves. The hurried nature of the effort works against thoughtful consideration of the problem. The result is an improvisation that, while it may not provide adequate shelter, is sufficient to reduce public pressure and hence the probability of more meaningful reform. Sustained pressure is necessary to bring about a comprehensive program to deal with consumer problems. *Sustained* is the key word; periodic outbursts of activity must be integrated and maintained over time. That is no easy task, but there is evidence that things may be moving in that direction. The full impact of consumers' efforts has yet to be felt, but important changes have been made already at all levels of government.

It is difficult to summarize these changes because they cover such a wide range of developments. To the student of consumer affairs, this is a happy problem, as it reflects the strength and vitality of the response to consumer problems. This response reflects rising consumer consciousness, which is necessary before substantive improvement can be expected. Many of the developments are concentrated at the state and local level. The federal system has its drawbacks, often representing duplication of effort and inadequate protection; at the same time, it has advantages. It allows a flexible response and enables consumers to pursue their goals by varied routes. We should look now at the various avenues by which specific forms of consumer protection are being pursued.

Recent Developments in Consumer Protection

The discussion thus far has dealt with consumer protection in the broadest sense. The more specific forms of consumer protection we are considering here fall into two categories:

1. Prohibition of specific fraudulent practices.
2. Clarification of consumers' legal rights, thus providing consumers with a better basis for protecting themselves.

Given the diversity of consumer protection, not all laws fall neatly into one category or the other. However, that very diversity makes the division useful, because otherwise it would be difficult to summarize developments in this area.

The first category deals with old-fashioned fraud. There is nothing new about con games, although they keep cropping up in new forms. Most of us like to get something for nothing, and that's a large part of what keeps consumer fraud going. Unfortunately, the great deal that looks too good to pass up often turns out to be an empty promise.* As noted in Chapter 1, Americans tend to romanticize the slick operator, but there is nothing very romantic about most consumer fraud. That point is underscored when you remember that fraud is practiced most often on the poor, the elderly, or other groups who tend to be isolated from the economic mainstream.

Because the laws that cover consumer fraud are usually enacted at the state level, the pattern of coverage is uneven. The examples that follow represent abuses that have drawn attention in most states. One illustration is *pyramiding,* a sales technique in which consumers are told they will get a product free if they can get just ten (the number varies) of their friends to buy it. Because the rate of increase is exponential, few consumers will be able to convince enough friends to buy the product. Just as someone always gets stuck with a chain letter, so some buyer will be stuck with the merchandise (usually at inflated prices). Distributorships are sometimes sold in the same manner; the consumer becomes a distributor, buying a supply of the product which will be "free" if he or she can get ten friends to become distributors. The result is the same.

Bait and switch advertising is another form of deception that has been attacked at both the state and federal levels. The bait is an ad for a product at a very low price. The switch comes when the consumer finds that the store is out of the product or that the product itself is literally junk. In either case, the consumer is pressured into buying a more expensive product. The practice still goes on, but laws now require that if a product is advertised at a special price, the product must be fairly represented and sellers must have adequate stocks on hand (if stocks are limited, specific limitations must be noted).

The word *sale,* in fact, is commonly abused. Before an item can be offered at a reduced (or sale) price, it must have been available at the higher price. This prevents firms from advertising "sale prices" that are in effect the regular price of the item. Other restrictions are placed on special sales (such as going-out-of-business sales or fire sales). A firm can't have a going-out-of-business sale unless it is

---

* A good rule of thumb to follow in such cases is: If it sounds too good to be true, it probably isn't true.

actually going out of business. Such regulations are generally local.

You should appreciate that almost any business practice is subject to abuse; given this range of possibilities, the number of specific laws dealing with those abuses is correspondingly large. Recent examples range from land sales to educational opportunities and from chest developers to acne cures. Fad diets offer obvious opportunities for fraud and have caused serious problems. New technological developments open new possibilities. Computer-controlled solicitation of sales over the telephone, for example, makes that area much more susceptible to abuse.

Abuse may be a better word to use in these cases than fraud, because some activities may be abused even when outright fraud isn't involved. Abuse is more likely when the issue is complex and there is a need for a great deal of information. Bill consolidation loans offer one example. These loans give consumers the opportunity to refinance existing debt; the new loan is used to pay off old ones. Repayment periods are generally extended so that monthly payments can be reduced. However, the loans that the borrower is paying off usually carry different interest rates, some of which are higher than others. The new loan is at a higher rate, but the finance company keeps the difference between the rate charged on the new loan and the rates on the old ones. All of this is complicated, which gives rise to abuse through misinformation. For that reason, many states have placed limitations on bill consolidation loans that have the effect of discouraging, even banning, this type of loan.

Because there are so many possible frauds, there is something to be said for a more general approach. Protection may be needed from certain abuses, but consumers also need the more general protection provided by a clearer specification of their rights. This is the second category mentioned above; the general aim is to make it easier for consumers to look after themselves. We have already discussed a number of examples of this type of protection. Most disclosure laws (such as truth-in-lending) fall into this category. So do regulations on warranties (these specify precisely what the rights and responsibilities of each party are). The new laws governing landlord-tenant relations (Chapter 7) are another example. In each of these examples, the effort is to avoid specific instances of fraud by specifying consumers' rights beforehand.

Ideally, this more general protection should go to the heart of the problem. To illustrate, consider the problems raised by door-to-door sales. One way to deal with the problems of fraud in this area is to pass specific laws banning specific types of sales. Given the range of possibilities, however, that is difficult to do. An alternative approach is to attack the conditions that are necessary for such fraud to be carried out. Fraudulent door-to-door sellers rely on high-pressure sales techniques; buyers are induced to make the purchase before they have time to think about the consequences. An answer to this problem is to give the buyer time to think, and that is precisely what *cooling-off* laws do. They give the consumer time (usually three days) after signing an agreement to withdraw from the sale.* This is particularly helpful when expensive contracts are involved [8, pp. 33–35].

When long-term contracts are involved, door-to-door sellers also need financing; most sellers operate on too small a scale to be able to afford to hold the buyer's contract until it is all paid. Instead, the contract is sold at a discount to a finance company, which then takes responsibility for collection. This is all normal business practice, and, because the finance company has come to own the contract as part of a legal transaction, it is said to be the *holder in due course*. Suppose, however, that fraud was involved in the original sale to the consumer. Until recently, the consumer would still be bound to pay on the contract and would have no recourse against the holder of the contract. Charges could be brought against the original seller (if he or she could be found), but not against the holder in due course. This made it easier for fraudulent operators to make the sale, sell the contract, and duck out of town. In a sweeping decision, the Federal Trade Commission ruled that any charges that a buyer could bring against a seller could be brought against subsequent owners of the contract [11 and 8, pp. 226–44]. This tended to dry up financing for illegal operations, because they could not get finance companies to buy their notes.

Cooling-off laws and the new holder-in-due-course regulations both illustrate the value of more general consumer protection. Without the advantages of high-pressure techniques and adequate financing, fraudulent operators are put in a more difficult position. Note too that legitimate businesses can continue to operate. Companies remain free to sell door to door and consumers remain free to buy. The changes only serve to curb possible abuses of the system by strengthening the consumer's position.

Some observers feel that increased *product liability* offers another avenue for generalizing consumer protection. This argument maintains that if producers were liable for damages caused by failure of their products, safer products would be forthcoming. A weak form of producer liability is implicit in the familiar pattern of automobile recalls; in that case, producers are required to notify owners of sig-

---

* Sellers must inform consumers of their rights. The cooling-off period applies only to contracts signed away from the seller's place of business.

nificant defects and pay to repair the defects. The producer therefore assumes responsibility for preventing accidents that could be caused by production defects.

Because no one likes the idea of producers passing off dangerously shoddy products on the public, the idea of producer's liability has some appeal. However, the idea carries some dangers, too. If producers were liable for all failures of their products, it is possible that only the most expensive products would be produced. Depending upon the character of demand, however, risky products might still be produced [27, p. 5]. In any event, costs would rise as producers added the costs of liability settlements to the prices of their products.

As the debate on producer liability has gone on in the courts, two critical questions have emerged. The first is: Was product failure caused by a random defect or was it due to some systematic production flaw? In the latter instance, the consumer has a much stronger case for arguing that the producer was negligent. The second question is: Did the producer know about the defect? If the answer is yes, there is a strong argument for saying that the producer should have done something about it and should therefore be liable.

The question of producer liability took a dramatic turn in early 1978 when a California jury awarded $128.5 million judgment against Ford Motor Company. The case involved the gas tank on the 1972 Pinto; the gas tank ruptured in a rear-end collision, killing the driver and seriously injuring the other occupant in the car [17, p. 1]. The jury maintained that Ford was aware of the design flaw, but did not correct it because of cost considerations [17, p. 17]. Ford is appealing the decision, but even if the amount of the award is reduced, the size of the judgment has awakened producers to the problem. It appears that in cases when negligence can be proven, tougher laws on producer's liability should be helpful to consumers; the value of the approach in the more general case is open to question.*

The preceding pages are full of references to court decisions and legal judgments. It should be clear that if a consumer is to carry a serious complaint very far, some legal assistance will be needed. Without such assistance, many of the recent efforts to extend consumer protection will be ineffective. In the case of a major complaint, the consumer may consider legal action; but if the amounts involved are small, the costs and bother of a court case may not seem justified. It follows that lowering the cost of legal actions to consumers should

---

* It is the case of the random defect that occurs despite precautions taken by producers that raises the most serious questions. A given percentage of defective units is possible even under careful quality control procedures.

expand the possibilities for consumers to follow up on their complaints.

Several approaches have been taken to this problem, the most direct being the actual provision of legal services to those who cannot afford them. *Legal aid clinics* have had considerable success with this approach, but it reaches only a small percentage of the population. For most consumers, *small claims courts* offer a workable alternative. Plaintiff and defendant act as their own lawyers in these courts, reducing the costs to consumers and offsetting the advantages that would otherwise go to firms with large legal staffs [12, pp. 195–99].

The structure of small claims courts varies from state to state. In most cases, procedures are simple and paperwork is kept to a minimum. However, in some states, *small* is interpreted literally, so that claims as small as $250 are considered too large for such courts. In some states, legal counsel is permissible (although not required). A workable system of small claims courts offers an indirect benefit to consumers. If businesses know that such recourse is available to consumers, there would be an added incentive to reach a mutually agreeable settlement out of court [4].

Another possibility open to consumers is the *class-action suit.* As the name implies, class actions are brought on behalf of a number of consumers (or a class) who have suffered in a particular situation. If a utility overcharges, for example, customers might bring a suit against the company as a class. The advantage in this case is that the amount of individual loss might be too small to warrant action; all customers, however, would have a considerable stake in the question and would therefore make action possible [12, pp. 184–185]. The impact of a successful class action is likely to be greater, too. If an individual consumer receives damages, the impact on the firm will be minimal. However: "the impact of having to make restitution in a class action, if judgment is rendered against the seller, may force the firm out of business or induce it to change its practices, preventing damages to others" [24, p. 15].

Unfortunately, the history of class-action suits is complicated; court decisions show numerous twists and turns. Traditionally, the courts took a very narrow view of class actions, maintaining that individuals each had to be able to show that they had suffered significant loss before they could undertake action. Then, the courts relaxed this view and seemed to encourage class actions. As such suits became more popular, interpretations changed again; not only did plaintiff have to show significant loss, but each individual who could be part of the suit had to be notified (or at least a good faith effort had to be made to notify all persons involved). That seemed to limit the use of class actions, but the situation changed again when federal courts suggested that state courts might be the appropriate place for such suits [12, pp. 184–94], leaving the situation unresolved. The courts may expand or redefine the role of class-action suits in the future. Until that time, class actions will continue to play some role in consumer complaints, but the dimensions of that role cannot be determined.

Study Questions

1. Identify the consumer interest in each of the following government policies. Which would you classify as consumer protection?

   a. Expanded trade relations with the People's Republic of China.

   b. The requirement that nutritional values be stated on all breakfast cereals.

   c. A vote on a bond issue for school construction.

   d. Legislation to allow no-fault insurance.

   e. Legislation banning discrimination in lending (or credit).

2. The following issues are more complex. Can you identify the consumer interest? Discuss the problems involved.

   a. A court decision that stops the construction of a power plant for environmental reasons.

   b. Safety (or "child-proof") caps on drugs.

   c. New legislation to require licensing of auto mechanics.

   d. Proposed standards to ban toxic substances from the environment.

3. Discuss the consumer backlash to protection efforts (the "leave-me-alone syndrome"). Do you think it will subside or grow? What are the implications for consumer protection.

4. Some utilities—power companies, for example—are privately owned and subject to government regulation, while others are publicly owned. Explain how these two approaches represent alternative responses to the same problem. Is it possible to generalize and say which one best serves consumer interests?

5. Many early regulatory efforts at the state level were declared unconstitutional. On what basis could such a judgment be made? How can you explain the rapid change in attitudes that accompanied the growth of regulation?

6. In most cases, consumers do not buy their telephones; they rent them from the telephone company instead. What impact

does this have on what customers actually pay for their phones? Is there any other significance to the fact that the company retains ownership of the phone?

7. Most observers agree that despite problems involved, there is a need for building codes:

a. What arguments can you give to support the need for such regulations?

b. Explain how they can be subverted to serve the interests of special-interest groups.

c. Can you think of another way to protect the consumer, thereby avoiding these problems?

8. What segment of the population gains the most from imposed standards? Since standards usually result in higher-priced products, which segment of the population bears the heaviest cost?

9. Why do you think consumer fraud is a more serious problem now than it was fifty years ago? What, do you feel, is the best way to combat it?

10. It may be argued that most consumer protection legislation benefits middle- and upper-income groups rather than low-income groups. This appears to be true with such things as boat and toy safety and controls on land sales. Considering the process by which legislation is enacted, explain why this result is predictable. What can be done to offset this trend?

11. Efforts to make legal protection available to the poor are often controversial. Can you explain why in the context of this chapter?

12. Do you think small claims courts offer a valuable service to consumers? What are the essential features necessary to make the courts effective?

Suggested Projects

1. Consumer protection cannot be effective if consumers are not aware of it. Conduct a survey to find out how much consumers actually know about the protection to which they are entitled. You will want to explore different aspects, including the following:

a. You may pick out a single law (as with tenants' rights—Project 2, Chapter 7) or sample a number of laws. Pick areas that affect consumers directly.

b. Set up hypothetical situations between buyer and seller

(misrepresentation of products, complaints, and so on) and see whether consumers would be aware of their rights under such circumstances.

c. Find out what people actually do when they have a complaint about a product or service.

d. Find out if consumers are aware of local consumer protection agencies or private consumer groups.

e. See how many regulatory agencies consumers can name. Do consumers know what the agencies do?

f. Can you identify cases in which consumers think they are protected when they actually aren't?

Do you think that consumers are generally aware of the protection available to them? If not, what could be done to improve awareness?

2. Does your locality have a small claims court? If so, find out what is involved in making use of it (forms, fees, and so on). Attend some sessions and report on the proceedings.

3. Review the most recent decisions involving class action suits. Is this approach serving as an effective mechanism for protecting consumers?

4. Find out how consumers actually feel about consumer protection. You may either:

a. Ask for consumer reactions to specific protection efforts (safety standards, for example), or

b. You could discuss the question with them more generally. Do you note any backlash? Do consumers want protection or to be left alone? Could it be that they want both?

5. Survey the consumer protection agencies in your area. Is there a single agency, or is responsibility shared among various units?

6. In conjunction with Project 3, list items for action on consumer protection, including what you see as the most pressing needs in your area.

7. In your area, what industries are regulated at the local level? At the state level? Research the activities of these regulatory bodies. How would you evaluate their effectiveness in protecting consumer interests?

8. Look into the history of consumer protection in your state or locality. When were the first efforts made? Do they follow the pattern discussed in the text?

9. Investigate the position that the chief political parties take on

consumer protection. Does it receive much attention in their literature? Is there a significant difference between the parties?

Bibliography and Suggested Readings

1. *Advertising Age.* February 13, 1978, pp. 1 ff.
   A report on the defeat of the proposed Agency for Consumer Advocacy and a summary of the administration's plans for adjusting to the bill's defeat. An interesting perspective.

2. American Bar Association. *Report of the ABA Commission to Study the Federal Trade Commission.* Washington, D.C.: Bureau of National Affairs, 1969.
   The ABA took a close look at the FTC and found it wanting. This report still represents a thoughtful consideration of the problems with the Commission.

3. Bain, Joe. *Industrial Organization.* New York: John Wiley and Sons, 1962.
   A standard reference work on industrial organization. Chapters 13–15 deal with the problems of government regulation.

4. "Buyer vs. Seller in Small Claims Courts." *Consumer Reports,* October 1971, pp. 624–31.
   An exploration of how small claims courts operate and how they can help the consumer. The survey of such courts is somewhat dated, but still useful in terms of possible improvements.

5. "Consumer Representation Plans." *Federal Register,* September 28, 1976. Washington, D.C.: U.S. Government Printing Office, pp. 42763–68.
   The published report of the proposal to incorporate a consumer representative in all federal agencies. This proposal was President Ford's alternative to an Agency for Consumer Protection.

6. *Cost-Benefit Analysis of Consumer Product Safety Programs: Final Report.* Directorate for Applied Science and Research Applications, National Science Foundation, APR 75-09984, 1978.
   A detailed report on cost-benefit relationships of safety standards, with emphasis on flammability standards. Contains a complete review of issues and procedures for students with a serious interest in the topic.

7. Dardis, Rachel, and Smith, Betty. "Cost-Benefit Analysis of Consumer Product Safety Standards." *The Journal of Consumer Affairs,* 11 (Summer 1977):34–46.
   A summary of research on the costs and benefits of the sleepware flammability standard. Concludes that the standard produced a net benefit, but does not include consideration of possible links to cancer.

8. Epstein, David G. *Consumer Protection*. St. Paul, Minn.: West Publishing, 1976.
   Subtitled "In a Nutshell," a compact look at a complex topic. Uses legal language, but should be understandable to most students. A good source for those who want to follow up on the topic.

9. *Establishing an Agency for Consumer Protection*. Committee on Government Operations, House of Representatives, 94th Congress (HR 7575). Washington, D.C.: U.S. Government Printing Office, June 1975. Hearings on the Agency for Consumer Protection. Contains a good survey of the arguments for and against the agency.

10. "FDA Approves Valproate for Epilepsy." *FDA Consumer*, April 1978, p. 23.
    The Food and Drug Administration's explanation of its decision to approve Valproate. The *FDA Consumer* reviews the agency's operations and is a good source of such information.

11. "FTC Rule on Preservation of Consumer Claims and Defenses." *Federal Register*, November 18, 1975. Washington, D.C.: U.S. Government Printing Office, p. 53506.
    The Federal Trade Commission's ruling against the holder-in-due-course doctrine. The rule extended consumer's rights to include subsequent owners of sales contracts.

12. Feldman, Laurence P. *Consumer Protection*. St. Paul, Minn.: West Publishing, 1976.
    An excellent survey of issues in consumer protection. Contains material on legal issues as well as regulatory structure. A balanced account.

13. Friedman, Milton. *Capitalism and Freedom*. Chicago: University of Chicago Press, 1962.
    Chapter 9 presents Friedman's analysis of occupational licensure. A very readable summary by the Nobel-Prize-winning economist. Whether or not you agree with Dr. Friedman, you must be impressed with his logic.

14. Fritschler, A. L. *Smoking and Politics: Policymaking and the Federal Bureaucracy*. New York: Appleton-Century-Crofts, 1969.
    A good case study of how the federal bureaucracy responds to pressure. As the subtitle indicates, this is an analysis of policymaking and as such offers valuable insights to consumers.

15. Galbraith, John Kenneth. *The New Industrial State*. Boston: Houghton Mifflin, Co., 1967.
    A fully developed statement of Galbraith's views on the firm as a planning system. He develops his idea of the "technostructure," a word that has entered the language in reference to the technicians who actually run the big institutions (public and private) in the economy.

16. Harris, Roy J., Jr. "The Stakes are Huge in Competitive World of Air-Crash Lawsuits." *Wall Street Journal,* May 22, 1978, pp. 1 ff.
    A report on lawsuits from the DC-10 crash in France and other crashes.

17. ———. "Why the Pinto Jury Felt Ford Deserved $125 million Penalty," *Wall Street Journal,* February 14, 1978, pp. 1 ff.
    A report on the Pinto product liability settlement. Contains a good review of how the jury reached its verdict and the implications of the judgment for other cases.

18. Hilton, George W. "The Basic Behavior of Regulatory Commissions." *American Economic Review, Papers and Proceedings* 62 (May 1972): 47–54.
    An excellent summary of many forces that affect regulatory agencies. A good introduction for those who are interested in material not generally contained in texts, yet still written in an understandable fashion.

19. Hofstadter, Richard. *The Age of Reform.* New York: Alfred A. Knopf, 1955.
    Classic study of the Progressive Era by a leading American historian.

20. "How Licensing Hurts Consumers." *Business Week,* November 28, 1977, pp. 27–29.
    A report on research showing the negative effects of licensure. There is a tendency to impose a high minimum level of quality, which denies the service to many customers.

21. Keeton, P., and Shapo, M. *Products and the Consumer: Deceptive Practices.* Foundation Press, 1972.
    Organized along casebook lines, this study focuses on primary problems of consumer protection. A good reference.

22. Kolko, Gabriel. *The Triumph of Conservation.* New York: Quadrangle Books, 1965.
    The revisionist view of American reform. Kolko's arguments, while often polemical, have been supported by more detached scholars in individual studies.

23. "Laetrile: The Political Success of a Scientific Failure." *Consumer Reports,* August 1977.
    The subtitle identifies Laetrile as a political issue, and that is certainly what it has become. However the issue is resolved, political pressure will play an important role.

24. Lane, Sylvia. "Economics of Consumer Class Actions." *The Journal of Consumer Affairs,* Summer 1973, pp. 13–22.
    An economic analysis of the impact of class-action suits. The analysis that the effect of class actions on consumer welfare may vary; the author concludes that they are still an important instrument in building an equitable economy.

25. Magnuson, Warren. *The Dark Side of the Marketplace.* 2nd ed., Engle-
    wood Cliffs, N.J.: Prentice-Hall, 1972.
    A graphic description of the suffering that attends so much consumer
    fraud; contains a call for more effective laws and better enforcement.

26. *New York Times.* September 16, 1977, 16:4.
    A report on Laker Airlines airbus service across the Atlantic. Laker's
    move set off a new round of fare cutting, which means lower prices
    for consumers, but, unfortunately, also means the fare structure is so
    complex that almost no one really understands it.

27. Oi, Walter. "The Economics of Product Safety." *Bell Journal of Eco-
    nomics and Management Science,* Spring 1973, pp. 3–28.
    This article has become a standard source on the subject. Oi shows
    that product liability requirements may result in more dangerous pro-
    ducts being produced. Highly analytical, but sections on perception of
    risk by individuals are straightforward and would benefit anyone inter-
    ested in the topic.

28. Oberg, S. R., and Trzyma, T. C., eds. *Consumer Protection Directory.*
    2nd ed., Chicago: Marquis Academic Media, 1975.
    As the name implies, this useful reference lists and describes various
    consumer protection groups. Coverage includes both private and public
    groups. Good source for information on protection at the state level.

29. Peltzman, Sam. "The Effects of Automobile Safety Regulation." *Journal
    of Political Economy* 83, 4 (August 1975):677–725.
    An investigation of the impact of auto safety requirements. The author
    concludes that these regulations have contributed to the growing num-
    ber of pedestrian accidents. A controversial viewpoint worth looking
    at.

30. ———. *The Regulation of Innovation: the 1962 Amendments.* Ameri-
    can Enterprise Institute, Evaluation Study no. 15, 1974.
    The study that concludes that efficacy testing by the FDA has limited
    innovation and therefore has had a harmful effect on public welfare.
    A complex methodology, but the analysis is worth considering. More
    general discussion of the impact of standards is also useful.

31. Robertson, Wyndham. "Tempest in Toyland." *Fortune,* February 1972,
    pp. 115–17.
    A review of how consumer action prompted action in the area of toy
    safety.

32. *Review of Procedures and Policies of the FAA and NTSB with Respect
    to the DC-10 Cargo Doors.* Committee on Interstate and Foreign Com-
    merce, House of Representatives, 93rd Congress (Serial #93–80).
    Washington, D.C.: U.S. Government Printing Office, March-April 1974.
    Congressional hearings on the case of the DC-10 cargo doors. Provides
    a review of what actually happened and explores a number of issues

relating to the way regulation actually works. Students will find the latter to be instructive.

33. Swagler, Roger M., and Harris, David H. "An Economic Analysis of Licensure & Public Policy: Evidence from the Social Work Case." *Journal of Consumer Affairs*. 11, 1 (Summer 1977):90–101.
A review of how credence qualities are involved in licensure. Suggests that there may be ways other than licensure to meet the public's informational needs. Also contains discussion of who benefits from licensure.

34. Troelstrup, Arch W. *The Consumer in American Society*. 5th ed., New York: McGraw-Hill Book Co., 1974.
See especially Chapters 16–17 for a summary of consumer protection.

35. Wilcox, Clair. *Public Policies Toward Business*. 3rd ed., Homewood, Ill.: Richard D. Irwin, 1966.
Good summary of government activities in regulation and antitrust.

-9-

Consumption and the Public Sector

The Nature of Public Consumption

Consuming Public Goods?

The next time you are with a group of friends, ask them to list the things they have used, or consumed, that day. The chances are that they will mention things like food, soap, books, gasoline, beer, and clothing. Maybe someone will even think of housing, electricity, and insurance. The odds are, however, that they will not mention police or fire protection, national defense, education, highways, sewage disposal, or street lights, and therein lies the paradox. The second grouping is made up of *public,* or *collective,* goods; these are consumed just as surely as the goods in the first group and make an easily perceived contribution to consumers' welfare. Anyone who has endured the chaos of a sanitation workers' strike or the fear that goes with a firemen's strike can appreciate how important public services are. Yet consumers still tend to think of consumption as limited to those goods and services purchased directly for themselves, omitting items purchased through taxes.

The oversight persists even though control of public goods is the subject of an ongoing political debate. While such matters as the level of defense spending are clearly political, it should be just as clear that they affect the consumer directly. An increase in defense spending means higher taxes or cuts in other areas of government spending like education, highway construction, and medical research. The consumer is affected either way. Similarly, the so-called tax-payers' revolt has emerged as a major political issue, but the question actually revolves around payments for public services. Again, a consumer issue is at the heart of the political debate.

There is no questioning the importance of public goods in the individual's budget. Americans purchased over $227 billion worth of public goods in 1977 by paying that amount in personal taxes. Even an individual's personal tax bill understates the consumption of public goods, since personal taxes amount to only about half of all government revenues. The rest comes from other tax sources and borrowing. Some of this may properly be classified as investment, but distinctions are unclear.

What is clear is that consumers *spend* a great deal of money through taxes. Table 9.1 shows that Americans spent nearly as much on taxes as they did on housing and home furnishings combined. Despite our well-publicized, and often lamented, love affair for the automobile, we spent almost $2.75 on public goods for every dollar we spent on automobiles; and for every dollar the American consumer managed to save, over three dollars went to the government in taxes. Among the principal expenditure categories, only food accounts for more than taxes. Yet the care and feeding of governments

Table 9.1 Total Personal Taxes and Selected Consumption Expenditures in the United States: 1967–77 (In billions of dollars)

	Personal taxes [a]	Auto- mobiles	Home furnishings	Food	Clothing	Housing	Personal savings
1967	83.0	30.5	31.4	108.5	40.3	71.8	40.4
1968	97.9	37.5	34.3	115.3	42.6	77.3	39.8
1969	116.2	40.4	36.3	122.5	45.7	84.0	37.9
1970	115.9	37.1	37.4	131.8	48.1	91.2	54.1
1971	116.3	43.8	39.4	140.6	50.5	102.7	57.3
1972	141.2	50.6	44.8	150.4	55.1	112.3	49.4
1973	150.8	55.2	50.7	168.1	61.3	123.2	70.3
1974	170.3	48.0	54.9	189.8	65.3	136.5	71.8
1975	169.0	53.9	58.0	209.5	70.2	150.8	80.2
1976	196.9	71.9	63.9	225.5	76.3	167.9	65.9
1977 [b]	227.5	83.8	70.3	246.3	82.6	184.5	67.8

Source: *Economic Report of the President, 1977*. Tables B-13 and B-21, pp. 272 and 282.
[a] Includes all federal, state, and local taxes paid by individuals, but not social security payments.
[b] Data for 1977 are provisional.

is still a primary expenditure for Americans; as such, it merits the same kind of attention given to private spending.

The point is underscored by looking at Table 9.1 in terms of the increases in the different expenditure categories. The amount paid in personal taxes rose 275 percent between 1967 and 1977. That increase reflects inflationary pressures on income and prices, which meant corresponding increases in income and sales taxes. Among private expenditures, only spending on automobiles kept pace with the increased tax payments. The average increase in spending for food, home furnishings, housing and clothing was 18 percent less than the increase for taxes. Thus, not only are taxes important, but they are becoming more important.

The Special Problem of Public Goods

Clearly, no treatment of consumer economics that failed to consider public goods would be complete. But if it is proper to speak of consuming public goods in the same way as consuming private goods, why not treat them together? The answer is that although both represent consumption, there is an important distinction between the two. With private goods you can purchase or not, and hence pay or not, according to your own individual taste. With public goods you have no such option.

Decisions about consuming public goods are made collectively. The entire community decides on the level of taxation and the pattern of expenditures. To illustrate this point, Douglass North commented that "the Seattle City Council voted to permit 21 murders, 104 rapes, 962 robberies and 417 assaults, as well as various numbers of lesser crimes in the first half of 1970" [15, pp. 114–20]. The city council, of course, did not vote on rape and murder, but it did allocate a specific sum to law enforcement. The level of crime followed from the level of enforcement. Some citizens might have wanted more enforcement, others less. Once a particular level was chosen, however, everyone had to accept it as an expression of the community's preferences.

This follows from the fact that public goods are by nature indivisible; they cannot be supplied to one person without supplying them to everyone. If you live in an apartment, your unit cannot very well be supplied with fire protection without the whole building being supplied [7, pp. 57–63]. Thus everyone benefits, whether you pay for the protection alone or whether everyone in the building pays. Similarly, if you pay to have a street light installed in front of your house, your neighbors will benefit from the light, even though you are paying for it.

When everyone benefits (potentially, at least), there is a strong argument for having everyone pay. This suggests an alternative statement of the same point. It is often said that there are *externalities* involved in the consumption of certain goods, which means that the benefit is external to (or goes beyond) the individual. Such is the case in both examples above, fire protection and street lighting. Education also involves externalities, for while it benefits the individual, it benefits the society as a whole, too. Thus, all taxpayers pay for education, whether or not they (or a member of their family) are actually in school.

These examples are reasonable enough, but the issue is not always so simple. Problems arise because not everyone benefits to the same degree from public goods. Individual consumption is based on individual preferences, whereas public goods are collective. Therefore, individuals cannot adjust the consumption of public goods to meet their own tastes. Suppose, for example, that you do not wish to consume so much national defense. You could write the Secretary of Defense and ask that your name be scratched from the next heat of the arms race, but that would only ensure that you would make it into some FBI file. You cannot even risk jail by not paying your taxes to support the military—in the manner of Henry David Thoreau—because the most important taxes are withheld before you ever receive your income.

This does not mean that it is necessary to build an entirely new analysis for public goods. Our conclusions about consumer strategies apply equally well to public goods. A change is called for, however, in that our analysis so far must be amplified and extended to account for the fact that the direct link between cost and benefit (or taste and consumption) is broken with public goods. For the consumer, the problem is still maximization of satisfaction on a given income. Because consumers lack *direct* decision-making power over the portion of their income that goes to public goods, they must exercise what power they have to ensure that public expenditures generally reflect their own preferences. In a small community made up of similar types of people, the problem may not be very serious. Even at the local level, however, divisions may exist, as illustrated by the increasingly bitter resentment local tax levies generate. In a larger community, such as a nation, consensus is even less likely.

This lack of consensus is reflected in debates about reordering priorities. Those who favor such a reordering are really saying they don't like the existing level or allocation of public expenditures. As the range of problems that the country faces becomes broader, and as more and more individuals develop their own perceptions of these problems, the public debate on such questions can only increase. We can predict, therefore, that the debate on priorities, goals, the allocation of public goods, or whatever name you choose to call it, will continue into the future.

Although there is considerable literature on these topics in public finance, political science, and public administration, it is usually not written from the consumer's point of view. The need is to analyze these ideas from the consumer's perspective, developing the notion of public goods as an extension of private consumption. Having said that, however, it is necessary to add that consumers themselves often act as if they do not see things in that light. Because this point colors the whole analysis, and therefore the consumer's perception of public goods, it must be explored before the specifics of the problem are considered.

The Underlying Bias

While public goods and services are purchased through tax payments, there is evidence that most people do not see it that way. Their attitude is reflected in everyday manners of speech. The typical consumer would say that he "bought a vacuum cleaner" or "bought a garbage-disposal." When similar services—such as street cleaning or trash collection—are publicly supplied, however, those same people would not speak of *buying* them, only of *paying* the taxes. This demonstrates a fundamental bias; with private goods, the focus is on the benefit, while with public goods, it is on the cost [9, p. 110].

Again, it is John Kenneth Galbraith who has served as the public's conscience in publicizing this double standard. He was among the first to note that we view even frivolous private goods with pride, but look at the most significant public goods with regret [9, 109–10]. Thus, the parent who grumbles about higher taxes for education will in the next sentence extol the virtues of his new electric can opener. There is an obvious inconsistency here; on the one hand, there is our infatuation with gadgets, on the other the view that

> Public services ... are a burden which must, in effect, be carried by private production ....
>
> At best, public services are a necessary evil; at worst they are a malign tendency against which an alert community must exercise eternal vigilance [9, pp. 109–10].

If it is not immediately clear to you why eternal vigilance should be required against such things as education, community health services, or public recreational facilties, you are beginning to see the point. Public goods are *different* from private goods because of the externalities involved, but they are not by nature inferior. They are provided, as private goods are, to satisfy particular wants. The fact that so many people miss this point and view government production as sterile may stem from simple shortsightedness, or it may reflect a reverence for the rugged individualist and the free enterprise system. Yet the need for government services is so inescapable that it seems obvious to ask Galbraith's question: How can "a system which still rejoices in the name of free enterprise in truth be so dependent on government?" [10, p. 296].

These ideas were organized earlier into one of the fundamental precepts of the Galbraithian system—the theory of *social balance*. It is generally recognized that most production is complementary; if there are to be more automobiles, there must be more steel, more rubber, more gasoline, and more junkyards. Since these are largely private goods, the market maintains a balance. However, more automobiles also require more roads, more traffic control equipment, more police, and more attention to the problems of congestion. These are public goods and their growth has generally not kept up with developments in the private sector.

In the extreme, this "private opulence and public squalor" leads to impaired economic performance (ask a business person how many important appointments he or she missed because of planes circling over crowded airports). In a positive sense, it can be said:

> By failing to exploit the opportunity to expand public production, we are missing opportunities for enjoyment we might otherwise have had. Presumably, a community can be as well rewarded by buying better schools or better parks as buying bigger automobiles. By concentrating on the latter rather than the former, *it is failing to maximize its satisfactions*. [9, p. 204, emphasis added]

That is an important observation about citizen-consumers. It suggests that their *perception of government may be inconsistent with their own self-interest*. The reason should be clear. Citizen-consumers use government services, paying for them with income they would otherwise have spent themselves to improve their well-being. Public goods thus emerge as an alternative to private consumption. Using opportunity costs as a measure, the benefit from public goods should equal the benefit from private expenditures.

In fairness to the consumer, it should be noted that the link between public goods and satisfaction often seems remote. Education, for example, bestows long-term benefits, which may not be immediately apparent. Other public services, like police protection, are most effective when they are least obvious. A crime wave brings criticism of police and charges that they aren't doing their job. However, when peace and quiet prevails, police receive less attention and are seldom credited with promoting tranquility.

This in itself underscores the importance of public goods. If citizen-consumers view public services as inferior or fail to recognize the contribution they make to individual welfare, their perception gets in the way of their own self-interest. It follows that if consumers actually want to maximize satisfaction, they must develop a strategy to deal with the consumption of public goods.

Controlling Public Goods

A Strategy for Public Consumption

Citizen-consumers cannot say they want to consume this much education or that many highways, the way they would if they were buying breakfast cereal or clothing. Decisions about collective goods are not made by individuals, but by the officials they elect to represent them. Even if the citizen-consumer is asked to express an opinion on a specific question, as in the case of a referendum on a school levy, the electoral process is still involved. This suggests that if the citizen-consumer is to have any hopes of maximizing satisfaction, it will be necessary to duck into the nearest phone booth and emerge as that mythical character known as the informed voter. You know how the script runs. Voters must take an interest in campaigns, learn the issues, identify the position of the candidates. and develop their own opinions so that (if they are not too exhausted) they can vote intelligently. Anyone who does less is automatically suspect and probably un-American.

Even with the dimensions of the problem only vaguely defined, it is clear that this view is naïve. The citizen-consumer is expected to vote for candidates who, if elected, will make decisions about the public goods the consumer receives. But when you consider all that is involved, the prospect is appalling. There is such a wide range of public goods that it is almost impossible for the voter to know what they are, let alone the candidate's position on all of them.

The magnitude of the problem facing citizen-consumers is now apparent. How can they hope to unravel all the issues involved in a vote on municipal bonds or annexation, let alone such things as agricultural price supports or tariff policy. They can't. Having been told all their lives that it is their duty to be well informed, when they find this to be an almost impossible task, they are likely to be filled with self-recrimination about their failure. The voter ends up as a frustrated nonparticipant, not the well-informed supercitizen of the textbooks.

The emphasis on the costs of information about public issues echoes the consideration of information costs related to private consumption. Is it valid to compare them? Consider the question for a moment. Consumers need information before they buy and will continue to seek it as long as the expected savings is greater than the cost of the search (Chapter 5, pp. 90–92). Similarly, voters must seek information, and if this analogy is correct, they should seek it only as long as the expected return is greater than the cost of obtaining the information. This leads to the surprising conclusion that it may be rational for the voter to be uninformed on at least some issues.

Anthony Downs, who helped pioneer this line of analysis, reaches a similar conclusion. He emphasizes that the political system, like the economic system, features specialization and the division of labor. Information gathering is among these specialties. As a result, large quantities of information are available if the individual voter seeks them out. Downs concludes that to reduce the costs of information "it may be rational for a man to delegate part or all of his political decision making to others . . ." [6, p. 233]. To delegate decision making, voters take the word of a trusted friend, or an independent research group, or newspaper, rather than investigate all the issues themselves.* It is still the citizen who votes, but his or her ballot is cast according to the direction of others in the sense that the responsibility for making the decision has been delegated. Most people behave in this fashion, since few make up their minds completely independently.

An election for judges will illustrate this theme. It is difficult to get enough information to make an intelligent decision in such cases. However, the local bar association or some other citizens' group usually makes endorsements. The voter who delegates responsibility to such groups has a sound basis for judgment. Those who do not will most likely have to vote randomly or according to whim.

Voters must exercise great caution in delegating responsibility. It is obvious that such responsibility can only be given to an individual or group that the voter has come to respect and that reflects the voter's own goals and aspirations. The selection process may be difficult, but it is rational so long as the cost of an incorrect decision is less than the cost of obtaining the information individually.

---

* Many people follow this practice in a negative fashion. If, for example they consistently disagree with a particular newspaper, they define their position by taking the exact opposite view to the view the paper takes. This is a rational approach, as long as one's enemies are chosen carefully.

Political parties may seem an obvious source of direction, but Downs issues a warning in that regard. Parties, Downs argues, are interested in maximizing votes, which is to say winning elections. They are not interested in a particular social state per se. Therefore, a rational voter

> cannot assume members of any party have goals similar to his own. But without this assumption, delegation of all political decisions to someone else is irrational—hence political parties can never be the agents of rational delegation. [6, p. 234]

This process of delegation helps explain the common phenomenon of seemingly indifferent citizens who suddenly become active when an issue touches them directly. The individual who never thought much about freeways becomes the bane of the city council when someone proposes a freeway through his backyard. It is common to criticize such people, charging them with indifference to all problems but their own. Yet they may be acting quite rationally if they feel that such decisions are too important to delegate, despite the high costs of information, communication, and action. At the national level, these costs are correspondingly higher, and such examples are less common.

It may seem that the preceding analysis does not fit with the earlier contention that the citizen-consumer needs to recognize the importance of public goods as consumption. The two are consistent, however, if the voter is delegating the right decisions to the right groups. Remember that we have held only that citizen-consumers should develop a strategy to deal with the issues that affect them, not that they should be informed on everything. Consumers who delegate some decision making have evolved a rational strategy to serve their self-interest at the least cost to themselves. Control and consumption of public goods, then, finally emerges as something quite like control and consumption of private goods. The difference is that with private goods, these principles are applied to the goods themselves, whereas with public goods, the application is a step removed. Citizen-consumers control public goods through the political process, but this added difficulty changes neither the basic problem facing consumers nor their approach.

The Level of Government—A Fable

In the American system, thinking about government in the singular is usually inappropriate. Citizens confront governments at all levels, so that while the Department of Defense is government, so are the New

York Port Authority, the State of Washington, the Cleveland Public School District, and the Omaha Public Power District—and that is just a sample. In 1972, there were 78,269 governmental units in the United States, of which 78,218 were local government.* [14, p. ii]. Some people see this smorgasbord of governments as the real solution to the problem of citizen control. They feel that big government is too remote to reach the people it is supposed to be serving. If citizens cannot control government because it has grown so far removed from their day-to-day lives, then the obvious solution is to bring government "back to the people."

There is certainly nothing new about the suggestion that individuals are best served by the governments closest to them. Its current popularity, however, can be traced to the tremendous growth in the federal establishment over the past generation. Since the country's problems have grown at least as fast as the government, there are grounds for maintaining that big government is not the answer. This view has recently emerged from within the federal government and is reflected in the program of federal revenue sharing with state and local governments. There is something to this idea. In terms of our earlier analysis, it is possible to contend that state and local governments can better serve the people. It stands to reason that the voter should be able to exercise more effective control over local officials. Individual voters may not feel they have much impact in a national election, but locally their votes, and those of friends, are very important. This is analogous to our earlier argument that consumers can be more effective in smaller markets; the logic is the same in both cases.

Furthermore, while issues may still be complex, they are likely to be less complicated than those at the national level; as a result, information costs are lower. This also relates to citizen-consumers' views of their self-interest, which should be clearer in local elections. Urban voters may be forgiven if they do not know where they stand on agricultural price supports, but they should certainly know what they think about the schools their children attend and the streets they travel to work.

Citizen-consumers have another element of control at the local level that they cannot exercise in national politics. If they really are opposed to policies in a particular area, they can "vote with their feet," and leave. True, a person can leave the country too, and some do, but this is an extreme step. It is not so extreme, however, to move from one area to another if you do not like the way things are going.

* There is, of course, just one federal government and only 50 state governments. In 1962, there were 91,237 governmental units.

Thus, those who feel that education should be well financed can congregate in areas where it is, and those who like low taxes can move to low-service areas.

Table 9.2 is only a sample of cities in different parts of the country, but it clearly shows the marked variation that exists in both taxation and public expenditures (and hence the level of services). Some care must be taken in interpreting these statistics. The amount of federal and state aid going to cities varies. Furthermore, if population is relatively sparse, services are going to be more expensive to provide on a per-capita basis; on the other hand, concentrations of population create new problems and costs rise.

Nevertheless, the variation is still marked. For every public dollar spent in Columbia, nearly $10 is spent in New York City and over $6 is spent in Boston. Even if costs are higher in New York, that still reflects a marked difference in public goods supplied (and may help explain New York City's ongoing financial difficulties). There are two ways to look at these differences. One is to assume that they reflect actual community tastes; in that case, they represent the level of public goods actually demanded in different cities. The other is to conclude that the variation shows that some areas are undersupplied with public goods.

Elements of both explanations are involved. To explain these disparities fully, it is necessary to explore economic organization, social structure, and historical development. It is logical to assume that the demand for public services will be higher in some areas than in others, but the extreme inequalities that exist clearly work to the

Table 9.2 Property Taxes and Expenditures Per Capita: Selected Cities: 1970

	Property Taxes	Expenditures[a]
New York, N.Y.	$234	$754
Chicago, Ill.	66	163
Minneapolis, Minn.	84	131
Columbia, S.C.	36	76
Birmingham, Ala.	23	91
Houston, Tex.	53	81
Denver, Col.	64	238
Los Angeles, Calif.	59	126
Boston, Mass.	345	481

Source: *County and City Data Book* [5, Table 6].
[a] Total expenditures per capita, excluding capital outlay.

disadavantage of some citizen-consumers. Balancing these needs will remain important in the years to come.

Regional variation in expenditures is not the only problem in this area. While the theory says that government closer to the people should be more effective, it doesn't always work that way. To illustrate, consider the tragicomic experience of a group of Long Island citizens who tried to have a traffic light installed. Installation of a traffic signal may seem like an insignificant undertaking, but you would have a hard time making that point with the parents from Port Washington, New York, who felt that such a signal was needed between their library and elementary school.

The area around Port Washington consists of four incorporated villages and several square miles of unincorporated area. It also includes seven special districts for such things as school, police, and sewer services. When the parents went forth in search of the traffic signal, they found that the school was in the township, but the library was in the village. As if that were not complicated enough, they discovered that the street that ran between the two "was a county road, but located in and patrolled by the Port Washington Police District, which is independent of the village, town and county" [11, p. 73]. If you are keeping score, that is four different jurisdictions within a matter of a couple of hundred feet. The parents found that while the county controlled traffic ligths on county roads, the town controlled parking on the street. Not surprisingly, the parents felt the whole venture was an exercise in windmill tilting as their request was passed from one jurisdiction to another.

A year after they had begun, the parents still had nothing to show for their efforts but a "No Parking" sign, which was recommended to the county "on the spurious theory that speeding drivers and anxious children would have a better view of each other" after the police rejected the request for a light [11, p. 274]. They had found that the fragmentation of responsibility among the different jurisdictions made it practically impossible to find out who had final authority. This in turn sheltered those with authority from public pressure, for they were able to hide among the many boards, commissions, and councils.

That is not to say, however, that groups in authority are immune from pressure. Well-organized citizens with specific goals operate among them effectively. The problem is that the goals of these citizen organizations often bear only faint resemblance to anything that can be identified as the public interest. If the special-interest groups are concerned about the general public interest, it is merely as a means to advance their own aims. Developments in New Orleans illustrate the point. The case revolves around that most American of monuments, the football stadium. Glittering new stadia—domed, of course —are supposed to be symbols of civic pride and accomplishment. At least that is what the people of New Orleans were told when they were asked to approve a $35'million stadium. They were also told, it is worth pointing out, that the stadium complex would be financially self-supporting and that no public funds would be involved in its operation [4, p. 178].

Only after the issue had been approved did anyone bother to point out that the referendum gave the Louisiana Stadium Exposition District (which again is local government!) unlimited authority to issue bonds and that these would be publicly guaranteed. It then developed that the stadium would probably not be self-supporting and that public money would be needed to subsidize its operation. That prediction has come true. The Superdome eats up many more dollars than it generates. Not only did construction run well over $100 million, but the expense of heating and cooling the structure costs the taxpayers money!

What had happened was that, in effect, the public had voted to allow the misappropriation of public money. The public had been "badly deceived," and taxes paid by all the people were going to benefit only a few people [4, p. 178]. The stadium is an impressive structure; unfortunately, it is as much a symbol of private manipulation of public interests as a monument to sport. It says something about present-day America that the battle of New Orleans is being fought in cities across the country. The shift of professional football from New York to New Jersey created a major political incident, and so did the related plans for the construction of a stadium. Some cities have fared better. In Seattle, the Kingdome was constructed under the careful scrutiny of a public board, while in Boston, a new stadium was financed through private commercial means and is doing quite well [4, pp. 104–105]. A scheme similar to that carried out in New Orleans was attempted in Minnesota, but it was uncovered before the vote. Minnesota fans may still have to shiver through their games, but at least their civic pride is intact.

The obvious point is that local government is not so well equipped to handle local problems as many believe. The problems of fragmentation and domination of special interests are merely representative of others that have been engendered by years of neglect and poor management. This happened because citizen-consumers let it happen, those same individuals who are now calling for local control. Volumes have been written on these developments. To explain them, it is necessary to consider public apathy, an increasingly mobile citizenry, structural changes in the economic and social life of the community, and the emphasis on national programs the federal government administers.

The problem is complicated by the differing forces at work on local government. On the one hand, there is an increasing demand for locally supplied services, such as police protection and education. At the same time, many problems are truly national in scope and therefore cannot be handled at the local level. This means that while local government is becoming increasingly important to citizen-consumers, it does not represent any magic formula that can be applied to all problems. Those who favor local government simply because it is local have unfortunately missed that rather obvious point. A two-step process is involved here: first to identify the areas for which local government can be effective and then to equip such government with the tools to do the job. Assuming that any local government can take on any problem is a good way to ensure frustration and failure.

The pattern of local government is most notable for its variation. In some areas, local government has shown the ability to serve individuals in their roles as both consumers and citizens. In other areas, citizens are showing displeasure—and in some cases, outright hostility—toward local government. The taxpayers' revolt, after all, began with consumers at the local level. Government cannot function effectively if citizen-consumers cannot decide what things they want government to do, what things they want to do for themselves, and what things they do not want done at all. The resolution of that issue, whatever form it takes, will show up first at the local level.

On Bureaucrats and Bureaucracy

The Bureaucratic Hang-up

If there is one outstanding feature of modern life, it is bureaucracy. No discussion of the consumer and public goods would be complete without considering it. While most of us like to think about government in grand terms, global strategies, and national goals, we are much less concerned with such things than we are with the elements of government that touch our day-to-day lives. Citizens may be concerned about foreign policy, but they seldom become as enraged about it as they do when the Department of Motor Vehicles makes a mistake in their automobile registration.

It can be argued that when people speak of making the government *responsive,* as they are increasingly prone to do, they really mean making the bureaucracy responsive. The bureaucracy has the power to make decisions that affect the citizen-consumer most directly. At the most superficial level, it is a problem of perception. Individuals see their own cases as unique, as not conforming to the general rule because of exceptional circumstances. To the bureaucrat, who sees thousands of such cases, the individual's case is no different from others, so it is treated according to established patterns.

A more fundamental problem with bureaucracy, however, goes beyond momentary inconvenience. It concerns bureaucratic intrusion and suggests that such things may impinge on democratic processes. Totalitarian states, like the Soviet Union, tend to be highly bureaucraticized, while pure democracy, as in the New England town meeting, features direct citizen control. The natural conclusion is that bureaucracy, if not itself undemocratic, is at least a threat to democratic principles [3, p. 103]. In this context, the growing bureaucracy in a country such as the United States is ominous and foreboding. Writing almost two decades ago, Peter Blau noted that "the more a person values equality, the more objectionable is the experience of being subjected to the controlling power of officials [3, p. 103]. As bureaucracy has grown over the years since Blau's writing, the cause for taking offense has intensified.

Any solution to this problem must surely take into account why the bureaucracy is there in the first place, which is to provide services. It may be unappealing, but it must be admitted that the bureaucrat is needed, for it is through the bureaucracy that a great deal of public consumption takes place. The legislature can pass enlightened laws and propose progressive programs, but it remains for the bureaucracy to carry them out. Therefore, anyone who rages against the bureaucracy for making society more complex has missed the point. It is the society that has made the bureaucracy more complex. As society has grown, so have the programs needed to deal with its problems. As a result, the bureaucracy needed to administer these programs has grown. To reduce the bureaucracy, it is necessary to reduce the complexity of the society, but that is unlikely since it is impossible to put the country in a time machine, twist a few dials, and return to the simplicity of the good old days.

It is clear that the citizen's position in the political system parallels the consumer's position in the marketplace. In both roles, individuals need to equip themselves to deal with their present environment. In this case, that means ensuring that the bureaucracy is responsive. The task of the citizen-consumer is to make sure that the bureaucracy functions as an agent of public consumption and that it does so with humanity and efficiency but without bias.

Efficiency and the Bureaucracy

Proper functioning of a bureaucracy cannot be achieved easily. Indeed, it cannot be achieved at all unless the general bias against public goods is removed. This bias works against bureaucrats too. An official in a private firm is an *executive,* while someone with a similar position in government is a *bureaucrat,* even though the former may be part of a larger bureaucracy than the latter.* There is no reason to cloak the executive in gray-flannel respectability while portraying the bureaucrat as a mean-spirited individual in eyeshade and sleeve garters.

Public bureaucracies in general are probably neither much better nor much worse than private ones, but they bear a much heavier burden of abuse. Some of it may be warranted, but citizen-consumers cannot expect better services until they are willing to improve the image of the public service. Beyond that, they must be willing to provide the necessary tools. This means modernization and professionalization. It also means more money, which will not sit well with the citizen-taxpayer. But since the citizen-consumer and the citizen-taxpayer are the same person, the need to pay in order to consume quality services is obvious.

Certainly there is room for improvement in public administration. Much of it arises from early neglect, rooted in public misconception. Public positions typically have been viewed in political as well as economic terms. Thus, through patronage, these jobs became the standard means for politicians to reward the party faithful. Even with the advent of civil service, efficiency too often took a back seat to political considerations. Efficiency is also hindered by the very nature of the job that the public bureaucracy must do. Most public services are labor intensive, meaning relatively large amounts of labor are required. Services in general—whether private or public—tend to show smaller increases in productivity than manufacturing. The relatively heavy labor input limits the application of the capital that is necessary to increase productivity.

It is difficult even to measure the productivity of public employees. In the private sector, success is ultimately measured by profits, but there is no similar standard for the public sector. Output itself may be difficult to define. What is the appropriate measure of output for teachers, police officers, or judges? If it is quantity alone that matters, then the number of students taught, the number of arrests made, and

---

* Companies like General Motors and AT&T have more employees and deal with larger amounts of money than most state and local governments in the United States.

the number of convictions handed down should do. However, most observers recognize that these quantitative measures are crude indicators at best. Nevertheless, increased pressures for accountability have forced such measures into use.

Using quantity as a proxy for quality of services may be counterproductive. If output per se is a measure of effectiveness, then there will be efforts to show more output for its own sake. The emphasis on numbers finally creates pressures for expanding the bureaucracy. That is doubly unfortunate, because bureaucracies generate their own momentum that creates additional pressure for expansion. Anyone familiar with any bureaucracy knows that it is a minisociety with its own status symbols and internal logic. Thus, a clever department head enhances his or her position by expanding the department's staff.

Left unchecked, these tendencies confirm a variation of Parkinson's law, that the amount of work will expand according to the number of people to do it. With more people, the available work is merely divided up into smaller and smaller portions. The bureaucracy then takes on a life of its own and becomes its own reason for being. Citizens, whom the bureaucracy is supposed to be serving, may be looked on as intruders. This problem is real enough, but it needs to be seen for what it is, a technical, organizational question. Too often, discussions of the topic take on emotional overtones that hardly contribute to a solution. How can the bureaucracy most efficiently do the job it is supposed to do? That is the question. Attacks against the bureaucracy are often really directed at the program that is being administered, a confusion that only clouds the picture and makes effective management more difficult.

Citizen control of the bureaucracy presents greater difficulty than the control of elected officials. The latter, at least, must be concerned about the next election. The bureaucrat, however, holds his or her position by either appointment or a civil-service test. The very professionalization called for above creates a problem. Well-trained professionals may see their responsibility in terms of their specific job, not in terms of the public. This is often a problem with local planning boards, for example, which tend to be preoccupied with technical questions.

A very delicate point arises. It is necessary to insulate the bureaucracy from political pressure and yet at the same time maintain public control and ensure that the bureaucracy is responsive. Balancing these two needs is difficult and requires continual review. The key here is the elected official. While bureaucracies are not responsible to the electorate, elected officials are responsible for the bureaucracy and are therefore vulnerable to pressure.

The public cannot, and probably should not, hope to dominate the day-to-day operations of government. The citizen-consumer's role is to establish the limits within which the bureaucracy will work and the ground rules that will govern its operation. This is very near to the point we reached about effective consumer protection. The important decision for the consumer is to decide in favor of effective protection. Once that decision is made, elected representatives can be presented with an ultimatum: Produce or be voted out. The same is true in this case; the decision must be applied to ensure action.

Some New Approaches

The Ombudsman

The traditional methods of citizen control of public goods have concerned us thus far. Recently, efforts have been under way to provide the citizen-consumer with additional instruments of control. These efforts have covered different approaches, most of which are still experimental. They deserve attention as a response to a basic problem. The developments examined here are offered to illustrate the direction that such efforts are taking, but they do not exhaust all possibilities.

It is not surprising in these days of imports that one of the best known of these attempts should be from abroad. The idea of the ombudsman comes from Scandinavia and has been widely adopted in Europe. The ombudsman is simply a public advocate, the representative of the public in government. He or she functions, as one authority noted, to

> provide protection and redress to the individual citizen against abuses by an increasingly remote, yet omnipresent administrative process ... (and) ... provide an institution capable of demanding certain standards of conduct and perhaps even of suggesting reorganization. ... [1, p. 236]

In terms of the previous discussion, the ombudsman becomes an information agent, helping the individual find his or her way among the maze of organizations that characterize modern government. He or she also ensures that citizens receive fair treatment before these various bodies. In a sense then, the function of the ombudsman is to even up the odds and give the citizen a fair chance against government organization.

The commonsense argument for the ombudsman is so compelling that it is not surprising that citizens' groups should be calling for the creation of such a position. The issue is not simple, however, since questions arise about the powers of the ombudsman, his or her responsibilities and position within the structure of government, and his or her relation to other governmental groups. There are also questions as to how effective an ombudsman could be, particularly at the federal level.* Nevertheless, various state and local governments have adopted the ombudsman proposal in one form or another. Though such operations are generally small scale, they have demonstrated their ability to help citizens in their dealings with government. Even critics of the idea indicate that it may hold considerable merit at those levels [12, pp. 246–55].

It would be a mistake to think of the ombudsman as a magic remedy to the problems that face the citizen-consumer. Such an office can cut the individual's information costs and promote an understanding of how government functions. Responsibility remains with the individual, however; if the ombudsman's office is to be more than a hand-holding operation, the citizen-consumer must be willing to demonstrate the kind of initiative I have indicated.

Decentralization

Involved is such an overworked word these days, that it is often difficult to tell exactly what it means. It is commonly used, however, in reference to a reform that has gained considerable attention. The logic behind its approach is simple and straightforward. If government programs are actually to serve the people, then the people should be involved in their formulation and administration. By extension, this line of thinking leads to decentralization and to community control of local programs, responsibility being returned to the people in the literal sense. Such proposals have taken two main forms. The first is direct citizen participation in government programs like the original Model Cities, where local residents are involved in the project from its inception. The second is the administration of existing institutions, such as city schools; in this case, responsibilities are taken from a central administration and vested in groups in various neighborhoods.

These experiments have met massive resistance from established

---

* As noted in Chapter 8, the proposed federal Agency for Consumer Advocacy would have functioned as a kind of ombudsman's office.

administrative units. Both power and money are involved, making the whole question hypersensitive. City officials do not want to see independent and potentially competitive sources of power springing up within the city. Nor do established organizations want to give up power to smaller units. Predictably, the results of such efforts are confused and confusing. Detached, objective evaluations are difficult to find, but certain shortcomings are evident. Senator Daniel Moynihan, who has worked on the question both in government and in private life, asked why such programs "have had a measure of success, but nothing like that hoped for?" He answers his own question with this disturbing observation:

> It may be we have not been entirely candid with ourselves in this area. Citizen particpation . . . is in practice a "bureaucratic ideology," a device whereby public officials induce non-public indviduals to act in the way the officials desire. [13, p. 33]

If this is true, then citizens' power is an illusion, and illusions seldom last. If local leaders try to develop programs that they feel are meaningful, differences in perception bring them into conflict with both local and federal officials. These often lead to disillusionment on the part of the citizens and resentment in the community at large.

Decentralization of administration has run into similar problems. In most large cities, the administration of government is so far removed from the individual that there is little identification between the two. Particular areas, representing racial or ethnic groups with their own traditions, typically feel that they are poorly served. The logic of decentralization is to give these people decision-making power over the policies that directly affect them.

There are a host of problems associated with decentralization. This seemingly simple proposal for fragmentation of power may reduce the ability to meet problems in a coordinated fashion. At the extreme, decentralization may destroy the city per se, reducing it to a series of neighborhoods. There should be an optimal mix of centralized and decentralized authority that offers the benefits of both cohesive action and community control. Were there no other elements involved, it could no doubt be found. Other elements are involved, however, complicating the already complicated question. These include racial, social, and economic questions that tend to escalate the level of rhetoric, if not the level of performance. Problems of entrenched power also develop and existing institutions resist any change. One New York official noted that the demand for decentralization has gone beyond merely administration to include policymaking. He continued:

> Skepticism about government processes has gone so far that unelected people—"community leaders"—demand that they be the adjudicators of policy; no Solomon arises to distinguish between the true community leader and the false community leader, so that the process of decision becomes further delayed. [19, p. 31]

Decentralization and community control offer urban dwellers nothing more than the advantages enjoyed by other citizens. Although citizens are free to move if they do not like their local government, this does not apply to the poor and to those who feel a strong attachment to an area. If these groups want more to say in government policy, they must seek it from the government they have. If you reverse this argument, it is possible to maintain that if there were more community control, the flight from the cities might be reduced as individuals found they could attain their goals without moving to the suburbs. America's preoccupation with bigness—the bigger-is-better syndrome—has resulted in the uncritical acceptance of continued growth in urban areas, even though this growth was unplanned and largely unpatterned.

The problems of urban congestion and the ongoing financial difficulties of many large cities—most noticeably, New York—should have laid the bigger-is-better idea to rest. Citizen-consumers have recognized the problem, and more and more of them are leaving urban areas altogether. For the first time in decades, it is rural areas, not cities and their suburbs, that are growing most rapidly. The new migration patterns offer opportunities for the future. Many experts feel that a population of about 250,000 is an optimal size for cities. This is large enough for efficient operation, but still small enough to be manageable.

This notion is borne out in Table 9.3, which compares the costs of city services per person in cities of different size. Cities of more than one million spend exactly three times as much per person as cities in the fifty to one-hundred thousand class do, and over twice as much as cities with populations just under half a million. While expenditures on highways are remarkably stable, most other areas show a marked increase. This is most dramatic with welfare costs, which are insignificant in the smaller cities, but account for the largest single expenditure category in the largest cities.* Unfortu-

---

* This reflects the fact that the poor are concentrated in the largest cities, which in turn shows the need for a national policy to deal with population movements.

nately, expenditures for parks and recreation—a quality-of-life cate-gory—are about the same in the largest and smallest group, but higher in between.

This suggests that better planning, controlled city growth, and a nationwide population policy are needed to ensure that cities of the future are not merely extensions of those we have. The goal should be more livable cities, where services are delivered efficiently. The periodic breakdown of public services in some of our big cities should underscore this point. The cities we have, however, must be managed. A practical method must be worked out that will involve the people in their own government and yet maintain efficient over-all operation. The word *community* in one sense means a group of people with shared experiences and aspirations. It is probable that such a feeling is necessary before the adequate delivery of public services is possible; in short, people have to care. If decentralization is needed to develop that feeling, then it should be pursued. The mere fact that improvement is possible should encourage whatever efforts are necessary.

A New Public-Private Mix?

By now it should be clear that when it comes to public consumption, the citizen-consumer is sitting on the horns of a dilemma. He or she is in an uncomfortable position and it is tempting to say he or she

Table 9.3 Expenditures Per Capita for Selected Categories, by City Size: 1971

Category	City size in thousands [a]		
	Over 1,000	300–500	50–100
All functions	$569	$271	$189
Education [b]	107	57	35
Highways	20	21	20
Public welfare	109	6	3
Hospitals [b]	47	7	6
Police and fire	79	48	38
Sewage and sanitation [b]	32	28	20
Parks and recreation	13	20	12

Source: *Municipal Yearbook*, 1973, pp. 98–99.
Note: All figures are rounded to the nearest dollar.
[a] There are 6 cities in the largest class, 21 in the middle, and 231 in the smallest.
[b] Includes capital outlay.

gets shafted either way. On the one hand (or horn), the citizen-consumer needs public goods. On the other, the very nature of such goods makes individual choices difficult, if not impossible. To attack the root of the problem, it is necessary to ask whether there isn't a better way to provide public goods, one that would account for externalities while still allowing more choice for the individual? There is nothing sacred about the way things are done now. Some goods, like highways and education, are both publicly and privately supplied (toll roads versus freeways; public schools versus private). To a lesser extent, the same thing is true of medical care.

It may be possible to ensure a larger measure of private control over the distribution of public goods. The volunteer army offers a recent example. Under the draft system, anyone selected for service had to serve or face imprisonment. Since defense is a public good, it was assumed that this loss of choice was warranted. With the volunteer army, the individual has a choice. If he or she joins, it is because service has been made sufficiently attractive.

The difficulties encountered in the actual operation of the volunteer army say something about the process of choice. The volunteer system is expensive because it takes money to make the service attractive. Furthermore, some complain that the quality of the army has suffered. If that is true, the problem may be with the military structure rather than with the volunteer system itself. In any event, the experience with the volunteer army shows the coercive nature of the draft and the degree to which individual choice was limited. The need, then, is to balance freedom of choice with the demands of national security.

Another example that is gaining acceptance is the so-called voucher system for education. This approach recognizes that externalities exist in education, but, its proponents argue, the monolithic structure of public education does not really serve the public effectively. Parents and students have little choice as to what type of school they attend. The voucher system would retain public support for education, but paradoxically, do away with public schools [8, pp. 85–107]. It would give parents (or students) vouchers financed out of tax revenues that could be redeemed in educational services. They could be spent on education at any school of the individual's choosing.

Advocates argue that this plan, by restoring competition to the educational system, would assure those who use the schools a wider choice and better quality. Because public support would reach the schools through the parent or student, schools that could not deliver adequate services would be driven out of business. A similar system is actually in use at the college level. Many states provide tuition grants that enable students to attend private colleges or universities. Proposed income-tax deductions for tuition expenses would have a similar effect.

Opponents of the voucher system maintain that vouchers would promote racial and socioeconomic segregation, and probably spell the end of public support for education. They point to the fact that vouchers were used in Virginia as a means of forestalling integration during the 1950s and 1960s. The advent of private "academies" in other areas where public schools have been integrated lends strong support to the argument. However, the potential advantages are sufficient to warrant further study of the question, with an eye to overcoming possible negative side effects. In this case, a new public-private mix may not be the answer, but it may at least force us to reexamine the way in which we approach these problems. If we can gain a clearer understanding of public consumption from that re-examination, the exercise will have been worthwhile.

The Taxpayers' Revolt

Growing numbers of citizen-consumers have apparently completed their own reexamination of public consumption. If their actions in the voting booth are any indicator, they weren't very impressed with what they found. Voters have been saying "NO!" to taxes in such a loud voice that they have been branded as revolutionaries. Thus, we have the taxpayers revolt, which might be called the *meat-axe approach* to public consumption. Rather than tinkering with the system, voters are forcing change by the simple expedient of cutting off money.

At this writing, it is impossible to give a full assessment of the taxpayer's revolt. California voters acceptance of Proposition 13, which cut property taxes to 1 percent of assessed valuation and limited tax increases, attracted such media attention that all sense of proportion was lost.* However, similar efforts are underway in other states and the California vote was not an isolated event. Voters across the country have been viewing tax proposals with increasingly critical eyes and have rejected new taxes even when that meant closing schools or cutting back on other essential services [16, p. 1]. Even if there is no revolution, the mood of the country is clearly running against taxes.

Taken at face value, the rejection of tax levies simply represents an expression of citizen-consumers' preferences for private consump-

---

* At present, the constitutionality of Proposition 13 is being tested in the courts.

tion over public consumption. If citizens say "no" to higher taxes, they are saying they would rather have the money to spend themselves instead of turning it over to a government for payments toward public goods. The implications of that decision, however, are far reaching, because of the externalities involved in public goods. For that reason, the entire question deserves closer attention.

As we examine the issue more closely, we'll see that the taxpayers' revolt embodies a number of points already mentioned. One example is the citizen-consumer's tendency to focus on the cost of public goods rather than the benefits. Citizens haven't been voting in *favor* of reduced police protection or poorer sanitation services; they have been voting *against* taxes. Voters may not appreciate fully that the consequences are the same in either case. If the taxpayers' revolt is simply another illustration of the bias against public goods, citizen-consumers are being dangerously short-sighted. Some voters, of course, recognize the implications of reduced taxation. They want to cut back on funding for public services. There is a strong feeling that citizens aren't getting their money's worth from taxes. These voters feel the public sector has grown fat and inefficient. To the extent that is true, cutting back on taxes would force government to become more efficient, but would not force any significant decreases in services provided.*

There is another, more divisive element in the taxpayers' revolt that appears particularly dangerous. Whatever consensus existed about the allocation of public goods seems to be breaking down. The public sector has grown rapidly and voters are showing their displeasure with the responsibilities governments have assumed. Remember that citizen-consumers don't benefit equally from public expenditures; in general, lower-income groups benefit more. That idea is borne out in Table 9.4. The benefit rates show (in percentage terms) the actual contribution that different types of federal expenditures make to the real income of individuals in different income groups. Thus, social security payments make up 28.6 percent of income for those earning under $3000, but make only an insignificant contribution to income for wealthy persons. Social security, veterans' benefits, and health expenditures are the most striking examples, but the pattern is the same across expenditure categories.

However, except for the very rich and the very poor, the tax system is proportional [18, pp. 38–40]. This means that most Americans pay about the same percentage of their income in taxes. The

---

* In the California case, this feeling was reinforced by a large state surplus. State officials were apparently not entirely candid about how much extra money the state had [2].

net effect is that individuals in the higher income brackets aren't receiving a dollar's worth of direct benefits for each dollar paid in taxes; such people would enjoy a net gain if one dollar were reallocated from public to private spending, because they would gain a dollar of private consumption but give up less than one dollar's worth of public goods. It is in this context that the comment of one Californian becomes significant. "It's those social services that annoy the heck out of me—social services for the colored, the Mexicans and so forth. Who wants to pay taxes that go for things like that?" [2, p. 28].

Such comments appear mean-spirited and they certainly don't reflect any notion of the externalities (benefits to the general public) involved in welfare payments. One might condemn such comments, but personal judgments ought to be tempered by an appreciation for the complexities of the situation. It is only natural for families pressed by inflation and higher taxes to look out for themselves first, especially when their fears are manipulated by vested interests (a role played by landlords in the California case, who stood to benefit mightily from lower property taxes) [2, pp. 26–28].

One element that has been overlooked in discussions of the tax revolt is the impact of internal migration. The people who approved Proposition 13 are the children and grandchildren of the families that swarmed to California in the 1930s and 1940s. They might well have seen higher taxes as a threat to their new economic status. Today's migration toward the so-called sunbelt represents a move from areas with higher taxes. Are these new residents of low-tax areas glad to have left higher taxes behind them, or will they begin

Table 9.4   Effective Benefit Rates by Family Income: 1973

Federal Expenditures	Income ($000)					
	0–3	3–5	5–10	10–15	15–25	Over 25
Highways	0.7	0.6	0.8	0.4	0.2	0.2
Education	0.7	1.1	0.7	0.6	0.4	0.4
Social security	28.6	41.3	11.8	3.9	1.7	0.9
Veterans	11.6	3.0	1.6	1.1	0.4	0.2
Agriculture	1.8	1.3	0.3	0.2	0.2	0.2
Health	11.0	4.3	1.7	1.2	0.6	0.4
Housing	6.7	3.4	0.6	—	—	—

Source: Singer, *Public Microeconomics* [18, p. 41].

to demand the higher level of services they previously enjoyed? The answer to that question will tell a lot about the pattern of local taxes in the 1980s.

I have used the word *complexity* several times in this discussion, which recalls my earlier comment about the relationship between government and the complexity of modern life. It is our complex society that creates complex (and expensive) government, not the other way around. Thus, voters may have misdirected their energies; governments, as visible symbols of society's complexities, bear the brunt of an attack that should be directed against the frustrations of modern life.

The future direction that the taxpayers' revolt will take cannot be predicted at this time. At some future date, we may look back on the whole episode and liken it to the story of the farmer and his mule. Before starting to plow, the farmer hits the mule with a two-by-four, "Just to git his attention." The tax revolt may be a two-by-four in the hands of citizen-consumers who want to get the attention of government. The action, while it seems drastic, may be necessary. In the previous sections, I've noted that change doesn't come easily; it may take an uprising of citizen-consumers to bring that change about. Falling profits are a signal of the need for change in the private sector. The taxpayers' revolt may serve that purpose in the public sector, bringing about positive reforms (such as those discussed earlier) that would otherwise be impossible.

If this is the proper interpretation, the taxpayers' revolt may be an encouraging development. If, however, voters simply want to turn away from community responsibility and indulge their individual desires, the picture is much less promising. Society's problems are real, and ignoring them by cutting off funds for public goods will only make the situation worse. Sooner or later, the problems will have to be faced; the longer the day of reckoning is put off, the higher the final price will be.

Study Questions

1. Some communities try to attract new industry and residents by stressing their low taxes. What does this tell you of the community's thinking about public goods? Do you think such policies are effective? Do you think they are desirable?

2. Many private and public goods are substitutes for one another. You can swim, for example, in a public or private pool and you could hire a guard or install alarms in lieu of police protection.

a. What other examples of this kind of substitution can you name?

b. If these goods and services can be supplied privately, why are they supplied publicly?

3. Public and private goods may also be complements, meaning they are used in conjunction with one another. Automobiles may be private vehicles, but they are used almost exclusively on public highways. Name some other examples of complementarity. What are the implications of this kind of relation?

4. Explain why the demand for public goods will be greater in communities that contain either high proportions of children or high proportions of elderly people.

5. For the citizen, what are the alternatives to delegating some political decision making? Are the alternatives either realistic or desirable?

6. Efforts are being made to revitalize local government at the same time that many local governments are being abolished. School consolidation, for example, is well advanced, and metropolitan government is being advocated (and adopted) in many urban areas. Can these two developments be reconciled? Explain.

7. One American worker in five is employed by some level of government, while in 1929, the figure was one in ten. Does that mean that public goods are twice as important now as they were in 1929? Are twice as many public goods supplied?

8. Can you relate your answer to Question 7 to the taxpayers' revolt?

9. There is growing evidence that many high school graduates cannot read. Relate this fact to your answers in Questions 7 and 8.

10. Discuss the differences between the controls that citizens have over elected officials and over members of the bureaucracy.

11. The old-style political boss, whose machine ran the city, had ward heelers to look after voters and hear their complaints. Carefully consider the advantages such systems held for citizen-consumers. How does the ombudsman's function differ from these early caretakers of the political system?

12. Public goods are supported out of tax monies on the assumption that everyone benefits. It is argued, however, that in many cases, the primary benefit goes to middle- and upper-income groups. If that is true, what is the impact of a policy of low tuition at state universities? Contrast the effects of a fee

charged at a state park (that can be reached only by automobile) and a fee at an ínner-city swimming pool.

Suggested Projects

1. Does your city or state government have an office of ombudsman or a similar office responsible for helping citizens with problems?

2. How many local governmental bodies are there in your area? Count not just city and county governments, but townships, schools, independent districts, and special authorities. What is the rationale for this sort of division? Do you think the public is well served under such a system?

3. The chapter began with the assertion that if you asked people to name the things they have consumed, they will not mention public goods. Try it on a random sample. What are the results? What does this suggest about how individuals perceive public goods?

4. Question 3 under Study Questions suggested that while automobiles are private and highways are public, they are nevertheless complementary goods.
   a. Calculate the taxes paid per mile a car is driven. This will require estimates of license fees, property taxes, and sales taxes, and also of miles driven and gasoline mileage (needed to calculate gasoline taxes per mile).
   b. Find out the cost of building and maintaining a mile of highway (the figures should be available through local highway officials and in national studies). How does this compare with the figures obtained in (a)?
   c. What other public costs are attached to automobile use?
   d. Are there externalities involved in highways? Explain.

5. The text did not discuss the specific taxes used to finance public goods; most areas rely primarily on taxes on property, sales, and income.
   a. What are the main revenue sources in your area?
   b. Sales and property taxes tend to be regressive (lower-income groups pay a higher percentage of their income in taxes) while income taxes are more progressive (higher-income groups pay a higher percentage). What is the implication of this fact for the provision of public goods?
   c. Would you say that in your area the cost of public goods

is borne equally by all income groups? What about the benefits?

6. Is there a group working to limit taxes in your area? If so, find out what they are trying to do, why they want to do it, and how they are trying to do it.

7. Are consumers satisfied with the quality of the services they receive? Conduct a survey to see if consumers feel they are getting their money's worth from their taxes (locally). Do consumers feel the quality of services have gone up or down?

8. Examine the regulations requiring citizen input in public projects (a call to city hall or the court house should put you in touch with the right people). Do you think these regulations are realistic? If possible, attend a hearing or open meeting held to obtain citizen input.

Bibliography and Suggested Readings

1. Abraham, Henry J. "The Need for an Ombudsman in the United States." In *The Ombudsman*, ed. Donald C. Rowat, London: George Allen & Unwin, 1965.
   The author outlines the functions of the ombudsman and builds a case for adopting such an office in the United States. While some of the statistics are now out of date, this collection of original articles is still one of the most comprehensive treatments of the ombudsman concept available.

2. "The Big Tax Revolt." *Newsweek*, June 19, 1978, pp. 20–30.
   A news report covering differing aspects of the taxpayers' revolt in the wake of the California vote on Proposition 13.

3. Blau, Peter M. *Bureaucracy in Modern Society*. New York: Random House, 1956.
   This little book remains a classic. It deals not only with the functions of bureaucracy, but also its place in a democratic society. An excellent introduction to the topic.

4. Burck, Charles G. "It's Promoters vs. Taxpayers in the Super-Stadium Game." *Fortune*, March 1973, pp. 104–107.
   When the Colosseum was built in ancient Rome, some Romans must have wondered if maybe there was not a better way to spend the money. That is still a valid question, even though pro football has replaced Christians vs. Lions. A good exploration of public benefits vs. private.

5. U.S. Department of Commerce, *County and City Data Book*. Washington D.C.: U.S. Government Printing Office, 1977.

Statistics and more statistics on American states, counties, and cities. Data on population, income, taxes, expenditures, and other categories.

6. Downs, Anthony. *An Economic Theory of Democracy.* New York: Harper & Row, 1957.
   The appropriateness of this classic work can be seen in the problems discussed in the text. Not only is the lucidity of Down's analysis to his credit, but also that he saw the problem before it had become popularized.

7. Due, John, and Friedlaender, Ann. *Government Finance: Economics of the Public Sector,* 6th ed., Homewood, Ill.: Richard D. Irwin, 1977.
   A public finance text that covers a wide range of topics. Even students with more limited backgrounds will find the book a useful reference.

8. Friedman, Milton. *Capitalism and Freedom.* Chicago: University of Chicago Press, 1962.
   More from one of America's most imaginative thinkers. Friedman's ideas, including the volunteer army and negative income tax, have had a strong impact on present-day American thought.

9. Galbraith, John Kenneth. *The Affluent Society.* Boston: Houghton Mifflin Co., 1958.
   The original treatment of the social imbalance theory, including forceful arguments for more careful attention to public goods.

10. ———. *The New Industrial State.* Boston: Houghton Mifflin Co., 1967.
    Treatment of the differences between perception and reality. A fairly complete summary of the Galbraithian system.

11. Kaplan, Samuel. "The Balkanization of Suburbia." *Harpers,* October 1971, pp. 72–74.
    A commuter takes time to reflect on what the proliferation of local governments means to a citizen who is trying to get something done. Well he might.

12. Krislov, Samuel. "A Restrained View." In *The Ombudsman,* ed. Donald C. Rowat. London: George Allen & Unwin, 1965.
    Another look at the ombudsman, this time from a less-than-enthusiastic supporter. The author nevertheless sees value in the office.

13. Moynihan, Daniel P. "Toward a National Urban Policy." In *Problems in Political Economy, An Urban Perspective,* ed. David M. Gordon. Lexington, Mass.: D. C. Heath and Co., 1971, p. 33.
    One of America's leading experts looks at the problems of the city and how they can be met. Both as an academician and a government official, Senator Moynihan has worked closely with urban problems.

14. *Municipal Year Book 1978.* Washington, D.C.: International City Management Association, 1978.

An excellent collection of data on city government. Includes both economic and political information.

15. North, Douglass, and Miller, Roger. "The Economics of Crime Prevention." In *The Economics of Public Issues*. New York: Harper & Row, 1971.
This reading, like others in the book, shows how economic analysis can be applied—and sometimes misapplied—to public questions. Other topics range from prostitution to major league baseball.

16. Perry, James, and Hayatt, James. "While California Votes on Taxes, Other States Mull Spending Limits." *Wall Street Journal,* June 6, 1978, pp. 1ff.
A news report on tax issues in California and similar efforts in other areas around the country.

17. Phelps, Edmund S., ed. *Private Wants and Public Needs*. Rev. ed., New York: W. W. Norton & Co., 1965.
A good collection of readings which, as the title suggests, deals with many of the questions discussed in this chapter. A good introduction for anyone interested in the subject.

18. Singer, Neil M. *Public Microeconomics*. 2nd ed., Boston: Little, Brown and Co., 1976.
Contains valuable information on actual impact of various public programs on consumers.

19. Starr, Roger. "The Decline and Decline of New York." *New York Times Magazine,* November 21, 1971, pp. 31ff.
The former executive director of the New York Citizen's Housing and Planning Council looks at the problems created by pressures for decentralization within cities.

-10-

Problems of the Low-Income Consumer

Special Problems of the Poor

The Forgotten Consumers

Among the numerous contrasts between the 1960s and the 1970s, none is more striking than the public's changing attitude toward poverty. During the 1960s, expressions of concern with poverty were translated into a variety of programs to deal with the problem. By the 1970s, however, most of the programs had been dropped (many of them in disrepute). Poverty had become a nonissue, attracting neither news coverage nor obvious public concern. As the poor became less visable, interest in their problems as consumers underwent a corresponding decline.

It would be simplistic to assume that public interest in the consumer problems of the poor passed as soon as the wave of violence that plagued American cities in the late 1960s receded. However, because those problems are complex and seem remote to most consumers, some dramatic stroke was necessary to force the issue into the public consciousness. Even amidst the scenes of blazing neighborhoods, it is unlikely that most people appreciated the subtlety of the distinction between robbing and looting made by a young man in Watts: "When you loot a credit store, you are just taking back some of the interest they have been charging for years ..." [13, pp. 56–57]. Yet his reasoning was based on conditions confirmed by the National Advisory Commission on Civil Disorders—that consumer-

246

related complaints were a primary source of unrest in the ghetto [16, pp. 139–40].

As we will see, identifying those complaints was easier than understanding them, but for now it is sufficient that we recognize that the problems are real. The very existence of those problems, however, represents a paradox. I have stressed that consumer problems are born out of affluence; because the poor are, by definition, not affluent, one might suspect that they are exempt from the problems of affluence. Just the opposite is true. Low-income consumers must face all the problems of consumers, problems brought about by the affluence they do not share. Not only that, but they must bear a particularly heavy burden, for the very fact of their poverty makes them less able to deal with these problems than middle-income consumers.

That is why the problems of low-income consumers deserve special attention. The poor receive few of the benefits and all of the problems of the modern, consumer-oriented society. It is a two-edged sword that cuts them both ways. Setting the problem up this way provides us with our general line of analysis; within this approach, there are two implicit points that should be brought out. The first is that while low-income groups deserve special attention, they do not require a special analysis. Elements of the analysis I've developed thus far can still be employed, but when poverty is taken into account, the results will be different. Our job is to take the analysis and ask: How does adding poverty into the equation alter the conclusions? The second point follows from the first: *The problem is poverty*. That may seem simplistic, but it is a necessary realization for improvement in the position of the poor as consumers. Treating the consumer-related problems of low-income groups is like treating the symptoms of a disease. The disease is poverty; the symptoms, however unpleasant they may be, are still only symptoms.

The Poor—A Profile

Poverty in the midst of affluence has bothered sensitive people for generations. Poverty is never pleasant, but when it is universally shared—as it was on the frontier and is in most underdeveloped countries—its sting is less painful. In the United States, however, the contrasts are clearly drawn. Table 10.1 shows that while the number of people living in poverty fell by over one-third between 1959 and 1976, nearly 12 percent of all Americans still lived below officially designated poverty levels in 1976.* The data also show that while

* Set at $5815 for an urban family of four in 1976 [8, p. 1].

poverty is not a unique problem of minority groups—the white poor outnumber nonwhite—in percentage terms, the problem is greater for nonwhites. Furthermore, improvement among nonwhites has been less rapid; while the number of whites living in poverty dropped by over 40 percent between 1959 and 1976, the number of poor nonwhites declined by only 25 percent. Note too that almost half the nonwhite poor are children, a figure that bodes ill for the future.

A closer look at Table 10.1 shows that, although Americans may have put poverty out of their minds, the problem hasn't gone away. The figures for 1975 (a recession year) are almost identical to those for 1970. The situation for whites improved in 1976, but among nonwhites the number of people below the poverty line was slightly higher than it had been in 1970. The percentage of nonwhites living in poverty did decline slightly between 1970 and 1976. Nevertheless, it is clear that the sustained progress made against poverty in the 1960s was not carried into the 1970s. A change in the political climate may have contributed to the lack of progress in recent years, but the erratic performance of the economy in the 1970s was also a significant factor.

Table 10.1   Persons Below the Poverty Level, Selected Years, 1959–76: With Detailed Characteristics for 1976

Year	Number below poverty level (in millions)			Percentage below poverty level		
	Total	White	Other	Total	White	Other
1959	39.5	28.5	11.0	22.4	18.1	56.2
1965	33.2	22.5	10.7	17.3	13.3	47.1
1970	25.5	17.5	8.0	12.6	9.9	32.1
1975	25.9	17.8	8.1	12.3	9.7	29.3
1976	25.0	16.7	8.3	11.8	9.1	29.4
Head of family	5.3	3.6	1.8	9.4	7.1	26.4
Minors [a]	10.1	6.0	4.1	15.8	11.3	38.3
Over 65	3.3	2.6	0.7	15.0	13.2	32.7
Not related [b]	5.3	4.2	1.1	24.9	22.7	39.5
1976 as % of 1959	63.2	58.7	75.1	. . .	. . .	. . .

Source: *Consumer Income:* 1976 [8, p. 21]

[a] Children under 18.

[b] Individuals not living as part of a family unit.

These figures might weigh upon the conscience of any American, but from the perspective of consumer economics, they take on added significance. They suggest that a good many poor people are permanently poor. People who have temporarily fallen on hard times may suffer, but they can hold on to the hope that things will get better. Many poor people have no such hope. This in turn creates what might be called a psychology of poverty, which itself has important ramifications on the consumer. Since life is unpleasant, there is a desire to escape it through material accumulation. Commenting on this, one observer noted that the problem facing the low-income consumer

> is all the more poignant when it is realized that this pursuit of goods and credit, which in turn makes him so vulnerable to callous exploitation, is in reality what has been called "compensatory consumption," a desire to infuse his existence with dignity denied him elsewhere by accumulating material goods. [13, p. 36]

The poor may be isolated from the majority culture, but they are not insulated from it. They are exposed to the same pressures and urges to consume known to other Americans. In an age of instant mass communications, the vision of the good life is constantly before them, being extolled as the model for which to strive. It is not surprising that the poor should want to escape the contrast between that vision and the realities of their own existence. There is no reason to assume that even without these pressures consumption patterns among the poor should be the same as those among other groups. In considering income elasticity, I noted that consumption patterns change with income. Beyond that, it has been stressed that the particulars of individual consumption are a matter of individual tastes.

There is no reason to assume that these tastes are the same across the entire population. No one would be surprised to find that a Baptist minister in east Texas has a different consumption pattern from a Unitarian pastor in New York; or that a stockbroker in Sioux Falls lives differently from one in San Francisco. Yet the poor are not usually given the benefit of the doubt. The difference between consumption patterns among the poor and the middle class is somehow taken as evidence of irresponsibility, whereas it is nothing of the kind. Consumers in general are too often judged against an ideal norm instead of some measure that accounts for the realities of their situation. The realities that the poor face make their problems all the more difficult. We must be sensitive to those problems without assuming a condescending and patronizing attitude, which is nearly as damaging as judging everyone against a norm. In this analysis, we can be content to let the facts of the situation speak for themselves.

The Crux of the Problem

In the last section I maintained that the everyday problems of consumers fall most heavily on low-income groups. To put it differently, these groups are the least capable, by virtue of their low incomes, of coping with the problems all consumers face. Consumer problems arise from the consumer's lack of leverage in the marketplace. This lack of leverage comes from inadequate information, a failure to understand market mechanism, and the smallness of the individual compared with the market as a whole. The low-income consumer is particularly vulnerable.

Middle-income consumers may be ill equipped to deal with all of the problems of the marketplace, but their dollar votes give them some leverage. Most businesses are responsive to threats of "I'll take my business elsewhere" or "I'll tell my friends about this." The other tactics—talks with the manager, letters to the company, and the possibility of legal action—are all available as alternatives to the consumer. Such tactics do not always work, but they do offer the chance for consumers to assert themselves in the market.

There is also the question of information itself. At least information is available to the consumer who can seek it out. Experience provides valuable information that can be augmented with government publications, private services like *Consumer Reports,* and assorted industry information. The mobile consumer can move around to collect more information when that is necessary. Contrast this with the condition of the low-income consumer, who, by definition, has less market leverage. It may be a matter of debate as to how well markets respond to economic pressure, but it is clear that without purchasing power, the consumer cannot exert influence. Low-income consumers are therefore unable to defend themselves through the market mechanism.

Low-income consumers are also less mobile. The poor have fewer private automobiles, and unless they are served by a particularly good public transportation system, the majority of their purchases are limited to stores in their immediate area. This represents a loss of leverage, since area merchants will be aware of these consumers' limitations. The same thing is true of information. There are costs attached to obtaining information, so it follows that those with lower incomes will be able to afford less information. The poor may have less information from experience because they make fewer repetitive purchases, have a narrower range of associations, and not as much overall market experience.* The rural poor, who in general are quite isolated and have the least experience with the market, are especially vulnerable.

The poor are also generally disadvantaged with regard to public goods, of which education is among the most important. While attempts have been made in recent years to improve education in poor areas, inequality of educational opportunities is still to be deplored. From the consumer's perspective, education is an important source of information and skills necessary for operation in the modern marketplace. The delivery of other public services, too, is typically deficient in low-income areas. Services like sanitation, parks, and libraries are often inadequate. The same is true of the quality of law enforcement, not only in police protection, but also in enforcing building codes and other consumer protection legislation. The rural poor are particularly hard hit, in many places receiving hardly any public services.

The same factors that work against low-income consumers in the marketplace work against them when they seek improved public services. Their lack of political leverage stems from the same factors that reduce their effectiveness in the market. Efforts already made at improved organization, particularly in urban areas, need to be intensified. Prejudice and discrimination complicate the poverty that is at the heart of the problem. Many prejudices work against the poor in general; the idea that they are lazy or deadbeats, for example. Racial discrimination is in this category. It denies opportunities to minority groups, limits their consumption possibilities, and generally weakens the will of the community to do anything about the problems that face the poor.

Taken together, these factors undermine the position of the poor in the marketplace. The consumer must draw on many resources in confronting the market; the poor, because they lack access to those resources, are systematically disadvantaged. The intensity of their disadvantage is magnified because the hazards that the poor face are greater than those that other consumers experience. Because of their vulnerability, the poor are the special targets of consumer fraud. Unfortunately, the legal system may be of limited help to the poor. If

---

* The poor, particularly in urban areas, will have some types of information that middle-income consumers lack. The street education that accompanies learning to survive in a ghetto environment may equip the low-income consumer to deal with some types of local consumer problems. The market in general, however is dominated by the majority culture, so information from a subculture may not apply generally.

they lack access to legal services, there is little they can do to protect themselves. One of the most unfortunate effects is the negative attitude that such developments create towards law enforcement and the legal system.

Being Poor is Expensive

The High Cost of Economy

One of the most inflammatory issues surrounding the low-income consumer is whether or not the poor actually pay higher prices for the things they buy. The ensuing debate has engendered more than its share of claims, counterclaims, studies, indignation, and confusion. It is necessary to conduct a more measured examination, separating the parts of the issue and analyzing each in turn.

One aspect that has been inadequately emphasized is fairly straightforward. The poor, by the fact of being poor, are denied many opportunities to save money that are available to affluent consumers. Buying goods in bulk, for example, may result in significant savings; poor consumers, however, seldom have the money needed to cover the initial outlay. Consumers who take advantage of sale items may also realize savings. This is true of durables, and also of nondurables, like food. The poor can be stopped by high initial costs or inadequate storage facilities (such as freezers) or both. Limitations on a consumer's mobility make it impractical to get to a sale, which also forces the low-income consumer to higher-priced alternatives.

It is in such common, everyday situations as these that the low-income consumer is hurt. Taken singly, none of them may be especially important; but together, they represent a potentially significant source of savings that is denied to the low-income consumer. It is often said that it takes money to make money, but it is equally true that it takes money to save money. Notice that in each case, the problem arises from the consumer's poverty. The normal workings of the system tend to put the poor at a disadvantage.

All of these factors are real enough, indeed costly enough, to the poor consumer, but they are not what is usually referred to in the poor-pay-more argument. That argument is more complex and rests on a different set of assertions. Not surprisingly, it is also much less clear and often more controversial. Thus, it is necessary to examine the question in detail, sort the issues involved, and attempt a systematic analysis.

Do the Poor Pay More?

The type of consumer fraud we are concerned with here does not involve the classical fly-by-night operation that bilks the consumer and then moves on. Rather, it concerns established businesses, which, it is charged, consistently take advantage of low-income consumers. It is maintained that many businesses in low-income areas overcharge their customers so that the poor pay more for similar products than their counterparts in affluent areas. This controversy first received serious attention with the publication of David Caplovitz's 1963 book *The Poor Pay More*. Caplovitz's study, carried out in New York City, suggested that low-income groups are victims of systematic gouging by ghetto merchants. Not only were prices in ghetto areas higher, but quality was lower than in middle-income neighborhoods; a variety of other questionable business practices also came to light [7].

The government, moved by increasing debate on the topic, began to investigate. A congressional subcommittee found, in making a personal check of a grocery store in Harlem, that

> packaged foods were found mismarked, frozen foods were half-thawed and the manager even admitted that after two days on the shelf, packaged meat was taken back to the butcher's block, repackaged, relabeled and redated. [18, p. 16]

The condition of the stores and their products have been a primary source of complaint. In Los Angeles, one ghetto shopper commented that store managers viewed their customers as a "bunch of animals," while a second was even more blunt: "The merchants don't give a damn about Watts. They take their money back to Beverly Hills and never spend a cent fixing up their stores" [21, p. 133]. In the face of such criticism, a more systematic study was instituted. The results were surprising. The Bureau of Labor Statistics in a 1966 study found "no significant differences in prices charged by food stores located in low-income areas versus those charged by stores in higher-income areas" [17, p. 122].

The Federal Trade Commission reported three years later after a survey in Washington, D.C., and San Francisco that there was no evidence that chain store operators "employ discriminatory policies which are designed to exploit low-income customers" [9, p. 3]. These findings were hardly consistent with earlier evidence and they certainly did not fit the poor's perception of their own situation. This is essentially an empirical question: Either the poor pay more, or they don't. Yet while the question can be simply stated, the procedures involved are sufficiently complex for conflicting evidence to be expected.

In making cost comparisons between high-income and low-income areas, it is not enough merely to compare the costs for a particular item in the two areas and then assume that all else is equal. On non-standardized goods, quality must be taken into account. There is also a question about which goods are being consumed in the two areas. The typical market basket of goods for a low-income family will differ from the supply for a middle- or high-income family. Suppose potatoes are cheaper at a market in a low-income area. That is going to be significant if people buy large amounts of potatoes. If, on the other hand, some luxury item is more expensive, it won't really matter if people do not actually buy it. It is necessary to know what goods people are consuming before a comparison can be made. This is difficult, because people are often buying different quantities and qualities of different items.

An equally important element to consider is that these purchases are made in *different kinds of stores*. While shoppers in high-income areas have a variety of stores to choose from, those in low-income areas do not. The facts of economic life lead large chain stores to locate in the most profitable areas. The ghetto does not qualify as a profitable area [9, p. 6]. Thus, the Bureau of Labor Statistics' study noted, while prices did not vary significantly if the same type of store is considered,

> prices are usually higher . . . in the small independent stores which are the most common in the low-income neighborhoods, than in the large independents and chain stores which predominate in the higher-income areas. [17, p. 122]

The FTC investigation reported similar findings, noting that competition among the chain stores forced price reductions, but since there were few such stores in low-income areas, similar reductions were rare* [9, p. 3].

Summarizing this situation, a report in the *Harvard Business Review* noted that the so-called mom and pop stores predominate in low-income areas. It continued:

---

* Comparisons between prices in small stores in low- and higher-income areas must be made with care. The latter tend to be either convenience stores or specialty shops, the small grocery having been driven out of such areas. Thus, they are not comparable to small groceries in the inner city.

Lacking economies of scale and the advantages of trained management, the "moms and pops" muddle through from day to day and, in the process, contribute to the oppressive atmosphere of such neighborhoods. Their customers generally pay higher prices, receive lower-quality merchandise and shop in shabby, deteriorating facilities. [2, p. 132]

Small stores tend to have higher operating costs than chain stores, which is why the small stores have problems in areas where the two compete. Other elements tend to increase prices in inner-city areas. Buildings are often old, increasing upkeep and insurance costs. Similarly, losses through theft tend to be high [17, pp. 339–41]. The most efficient stores want to locate where costs are low and revenues high. That keeps them out of low-income areas.

This discussion has concentrated on food stores because there is more literature on the subject and because everyone has to buy food. However, the same pattern is evident with other types of establishments. Big department stores and discount stores tend to stay away from low-income neighborhoods. In the case of consumer durables, there is more substantive evidence of abuses in low-income areas. These abuses cover a range of business practices and are not limited to price alone; credit policies, service, and the quality of the merchandise itself can have a most significant effect on the consumer. Studies have confirmed that furniture and appliances tend to cost more in low-income areas than comparable merchandise bought elsewhere [22]. Another Federal Trade Commission study in the District of Columbia found that, on the average, durables cost 60 percent more in low-income areas [10, p. x]. Other abuses, such as failure to mark price and bait-and-switch tactics, have been reported repeatedly.*

Higher prices, however, tell only part of the story. Credit abuses are equally common and may be more damaging. As we will discuss more fully below, the use of retail credit is more common in low-income areas and the interest rates charged are higher [21]. Identifiable interest charges run as high as 80 percent, but in many cases recordkeeping is incomplete; the actual rates charged could be even higher, and it is possible that merchants could simply continue adding interest indefinitely.

These abuses show the clear need for more vigorous enforcement

---

* The failure to mark price leads to a kind of price discrimination. The seller can name an initial price which is exorbitant, and then lower the price if the buyer complains. The buyer, however, may accept a price above the minimum the seller would accept; lower-income consumers are literally charged what the market will bear.

of existing consumer protection legislation. However, there is more involved than simply lax enforcement. It is one thing to stop exploitation of the poor, but the real need is to *do something about the conditions that give rise to the exploitation.* This is where the problem becomes really difficult. Ask yourself, "What's to be done about the situation?" The poor pay more because of the economic complexion of the community. Because of poor profit potential, only small stores with captive markets can survive in low-income neighborhoods. Because markets are captive, consumers are subjected to abuses.

Thus, the real problem is that, from a *social* point of view, the market has failed. It is important to emphasize the word *social,* because in economic terms, the market is operating precisely the way you would expect. It is allocating resources to areas with dollar votes. If those dollar votes were more evenly distributed, the problem would largely be solved. Again, the problem is poverty. The basic way to attack the problem is to go to its source and attack poverty, but that is hardly an operational solution. Poverty has proven stronger than the public's will to deal with it. Even with a change in attitudes, the process would be time-consuming. Thus, while reducing poverty should be maintained as a long-run goal, something more immediate must be done about the problems that millions of people confront in the marketplace everyday.

Unfortunately, it is easier to agree that something needs to be done than to agree on what that *something* is. Various types of government subsidies have been tried, including low-interest, federally backed loans and subsidized insurance programs for ghetto businesspeople. While these have met with some success, technical and managerial advice is still needed. Such businesses also suffer from a chronic shortage of capital. Most important, the fact that the area is a poor market remains as much of a problem for the ghetto businessperson as for any other.

Furthermore, these solutions treat the problem in isolation, as if it affected only one part of the community. In fact, it is a social problem, which means it has to be considered in terms of the whole community. The solution must be developed on a communitywide basis, not in low-income areas alone. The society may not be able to do very much about poverty in the short run, but it can do something about the impact of poverty. One possibility is providing subsidies, through tax reductions or outright grants, to induce businesses to locate in low-income areas. If the subsidy equated profit levels in low-income stores to those in other areas, the poor would benefit from the access to lower-priced goods. An alternative approach would be to force large stores to locate in poor areas. This would not be possible in all cases, but, since public licensing of most types of business operations is required, government has some leverage in the matter.

The public at large would pay in either case. In the first instance, the subsidies would be paid out of tax monies. Under the second alternative, stores would have to raise prices throughout the community to make their ghetto operations profitable. Thus, consumers outside the low-income area would pay a subsidy in the form of higher prices. In a positive vein, additional resources could be directed toward ghetto businesses. The efforts already under way have not been integrated into a comprehensive program. Ongoing financial support is necessary; but, perhaps more important, programs are needed to develop managerial skills and provide assistance with management problems.

This discussion has been based on an urban setting, balancing conditions in one part of the city against conditions in another. For the rural poor, however, such adjustments may not be possible. Those living in depressed areas or as tenant farmers, migrant workers, or reservation Indians, are among the most needy. However, their isolation and scattered settlement patterns makes coordinated effort difficult. Furthermore, because they are less in evidence, they may not attract the same attention with their problems as the urban poor. The plight of such people as consumers is not going to be easily cared for. Community and rural development programs may help and cooperatives offer some hope. To help these people effectively will require increased economic opportunities for the rural poor, and also increased options for them as consumers. It is difficult to see how this can be attained without public support.

Understanding the Low-Income Marketplace

Recognizing Differences

For the sake of truth, it should be noted here that no one really understands all the forces at work in the low-income marketplace. The problems identified above can be linked to both the structure of the marketplace and the characteristics of low-income consumers themselves, but the precise nature of the interrelationships is unknown. Speculation on the subject is much easier to find than definitive answers. What is becoming clearer, however, is that the market environment in which low-income consumers operate is different from that faced by consumers at large. The failure to recognize those differences has lead to confusion and misinterpretation.

By way of analogy, consider the comparisons and contrasts between two games, cricket, and baseball. Both are team sports in which a batter tries to hit a ball with a bat; both have hits, runs, fielders, pitchers, and outs. Despite these obvious similarities, however, an American who goes to a cricket match expecting it to be like a baseball game is going to be confused and annoyed. The frustrated fan will come away feeling that the game makes no sense at all, that it isn't played by the proper rules, and that the players themselves behave in an unexplainable, if not irrational, fashion. Cricket, of course, makes sense (at least to the British) if one knows the rules and can understand what is going on.

In a similar fashion, efforts to interpret the behavior of low-income consumers by the rules that apply in the marketplace at large will lead to confusion about what is actually going on. I have stressed throughout this book that it is wrong to judge one group by the standards of another, and yet that is what is precisely what has happened to the poor. Their behavior as consumers is judged *as if* they faced conditions similar to those confronted by more affluent consumers. Because the poor face a different set of conditions, their behavior will be different. That behavior cannot be understood unless the conditions are understood.

This means the low-income marketplace must be dealt with on its own terms. However, as noted earlier, it does *not* mean that a whole new analysis must be developed. Like all consumers, the poor face problems of uncertainty, choice, information, and power; however, because of the special problems that the poor face, these problems will be worked out differently. Shopping behavior offers one obvious example.* It is maintained that the poor are careless and indifferent shoppers. However, when such elements as lack of mobility, high cost of information, discrimination, and limited options are considered, their behavior might be interpreted quite differently [1, pp. 83–84].

Another feature of the low-income marketplace that deserves further attention is the personal nature of market relationships. I have stressed that modern markets tend to be impersonal, and that is certainly the general case. However, in the low-income marketplace, personal relationships appear to be much more important. Systematic evelution of this point is lacking, but the role of personal buyer-seller relationships crops up too often to be mere chance [4 and 12]. It

---

* The heavy use of retail credit, which is one of the outstanding features of the low-income consumer, is another example; it is discussed in the following section.

may seem strange that personal contacts should be so important when one considers how the poor are exploited in the market; yet it may well be that the personal nature of market relations contributes to that exploitation. In any event, the question deserves more serious study.

Additional study is also needed on differences among low-income groups. We have been speaking of *the poor,* when in fact low-income consumers represent a diverse population in terms of race, geographic locale, and cultural backgrounds. Most studies of low-income consumers have focused on urban blacks. Less is known about other low-income consumers, although the work that has been done suggests that differences exist. The fierce independence of the Appalachian culture, for example, apparently affects the consumption behavior of rural whites in that region [19]. A recent study of Spanish Americans in New Mexico suggests that their market behavior exhibits few of the traits associated with the urban poor [15].

The emphasis here on the special conditions of the low-income marketplace recalls similar points raised earlier in this chapter. This discussion was meant to focus those more general remarks and underscore their significance. It should now be clear that more careful study of the forces that bear upon the low-income consumer is needed. A better understanding of those forces is essential if effective means of dealing with the problems are to be developed. Furthermore, public support for such efforts won't be forthcoming until misconceptions about the poor as consumers are dispelled.

The Problem of Credit

The heavy use of retail credit is one of the most distinctive features of the low-income marketplace. In urban areas, up to 93 percent of durable purchases by the poor are made on credit, which contrasts with 27 percent for more affluent consumers [10, p. ix]. The availability of credit may be the dominant factor in the purchase decision. Many discussions of the use of credit among the poor contain the suggestion that such behavior is inappropriate and perhaps irresponsible.

Before we can draw any conclusions, however, we need to ask why low-income consumers rely upon credit so heavily. The obvious answer is that they need to; without credit, their consumption options would be sharply limited. One might say, though, that options should be limited; if credit merely enables the poor to live beyond their means for a time, then trouble will finally result. To evaluate the situation, we need to remember that in Chapter 4 we discussed the general question of debt in the context of uncertainty. That suggests that if the poor use credit differently, they face different prospects with regard to the future than other consumers.

In fact, that is the case because the poor face greater income uncertainty than other consumers. In 1976, only about 12 percent of the poor held full-time, year-round jobs, which contrasts with 42 percent of those above the poverty line* [8, p. 25]. Less certainty about the future means less information and a narrower base for planning future strategies. As Alan Andreasen has pointed out, the use of debt could be involved in a variety of rational approaches to the problems of added uncertainty [1, p. 182]. These range from the assumption that things will get better to a belief that whatever happens, there isn't much to lose.

The point is that the heavy use of credit among the poor is not in and of itself evidence of irresponsible behavior. Further investigation is needed to clarify the situation, but debt among the poor may well represent a consistent and rational strategy for dealing with a serious problem. However, that doesn't explain why the poor rely upon credit from retailers rather than other, less expensive, forms of credit. The answer to that question is rather straightforward; the poor generally don't have access to cheaper forms of credit. Banks, savings and loans, and credit unions may offer credit at lower rates, but the low-income consumer, who is perceived as a greater risk, usually doesn't qualify, leaving personal finance companies and credit from the retailer. The former may be rightfully maligned, but it must be understood that they provide a definite service to the poor. Even if their rates are high, they at least make credit available. It is in this sense that such companies are often referred to as the "poor people's bank." It is worth noting that personal finance companies report lower default rates on loans than commercial banks, despite the fact that the latter supposedly lend to lower-risk customers [12].

The retailer, however, remains the most important source of credit to the poor. For more affluent consumers, a purchase on credit may reflect a whole series of decisions; the average consumer decides whether or not to buy, where to buy, whether or not to use credit, and where to obtain that credit. Those four decisions are not necessarily related; indeed, it is considered a good practice for consumers to *shop* for credit just as they shop for products. For the low-income consumer, however, the questions are so closely related that there is really only one question: whether or not to buy. Once that decision is made, the purchase will be made at a store that offers credit; the

---

* Percentages apply to persons fourteen years of age or older.

source of the product and the source of credit are the same.* As a result, *credit practices among the poor cannot be isolated from buying patterns.* The two go together and must be treated as part of the same process [4, pp. 319–21].

As mentioned in Chapter 5, all of this means that disclosure of additional information about interest charges (truth in lending), will have minimal impact on the poor. Research supports that point [4]. If the poor have few credit options, and if purchase and credit decisions are bound together, then knowing about alternatives is of limited value. Again, however, the personal nature of the low-income marketplace appears to play a role. Consumers want to return to familiar surroundings [4, p. 320]. Finance companies also devote a great deal of personal attention to their customers, so that transactions appear to be more than just business arrangements.

It should be clear by now that credit use among the poor represents a complex set of behaviors. Little can be done about the abuses of credit until those behaviors are understood more fully. Efforts to deal with the problem thus far have concentrated on preventing excessive interest charges. There is a need for such efforts, but it is also necessary to remember that high interest charges themselves are not the problem. Simply holding down interest rates may even make matters worse. Interest-rate ceilings are often promoted as a way of making credit more available, but if the ceiling is set too low, it may cut off credit altogether. If lenders cannot obtain the market rate on their money, they won't lend; consumers would then either be cut off from credit or forced to go to alternative (and probably illegal) sources [14, pp. 340–42].

There is definitely a need to prevent individual abuses of credit charges, but, from an overall point of view, it is probably better to try to increase supply rather than artificially hold down interest rates. This means that alternative sources of credit must be made available. One possibility is to insure loans to low-income consumers. The loan could be provided through conventional financial institutions at a more favorable rate because the guarantee would reduce the risk to the lender. If the borrower repaid the loan on schedule, no additional costs would be involved. Only when the borrower defaulted would the insurance become a factor. A scheme similar to the Federal Deposit Insurance Corporation (through which bank deposits are insured) could be used to spread the risk associated with loan guarantees.

Remember that there is nothing new about the federal government

---

* A point that is missed by those who condemn the poor for not shopping for credit.

guaranteeing loans. The government has loan programs for farmers, moderate-income consumers (FHA 235), small businesses, and students. A loan-guarantee program for the low-income consumer would therefore not represent any great innovation. Such programs have been instituted in specific instances, such as loans for housing rehabilitation.

Increasing the availability of credit should help the low-income consumer, but will not itself take care of the problem. More needs to be known about the purchase-credit decision in order to know precisely what the consumer is doing. Education is also needed in this regard. There is evidence that low-income consumers don't know what is involved in the terms of many loans; furthermore, the poor may not seek alternative forms of credit because they feel they wouldn't qualify, even though they might. Clearer perceptions of the reality of the situation should, in both cases, enable the low-income consumer to carry out plans more effectively [4, pp. 319–22].

Finally, we should note again that there is no single pattern of credit use among the poor. Low-income blacks tend to use credit more than whites of a similar income level [4, p. 319]. Cultural variations also make a difference. The lower use of credit among Spanish Americans appears to be related to close-knit family organization [15]. Therefore, it is easy to overgeneralize. It does appear, however, that the problem is not simply credit availability or interest charges; rather, the whole market environment is involved, including both market structure and the characteristics of the low-income population. An understanding of the fact provides a point of departure for further study.

Discrimination and Consumption

No discussion of the problems of the low-income consumer would be complete without considering discrimination. I have referred to discrimination several times in the preceding pages because the poor bear a heavier burden of discrimination than other consumers. Discrimination may be best thought of in political, legal, or humanitarian terms, but it does have an economic side that directly affects consumption. Its results are sufficiently important for the subject to warrant a close examination.

Suppose you are looking for an apartment and you find two equally priced units. One is clearly preferable to the other in space, condition, and location. Now suppose that the landlord of the better apartment refuses to rent to you, so you are forced to take the inferior one. What does your choice of apartments—your consumption pattern—

say about your own preferences? It says very little because you were not allowed to express your preferences; the choice was dictated to you. Consumption patterns among the poor reflect a similar lack of choice. Analyzing these patterns as though they are the result of free choices will introduce a significant error, for consumption choices among the poor are artificially limited. The word *artificial* here means that considerations besides taste, price, and income enter into the decision.

The theory of consumer choice is developed around these elements. Given the level of their incomes, consumers are free to buy the combination of goods that brings them the highest level of satisfaction. If discrimination is involved, however, consumers do not enjoy that freedom. So it is that, among the poor, observed consumption patterns may say very little about actual preferences. These patterns do show what the poor consumed with the choices they had, but they do *not* tell how the poor would have spent their money if their choices had not been restricted. Restricted choice has troublesome ramifications. Housing is a good example. At any time, there exists a given amount of housing, a certain percentage of which will be suitable for low-income groups. Discrimination restricts the supply of housing for the poor by denying them access to units that would otherwise be available. Since the number of poor people seeking housing has not changed, but the available supply has decreased, the price of the remaining accommodations will be driven up.

Higher prices are the immediate effect of discrimination, but its long-run impact may be even more damaging. Discrimination results in overcrowding in poor neighborhoods, and this in turn contributes to a rapid decline in living standards. Carry the process very far and you have all the conditions that have come to be associated with ghettos. Discrimination in this case worsens an already difficult problem.

The impact of discrimination on the poor goes beyond limiting their choices in the marketplace. Job discrimination limits employment opportunities and thus perpetuates poverty. Educational discrimination is even more insidious. If the poor are denied equal access to education, they will be permanently handicapped. Lacking skills, they will not qualify for good-paying jobs that offer an escape from poverty.

Society as a whole also suffers from discrimination. The poor become its wards instead of being productive members. As a result, the society must bear the high cost of welfare payments and elevated crime rates in low-income neighborhoods. More important, the contribution that low-income individuals could make to society is lost.

As a result, the well-being of society is reduced. This is an important point because although it is fairly obvious that discrimination hurts the person against whom it is directed, the total effect of discrimination is not so clear. Suppose a woman who does not like blacks is looking for a job; she has two offers, of which the better one involves working closely with blacks. Clearly, it will cost her to indulge her prejudices, because to do so she would have to accept an inferior position.

The same thing is true for employers. The businessperson who hires workers on some basis other than productivity places himself at a disadvantage. If a businessperson refuses to hire the most qualified applicant because of race or sex, he or she will have to be content with a less productive worker. This will raise costs; the employer who does not discriminate will therefore enjoy an advantage [11, pp. 109–10]. One of the best examples of this was the integration of major league baseball. It is hard to imagine, but until after World War II, the majors were for whites only. When the color bar was broken in 1946, owners could not afford to ignore the talents of black players. Those who did cut themselves off from players of outstanding ability and their teams suffered accordingly.

Gary Becker has shown that discrimination can be analyzed in the same fashion as tariffs [3]. Tariffs increase the cost of imported goods and hence lower the overall level of satisfaction for the economy. Discrimination does the same thing. Employers who discriminate raise their costs and lower their output from a given amount of resources. As a result, the economy is worse off than it might be. If one person discriminates against another, both lose in economic terms. To the person doing the discriminating, that discrimination becomes a product to be consumed. The person with a taste or preference for discrimination pays for it, just as a person with a taste for fine wine pays for the best vintages. This formulation helps explain why discrimination is so difficult to stop.

During Prohibition, it was illegal to consume alcoholic beverages, and even now there are restrictions on when, where, and by whom they may be consumed. Yet tastes were such that people were, and are, willing to break the law in order to drink. Similarly, those with a taste for discrimination may be willing to break the law and face higher costs in order to satisfy their preferences. That is hardly an encouraging thought for the person who is being discriminated against. It does suggest the need for strict and vigorous enforcement of antidiscrimination laws. Since discrimination is a commodity, if its price is set high enough, most people will cease to consume it.

You may have noticed that there has been no mention of the human cost of discrimination. That is by design, as it shows that one need not be a humanitarian to appreciate the costs of discrimination. Those who consider themselves hard-headed realists interested only in dollars and cents would do well to consider that fact. When the human factor is introduced, the costs are magnified. Though these costs are more difficult to quantify, they are no less real.

The market is often condemned for being cold and impersonal, yet in this case the problem lies in the fact that personal distinctions are made. It is people, not markets, who make distinctions based on race or religion. For the low-income consumer, the elimination of such distinctions would mean expanded choices and hence an improved standard of living. Any treatment of the problems of the poor must deal with that fact.

Increasing Market Leverage

I have noted throughout this chapter that the poor typically lack the power to contend with the marketplace. Therefore, it seems appropriate to close our discussion by considering ways in which market leverage among the poor can be improved. As in the general case, that improvement can come though public protection, private organization, or some combination of the two. However, special consideration must be given to the unique conditions that characterize the low-income marketplace.

I indicated in earlier chapters that many of the programs that are commonly thought of as consumer protection are of limited value to the poor. Information policies, for example, have their greatest impact among more affluent consumers. Efforts to promote safer products through the imposition of standards may be harmful to the poor if the standards mean restricted choices and higher prices. As noted in a previous section, limitations on interest rates may also hurt the poor because they will be the first to be denied credit.

The low-income marketplace sometimes frustrates consumer protection efforts for inexplicable reasons. For example, a study of used car prices in three Midwestern states showed that those with incomes of under $6000 paid up to 10 percent more for a used car than higher-income consumers paid for a comparable model [20, p. 2]. The study was conducted to evaluate the impact of a 1974 Wisconsin law requiring disclosure of information about used cars. It was found that the law improved the "deals people of all income levels were able to get, [but] it reduced the disparity among income groups not at all" [20, p. 2]. Neither the higher prices paid by lower-income consumers nor the failure of the disclosure law to reduce the differential could be explained. To the extent that dealer fraud is involved, the researchers warned that faith in

> disclosure regulation as a strategy for giving leverage to the low-income consumer would be misplaced. It may only increase restrictions on decent dealers who would abide by the law to maintain their reputation, while rotten dealers would continue to ignore the legal regulations in all but the most symbolic ways. [20, p. 6]

These examples are consistent with Alan Andreasen's contention that most consumer-related policies are in response to middle-class concerns. Andreasen argued that when compared to the problems of the middle-income consumer:

> the problems of the disadvantaged are in important respects qualitatively different, and while the middle class may think they recognize these differences, they do not understand them well and it may be impossible for them to have much direct impact on them anyway. [1, p. 180]

To the extent this is true, a great deal of consumer protection legislation is largely irrelevant to low-income consumers.

This does not mean that consumer protection legislation cannot help the poor. Cooling-off laws and the bait-and-switch advertising could be most helpful if combined with the proper amount of enforcement and education. However, the fact remains that the needs of middle- and low-income consumers may not match. It follows, then, that some mechanism is needed that will enable low-income consumers to look after their own needs (assuming that if they don't, no one else will).

That mechanism appears to be available in the form of a combined private-public effort. The phrase *public effort* does not mean a commitment to large-scale programs; that was tried in the 1960s through the Office of Economic Opportunity, which supported the development of neighborhood consumer groups. Their level of community support showed that they were fulfilling a real need. Unfortunately, many of these organizations endured stormy existences and generated antagonism within the community at large. The community power structure took offense at their activities and the groups came to be looked at as troublemakers. As funding for OEO was reduced and the office was finally dismantled, support for such efforts was phased out. Some groups continued to operate, but at a reduced level.

There is a footnote to this story. Much of the money that had been channeled through OEO was diverted to state and local governments in the form of federal revenue sharing. Local officials, once they gained control of the money, could hardly be expected to continue support for programs of which they didn't approve. Local governments reflect the local power structure, and such groups have a vested interest in the status quo. Because the poor, almost by definition, want things changed, there are significant possibilities for disagreement. Questions therefore arise about how well local governments can direct programs to deal with the problems of low-income consumers.

There is, however, a role for the public in terms of ensuring that low-income consumers have access to the means to protect their own rights. Public involvement need not be limited to *enabling* the poor to look after their own interests, but that does emerge as the critical element. In practical terms, this means legislation that guarantees the rights of the poor, adequate enforcement, and access to legal services for the poor. The question of legal services is most significant, because laws are meaningless unless they are enforced.

The poor themselves become the active element in the equation. Individually, of course, low-income consumers have little leverage; but when organized into groups, they can exercise power. The advantage of this kind of approach is that it doesn't tell the poor what they should be concerned about; neither does it depend upon the goodwill and sustained interest of more affluent consumers (who have their own problems to worry about). Instead, it lets low-income groups decide for themselves which problems are important, and then provides them with the means to deal with those problems.

These suggestions may sound unrealistic, but in fact they have been proven effective. The key, of course, is organization, and organization is difficult. However, if an issue isn't important enough to prompt low-income consumers to organize, it probably won't be important enough to move anyone else to action. Groups *have* organized effectively. One successful group is Philadelphia's Consumer Education and Protective Association (CEPA). This association works among the poor to promote consumer education, to investigate complaints, and encourage legal reform. The group has also supported more direct action with boycotts. The causes that CEPA and groups like it have uncovered testify to the needs of low-income consumers [13, pp. 46–52].

The rent-strike movement provides another illustration. It was the poor themselves who defined the problem and took action. They were successful because they were organized and had access to legal expertise. As a result, they were able to bring about fundamental changes [5]. Legal-Aid Societies and other groups that bring legal services to the poor have played an important role in these developments. With such services, the courts can serve as an effective means of protecting and expanding the rights of the poor.

The approach outlined here takes into account the realities of the situation. It accepts the differences in perception between the poor and the more affluent; it also accepts that the public mood does not seem supportive of large-scale antipoverty efforts. These two elements may well be related. The public's lack of support in part reflects frustration with earlier programs. Many of the programs were not given a fair trial, but the problems encountered suggest that the various policies were geared to others' conceptions of the problems of the poor. It isn't surprising, then, that misunderstandings and even conflict developed.

The last decade has demonstrated that, although it is easy to say that the poor need better jobs, expanded educational opportunities, and access to a wider range of services, attaining such goals is difficult. Statistically, the 1970s showed little progress for the poor. No one knows what the 1980s hold or what the impact will be of advances that have been made in education and employment opportunities. We should not underestimate the cumulative impact of small changes; neither should we underestimate the problem of poverty. This leaves the question where it has always been: unresolved. It is clear, however, that until there is a resolution of the problem of poverty, there can be no final resolution of the problems that the poor face as consumers.

Study Questions

1. Discuss the special features of the low-income marketplace that set it apart from the market at large. Are these differences due to the fact of poverty, the structure of the market, the poor themselves, or some combination of the three?

2. In Chapter 7 it was argued that individual consumers have more leverage in small neighborhood stores. This is the type of store that low-income consumers most commonly shop at. Does the argument still hold? Explain.

3. What kinds of consumer protection would be most helpful to the poor? What types could actually be harmful?

4. What parallels can you draw between the problems faced by college students living near a large university and those faced by low-income consumers? Show how the problems in each case arise from similar factors.

5. Many college students have incomes below the poverty level

and thus could be officially classified as poor. Even though they have similar incomes and face similar problems, what is the basic difference between college students and low-income consumers as discussed in the text?

6. Why should low-income consumers in smaller cities be relatively better off than consumers with similar incomes in larger cities?

7. Efforts to build low-income housing outside of low-income neighborhoods have been resisted in many communities. If such projects are carried through, however, they help reduce the problems of the poor as consumers. Explain why that is so.

8. In almost any city, low-income neighborhoods feature boarded-up stores and empty commercial buildings. Does this provide any insights into the problems of poor consumers? What does it suggest about possible solutions to those problems?

9. Problems that the rural poor face receive less attention than problems of urban poverty. Which group is better off as consumers, do you think? Explain.

10. "If the poor had any pride, they wouldn't live as they do, they could at least find decent housing." Comment.

11. Explain how the enforcement of antidiscrimination legislation can be considered a form of consumer protection.

12. The discussion in Chapter 4 indicated that the smaller the down payment and the longer the payment period, the higher the total interest charge on a loan. What is the relevance of that fact to the low-income consumer?

13. Would a loan-guarantee program such as that discussed in the text have a significant impact on interest charges paid by other borrowers?

Suggested Projects

The obvious project in this chapter deals with the poor-pay-more controversy. That is a considerable undertaking, however, and classes may want something less complex. Thus, a number of alternatives are offered that deal with the question but avoid the technical difficulties in a full-scale investigation.

1. Several assertions were made in this chapter about low-income consumers, including such things as their lack of mobility and their limited choice of stores. These can be checked by using United States census data. Large cities are broken up into cen-

sus tracts; data such as income, automobile registration, and commercial establishments are given for each tract. Review these data for your city or some nearby city. What patterns emerge? Incidentally, census data are valuable as a research tool; students with an interest in these questions should become familiar with such statistics.

2. Impressions can sometimes be misleading, but they do provide a basis for judgment. Spend some time browsing through stores in a low-income shopping area. Do you consider it a favorable environment? Make notes on the quality of merchandise offered, including produce and meats in groceries. Do you think quality varies from that available in other parts of town? Discuss.

3. Those interested in a more systematic study may actually want to make a survey of prices in various parts of town. This must be done with care; it is also important to be discreet, since merchants (and sometimes consumers) are sensitive about questions on pricing.

   In undertaking such a survey, there are two important points to keep in mind:

   —Be sure that comparisons are made between comparable products and comparable types of stores.

   —Be sure that you pick products that are actually being purchased.

   The first point relates to the discussion in the text concerning the differences between large stores and small stores, product sizes, quality, and so on. The second concerns expenditure patterns of different income groups. Expensive cuts of meat, for example, are not commonly consumed in low-income areas. Similarly, comparisons of price on a large-console television-stereo combination would be misleading.

   The Department of Agriculture publishes suggested grocery lists for different income levels; these might be used as a basis for comparing food prices. For other items, select products that you could reasonably expect residents of the area to consume.

   It is probably best to make the survey relatively short. This might provide less information, but it will be easier to conduct and probably give you truer information. In interpreting the results, discuss possible sources of error or biases.

   For additional information, check citations 2, 7, 9, and 10 in the Bibliography. Also, see Appendix.

4. The credit problems facing low-income consumers were discussed at length in the text. Conduct a survey to see how

interest charges vary in your area. Check conventional financial institutions, personal finance companies, and individual merchants. Be sure to include all costs of credit, not just the interest rate.

5. If there is a legal aid society or similar group in your area, invite a representative to speak to the class on the legal problems of the poor.

6. What sorts of programs are under way in your area to help low-income consumers? Survey private efforts, as well as those undertaken by state, local, or federal governments. Evaluate the effectiveness of these activities.

Bibliography and Suggested Readings

1. Andreasen, Alan. "The Differing Nature of Consumerism in the Ghetto." *The Journal of Consumer Affairs,* Winter 1976, pp. 179–190.
One of the best recent articles on the low-income marketplace. Andreasen stresses the differences between the problems confronting the poor and those faced by more affluent consumers. Analysis is excellent. If you want to read more on this topic, start here.

2. ———. *The Disadvantaged Consumer.* New York: The Free Press, 1975.
A more comprehensive review of the problems of low-income consumers. Contains a good review of research and analysis of the problem. Particularly strong in terms of identifying the basic problems and suggesting ways of dealing with them.

3. Becker, Gary. *The Economics of Discrimination.* 2nd ed., Chicago: University of Chicago Press, 1971.
The classic economic analysis of discrimination since its first publication in 1957. The analytical going is a bit heavy at times, but even the novice can get something from this penetrating work. It is also valuable in illustrating the imaginative use of economic theory.

4. Brandt, William, and Day, George. "Information Disclosure and Consumer Behavior: An Empirical Evaluation of Truth-in-Lending." *University of Michigan Journal of Law Reform.* 7 (Winter 1974): 297–328.
An excellent study of the impact of truth-in-lending legislation. Particularly valuable in analyzing how such legislation affects low-income consumers.

5. Brill, Harry. *Why Organizers Fail.* Berkeley, Calif.: University of California Press, 1971.
Excellent as a study of consumer organization among the poor. Particularly good in relating the efforts of the poor to the power structure of the community.

6. Caplovitz, David. *Consumers in Trouble*. New York: The Free Press, 1974.
A look at debtors in default. Emphasis is on problems of lower-income consumers, with special attention to the role of consumer fraud.

7. ———. *The Poor Pay More*. New York: Free Press, 1967.
The original inquiry into the problem. While Caplovitz's methodology has been questioned, he may be credited with focusing public attention on this serious problem.

8. *Consumer Income: Money Income and Poverty Status of Families and Persons in The United States: 1976*. (Advance Report). Bureau of the Census, U.S. Department of Commerce. (Series P-60, #107). Washington, D.C.: U.S. Government Printing Office, 1977.
Statistical information on American incomes. A more detailed final report on these data is published each year.

9. *Economic Report on Food Chain Selling Practices in the District of Columbia and San Francisco*. Government Operations Committee, U.S. House of Representatives, 91st Congress. Washington, D.C.: U.S. Government Printing Office, 1969.
A study of food prices, which suggests that the problem centers on the types of stores available.

10. Federal Trade Commission. *Economic Report on Installment Credit and Retail Sales Practices of District of Columbia Retailers*. Washington, D.C.: U.S. Government Printing Office, 1968.
The study shows that credit abuses are common. The abuses included not just high rates, but extra charges and sloppy recordkeeping.

11. Friedman, Milton. *Capitalism and Freedom*. Chicago: University of Chicago Press, 1962. Especially Chapter 7.
Not surprisingly, Friedman sees discrimination in terms of market forces and therefore has little sympathy for legal restrictions. Required reading for anyone interested in the topic.

12. Legal Aid Society of Polk County, Iowa.
Legal Aid brings legal services to the poor and investigates problems facing the poor. In Iowa, the society successfully prosecuted a landmark case expanding the rights of tenants.

13. Magnuson, Warren, and Carper, Jean. *The Dark Side of the Marketplace*. 2nd ed., Englewood Cliffs, N.J.: Prentice-Hall, 1972.
Short on analysis, but a good introduction to the problems of fraud and deception among the poor.

14. Maynes, E. Scott. *Decision-Making for Consumers*. New York: Macmillan, 1976.
A good discussion of credit and impact of interest rate limitations.

15. Mitchell, Glen. "Credit and Marketing Practices Among Low-Income Spanish Americans." Private publication. Las Cruces, New Mexico, 1976. Summary published in *Proceedings, 22nd Conference of the American Council on Consumer Interests.* Columbia, Missouri, 1976, pp. 125–33.
A report on credit practices and consumer behavior among Spanish Americans in New Mexico. Finds that their behavior is markedly different from urban consumers with similar incomes.

16. *National Advisory Commission on Civil Disorders: Reports.* Washington, D.C.: U.S. Government Printing Office, 1968.
A review of the causes of the civil disturbances of the 1960s, including the role played by ghetto merchants and their excesses.

17. National Commission on Food Marketing. *Special Studies in Food Marketing.* Special Studies, #7 and 10.
Additional evidence on variation in food prices.

18. "Paying More for Being Poor." *Time,* December 1, 1967, p. 16.
A report on congressional investigations of prices in the ghetto.

19. *Poverty, Rural Poverty and Minority Group Living in Rural Poverty.* Institute for Rural America. Spindletop Research: Lexington, Ky., 1969.
A report on rural poverty in Appalachia.

20. Skidmore, Felicity. "The Used Car Rip-Off," *Focus,* Institute for Research on Poverty. 2 (Spring 1978).
A report on variations in used-car prices and the limited impact of disclosure laws. The institute is part of The University of Wisconsin, Madison, and produces a variety of good material on poverty.

21. Sturdivant, Frederick D., ed. *The Ghetto Marketplace.* New York: The Free Press, 1969.
This collection of readings remains a valuable introduction to anyone interested in the problems.

22. ———. "Better Deal for Ghetto Shoppers." *Harvard Business Review,* March-April 1968, pp. 30–39.
This widely quoted article has become something of a classic. Emphasis is on structure of the ghetto marketplace.

-11-

Emerging Issues for the 1980s

The Dilemma of the Female Consumer

Changing Perspectives

Thus far I have covered topics that are generally recognized as areas of consumer interest. However, the marketplace is not static. It changes in response to new economic, political, and social forces. Such changes mean that consumers must contend with new conditions, and new conditions mean new sets of problems. Given the range of possibilities, it would be impossible to identify, let alone analyze, each individual problem. Thus, although the problems discussed in this chapter are important in and of themselves, they are also intended as illustrations of emerging areas of consumer concern. The discussion is meant to show how the general analysis developed throughout this book can be applied to different kinds of problems.

These applications are particularly important because it appears likely that consumer problems in the 1980s will be interpreted from the perspective of particular groups.* That is, there will be less discussion of *the* consumer, and more talk of the *female* consumer, the *black* consumer, or the *elderly* consumer. In the face of consumers' plural interests (or lack of common interests), this is a logical development. Because *the* consumer interest is difficult to define, consumers' interests will be expressed through more specialized groups focusing on the consumer issues that affect them.

* This contention is consistent with the discussion in Chapter 7.

In the case of the female consumer, the range of problems really isn't limited very much. Women make up over half of the American population, so most problems that affect *the* consumer also affect the *female* consumer. By extension, we can see that because all women are consumers, it is difficult to speak of problems in this area without considering the broader issues of the women's movement. I will try and limit the discussion here to the narrower question, but you should note that there are similarities between the efforts to expand the rights of consumers and similar efforts regarding women's rights.

The most obvious similarity is that the same people may be involved in both cases. There is evidence that women who support the feminist movement also tend to be more actively involved in consumer issues [1]. Beyond that, the two movements share common problems. Efforts by the women's movement to call attention to the special problems of women have suffered many of the same difficulties faced by consumer advocates. Just as many consumers are openly antagonistic toward efforts at consumer protection, many women seem to resent the efforts of feminists to secure women's rights. Witness the division among women's groups in the battle over the Equal Rights Amendment.

When it comes to their roles as consumers, however, women do share a common set of identifiable problems. The perspectives on those problems may vary, but most observers must now admit that past assessments of the female consumer were characterized by an ironical kind of double vision. On the one hand, women were accorded a key role as household decision makers about consumption; at the same time, those decisions were often made to appear trivial, reserving the really important decisions for men. If we believe the stereotypes, the woman who supposedly knows how to run a household is too easily distracted by the thought of a new dress to concentrate on the complexities of insurance or credit. It is obvious that the two portrayals don't go together; recognizing that, we can look more closely at the substantive issues involved.

Household Production and Consumption

In considering the female consumer, we need to retrace our steps and consider again the consumption options confronting the household. In Chapter 2, I indicated that those options were defined by tastes, prices, and income, where income was treated in money terms. That is the conventional approach, but the household's consumption options are also affected by the things it produces for its own consumption. If a meal is prepared or a lawn is mowed, the household's consumption opportunities are expanded, regardless of who does the cooking or the mowing. Despite specialization, then, a great many consumption activities are linked directly to household production.

Household production may be carried on by any member of the household, but traditionally women have been—and remain—particularly important in this regard. Estimates of the total value of household production vary and are obviously related to the size of the family and the number of children. However, for a family with children, a figure of over $10,000 a year appears to be a conservative estimate [18]. That figure means the average family consumes over $10,000 a year in goods and services it provides for itself.*

There are two important points to note here. The first is simply to emphasize the contribution that household production makes to the family's standard of living. Despite renewed emphasis of the value of work in the home, we still use the phrase "going to work" to mean a job in the marketplace. The value of work in the home, however, should be recognized because it makes a significant contribution to the family's total consumption possibilities. The second point should now be obvious. When a woman enters the labor force and takes a job in the market, she isn't simply "going to work"; she is substituting one kind of work for another. In the case of the working wife, therefore, money earned in the market does not represent a simple addition to income. The value of household production given up must be considered.

The choice between market and nonmarket production represents a fundamental determinant of the family's overall consumption pattern. For example, younger couples are tending to postpone the birth of their first child, limit the number of children they have, and choose apartments or condominiums over single-family homes. In each case, the choice favors reduced household production, which frees more time for market production. With increased money income, families can afford to purchase goods and services that they formerly produced for themselves; hence, the increased number of meals eaten away from home and the growth of child-care alternatives.

A number of other changes have been forced on the marketplace as women become more involved in production outside the home. Stores, for example, are extending their hours of operation to accommodate women's work schedules. The increased emphasis on convenience may itself reflect the increased value placed on women's

---

* These figures, however, are not counted in national income; for that reason John Kenneth Galbraith calls household production a "convenient social virtue," meaning it is a way of getting the dirty work done [15, p. 30].

time.* It is ironic that the value of household production was largely ignored until women increased their labor-force participation. Now, however, it should be clear that one cannot understand the changes underway in either the marketplace or families' consumption patterns without understanding the role of household production.

Women in the Labor Force

Increased labor-force participation among women was one of the most significant economic developments during the 1970s (labor-force participation simply means the person is either working or looking for work outside the home). There is, of course, nothing new about women working outside the home; the difference now is that *more* women are working outside the home, and they are working *longer*. Younger women have always had relatively high labor-force participation rates, but as women married and established families, they tended to confine themselves to household production. That pattern is still evident, but to a much lesser extent. Women in the twenty to twenty-four year old age group still have the highest labor-force participation rates (64 percent in 1976), but the decline after that is neither pronounced nor sustained. The average labor-force participation rate for women twenty-five to fifty-five is over 55 percent [23, p. A-12].

Overall, nearly 38 million women (over age sixteen) were in the labor force in 1976, which meant that two workers out of every five in the civilian labor force were women [23, p. A-12]. Not surprisingly, participation rates are higher for women who are unmarried or divorced, but over half of all married women between ages twenty and fifty-five work outside the home. It follows that there are increasing numbers of working mothers. Between 1970 and 1976, the proportion of children whose mothers were in the labor force showed an average annual increase of 1 percent a year; in 1976, 46 percent of all children under the age of eighteen had mothers in the labor force [5, p. 41].

We are interested in women as consumers, not as workers, but the obvious relationship between the two means that we have to consider the implications of increased female labor-force participation. I touched on this question in the previous section, when discussing

---

* Which itself reflects a bias, because work in the home makes the woman's time valuable, even if no dollar wage is paid. There is, however, less flexibility in work schedules outside the home; also, most women who work outside the home still engage in considerable amounts of home production.

the change in household production and consumption patterns. The other obvious conclusion is that as more women work for wages and salaries, women have more money to spend on consumption in the marketplace. In this respect, the so-called earnings gap between men and women becomes especially important.

Among workers with full-time, year-round jobs, women earned only 57¢ for each dollar earned by men; but differently, the median earnings of men in 1974 were 75 percent greater than median earnings for women. Furthermore, the gap is growing; in 1955, men's earnings on the average exceeded women's by only 56 percent [12, p. 6]. These trends show that women are still concentrated in lower-paying jobs where possibilities for advancement are limited. The growth in labor-force participation among women also means that a larger percentage of women are at or near entry-level salaries.

The differential between men's and women's earnings increases with education. For workers who didn't complete junior high school, men earn on the average 57 percent more than women. Among college graduates, however, the figure is 71 percent [12, p. 10]. For recent college graduates, the situation is different; a study of six different fields in 1975 showed virtually no difference between starting salaries for male and female graduates (although variations existed among the fields)* [12, p. 11].

These figures suggest that if women have access to better-paying jobs and opportunities for advancement, the earnings differential should decline. Those conditions, however, underscore the importance of programs that ensure women equal treatment in the labor force. To the extent that discrimination against female workers continues, women's consumption opportunities in the marketplace will be reduced. This is particularly important because most women work out of economic necessity; labor force participation drops sharply for women who are married to men earning over $20,000 a year [23, p. A-28]. This means most working women are either heads of household or come from middle- or lower-income families. Discrimination, then, poses a real threat to the family's standard of living and, for some families, may contribute to a perpetuation of poverty.

Women in the Marketplace

Even in the days when everyone agreed that "a woman's place is in the home," most people would have admitted that women belonged

---

* The fields were accounting, engineering, liberal arts, marketing-retailing, business administration, and science. Engineers and accountants (traditionally male fields) had the highest starting salaries.

in the marketplace too. Housekeeping was *women's work,* so it followed that buying the things that were needed to keep house was also woman's work. Attitudes about a woman's place have changed, but the paradoxical role of the female consumer has lingered on. As consumers, women are at once considered expert and incompetent, calculating and frivolous.

The stereotype is maintained in advertising. The use of women as sex objects in advertising is declining, but advertising still presents a narrow perception of women. Women are typically shown in the home, and except as adornments, are less likely to appear in ads for cars, home appliances, insurance, and banks [7]. In the sample of 321 network television advertisements discussed in Chapter 6, the majority of the ads relied upon traditional sex roles; however, only about 12 percent of the ads exaggerated those roles or treated women as adornment [26].

Part of the problem with advertising is that women do make most of the purchases in certain product categories (particularly home products), so it is logical that women should appear in the ads. Again, the traditional view of the woman's role emerges and it may emerge at an early age. Little girls play with toy kitchens, little boys with toy cars. To the extent that children come to believe that these are the things they should be concerned with, that belief will be reflected in their behavior as consumers.

In the markeplace, then, women must contend with a pervasive kind of prejudice. If a woman is asking questions about cars, she may have trouble getting anyone to take her seriously. She may also find that no one listens to her when she talks about insurance or credit, regardless of how knowledgeable she is. It doesn't matter that most men don't know very much about either cars or insurance; there is a presumption that men know about such topics, which marks each man as an expert by virtue of his sex.

It is hardly an exaggeration to say that, in the traditional view, women were given a great deal of authority over consumption decisions that didn't really matter. Women were considered competent to make routine purchases, to act, in John Kenneth Galbraith's phrase, as crypto-servants [15, p. 33]. Galbraith contended that:

> The administration of consumption resides with the women. This involves much choice as to purchases—decisions as between different cake mixes and detergents. . . . [women have] . . . *the power to implement decisions,* not to make them. Action, within the larger strategic framework is established by the man who provides the money [15, pp. 35–36, emphasis added].

Actual research on family decision making provides some evidence for Galbraith's view. Women are most likely to make day-to-day decisions; when the purchase of something like a car is involved, the husband makes the decision to buy, but the wife influences decisions about color and style [9, pp. 244–45]. However, patterns of family decision making vary widely. For most families, the decision to buy a house is a joint decision, and in many families, husband and wife share equally in important decisions [9, pp. 252–57]. The degree of joint decision making suggests that popular perceptions haven't caught up with practice.

As a result of this lag in thinking, women must still deal with misconceptions about their role in the marketplace. For the growing number of women who are either unmarried or heads of household, this presents a particular problem. They have to make decisions that routinely bring them in contact with automobile mechanics, insurance salespersons, and credit officers. There is no evidence that women handle such decisions much differently than men do, but most women face more of a challenge. Women have learned that they can be as assertive as men and that those portions of the marketplace that had previously been reserved for men are not so terribly complex as had been supposed.

There is one area, however, where women faced particular difficulty. When it came to obtaining *credit,* women found that prejudice hardened into discrimination and that neither competence nor economic resources could overcome the problem. You will recall from the discussion in Chapter 4 that debt management is an important resource to the consumer. Denying a woman access to credit denies her the use of her future income. Therefore, her present choices are limited and her level of satisfaction is reduced. Part of the problem was that women were (and to some extent, still are) viewed as temporary participants in the labor force. Thus, women were either denied credit or were subjected to a series of personal and potentially embarrassing questions (such as plans for a family), which no one would have thought of asking a man. Married women found that they could not obtain credit on their own, a problem that became significant for those who were later widowed or divorced.

As more and more women became interested in credit, the question drew increasing attention. The result was the Equal Opportunity in Credit Act of 1975, which banned lenders from discriminating according to sex or marital status [3, pp. 173–74]. Because discrimination in such cases is often difficult to prove, the act hasn't solved the problem. However, the law has given women a legal basis on which to pursue their rights to credit and has forced lenders to deal with credit requests on a more objective basis.

On the basis of our discussions here, it should be clear that most of the problems that women face in the marketplace are the result of long-standing biases and well-established social attitudes. The changes that have taken place in the market, therefore, reflect both the growing importance of women in the economy and a gradual change in the society itself. There is every indication that these changes will continue into the future, suggesing that gender will be less of a factor in the marketplace of the 1980s. This doesn't mean the process was fair—women should not have had to fight for rights that were supposedly theirs to begin with. It does mean, however, that when it is forced to, the market can adapt.

Consumers in the Classroom

"A Middling Standard"

Fortunately for our analysis, the problems faced by students as consumers of education are narrower in scope than those faced by women. The problems may be complex, but at least we are dealing with a specified group and a common set of problems. Most readers of this book are already familiar with those problems. If you have ever wondered why the students on campus aren't as friendly as those described in the catalog, why Professor Jones is still teaching (even though he obviously hasn't changed his notes since World War I) or whether your studies in college are really going to benefit you later on, then you know about the problems of the student consumer.*

American student-consumers face a unique set of problems that can be traced to the manner in which higher education developed in this country. Two words characterize that development: *diversity* and *accessibility*. Unlike most European institutions, American colleges grew up independently with their own standards. This encouraged a variety of approaches to education, but made comparisons among institutions difficult. Each institution defined its own goals and made its own judgments as to what constituted quality education. The system contrasts sharply to the British system, where students in all institutions follow a common curriculum and are expected to pass common tests.

---

* Most of this discussion is appropriate for students at any level, but because choice is greater in postsecondary education, the analysis will be confined to that level.

As American colleges and universities developed, they became accessible to a wider range of students. A college president during the nineteenth century maintained that "All classes have contributed to the establishment and support of colleges, and all classes have reaped the benefit" [30, p. 5]. There is more rhetoric than truth in that statement, but by European standards, American universities were relatively open. During his travels through the country in the early nineteenth century, Alexis de Tocqueville noted that "A middling standard is fixed in America for human knowledge," suggesting that education was meant to serve the needs of a broader segment of the population [10, p. 52]. However, as the educational mandate was broadened, the goals of education became more obscure. Education was meant to offer something for everyone, but that meant no one could be quite sure what education was supposed to do.

Any consumer who confronts a situation in which there is no standard for judgment, and in which the purpose of consumption is itself unclear, is going to have problems. However, that is precisely the problem faced by students making decisions about postsecondary education. By the 1960s, that fact had dawned on students who began a well-documented (and sometimes violent) campaign for change. During the 1970s, student protests subsided, but new forces were at work. These included new pressures for accountability, which in turn were tied to budgetary concerns and a certain disillusionment with education. Renewed vocational interest on the part of students has also played a role. Finally, changes in public policy have had their impact, as financial aid began to go directly to students rather than to institutions (beginning with veterans' benefits and continuing with Basic Educational Opportunity Grants and certain state tuition-grant programs).

Students as a Special Case

It seems logical to designate students as consumers because they are the recipients of educational services. However, while the term provides a convenient analogy, the designation may be inappropriate in a more comprehensive sense. There are important differences between students as a group and consumers in a typical market setting. These differences offer insights into the unique characteristics of student-consumers and help identify the proper way to approach the question [29].

One of the major differences between students and consumers per se lies in the matter of sovereignty. I have stressed throughout this book that consumers maximize their satisfaction by making independent choices according to their tastes. The individual—and *only* the individual—knows what is best for him or her. As any student knows, however, that idea won't get you through registration. Education is permeated with a kind of paternalism that is lacking in the marketplace. The implicit assumption is that someone else knows what is best for the student-consumer. Students come to learn from those who already know, and it is the latter who decide what is to be learned.

Significantly, the more objective the outcome, the stronger this tendency is likely to be. Students in liberal arts are allowed the luxury of choosing electives (and some students may even structure their own programs), but students in engineering and other pre-professional programs must adhere to a rigid curriculum. The student, therefore, must accept decisions about the educational process that others have made.

The second major difference between students and consumers in the market can be summarized under the heading of *goals and objectives*. Individuals generally buy products for a specific reason and have an idea of what to expect from the product. Because consumers are seldom expert, the evaluation process may be imprecise, but expectations about how the product should perform at least provide some basis for evaluation. As I've noted, the consumer of education may not have such a basis for judgment because he or she lacks a simple standard of evaluation. If they are stated at all, objectives are usually too general to be operational. Moreover, because education is a complex product, students are likely to have multiple goals, which automatically complicates the evaluation process. The following summary of possible educational objectives illustrates the point and identifies another special characteristic of the student-consumer.

Education as Investment. Whereas consumption is a process that produces satisfaction, investment defers present satisfaction in favor of a larger return in the future. Education may produce satisfaction, but investment aspects are equally obvious, given the significant financial expenditures and foregone earnings involved. Thus, one of the classic goals of education, to improve future economic potential, identifies the student as an investor rather than a consumer. The obvious analogy between business investment in real capital (plant and equipment) and investment in human capital (students and education) has lead economists to develop their analysis of education in those terms. The analysis is based on the idea that investment in training will generate a flow of earnings over time; in equilibrium, marginal costs and benefits should be equal.

From the student's perspective, however, there are two serious problems. The first is that the flow of benefits cannot be accurately measured; that is, the rate of return on education cannot be measured beforehand. Secondly, the specific nature of the production process is unknown. Students lack information on precisely how educational inputs are combined to provide a certain kind of output.* To the extent, then, that investment is the primary goal of education, the most important information is unavailable.

Social Considerations. Students may seek postsecondary education (especially the more traditional types) for reasons of status or in order to improve social position. Possibilities include both the generalized sort of status that goes with being college educated and the more particular kind associated only with certain colleges and universities.

A Fuller Life. This is hardly a very specific concept, but it is commonly associated with education, most especially the liberal arts. Education is presumed to develop talents and the ability to enable the individual to draw upon and appreciate a wider range of experiences. This idea is clearly subject to wide personal variation and numerous interpretations.

Short-Run Expedience. This category includes a variety of possible objectives and nonobjectives. They include such things as having a good time (short-run maximization of pleasure) or going to school because there doesn't appear to be anything better to do. Students might continue their education to please their parents or peers or avoid some less desirable alternative (such as military service).

By way of summary, three difficulties may be identified with objectives. Objectives may be inadequately specified, meaning there is no clear notion of what is to be maximized. When multiple objectives exist, attaining one may act as a constraint on reaching another (and when goals conflict, a reevaluation may be required). Finally, even when goals are specified and consistent, the information necessary to fulfill them may not be available. The obvious implication is that educational objectives need to be more clearly specified, a conclusion which itself points to the need for more information. Thus, our analysis of information from Chapter 5 should serve us in this case.

---

* Instruction, for example, is important, as are resource materials such as libraries. However, the precise contribution that each makes to education is unknown. Will excellence in instruction make up for deficiencies in library holdings, and if so, to what degree?

Students' Informational Needs

Our discussion of search, experience, and credence qualities of information can be applied to education.* Search qualities include such elements as the size and location of the institution, number of volumes in the library, and the level of tuition and fees. Information from search and experience may be complementary, as in the case of the library which cannot be judged until some time has been spent working there. Other experience qualities revolve around what might be called the tenor of campus life (particularly social life). However, it is the credence qualities—the manner in which education is produced and its ultimate value—which are in the long run the most important to students. By definition, this information is unavailable.

It should now be clear that when the educational objectives listed above are evaluated in terms of their informational requirements, *the kinds of information which students need to specify their objectives are unavailable.* The difficulty arises because most objectives are stated in terms of either experience or credence qualities, but prospective students cannot obtain information in either category. Whether the student is after social status, a fuller life, or just a good time, no judgment can be made without actually attending the school. The investment value of education is even more of a problem, because it cannot be tested until years later.

In most cases, then, students must rely upon proxies for experience information. These might include a visit to the campus to sample life there (often under carefully orchestrated conditions) or, more commonly, drawing upon the experience of friends. Increasingly, however, institutions seek to promote an image of themselves through their publications, thus conveying something about experience qualities. The institution may, for example, stress personalized aspects in an effort to indicate that the institution cares about students. Obviously, such efforts are subject to abuse. These deceptions may not involve great distortions, because most institutions have their truly appealing features. However, these features may not be representative of campus life or unique to that campus.

Because prospective students cannot evaluate the information they are receiving, institutions are left with a great deal of latitude, which, in some cases at least, they put to use. An institution can assert that upon graduation, students will "be confident that they have received one of the best educations possible," knowing that the claim cannot

---

* Search information is gained prior to purchase, while experience information can only be obtained by consuming the product. In the credence case, information cannot be evaluated even after the product is consumed without facing prohibitive information costs. Chapter 5, pp. 92–95.

be proven wrong. Similarly, because the precise manner in which educational inputs combine is unknown, it is possible to say that a "liberal arts education, without sacrificing the breadth and depth of learning, leads to a career." * No one can prove that it doesn't.

All of these elements bear upon the student and suggest something about the likely pattern of the decision process. Because credence qualities cannot be evaluated, they may well be dealt with at a subjective level. This places search and experience qualities in a new light, because they are likely to become important not only in their own right, but as proxies for credence qualities. Two possibilities exist. One is that search and experience qualities become proxies in the true sense. In this case, the size of the library or the degree of personal attention students receive become measures of the ultimate value of the education. Neither may serve as a very accurate measure, but they are at least measures, and may therefore assume qualities that they possess to only a limited degree.

The second possibility really amounts to decision by default. Information on search qualities is available, but it is expensive and its real significance may be unclear. Definitive information on credence qualities is not available. That leaves experience qualities. Information in this case may be second hand or highly impressionistic, but at least it represents something to which the student can relate. This suggests that experience qualities may assume more importance in the student's decision than they actually warrant.

Protecting the Student Consumer

You will recall from our earlier discussions that, in the case of credence qualities, efforts to provide the consumer with information will have limited impact. Given that limitation, some form of government intervention is generally necessary to protect the consumer. That is the general pattern in education too, but in this case, consideration is given to the special features of education (the Food and Drug Administration may test drugs for efficacy, but no such test has been devised for universities). Therefore, it would be improper to say that postsecondary institutions are *regulated;* rather, the government has intervened in specific areas to protect students. For the purposes of our analysis, we can identify three problem areas: *student rights, fraud,* and *program quality.*

In the area of *student rights,* changes have been significant and action has been definitive. Some of the changes came from inside

---

* Quotations are taken from recent materials that colleges have supplied to students. Because the statements are only meant to illustrate qualities of information and no implication of judgment is intended, sources are not given.

the universities themselves. The student protests of the late 1960s and early 1970s prompted universities to grant students a larger role in decision making. In most cases this promoted the establishment of grievance procedures for students, a reinterpretation of conduct rules, and a general dismantling of the regulations that had governed students' lives outside the classroom.

These actions only confirmed trends that were already underway. In a series of decisions in the late 1960s, the courts struck down the idea of *in loco parentis,* thus guaranteeing students their personal rights within the institution [28, p. 19]. Other decisions upheld students' constitutional rights. The courts maintained that students have the same rights to free speech and due process as any other citizens [8, p. 19; 22, p. 77]. Thus, as far as conduct and discipline were concerned, postsecondary institutions ceased to be laws unto themselves; institutions could not enforce rules that violated the students' rights as citizens.

In the case of *fraud,* government actions have concentrated on nondegree institutions (vocational and proprietary schools) [20, p. 12]. Fraud in this area became a problem when it was discovered that most states had few regulations to control educational institutions. Thus, the fly-by-night operator who might otherwise have gone into aluminum siding, set up shop as a trade school and began offering unsuspecting students the chance to train for big salaries as truck drivers, computer operators, or artists. The con man in academic garb didn't change his method of operation very much; it was still a matter of "take the money and run." One or two weeks into the course students would find that the school was closed, their instructor was gone, and their money (paid in advance, of course) was lost.

The problem became acute because the federal government was providing educational benefits that veterans could use for whatever training they wanted. Thus, clever operators were in essence getting federal funding for their schemes.* Some of the worst abuses in this area were handled at the state level through relatively simple bonding arrangements. Schools were required to post performance bonds to cover any losses that students might suffer. The Federal Trade Commission also became involved with a set of regulations protecting students in proprietary schools [2]. The FTC has now brought charges against one of the nation's largest correspondence schools, maintaining that the school misrepresented students' financial obligations and made false claims about potential earnings [6, p. 12].

---

* When federal student loans are involved, the government has been unsympathetic to the student. Students have been required to repay loans even though they were the victims of fraud.

One of the reasons that fraud in vocational schools has attracted more attention is that it is easier to detect. Objectives can be clearly stated ("become a truck driver"), outcomes can be evaluated (you either learn to drive a truck or you don't), and the quality of the product can be assessed (you are either employed or you aren't). Given that set of circumstances, fraudulent or inferior schools will be exposed. Note, however, that none of those conditions apply to traditional four-year institutions. Hence, it is much more difficult to evaluate how well those institutions are doing their job.

Fraud, therefore, becomes difficult to define and may rest in the eye (or mind) of the beholder. In what can only be described as a whimsical example, a student at Columbia University refused to pay back tuition because the university had failed to provide him with "wisdom, truth, character, enlightenment, understanding, justice, liberty, honesty, courage, beauty, and similar virtues and qualities" [21, p. 83]. He collected that list of virtues from various Columbia publications and mottos on campus buildings. The court dismissed the case on the grounds that Columbia had never promised to deliver those qualities. This case is obviously extreme, but it illustrates how difficult it is to tell precisely what it is that universities are supposed to do.

Even when the charges are much more specific and the complaint is serious, the courts have been reluctant to intervene. The question of *program quality* has therefore been left to the institutions themselves. The situation here contrasts with questions of students' rights in which the courts have intervened. The courts' hands-off policy toward classroom questions has been tested in a variety of cases, one of the most significant of which was brought by a Vermont medical student. He claimed that he had not been graded fairly (as the result of which he was dismissed from school). The court rejected his claim, just as courts have failed to uphold other complaints against programs that failed to meet anticipated standards [21, pp. 98 & 102]. In an important decision in 1978, the Supreme Court failed to support the complaint of a medical student from Missouri who was dismissed from school just before graduation because of her personal grooming habits. Even though the student's academic record was outstanding, the court said that decisions about program rested with the institution [21, pp. 103–104]. Some have interpreted this decision to mean that students do not enjoy the protection of requirements for due process with reference to academic questions.

It is obvious that the courts do not want to get involved in questions of grading and program quality. You can imagine the confusion that would result if you took Professor Jones to court because he gave you a C when you felt you deserved at least a C+. The courts are not well equipped to decide such questions and have therefore avoided them. The courts have put their faith in the professional competence of institutions and individual instructors. That may seem to give institutions a blank check, but it has put pressure on institutions to be more specific and to be able to deliver on their promises.

At most four-year institutions, students are protected by the accrediting process. Institutions are accredited by regional associations, but individual programs (such as public health) or schools (such as business) may also be accredited by their respective professional groups. Accreditation is a private process, but in this case it serves a quasi-public function [24]. Accreditation is a form of licensing, and therefore carries all the accompanying dangers. As in the case of other professional services, the student's need for protection must be balanced against the value of competition and accessibility.

We should note finally that additional efforts are being made to provide students with better information. Those efforts were championed by the National Task Force on Better Information for Student Choice [13]. The task force found that critical information on such matters as financial aid or refunds might be unavailable and that other information might be incomplete (regarding admissions, for example, so an institution might appear to be highly selective when in fact it isn't). Better information can be provided; if seventy-five of the ninety-four students in last year's premed class were accepted into medical school, that information should be useful to prospective students. If different institutions provide information in a similar format, students will be able to make comparisons and reach sounder conclusions.

For all of that, we must remember that we are dealing with credence qualities, which means that the best information represents only an imperfect solution. It also means that information must be interpreted and that such interpretations should include emphasis on the limitations of the information itself. If students come to recognize those limitations, they will also be able to recognize when institutions are making claims without substance. There may be no final answers, but, at the very least, things would work better if everyone involved recognized that fact.

The Consumer and Health Care

Sorting Out the Issues

In discussing the problem of medical care, we are not talking about the needs of a particular group; the problem obviously affects all consumers. However, the issue is specific and we can therefore focus on it as a well-defined aspect of consumers' overall concerns. There is certainly no question that consumers are concerned about medical care. That concern stems from two critical issues: *cost* and *quality*. The cost of medical care has more than tripled since 1960, with hospital costs rising even faster; the average American family now spends 10 percent of its budget on medical care [4]. Despite the added costs, concerns about the quality of health care have increased. Malpractice suits have become regular features in the news.

These facts are obvious, which is worth noting because the most obvious features of the problem may obscure the real issues involved. The question of quality, for example, is usually discussed in terms of malpractice. However, recent studies show that a small percentage of doctors are responsible for most malpractice suits [25]. These cases, of course, deserve attention, but other aspects of the quality question may be more important. One is the problem of unnecessary surgeries. Some estimates suggest that as many as *one-half* of all the surgeries performed under private medical plans are unnecessary [16, p. 67]. Such estimates are obviously a matter of debate, but there is no denying that the frequency of surgical procedures varies across the country. New Jersey, Pennsylvania, and Ohio are contiguous states; all three are highly industrialized; however, a citizen of Ohio is three times as likely to have surgery as a resident of Pennsylvania, but only half as likely as someone in New Jersey [16, pp. 263–64]. Either too many or too few surgeries are being performed.

Another significant aspect of the quality question is the distribution of health care over the population. The problem is most pronounced for lower-income groups; a comparison of the poor with moderate- and upper-income groups shows that among the poor:

The infant mortality rate is 75 percent higher;
The incidence of heart conditions is four times greater;
The percentage of persons with limitation of activity from chronic condtions is twice as high [32, p. 7].

One can only conclude that the poor do not receive the quality of medical care received by more affluent consumers. Even among the latter, however, there is no assurance that the quality of care received is appropriate to their needs.

The question of the cost of medical care is similarly complex. Private medical insurance helps ease the problem, but insurance costs are rising too. Public programs, such as Medicare, seem to have put increased pressure on costs and have produced complex bureaucratic procedures. Plans for national health insurance are being debated in Congress, but are lagging because they may cost too much. If we look only at costs themselves, there doesn't seem to be any way around the problem.

The discussion here suggests that while cost and quality considerations are important, they are merely reflections of more fundamental shortcomings of the health-care system. In considering those more basic problems, *system* is the key word. The preceding paragraphs indicate difficulties with the entire system by which medical care is delivered. To understand these difficulties, we need to look at the entire system, but before we do that, we should take note of some special characteristics of medical care.

Special Considerations

Whether we are talking about the demand for medical care from patients or the supply of such care from doctors, the provision of medical care involves a number of special characteristics that deserve attention. On the demand side, one of the most obvious features is the *credence quality* of medical care. Most patients cannot evaluate the quality of care, even after the care is received. In this case, "quality of care" refers to more than whether the right drug was prescribed or whether the surgery was performed correctly. Quality refers to the whole process of diagnosis. If your family doctor tells you that you need to see a specialist, you may either accept his or her advice or seek another opinion; you are in no position to make the judgment yourself. Obviously, then, some method is necessary to ensure that those practicing medicine are competent. As we'll discuss more fully below, the method chosen in the United States—licensure—has had important ramifications for the structure of the profession.

The other distinguishing feature of the demand for medical care is that it is irregular and uneven. As in the case of food, clothing, and shelter, you need medical care on an ongoing basis, but, unlike the other examples, you don't know when [32, p. 105]. Also, unlike eating, you can postpone medical care even when you need it. Thus, it may be appropriate to think that at any time, a reserve demand for medical care exists (that is, consumers would seek such care if it were available at a low enough price). The optimal level of medical care is itself difficult to specify; how much care do you need to be healthy?

A related question, which may be viewed from the perspective of supply or demand, is the definition of medical care itself. Does medical care involve more than simply the treatment? If so, it takes on a social-psychological dimension in which interactions between the patient and care giver become important. "Care giver" is a somewhat awkward phrase, but it is appropriate here. Is a shot administered by a nurse the same treatment as (the same) shot administered by a doctor? A midwife might provide precisely the same services as a doctor, but would the prospective mother perceive them in the same way?

As discussed in Chapter 3, goods and services are made up of bundles of characteristics, and medical care is no exception. The particular characteristics that people come to expect from medical care (such as personalized attention) may not relate directly to the quality of treatment per se. However, treatment that is offered without those characteristics might be rejected by consumers. There may also be a kind of snob effect at work; people come to expect treatment from specialists and therefore equate that level of care with quality, even though a general practitioner (or even paramedic) might really be better suited to their needs.

In discussing the supply of medical care, the licensing provisions mentioned above are an obvious consideration. However, other elements deserve attention also. One is the special role that capital plays in this case. In the general case, capital enables workers to be more productive, so that a given output can be produced with fewer workers. That isn't necessarily true in the case of medical care. Capital, in the form of the sophisticated equipment associated with modern medicine, enables doctors to do more things and in that sense improves the quality of care; however, doctors are not necessarily freed to see more patients.

The way in which the word *specialization* is used offers a clue to this situation. Throughout this book, I have used specialization to mean the dividing up of a particular task. In medicine, the word specialization means more than dividing up care; it means that the specialist delves more deeply into that particular problem. As a result, specialization has its primary impact on the quality and scope of the service delivered rather than the quantity of the service. To the extent that consumers' problems with medical care result from restrictions on quantity, increased specialization may not be the answer.

Is Structure the Problem?

We might summarize the preceding section by asking whether health-care delivery is currently structured in a way that best meets the special needs of consumers. The question of structure is itself dominated by the licensing system for the medical professions. The general issues involved were discussed in Chapter 8 (pp. 190–193) and need not be recounted here. It is sufficient to note that licensure restricts entry into the profession (thus limiting output) and is biased toward higher-quality services. Because of the difficulties with substituting capital for labor in medicine, some observers have suggested the use of physicians' assistants in cases when less medical training is required.

One study estimated that physicians' assistants could have a significant impact on productivity, increasing the number of patients a physician could deal with by up to 74 percent [17, p. 464]. The findings showed that an efficient medical practice could deal with 147 patients per week; the use of physicians' assistants could raise that figure to 265 [17, p. 466]. Because physicians' assistants are less expensive, the amount of medical care delivered per dollar would be greatly expanded. Assistants are not the only possibility in this case; in addition to midwives, nurses could assume functions currently carried out by doctors.

Not surprisingly, these suggestions have not been received well by the medical profession. Some doctors see assistants as more of a bother than a help, and others worry about the quality of care and the impact on the doctor-patient relationship. Nurses have resisted the idea also. They are anxious to see nursing develop an independent professional image and do not want to be thought of as doctors' aides [32, pp. 33–34]. The acceptance of auxiliary medical personnel by the medical establishment would be essential to their success. Patients would be more likely to accept such treatment if they knew the doctor approved.

This issue obviously involves the question of defining medical care (as discussed in the previous section). The use of auxiliaries would change the nature of the service and would affect the doctor-patient relationship. However, that relationship has already changed and the costs of services may encourage consumers to rethink the kind of care they are willing to accept. These issues, however, are really secondary; no widespread changes will be made until adjustments are made in the licensure system.

A related issue concerns the distribution of medical resources by both geographic area and type. It is not simply the number of medical doctors that matters; it is equally important to consider where those doctors are and what specialties they practice. We have already noted that specialization does not necessarily increase productivity, which means that large numbers of specialists may not contribute toward meeting the bulk of medical care needs. The regional distribution of doctors shows a concentration in the Northeast and, within any region, there are more medical services available in urban areas* [32, pp. 43–46]. Thus, consumers in rural areas may suffer and many small communities have few if any medical services.

The same pattern of distribution is evident with reference to hospitals. In this case, however, a new element is involved. As noted earlier, hospital costs have risen more rapidly than the overall costs of medical care. It is a simple fact that hospitals are expensive to build, equip, maintain, and operate. It is particularly expensive for a hospital to have the latest treatment facilities, which means that needless duplication in this area is extremely costly to consumers. Until recently, however, there has been very little health planning. The result is that areas may be oversupplied with expensive treatment facilities, but undersupplied with more basic and widely needed facilities. More attention is now being paid to increasing outpatient care and to medical facilities for those who don't require extensive care (recovery centers). However, the failure to act on these problems sooner has had an adverse affect on consumers in terms of both costs and overall quality of care.

It should be clear that simply tinkering with the health-care system is not going to take care of the problem. Proposals to increase the numbers of doctors do not account for the problem of distribution. Plans to increase medical insurance do not account for the structural rigidities and need for increased productivity. Increased aid to hospitals doesn't account for the need for health-care planning. These are only some of the problems that must be taken into account; but if they aren't, attempts to deal with the problem of health care may make the problem worse. This doesn't mean we have to do everything before we can do anything, but it does mean we have to look at the system as a whole and think in terms of solutions that deal with the whole system.

Proposals for Health-Care Reform

None of the current plans for health-care reform really deal with the problems of the entire system. Some, however, do show promise. Presently, health care is organized around fees paid for services, with private (such as Blue Cross-Blue Shield) or public (such as Medicare) insurance plans covering some of the fees. For those with coverage, this approach offers a workable solution. However, because the approach is becoming increasingly complex and expensive, and because it fails to cover a large segment of the population, the need for an alternative has become clear.

* Concentration based on physicians per 1,000 in population

The most commonly discussed alternative is some form of national health insurance. Most industrial countries already have some form of national health care. In areas such as Germany and the Scandinavian countries, the system works well; Great Britain, however, has had ongoing problems with its national health-care plan, problems that have been well publicized in this country. As a result, terms such as "socialized medicine" have taken on negative meanings.

A variety of national health-care plans have been proposed in the United States. The various proposals differ both in terms of coverage offered and methods of financing. Broadly speaking, there are two main categories. One would expand the role of private insurance companies, with the federal government paying part of the cost of premiums. The other would be closer to a true national health-insurance plan, financed in the manner of the present social security system. At this writing, the latter approach has more support, but implementation of a comprehensive plan does not seem likely soon [32, pp. 139–46].

Part of the problem with most national health-care proposals is that they do not deal with the structural problems identified above. Thus, national health insurance would add additional burdens to a system that has trouble supporting the weight it already bears. A plan requiring patients to pay part of the cost would take care of part of the problem, but no solution is possible without dealing directly with the special demand and supply conditions in medical care.

Health Maintenance Organizations (HMOs) offer an alternative approach to medical care. HMOs are essentially prepaid plans in which the consumer pays a set fee per month and is therefore entitled to a stated range of medical services [11]. Under this system, you don't pay for services individually; rather, you pay and then go for whatever services you need. The Kaiser medical group, which originated in California, is the best-known HMO.

The federal government endorsed the HMO idea in 1973 with the passage of the Health Maintenance Organization Act. However, the act was so restrictive that it was not until additional legislation had been passed that it had any impact [11]. The strong suit of HMOs, as the name implies, is health maintenance. The system encourages preventive medicine and routine care; to the extent that such care reduces the chances of major illnesses later, there would be a net savings to consumers and society. HMOs, however, have their drawbacks. Some consumers complain that treatment is impersonal. Costs remain a factor also, and, in many cases, HMOs are not any cheaper than conventional medical care.

As I noted, none of these proposals offers a comprehensive approach to the health-care problem. However, the various plans are not inconsistent and may therefore be viewed as parts of a more general approach. For example, national health insurance can be linked to the encouragement of Health Maintenance Organizations. Both of these could be integrated into a system featuring more effective planning and more flexible licensure requirements. Thus, a comprehensive, systemwide attack on the problem is possible. What appears to be needed at this time is a true national debate on the issue. Consumer concerns need to be clearly identified and specific attention must be given to questions such as the definition of medical care. With priorities in mind, a system that better serves consumer needs could be developed. If, however, we continue to deal with the problem from a narrow perspective, the chances of significant improvement appear slight.

Other Issues: A Brief Review

The Very Special Problem of Funerals

The topics covered thus far range over a great deal of material. In this concluding section, we will look at some more specific issues in an effort to at least point out problem areas. Funeral practices represent one such area that has attracted increasing attention. The evidence suggests a considerable amount of abuse. The potential for abuse is heightened because survivors probably have not made arrangements in advance. In the emotional turmoil following the death, the survivor can be easily misled and encouraged into extravagance "as a sign of respect for the deceased."

No other purchase a consumer makes is really comparable to a funeral. Nevertheless, many of the issues involved are already familiar to us. Once again we encounter the problem of licensure; the funeral industry is heavily restricted as a result of lobbying by funeral directors at the state level. Specified procedures must be followed for the disposition of bodies, which in most cases require the services of a funeral director. The funeral industry may be a classic case of a special interest group using the law to ensure its market, while at the same time restricting entry to the profession. Thus, the industry is essentially monopolistic, even though it is made up of many small firms [14, p. 85].

A second familiar issue is the ban on price-related advertising. As we discussed in Chapter 6, most quasi-professional groups discourage advertising as being undignified; given the special role of dignity in the burial ceremony, that argument has been used with special force by the funeral industry. In fact, the ban on price advertising for funerals appears to be simply an anticompetitive practice [14, pp. 419–23]. Because the consumer lacks information on what a funeral should cost, and because of the special difficulties involved in searching for information, he or she is especially vulnerable. The consumer is dependent upon the funeral director for all advice and information (although a member of the clergy may provide useful suggestions). Given the situation, the consumer is not in a good position to think clearly of alternatives and may easily be misled into thinking that services that are not required are mandatory. The consumer is also susceptible to the Veblen effect and may be encouraged to stage a showy funeral as a sign of respect.

These abuses are not confined to the rich. In one rural area, a mother delayed the burial of her dead infant because she did not have the $2,000 she had been told a funeral would cost. In a coal-mining region, funeral directors are reported to have raised the price of all funerals $200 after the United Mine Workers increased death benefits by that amount. Part of the reason such practices are possible can be traced to the general societal attitude toward death; most people don't even like to think about the issue. Death is almost an unspoken word. This provides the funeral director with a special kind of status and leaves the consumer in an especially awkward position.

A number of alternatives have developed to conventional funeral arrangements; all of them have been fought by the organized funeral industry. One is the "preneed" arrangement, which is a polite way of saying that plans are made prior to death. This approach, which makes burial something more of a conventional purchase, was championed by cemetery operators who felt that they were at a competitive disadvantage in traditional arrangements. In some cases, these plans were sold door-to-door using a hard-sell technique [14, p. 414]. However, legitimate operators offer consumers an alternative to traditional methods of purchase.

Memorial societies offer consumers a different kind of alternative. These groups represent a kind of cooperative, although they do not provide services directly. Rather, they provide members with information and advice, enabling those who so desire to arrange simple, economical funerals. The Federal Trade Commission report on the funeral industry indicates that the industry's response was one of "vituperative hostility," and individual directors were advised not to cooperate with memorial societies [14, p. 417]. However, because of their collective purchasing power, the groups have met with some success.

The most recent development in funerals are so-called direct-disposition companies. These companies do not offer the range of services or equipment that is provided by funeral homes. As their name implies, they provide direct disposition of the body (usually by cremation) at a cost of one-half to two-thirds below that commonly charged by funeral directors [14, p. 420]. The approach is much more direct, with little of the ceremony currently associated with funerals (although ceremony can of course be provided independently, at a church for example).

As was suggested earlier, funeral directors have been able to structure the industry to serve their own interests because most people wanted to avoid the issue. The artificially high prices consumers have paid is the cost to them for turning the question over to others. A general reassessment of practices, however, now seems to be underway. At this writing, the FTC's Bureau of Consumer Protection has just completed a massive study that is highly critical of the industry; it appears that a series of proposals for reform of the industry will be forthcoming. I have noted several times that there is an emotional element involved in most consumption; in this case the emotional element is obviously important. It appears, however, that looking at the question in a more objective manner would serve the consumer's interest. Objectivity here is not incompatible with reverence, but simply means that the consumer's desire for dignity not be commercially exploited.

The Elderly Consumer

As a group, the elderly might qualify as the forgotten Americans. The elderly are less visible and more easily ignored than other groups. In the past, they also tended to be more passive. That situation is changing, however. Part of the reason is that the elderly population is growing; a lower birth rate means that the median age in the United States is rising and the over-sixty-five group is one of the fastest growing segments of the population [19]. Furthermore, the elderly have begun to organize and press their demands more effectively.

Older American consumers face many of the problems we have already discussed. Discrimination and prejudice are common, and even well-meaning individuals may suffer from misconceptions. The idea that the elderly are infirm or even senile permeates thinking, even though neither condition is typical. Again, the whole question of aging is one most people would like to avoid (and in a youth-oriented culture, avoidance is encouraged); thus, it is easier to carry on with misconceptions than it is to face the realities of the situation.

All of this serves to isolate elderly consumers, cutting them off from the mainstream of cultural, economic, and social life. That isolation has become a characteristic of the elderly consumer and creates special problems. When the isolation is physical (in rural areas, for example), as well as emotional, problems are compounded. The consumer who craves social contact is especially vulnerable to fraud. The consumer may be thankful for the attention that he or she is receiving and that gratitude may cloud judgments. Even in cases when the consumer isn't physically removed from others, isolation serves to reduce satisfaction [31, p. 166].

Income is a particular problem among the elderly. Because most are retired and on fixed incomes, inflation is a real threat. Beyond that, many of the elderly are simply poor, which means they must confront many of the problems discussed in the previous chapter. Older people may literally be forced into poverty because they are not allowed to work or are unable to do so. For those who have grown accustomed to a higher standard of living, the problem may be particularly difficult. In discussing female consumers, we noted that the question of earnings could not be separated from consumption. That is true in this case also, although *earnings* may take on a slightly different connotation. Social security, private retirement benefits, and annuity programs take on special meaning (and have, of course, an impact on the entire population). Changes such as increases in social security payments and the vesting of pension-fund benefits have had a positive impact on elderly consumers.

Work itself is also an issue here. The elderly's right to work is limited by forced retirement at age sixty-five. Any forced retirement age is essentially arbitrary and illustrates a problem definition in actually identifying *the elderly*. It seems foolish to say that someone who is sixty-six is elderly, but someone who is sixty-four is not. Some people are more active and alert in their eighties than people half their age. In professions that do not have forced retirement (such as medicine and politics), individuals over sixty-five continue to make contributions. Mandatory retirement may therefore have both direct and indirect economic impact. It directly raises the cost of such programs as social security and indirectly imposes costs as more productive workers are forced out of the labor force.

For these reasons, significant changes have been made in retirement laws. The mandatory retirement age is being raised gradually to seventy for private firms and will be abolished for government employees. Those who fear this development should take note of another trend. At the same time that the retirement age is increased, more and more workers are taking *early retirement*. Some retire early so they will have more time to enjoy themselves. However, many workers who retire early begin second careers that they can continue for the rest of their lives. It appears that a much more diverse pattern is developing. Some workers will continue at their jobs longer, while others will leave sooner. This wider range of choices is a healthy development and is certainly more in keeping with the diversity that exists within the population. An economy that is built upon choice should not deny choices to people simply because of their age.

As the elderly obtain a wider range of choices, misconceptions about aging should be dispelled. Seeing the elderly in different roles should help the total population develop a truer perception of the situation, which in turn should make it easier to deal with actual problems. For example, many of the elderly are less mobile and have problems of access to buildings and transportation. These problems need to be dealt with, but should be treated like any other consumer problem and not generalized as characteristics of an entire group. We generally think of integration in racial terms, but it is really integration that we are talking about here. As the elderly are better integrated into the total population, many of their consumer problems will be taken care of. Some of the consumer problems of the elderly, such as lack of mobility, are tied to age. The more significant problems, however, arise because of the way in which society has treated the elderly. Most of those problems can be traced to economic and social isolation. Once again, then, consumer problems arise out of a larger social problem.

Summing Up

I noted at the beginning of this chapter that the problems under consideration were meant to illustrate how the analysis developed earlier could be applied in different situations. Now that we have analyzed the problems, you should see a number of common themes. As illustrations, consider:

Information problems, especially credence qualities in education and medicine;
Licensing issues in medicine and the funeral industry;
Discrimination in the cases of women and the elderly;
The relationship between employment opportunities and consumption opportunities.

We could talk about other special groups–the handicapped, children, or rural consumers—or other problem areas—legal services, transportation, or repair work—and the issues would be similar.

In each case, specific elements might be involved that are unique to the situation (with children, for example, there are special developmental considerations). However, the same basic issues are involved in the analyses of different problems. This tends to confirm our initial proposition in Chapter 2 that consumer problems can be traced back to the assumptions of the theory of consumer choice. Thus, we can see problems of rationality (or choice), uncertainty, information, and sovereignty. The difference is that now we have a better understanding of the complexities involved in each of those areas.

We should also understand that economic change has both direct and indirect effects on consumers. I identified the direct effects when I said that consumer problems grow out of our highly specialized economy. However, specialization also changes the income distribution, the role of different groups (such as women and the elderly), and causes social strain. These changes ultimately affect consumers also. Indirect effects such as these may be more difficult to deal with because they grow out of broader social problems.

Study Questions

1. We have spoken before of consumers' perceptions getting in the way of their self-interest. Indicate how this is true for each of the topics discussed in this chapter.
2. Have you ever seen a woman selling used cars or major home appliances? What does that say about perceptions of women's roles?
3. What is the implication of more flexible policies on maternity leave for women's long-term gains in the labor market?
4. Many successful realtors are women. What does this tell you about patterns of family decision making?
5. If health care were cheaper, would consumers use more of it? Is this good or bad? What problems does it raise?
6. We have emphasized the cost of improving the delivery of health care. What economic gains (or savings) might attend such improvement? Would there be savings involved for society as a whole?
7. Because of demographic changes, the number of students graduating from high school will drop sharply during the mid-1980s. How can students take advantage of this buyers' market? Are there any dangers in the way colleges and universities might react?
8. The differential between the lifetime earnings of high school

and college graduates is narrowing. What does that mean about higher education as an investment? What does it mean for choices between four-year programs and shorter programs?

9. We indicated that funerals represent a unique consumer problem. However, can you think of similarities between funerals and other decisions consumers face?

10. Many of the elderly are poor. Many are also women. Nevertheless, the problems of the elderly consumer extend beyond those of either the poor or women. Explain.

Suggested Projects

1. Review the way in which women are treated in advertising. Look for examples of sexual exploitation, adornment, stereotyping, and nontraditional portrayals. Discuss.

2. Send a male and a female student on comparative shopping trips. They should go separately, but each should go to the same stores, ask the same questions, or bargain on the same items. Are there any differences in the way the two are treated? Can these differences be traced to sex?

3. Review proposals for national health insurance. Compare the alternative plans and evaluate them in terms of our discussion in the text.

4. Does your community (or region) have any kind of health-care planning? Discuss the question with hospital administrators or local United Fund officials.

5. Check the Yellow Pages for the number of doctors in your city; compare availability according to specialty. Look for phone books of other cities in the library and make similar comparisons. If you can, get data on all the doctors in your state (check with the reference librarian). How does the distribution vary over the state?

6. Evaluate your college or university catalog. Is the information you need presented clearly? Is there any evidence of misleading information?

7. Does your campus have an ombudsman? If so, talk with him or her about how the office works. If not, does any other campus official fill that role?

8. Check the grievance procedures for students on your campus. Do you feel they are adequate to give students a fair hearing?

9. Do any funeral directors in your area advertise? If so, evaluate the advertising.

10. What alternatives to traditional funeral homes are available in your area? If there is a memorial society, meet with members to find out how it works.

11. What services are available to the elderly in your area? How many of these are directed toward consumer problems? Do the elderly make use of them?

Bibliography and Suggested Readings

1. Abdel-Ghany, Mohamed, and Godwin, Deborah D. "Feminism and Attitudes Toward Consumerism." Unpublished paper, School of Home Economics, The University of North Carolina at Greensboro.
   A study that finds that women who are more activist as consumers are also likely to support the women's movement. An interesting investigation of the common ground between the two movements.

2. *Advertising, Disclosure, Cooling Off and Refund Requirements Concerning Proprietary, Vocational and Home Study Schools.* Federal Trade Commission. Washington, D.C.: U.S. Government Printing Office, May 15, 1975.
   The Federal Trade Commission regulations for nondegree institutions.

3. Ahern, Dee Dee, and Bliss, Betsy. *The Economics of Being a Woman.* New York: McGraw-Hill Book Co., 1976.
   A look at the problems of the market from the female perspective. Largely journalistic and nonanalytical, but provides good introduction.

4. Bureau of Labor Statistics. *Distribution of Consumption Expenditures by Consumption Unit.* Washington, D.C.: U.S. Government Printing Office, 1975.
   Data on how households spend their money. Information is based on surveys and includes comparisons with earlier periods.

5. *Children of Working Mothers.* Special Labor Force Report 205, Bureau of Labor Statistics. Washington, D.C.: U.S. Government Printing Office, 1977.
   Data on children in families with working mothers. Indicates a major change in this area.

6. Clark, Tinney S. "FTC Accuses Extension School of False Claims." *The Chronicle of Higher Education,* June 26, 1978.
   Brief account of the FTC's actions against a large correspondence school.

7. Courtney, A. E., and Whipple, T. W. "Women in T.V. Commercials." *Journal of Communication,* 24, 1974.
   A detailed study of sex-role stereotyping in advertising. Part of an extensive literature on how women are presented in advertising. Includes

discussion of authority figures and the use of male voices even when women are in the ad.

8. Davidson, Robert H., and Stark, Joan S. "The Federal Role." In *Promoting Consumer Protection for Students*, Joan S. Stark, ed., New Directions for Higher Education 13, San Francisco: Jossey-Bass, 1976.
   A discussion of consumer issues involved in education. Along with 28, below, this collection of readings offers one of the most complete treatments of the topic.

9. Davis, Harry L. "Decision Making Within the Household." *Journal of Consumer Research,* March 1976.
   An excellent review article on family decision making. Covers the entire range of decisions and participation patterns. An excellent source for those interested in the topic. Bibliography is extensive and useful.

10. De Tocqueville, Alexis. *Democracy in America.* trans. Henry Reeve, ed. Phillips Bradley, Two Volumes. New York: Alfred A. Knopf, 1956.
    A genuine classic. One of the most famous accounts of America by a foreigner. Details American life (and consumers) in the early nineteenth century.

11. Easton, Allan. *The Design of a Health Maintenance Organization.* New York: Praeger Publishers, 1975.
    A good review of Health Maintenance Organization plans and how they operate.

12. *The Earnings Gap Between Women and Men.* U.S. Department of Labor, Washington, D.C.: United States Government Printing Office, 1976.
    Information on earnings for men and women. Includes discussion and interpretation of the statistics, especially the gap between men and women's earnings.

13. El-Khawas, E. H. *Better Information for Student Choice: Report of a National Task Force.* The National Task Force on Better Information for Student Choice, March, 1977.
    The report of the National Task Force. Includes recommendations for improving both the quality and quantity of information that goes to students. The task force represented a coordinated effort by participating colleges and universities to deal with students' informational needs.

14. *Funeral Industry Practices.* Bureau of Consumer Protection, Federal Trade Commission, June 1978.
    A massive study of the funeral industry that constitutes the best review available. The key source for anyone interested in the problem. Will probably serve as basis for new set of FTC rules.

15. Galbraith, John Kenneth. *Economics and the Public Purpose.* Boston: Houghton Mifflin, 1973.
A broadly reflective review of Galbraith's thoughts. The section on women as crypto-servants has become a classic.

16. *Getting Ready for National Health Insurance: Unnecessary Surgery.* Hearings before the subcommittee on Oversight and Investigations, Washington, D.C.: U.S. Government Printing Office, 1975.
Congressional hearings on health care, with the emphasis on unnecessary surgery. Reports large variations over the country. The problem appears to be particularly pronounced for gynecological difficulties.

17. Golladay, Frederick et al. "Allied Health Manpower Strategies: Estimates of the Potential Gains from Effective Task Delegation." *Medical Care,* November-December 1973.
Estimates of how the use of physicians' assistants could increase medical productivity. Concludes that the approach warrants consideration.

18. Gronau, Reuben. "Home Production—A Forgotten Industry." Unpublished paper, National Bureau of Economic Research and Hebrew University, August 1977.
Calculations of the value of household production. Gronau's published work includes a variety of related topics, which should be of interest to students. Somewhat analytical, but still manageable.

19. *Household and Family Characteristics: March 1976.* Current Population Reports. Bureau of the Census, U.S. Department of Commerce, Series P-20, No. 311. Washington, D.C.: U.S. Government Printing Office, 1977.
Detailed information on American households. Valuable source.

20. Magarrell, Jack. "Consumer Protection Focuses on Non-Degree Institutions." *The Chronicle of Higher Education,* June 26, 1978.
A news account of the Federal Trade Commission's activities in education, which suggests that the FTC should pay more attention to degree-granting institutions.

21. Mancuso, John H. "Academic Challenges in the Courts." In *The Many Faces of Educational Consumerism.* ed. Joan S. Stark, Lexington, Mass.: Lexington Books, 1977.
A detailed account of the changing legal framework of education. Shows that the courts have been willing to intervene in cases involving personal rights and conduct, but not when academic issues are concerned. Includes legal citations.

22. ———. "Legal Rights to Reasonable Rules, Fair Grades, and Quality Courses." In *Promoting Consumer Protection for Students.* Joan S. Stark, ed. New Directions for Higher Education # 13. San Francisco: Jossey-Bass, 1976.
A similar presentation of material covered in 21.

23. *Marital and Family Characteristics of the Labor Force in March 1976.*

Special Labor Force Report 206, Bureau of Labor Statistics, Washington, D.C.: U.S. Government Printing Office, 1977.
Statistics on the marital status and family membership of workers. Part of The Bureau of Labor Statistic's series that details various aspects of the labor force.

24. Orlans, Harold. *Private Accreditation and Public Eligibility.* Lexington, Mass.: Lexington Books, 1975.
A good review of academic accreditation, including the degree to which governmental bodies rely upon this private process.

25. Schwartz, William B., and Komesar, Neilk. "Doctors, Damage and Deterrence: An Economic View of Medical Malpractice." *New England Journal of Medicine,* June 8, 1978.
One of the most detailed studies available on malpractice. Suggests that a few doctors are responsible for most malpractice suits. The *New England Journal of Medicine* is one of the nation's most prestigious medical journals. As in this case, its articles may be of interest to the general reader.

26. Scott, Nan E. "The Relationship Betwen Sex Role Stereotyping and Information Content in Network Television Advertisement." Unpublished Ph.D. dissertation, University of Tennessee at Knoxville, 1978.
A study that relates the manner in which women are presented in advertisements to the information content of the ad. Found that women were presented in a less stereotypic way in ads which had higher information content.

27. Scott, Rosemary. *The Female Consumer.* New York: John Wiley and Sons, 1976.
Provides a British perspective on the woman in the marketplace. Particularly good in terms of the impact of traditional roles played by men and women and how that effects the way women are assumed to act.

28. Stark, Joan S. *The Many Faces of Educational Consumerism.* Lexington, Mass.: Lexington Books, 1977.
The best single source on consumer issues in postsecondary education. Includes a general discussion of the topic in addition to a series of papers on particular issues. Contains extensive bibliographies.

29. Swagler, Roger M. "Students as Consumers of Postsecondary Education: A Framework for Analysis," *Journal of Consumer Affairs,* Summer 1978.
An analysis of student's informational needs based on the search, experience, and credence qualities involved. Provides the basis for the approach taken in this chapter.

30. Tewksbury, Donald G. *The Founding of American Colleges and Universities Before the Civil War.* Archon Books, 1965.
A review of the development of American higher education. Comments by nineteenth century educators are particularly useful in showing the

implicit faith of Americans in the value of education. Contrasts with the present are telling.

31. Waddell, Frederick E. "Consumer Research and Programs for the Elderly—The Forgotten Dimension." *Journal of Consumer Affairs,* Winter 1975.
A good introduction to the problems of elderly consumers. Emphasizes the role of isolation and the vulnerability of the elderly to fraud.

32. Ward, Richard A. *The Economics of Health Resources.* Reading, Mass.: Addison-Wesley Publishing Co., 1975.
An excellent reference on the problem of health care. Provides a comprehensive yet concise, review of the issues. The analysis is complete, but is presented in readable form. Appropriate for anyone interested in the topic.

-12-

The Future of the Consumer Society

A Flawed Utopia

"Emptiness, emptiness . . . all is empty," says the Speaker in *Ecclesiastes,* "What does man gain from all his labor and toil under the sun?" [I, iii]. The answer that the ancient Hebrews gave to that question is not known, but more and more people today find such questions bothersome and unsettling. That fact alone should give us reason to pause. Only a few years ago it would have been sufficient to answer that "labor and toil" had brought the unparalleled accumulation of material wealth—but no more.

The quote from *Ecclesiastes* was written over 2,500 years ago. While such questions are not new, the perspective from which we view them is. In earlier times, when most people lived at or near subsistence, the goal of satisfying material wants seemed sufficient. Now, most people in most Western economies can not only satisfy their daily needs, but enjoy refinements that even their grandparents hardly dared dream about. That is a considerable achievement; but despite all this abundance, people have increasingly come to wonder if they are really any better off. What has really changed, then, is our idea of *better off* or *well-being*. These concepts have always been tied to the accumulation of material goods, the more affluent person being better off.* Now well-being is interpreted much more broadly. Wealth still plays a part, but it is now only one aspect of the definition rather than the definition itself.

---

* Statements like "Money can't buy happiness" are favored by people who have neither.

It is not surprising that these changes should be most noticeable in the affluent United States. They are reflected in a variety of subtle ways, of which attitudes toward job satisfaction offer one illustration. People who have been out of work for some time will not be too particular about the kind of jobs they get; if they express any preference, it will probably be for a job that offers steady income. Yet in a survey of heads of households in the United States, George Katona found that only 34 percent gave job security the highest priority; almost the same number, 35 percent, ranked job satisfaction highest. By contrast, in Germany 70 percent put job security first and only 10 percent gave top priority to satisfaction [11, pp. 126–27].

You may recognize in this discussion the recurrence of several themes touched on before. With affluence, consumption itself becomes complex and its very definition changes. Consumers become less concerned with the good itself and more mindful of the combination of characteristics it possesses. By extension, then, the consumer's perception of consumption as a whole changes with rising incomes. To many people, these changes have been unsettling. Gailbraith noted that, until recently, success was defined in rather narrow, economic terms. He states that now, however,

> Few will admit publicly to believing that the accumulation of wealth is the only measure of virtue. We have now a much more incoherent set of goals.... All of this, of course, has an aspect of chaos for people who were reared to believe in the simpler tests of economic performance. [8, p. 72]

Consumers today have realized the dreams of centuries, only to discover that those dreams were too small. The standards of measurement have been changed so that yesterday's utopia becomes today's stark reality. When the goal seemed to be within reach, it slipped away. Just as increased production is no longer a universally accepted goal for the economy as a whole, the additional accumulation of material goods is not accepted as the goal by all consumers. While fate has never dealt kindly with utopians, it is because their vision of the good life was dismissed as an impossible dream. Most utopian thinkers envisioned a world in which an individual's material needs would be fulfilled but subordinated to a sense of community, religious conviction, or love of humanity. In retrospect, that may seem like a vain hope. Yet in recognizing materialism itself as an inadequate goal, the utopians proved particularly discerning. To date, only the material aspects of their dream have been attained, and the results are decidedly nonutopian.

Consideration of the consumer's problems ultimately turns out to be an analysis of a flawed utopia. That may seem like a contradiction in terms, but it provides a useful point of view. The varied elements that intertwine in this analysis, while they ultimately converge, often seem to be moving in different directions. Analysis involves so many factors and they operate at so many different levels that it is difficult to bring them all into focus at the same time. In facing this situation before, we tried to take the problem apart and look at its various components. That seems like the most profitable approach in this case too, but caution is required, because the way the different parts fit together is especially important. Understanding them in isolation is insufficient; it is necessary to understand how they interrelate.

To do that requires the recognition that the problems of the consumer society sprang from a variety of sources. Some of the problems can be traced to specialization, which makes greater affluence possible and isolates the consumer. Greater affluence, in turn, works changes on the consumer; it changes both the pattern and the character of consumption. At the same time, various outside forces are working on the consumer. These include not only changing attitudes but technological constraints as well.

Working together, these forces have tarnished the cherished goal of affluence. Our purpose now is to see precisely how they have done it. In tracing the different elements and identifying the contribution each makes to the overall picture, we can reasonably assume that despite all the changes that have taken place, consumers' fundamental goals have not changed. That is, consumers would rather be better off than worse off. If people still prefer to be better off, but feel that they aren't, then the problem must lie within the definition of "better off." I suggested that earlier, when I indicated that it is no longer possible to equate well-being with material accumulation. The problem now is to find out precisely what is meant by the phrase.

The Realities of the Consumer Society

Hassled, Harried, and Humbugged

The most obvious drawback to the consumer society, with all its splendid affluence, is that it is a lot of bother. The accumulation of material goods itself creates problems, and the more sophisticated the goods, the greater the problems. This is the most basic aspect of the question; it has nothing to do with lofty notions of the meaning of life or the ultimate consequences of consumption. Rather, it concerns the simple fact that the more you have, the more you have to go wrong.

Let us take a mundane example, a lawn mower. The term power applied to lawn mower is a misnomer; all lawn mowers are powered, it is just that some are powered by people, while others are powered by machinery. The latter can make the job of cutting grass a lot easier, but at a price. Power lawn mowers are not just more expensive to buy than hand mowers; they are more expensive to maintain. Gas, spark plugs, tune-ups, starters, and a lot of other things are necessary to maintain what looks like a relatively simple machine. People with hand mowers do not share these problems. They may have sore backs, but they are spared the frustration that goes with owning a power mower.

Power mowers are only one example of devices that are supposed to simplify life but often end up making it more complex. Vacation homes are fine, but they mean two water heaters to worry about, two lawns to mow, and two roofs to leak. Similarly, color television is more of a problem than black-and-white; television more of a problem than radio; radio more of a problem than books, and so on. You can supply additions to the list yourself. In the extreme, this argument leads to the enslavement of individuals to their material belongings. Most people probably do not feel enslaved but they are certainly more than a little aggravated. Our lifestyles have grown so complex and so dependent on so many things that the chance of any one thing's going wrong is greatly increased. Since things are so interrelated, when something goes wrong, everything else is affected.

The culprit in this case is *time,* or rather the lack of it. Despite all the publicity given to the explosion in leisure time, the average number of hours worked per week has not declined much in the last quarter century [12, pp. 28–31]. Therefore, consumers must try to cram more consumption into the time available. One way to do this is to avoid consumption activities that by their very nature require large amounts of time—leisurely drives in the country and multi-coursed French meals.* Increased pressures on (and hence value of) time make these activities too expensive.

Another approach to the problem is successive consumption, meaning that different activities follow each other rapidly so that the pace becomes hectic. Finally, there is consecutive consumption or the overlapping of consumption activities. People talk and watch television, socialize and play tennis, and eat and conduct business. These

* Time pressures have an impact on sports too. Golfers use carts to get around the course more quickly and each year there is a new proposal to "speed up" baseball (which, with its disregard for time, is obviously a surviver from a more leisurely age). Indoor sports are affected too. Linder notes that time pressures leave less time for sex and quotes Ovid, "Love yields to businesses; be busy and you will be safe" [12, p. 87].

tendencies may help explain the decline in the number of books Americans read because it is difficult to read and do anything else.

According to Staffen Linder, the collective impact of these tactics is to accelerate consumption. However, acceleration also requires the substitution of goods for time in consumption, and, as noted in the power-mower example, this creates problems [12, pp. 77–93]. You should also recall the discussion from Chapter 7 where we noted that what we call *consumption* involves not just use of the product, but also maintaining the product. As consumers acquire more and more products, the maintenance problem increases. There follows the frustration with things that don't work and the irony of wasting time over time-saving products. The net result of all this is a feverish pursuit of leisure-time activities, a pursuit that is ultimately exhausting. There are limits to both the amount of consumption that can be crammed into a given amount of time and the degree to which goods can be substituted for time in consumption. When those limits are approached, frustrations mount. As a result, more and more consumers are questioning mass consumption not because they find it boring or distasteful, but simply because it is too much trouble. These factors affect (or afflict) some consumers more than others. Most consumers, however, find themselves confronting these problems at some time or another. The drive for simplicity and the return to so-called natural pleasures reflects the fact that they provide the easiest path. All of this is difficult to face for people who have been raised in a society that glorifies material things, but more and more people are coming to accept the need for change.

Deep Down It's Shallow

While most people find that life in the consumer society is hectic, they are still trying to cope with its difficulties. Some, however, have carried their questioning a step further; they look at mass consumption and wonder what it has gotten us. If one believes the images that Madison Avenue flashes across the television screen, the paramount achievement of all of this is a clean bathroom bowl. The modern consumer, as portrayed in advertisements, seems to be concerned with little else. It is no wonder that real consumers have begun to question whether it has all been worth it. People find that increased consumption does not necessarily bring increased satisfaction. Particular wants may be satisfied, but life itself is not satisfying. As George Katona has noted: "*Excessive* materialism is not a necessary consequence of increased well-being or of striving for further well-being" [11, p. 200, emphasis added].

Additional words from *Ecclesiastes* are worth considering:

> What reward has a man for all his labor, his scheming and his toil here under the sun? All his life long his business is pain and vexation to him; even at night his mind knowns no rest. This too is emptiness. [II, xxiii]

Though thousands of years separate George Katona and the Speaker in *Ecclesiastes,* they are both making the same point. The accumulation of material goods does not in itself guarantee a full and satisfying life. Indeed, its "pain and vexation" may detract from that goal. Galbraith was saying something similar when he observed that in any definition of well-being,

> Intellectual purpose has some role, new modes of life have some role and artistic purpose has some role. The sense of whether one is living a reflective and tranquil existence has begun to take on some meaning [8, p. 72].

"A reflective and tranquil existence"—that single phrase sums up the changes that affluence has worked on the consumer. Would anyone have thought of asking a person in a 1930s breadline if life was tranquil? It is highly unlikely. When people face serious economic dislocation, they are concerned with where their next meal is coming from. Reflection and introspection are luxuries that cannot be afforded until immediate needs have been fulfilled. These new goals may be incompatible with the old. A hassled consumer has little time for reflection. The continual pressures of modern life that beset the individual make tranquility at once more attractive and more difficult to attain. That frustration and even hostility should result is easy to understand.

It is not difficult to see why today's radical thinkers have played on this theme, stressing alienation [9]. Paul Baran speaks of the "lethal fragmentation of the human personality under capitalism," and pleads for individuals to be considered as human beings, not as consumers [1, p. xvii]. In this text, the words *individual* and *consumer* have been used interchangeably, yet it is easy to lose sight of the fact that consumers are people and the *consumer society* is *human society.*

Daniel Bell, a sociologist, was also concerned with fragmentation, identifying what he termed *disjuncture* among the various parts of modern life. Disjuncture simply means there is no relationship among the different aspects of life and no logic to the whole. Work hours are dominated by the work ethic and the drive for efficiency, but consumption is based on "the fun morality" and motivated by "the institutionalization of envy." [3, pp. 22 & 71] Bell notes:

> The characteristic style of industrialism is based on . . . efficiency, least cost, maximization, optimization and functional rationality. Yet it is this very style that is in conflict with the advanced cultural trends of the Western World, for modernist culture emphasis anti-cognitive and anti-intellectual modes . . . [3, p. 84]

According to Bell, then, the mass consumption society lacks any glue to hold it together. Without a common logic or unifying theme, the contradictions implicit in the system will ultimately pull it apart. Ultimately, the cultural aspects of mass consumption may be more important than economic elements.

The problems discussed here have become increasingly common, a fact that has been duly recorded by the media. Unfortunately, this focuses attention on some of the more intense reactions to mass consumption. The counterculture receives close attention and life in the commune is well documented. However, the extremes affect only a tiny part of the population and are less significant than the more subtle changes that are evident in the behavior of large numbers of people. As Katona noted, workers are increasingly concerned with job satisfaction. Young executives are turning down promotions because it would require them to move, even though they know such actions slow their climb up the corporate ladder. In recognition of these trends, large firms are reexamining their personnel policies. Some now question the value of shifting people around just for the sake of a move. Others offer time off for public-service activities.

Since it is difficult to obtain a true perspective on these changes, it is easy to exaggerate their importance. Every era has its dropouts. American history tells the story of many utopian communities, like Brook Farm and New Harmony, and also religious splinter groups like the Shakers. Recently, the years between the two world wars had their lost generation and featured Mencken's stinging satire on American life. In the past, however, such reactions were limited to fringe groups or elites. Now they are making an appearance in the American mainstream. That appearance coincides with a much broader reaction against modern, technological society. Rationalism and scientific inquiry, which have been the basis for most modern thought, face a growing challenge. There is a new emphasis on the senses, on feeling as opposed to knowing. Introspection and intuition have taken on new status, and so have mysticism, the supernatural, and exotic religious forms.

These reactions taken together show a dissatisfaction with modern life and all its complexity, and, by extension, the consumer society, itself an outgrowth of centuries of scientific invention and innovation. Mass consumption is such an integral part of the society as a whole that it is very difficult to analyze it as a separate question. The problems of consumption are the problems of modern society.

A House Divided

The points discussed thus far have been internal, growing out of the character of the mass-consumption society itself. One aspect, poverty in the midst of affluence, must be considered in a broader context. Poverty acts, or has the potential to act, as an external constraint on consumption patterns. Chapter 10 dealt with the details of the problem. Now we need to look at the question more generally and see where poverty fits in the overall pattern of the consumer society. It is also necessary to look at poverty in the international context, which means reversing the sequence and considering the problems affluence creates in the midst of poverty.

It is doubtful if many low-income consumers are overburdened with material goods or feel bored and unfulfilled with consumption. Individuals are not very likely to worry about the real value of a third car or a second house if they are not sure about their next meal. While most consumers struggle with affluence, the poor must deal with a more immediate concern, scarcity. Such an unstable situation, if it endures, threatens the whole society. That the situation contains the roots of violence was well demonstrated in the 1960s; but violence is not the most serious threat. An affluent society that learns to live with poverty develops a callous disregard for its own problems; that sort of blindness must ultimately be self-defeating. If a society cannot respond to poverty, it can hardly be expected to respond to other, more subtle problems it faces.

A willingness to accept poverty can only mean that the society has become self-seeking and self-indulgent, hardly attributes of a vital, problem-solving people. Such a society is headed toward more serious problems. It is in that sense that poverty acts as an ultimate constraint on mass consumption. Even so, this is only a partial effect. The problems of affluence and poverty exist among countries as well as within countries. The world is divided into "haves" and "have nots," and most countries belong in the latter category. Areas like Western Europe, North America, and Japan are the exceptions. From a world view, the proportions are turned around and the problem is affluence in the midst of poverty [16].

Until recently, most Americans did not look at this situation in terms of its implications for mass consumption. However, like all affluent countries, America depends on resources drawn from low-income countries. American affluence depends not only on Arab oil, but Bolivian tin, Zambian copper, Brazilian coffee, and Canadian timber.* Americans tended to take this for granted, even when it became clear that we were consuming a disproportionate share of the world's resources. Even though the United States has only about 6 percent of the world's population, over one-third of the world's resources is needed to keep its mass-consumption society going. The Arab oil boycott of 1973–74 graphically illustrated American vulnerability, at the same time representing only the tip of the iceberg. Similar efforts on other products may not produce boycotts but could contribute to rising prices and possible shortages.

Part of the problem lies in the perspective of consumers in the industrial countries. Because of their affluence, they tend to look on the world resources as their own preserve, finding it difficult to comprehend the situation of people in less developed countries. Tourists, for example, fly halfway around the world to view game animals in East Africa without giving it a second thought. Yet within that area, competition exists between the game animals and the domestic herds of local inhabitants. Bitterness arises over claims that the latter suffer for the sake of rich tourists. This perception gap needs to be closed, as it poses a real threat to world economic stability. That threat clouds the future of both mass consumption in the industrial countries and the newly won increases in the standard of living in less developed countries. A difficult reassessment is necessary, but the pain will be much greater if the matter is ignored until it has reached crisis proportions.

The New Imperative

Resource availability deserves close attention. There are limited supplies of mineral resources and conventional energy sources, which raises the point whether affluent consumers can really afford the lifestyle they have developed. The final constraint on the mass-consumption society may be that it is too expensive. Excesses will have a twofold consequence. The first aspect is that critical resources may be exhausted. Even if they are not, there is the broader issue of how rising demands of mass consumption affect the environment. Increased production is required to meet these demands, and that places increased stress upon the environment.

---

* Canada, of course, is a rich, industrial country, but it is a principal supplier of raw materials to the United States. The Canadians have become increasingly uncomfortable in this role and have taken steps to preserve their resources for their own use.

Pollution is not new, but it was only after prosperity became well established that the problem became a main concern. The first concern of a poor economy is generating income; that the environment is damaged in the process is of secondary importance. To most people, a full stomach is more important than clean air and certainly more important than vague threats of future calamities. Thus, while affluent economies cannot afford to ignore the environment, less affluent ones cannot afford to consider it.

The public at first discounted environmental concern as extremism, and some of the gloomier predictions probably were. However, the seriousness of the problem soon became apparent as smog alerts were declared in large cities and floods caused by denuding of the countryside became more severe; specific problems, such as oil spills, were also recognized as serious threats. Environmental limitations began to loom as a plausible constraint on future growth. Even when those limitations were not immediate, people came to realize that their well-being was endangered because of environmental decay. Life in a city full of smog, noise, and congestion is not much fun. With this recognition, the environment came to be viewed as a part of consumption itself. Increases in one type of consumption— traditional goods and services—were endangering another, the environment.

It is possible to pick almost any area of American life and find examples of resource waste. Buildings are constructed so as to require year-round climate control, with no possibility of even opening the windows. Products are elaborately packaged in expensive containers. The ubiquitous aerosol can has become the symbol of this waste. Though pressurized containers are expensive and not very efficient, they are convenient, which explains why products as diverse as paint, deodorant, cheese, and frosting are packaged this way. It is in transportation, however, that the problem is most glaring. The American transportation system has grown up almost wholly around the private automobile. Few large cities have adequate public transportation systems, and this lack is still encouraged by government policy. The federal government is much freer with financing for highways than it is with monies for developing alternatives. The government has mandated fuel efficiency standards for automobiles (which mean smaller and lighter cars), but large quantities of resources are still used in the production and operation of automobiles.

The need for conserving resources was first dramatized by the Arab oil boycott of 1973–74. Consumers may have forgotten those cold winter mornings spent waiting in line for gasoline, but shortages in other areas have kept the resource problem in the news. A succession of cold winters (and a coal-miners strike) caused problems for many consumers and meant economic dislocation for some areas. Even when energy was available, consumers found that costs were spiraling upward. Judged by an absolute standard, these problems have not been severe, but that in itself shows how vulnerable the mass consumption society is to resource shortages. What would happen to our standard of living if there were a true crisis?

Various answers have been suggested to this question, but most of them overlook why our consumption patterns are so resource intensive. I noted earlier that consumers substitute goods for time in consumption; time is more valuable and is therefore conserved. The word *waste* is subject to reinterpretation when we consider the total cost of consumption to be the cost of goods *plus* the cost of time involved. We are apparently wasteful in our use of goods in order to conserve time and hence reduce the *total cost* of consumption. Gary Becker noted this point explicitly; Americans, he wrote:

> are simultaneously supposed to be wasteful—of material goods— and overly economical—of immaterial time. Yet both allegations may be correct and not simply indicative of a strange American temperament, because the market value of time is higher relative to the price of goods there than elsewhere. That is, the tendency to be economical about time and lavish about goods may be no paradox, but in part simply a reaction to a difference in relative costs. [2, p. 514]

The obvious logic of that argument makes its implications even more disturbing. The relative prices of time and goods makes apparently wasteful behavior rational for consumers, which helps explain why most appeals for conservation have minimal impact. It is not that consumers are simply selfish and insensitive; rather, consumers recognize that conserving goods (and resources) represents a more expensive alternative that is against their short-run self-interest. *It follows that significant savings in resources won't be achieved unless the cost of goods is substantially raised or the cost of time is substantially lowered.*

Some recent policy decisions reflect a recognition of these alternatives. For example, some states have banned throw-away bottles [15]. If you have paid a deposit, the effort required to return the bottle is worthwhile. Put differently, it will cost you more to save time by not returning the bottle. The deposit changes the relative price of time and goods, making the latter more expensive (and hence lowering the relative cost of time). The bottle ban is a relatively minor example, but it shows the kind of policies that may be necessary to have a significant impact on individual's use of resources.

Such a prospect may lack appeal because it raises the possibility of government interference in consumption activities and a dramatic change in those activities. Such a change, if it is severe, could cause serious social strains. To avoid those strains and to ensure that required adjustments are made as equitably as possible, policies must be carefully devised. Above all, those policies must be structured in such a way as to make conservation the economically rational alternative for consumers. Policies that do less will simply be tinkering with the fringes of the problem.

At this writing the prospects do not look very encouraging. Vested interests may fight against changes (as in the case of the bottle ban) or use those changes as a source of windfall gains at the consumer's expense (as in the case of the deregulation of natural gas). It is clear, then, that consumers as citizens need to take an active part in the policy-making process. Given the difficulties that citizen-consumers face in that regard (Chapter 9), the task isn't easy. However, as consumers come to recognize the fundamental issues involved and the degree to which their day-to-day lives could be affected, they will also recognize that it should pay them to become involved.

Toward a Reconciliation

An Obvious Conclusion

I have outlined the main elements involved in the future path of the mass-consumption society. Despite the diversity of the forces at work, there is a common unifying factor. In every case, conditions have changed so that old assumptions are being called into question. It was always assumed that increased consumption would increase well-being, but increasing numbers of people find consumption either a bore or a bother. It was assumed that the problem of poverty would either take care of itself or at least exist quietly, yet neither has happened. It was assumed that resources would always be available and that the earth would regenerate itself, though neither seems to be true. Any society works on a set of premises or assumptions that give it a sense of continuity and stability. When these are shaken, repercussions are felt in every aspect of life. It should not be surprising then that these changes have shaken the life of the modern consumer. These are not superficial changes; there is nothing cosmetic about them. They represent a fundamental alteration in the approach to consumption, with affluence acting as the agent of change.

This is clearly a time of transition. That much is certain. Unfortunately, during any such period, the precise character of change is uncertain. Different forces are pulling in different directions at different speeds and until they work themselves out the final result will be unclear. Therefore, it is dangerous, even reckless, to predict the precise path of future events. This should be sufficient warning against overgeneralizations and prepackaged conclusions. While the caution should be taken to heart, there is still something that can be said about the most probable course of future developments from the pattern of cumulative trends. This is hardly a sweeping claim, but it is all that anyone could justify at this point.

The Future—Prospects and Patterns

The surest clue that significant change is under way is the present questioning of the assumptions that have guided modern economic development. Unless people feel that conditions have changed, they will not feel the need to change the basic principles on which they operate. The need that increasing numbers of people now feel for such a change indicates that the consumer society has moved into a new phase.

In Western countries, particularly English-speaking ones, consumption has traditionally been viewed as a private affair based on choices of individuals. This intensely personal aspect of consumption may now be giving way to a new sense of community based on a recognition of interdependence among consumers. Differences in this pattern may be observed among the affluent economies. The idea that individuals maximize their welfare by private market choices never took hold in Europe to the degree that it did in Great Britain and the United States. A sense of paternalism was retained in Europe that protected the consumer from many of the vagaries of the market. This sense was also reflected in attitudes toward change, which Europeans tended to resist, but Americans embraced.* Much of this resistance has broken down with recent economic advances in Europe; George Katona found, however, that in terms of attitudes and expectations, the European countries are still more "traditional," while the United States is more "dynamic" [11].

There is a paradox in the differentiation, which the Europeans, who have long suffered under such distinctions, are quick to point out. What has all this dynamism gotten the United States? The United States was the first to develop a mass-consumption society and therefore the first to face its problems. The Europeans can now

---

* Katona quotes the European commentator and politician J. J. Servan-Schreiber, who said that Europeans "continue to suffer progress rather than pursue it" [11, p. 201].

afford to be smug and suggest that their more plodding approach may in the long run turn out to be superior. Related to future developments, however, is an important point that Katona has found; despite the problems in the United States, American consumers are much more optimistic about the future than Europeans [11, pp. 41–59]. Significantly, the differences are not restricted to older people. The differences are actually greater among younger people [11, p. 201].

This suggests that Americans have not given up on the consumer society despite their problems. It also suggests that those who predict dramatic change or expect the American consumer to make an about-face are bound to be disappointed. Change can be significant without being abrupt. Just as a building can be completely remodeled without altering its basic structure, the consumer society can undergo fundamental change without being dismantled and replaced. These realizations provide a framework for analyzing current developments as well as a good hint for future direction. You will recall that each of the four points discussed under the realities of the consumer society pointed to a depressed level of consumption in the future. Interpreted within the traditional framework, this would represent a significant movement away from mass consumption. The key phrase is "traditional framework," which implies the consumption of goods and services in the classic sense. However, with affluence, this traditional view is too narrow. Affluence changes the character of consumption, changes what is being consumed. Two important concepts employed earlier should help clarify this idea. The first is Kelvin Lancaster's redefinition of consumption; in this context, we could say that the particular set of characteristics that people consume changes with rising income.

The argument that "goods are not goods" can be related to qualities such as status and convenience, but simplicity is also a characteristic, as are a sense of contentment and peace of mind. Even Galbraith's "tranquil existence" reflects a specific set of characteristics attributable to a particular consumption pattern. With affluence, people can afford to consume more of those particular characteristics. It may happen that the consumption of those characteristics will interfere with other forms of consumption. At one level, it is simply a question of deciding which is more important. People who value tranquility will simplify their lives accordingly.

There is a bit more to it than that, however. The consumption of tranquility requires time, and that brings us to the second important concept. Earlier in this chapter I recounted the difficulties consumers encounter with respect to time. That discussion drew on the earlier definition of consumption as any activity through which consumers combine time and goods to produce satisfaction [Chapter 3, pp. 35–37]. That definition doesn't distinguish between leisure and other time; all activities require varying proportions of both time and goods. It is therefore more appropriate to think in terms of an overall pattern of time allocation than to designate a particular type of time as leisure. In such a case, we should see a change in the way in which consumers are allocating their time, and in fact we do.

People are beginning to view time in a properly creative sense. This means more than simply relaxation, but involves the opportunity for individuals to develop their full range of talents. This is shown in growth of adult education programs and through interest in the arts and the highly individualized hobbies and crafts that are now available. The amazing number and success of *how-to* books attest to the strength of such interests. Commentators have noted that Americans are increasingly interested in themselves; the "me generation" is introspective and seeks personal gratification. These tendencies are difficult to interpret, but may be viewed as an effort to come to grips with a changing situation. Having failed in their effort to cram more consumption into limited amounts of time, consumers are being forced to reassess what they do and the way they do it. Thus, the intensely personal concerns exhibited today may reflect this reassessment rather than a rejection of social concerns.

We have heard for some time that people should "do their own thing," and while that is an unfortunate phrase, at least we now realize that people have a thing to do. In a sense, that realization gives people the chance to become more human. If affluence means anything more than a clean bathroom bowl, it must mean that people have the opportunity to develop their own humanity. That point hasn't been fully appreciated, particularly by those who view these developments as a triumph of the grasshoppers over the ants.

The grasshopper theory involves images of a nation full of indolent people; ambition, innovation, and progress become things of the past and the economy stagnates. If you think about it for a minute, you will see that such fears are unrealistic. People are not about to turn their backs on materialism; they are too fond of it. However, more people now view materialism as a means rather than an end. The end is satisfaction, the attainment of which requires both material goods and time.

This means work remains important, but attitudes toward work are changing. As noted in Chapter 3, the activities approach we're discussing here blurs the distinction between work and nonwork. As more and more Americans express a preference for jobs that are in some way satisfying, work becomes more than merely a way to earn money. It too becomes a form of consumption. People are increasingly unwilling to segment their lives into "work" and "living." They are looking for employment that offers them some sense of fulfillment, showing again a broad view of well-being. Employers are finding that to make their jobs attractive, they must emphasize opportunities for personal satisfaction on the job.

When these opportunities are minimal, problems develop. Studs Terkel's *Working* provides individual accounts about how people feel about their jobs and indicates that many workers are unhappy [18]. Assembly-line jobs, in particular, may pay well, but are largely boring and repetitive. Workers develop the so-called blue-collar blues, with corresponding increases in absenteeism and labor turnover and decreases in performance. To counteract this, firms increasingly move workers to different jobs on the assembly line. In other cases, the assembly line has been broken up; workers are responsible for producing an entire unit, with appropriate rewards for quality work.

All of this points to a large-scale redefinition of consumption. The reinterpretation of consumption has actually been under way for some time, although people may not have been aware of it. Pets, particularly dogs, offer an example of goods that are being *consumed* as before, but for quite different reasons. The American Kennel Club retains a classification of "Working Dogs," which illustrates the change. At one time, all dogs were working dogs; if they did not work, they were not kept. Now, except for a few farm animals and creatures kept by their masters for security, dogs are consumption items.

A similar change is evident with children, if you will allow the comparison. When society was primarily rural and agricultural, children were an important source of labor; they also were a sort of social security for their parents. Few children today perform either of those functions; they represent instead a very expensive and time-consuming form of consumption. This helps explain why more young couples are limiting their families; they cannot afford not to. More properly, they prefer to vary their consumption rather than taking it all in the form of children.

What is happening, then, is that people are consuming more, not less, but they are also consuming differently. They are much more sophisticated in their consumption. There is no reason to assume that these trends will not continue into the future. The opposite can be expected—there is every reason to suspect that the trends will become more pronounced. Abba Lerner proved remarkably perceptive about the world of the 1980s when he suggested:

> Perhaps the only possibility of a state of plenty lies not in the increase of goods, but in the reduction of wants. If a culture of simple living on Gandhian lines should be universalized, it might indeed be possible to provide fully for the requirements of all. [3, p. 266]

On the face of it, that might not seem very probable. Despite the interest in Eastern religions, it is unlikely that many people are going to begin living like Indian ascetics. If, however, you substitute *re-direction* for "reduction" and interpret "Gandhian lines" to mean a *concern with the quality of life*, then the possibility seems much less remote.

Despite present trends, some might argue that things will not work out this way. They can point to examples of self-indulgent consumption that suggest a much less promising future. However, it is not a question of the continuation of the consumer society in its traditional form versus the sort of transition discussed here. If the trends identified here do not assert themselves and gain ascendancy, the mass-consumption society is in serious trouble. If mass consumption cannot adjust to both the needs of individuals and the realities of world resources, then it is surely doomed. Those who lack a taste for apocalyptic visions will see that there is really no alternative. It is not an *either-or* matter, but rather *if-then*. If the adjustments that are already under way continue, then the prospects for the future are encouraging indeed; if not, there is little reason for optimism.

Here, again, perspective is important. It is easy to get carried away with dreams of bright or dismal tomorrows. The typical consumer, however, does not think about such things very much. Most of us are small thinkers most of the time. Even college professors, who have more time for such reflections than most people, are preoccupied with mundane questions of tenure, raises, or how to pay for braces on the children's teeth. This is probably a good thing. As people quietly go about the business of living their own lives, they may unobtrusively come to many of the same conclusions outlined here. As they do, the accumulation of small, subtle changes will produce a significant alteration in modern society. That may be the ultimate significance of the consumer revolt. "It is," to close with Galbraith's words, "a revolution not in economic forms, but in values" [8, pp. 71–72].

Study Questions

1. One of the great themes of American history has been the democratization of areas that were previously the reserve of elites. Thus, art and literature broadened their appeal to serve a mass audience. The widespread concern with the quality and significance of life represents a continuation of this trend. Can you give any other examples of this process? What is the significance of such developments for the consumer society?

2. Occupational fields like journalism, the law, and teaching, which offer flexibility and some freedom from routine, are becoming increasingly popular. Explain this development in terms of this chapter. What changes will this bring about in other types of employment?

3. In Chapter 1, recent reactions to materialism were described as *conspicuous nonconsumption*. That is not entirely accurate. Why?

4. In *Porgy and Bess,* Porgy sings, "I've got plenty of nothing, and nothing's plenty for me." Would most people agree with that? If nothing is not plenty, what is?

5. People who are unemployed typically expend a great deal of effort searching for jobs that will reduce the leisure time they have. If they are successful, they will then spend equal amounts of effort to eke out a bit more leisure. Does this sort of behavior make any sense? Explain.

6. One worker to another on Monday morning: "I'm glad to get back to work so I can recover from the weekend." Comment.

7. A century ago, workers were pressing for a 60-hour work week and a 12-hour workday.
   a. Can you compare what leisure meant to workers then with what it means to today's workers?
   b. There has been an obvious explosion of leisure time in the last 100 years. Why, then, should leisure remain such a scarce commodity?

8. In mid-1974, the Japanese finance minister said that Japan would have to lower its growth rate to avoid increased criticism for depleting world resources. In what way is that a historic comment? Could it have been made a generation ago? Discuss.

9. The world of the future, as science fiction portrays it, features a computerized life of leisure. What would be the value of leisure under such conditions? Would work—any work—be valued differently from the way it is now valued?

10. Indicate how the manner in which consumers value time shapes their entire consumption pattern.

11. New consumption forms, like traditional ones, may contain internal contradictions. Thus, the peace and quiet of a remote cabin hideway may be highly valued, but if everyone sought such a refuge, the countryside would be overrun. Is there any way around this kind of problem? Discuss.

12. The coming years are not going to be easy ones for consumers. What sorts of people are going to find the adjustment most difficult? Is there any way these difficulties can be eased?

13. Do you think changes in consumption patterns will make public goods more or less important? Explain. Will changes in the composition of private consumption also call for new forms of public consumption? Discuss.

Bibliography and Suggested Readings

1. Baran, Paul. "A Marxist View of Consumer Sovereignty." In *The Political Economy of Growth*. New York: Monthly Review Press, 1957.

2. Becker, Gary. "A Theory of the Allocation of Time." *The Economic Journal*, September 1965, pp. 493–517.
   Along with Linder [12], this article represents the starting point for students interested in the question of the allocation of time. The analytical going gets a bit heavy at times, but students should still find it useful and insightful.

3. Bell, Daniel. *The Cultural Contradictions of Capitalism*. New York: Bantam Books, 1976.
   A distinguished sociologist takes a look at modern American culture and finds that the parts don't fit together very well. Bell's idea of disjucture suggests that one part of the individual's life may not make sense in terms of another. A thoughtful reexamination of our basic assumptions about mass consumption .

4. *Ecclesiastes*, in *The New English Bible*. New York: Oxford University Press, 1971.
   One of the most thoughtful, and many feel most beautiful, books in the Old Testament. The questions it raises are at once timely and timeless.

5. Ewen, Stuart. *Captains of Consciousness*. New York: McGraw-Hill Book Co., 1976.
   A somewhat radical look at mass consumption, with emphasis on the role of advertising and the media. The author suggests that consumers are being manipulated in a thorough going fashion. Contains some good historical material.

6. Galbraith, John Kenneth. *The Affluent Society*. Boston: Houghton Mifflin Co., 1958.
   In the context of this chapter, it is clear that Galbraith understood the process of affluence before most people were aware of it. A good starting point for anyone interested in the topic.

7. ———. *Economics and the Public Purpose*. Boston: Houghton Mifflin Co., 1973.
   Galbraith continues the line of thought developed in his earlier work. As the title implies, he is not convinced that the public interest and the interest of the economy as currently organized are the same.

8. ———. As interviewed in *Forces*, no. 22, 1973, pp. 71–75.
   Reflections by Galbraith in this Canadian journal.

9. Gintis, Herbert. "Consumer Behavior and the Concept of Sovereignty: Explanations of Social Decay." *American Economic Review, Papers and Proceedings*, 62 (May 1972):267–78.
   A radical economist looks at the alienated consumer.

10. Hirst, I. R., and Reekie, W. D., eds. *The Consumer Society*. London: Tavistock Publications, 1977.
    The book contains a series of original articles on aspects of the consumer society from a British perspective. Topics range from public and private consumption through advertising to housing. Thus, coverage is similar to topics discussed here. Worth looking at.

11. Katona, George, Strumpel, B., and Zahn, D. *Aspirations and Affluence*. New York: McGraw-Hill Book Co., 1971.
    An excellent comparative study of trends in consumption patterns and consumer expectations in Europe and the United States. Some of the descriptive data are dated now, but the book remains one of the best sources available on the subject.

12. Linder, Staffan B. *The Harried Leisure Class*. New York: Columbia University Press, 1970.
    Essential for anyone interested in how time affects consumers and consumption. A readable, enjoyable account, including numerous discussions and illustrations of basic points. Recommended for anyone who has ever wondered why there isn't enough time for anything.

13. Lerner, Abba P. "The Politics and Economics of Consumer Sovereignty," *American Economic Review, Papers and Proceedings* 62 (May 1972):258–66.

14. Morgan, Edmund S. *The Puritan Dilemma*. Boston: Little, Brown and Co., 1958.
    This book is a little classic. It covers the life of John Winthrop, one of the founders of Massachusetts Bay Colony. That may seem like a long way from mass consumption, but Morgan emphasizes that the Puritans

had a clear perspective on consumption. Their view helps in understanding our problems today.

15. Murphy, Patrick E. "A Cost-Benefit Analysis of the Oregon 'Bottle Bill.' " In *Consumerism.* eds. David A. Aaker and George S. Day, 3rd ed. New York: The Free Press, 1978.
An analysis that suggests that Oregon's ban on nonreturnable bottles has been a success. The other readings in this volume are valuable, covering a wide range of consumer issues.

16. Myrdal, Gunnar. *An International Economy.* New York: Harper & Row, 1969.
A sympathetic treatment of the problems of less-developed countries by the noted Swedish economist. Myrdal has continually emphasized the policy implications of international income variations.

17. Scitovsky, Tibor. *The Joyless Economy.* New York: Oxford University Press, 1976.
A detailed look at human satisfaction and contemporary lifestyle by a noted economic theorist. As the title suggests, he thinks something has gone wrong. The book is nontechnical. It is worth noting that only a few years ago, economists showed little interest in such topics.

18. Terkel, Studs. *Working.* New York: Pantheon Books, 1974.
Studs Terkel's account of "people talking about what they do all day and how they feel about it." The book suggests that most people feel their jobs are a bore, which in turn shows why more and more people are seeking on-the-job satisfaction. Good reading.

19. Zahn, Ernest. "The Consumer Society: Unstinted Praise and Growing Criticism." In *Human Behavior in Economic Affairs,* ed. Burkhard Strumpel, et al. San Francisco: Jossey-Bass, 1972, pp. 433–51.
A highly relevant paper in terms of this chapter. Especially strong in tracing intellectual attitudes toward the consumer society in the past quarter century. As good a summary of the question as there is available.

Appendix

As mentioned in the Preface, the projects included at the end of the chapters are based on the idea of the marketplace as a laboratory. All students are consumers, and the projects are intended to relate their daily problems to the material covered in the text. In this relation, the projects show theory in action and stress applying concepts to real-world conditions.

If one includes controlled conditions in the definition of a laboratory, the market does not serve very well. So many different forces are at work in the marketplace that they are difficult to isolate. The variation leads to all the methodological problems with which researchers in the social sciences are so painfully familiar. The projects in this book will provoke problems. Many of them involve sampling or surveys, subjects that in themselves provide sufficient material for several courses. In using these projects myself, I have found two successful approaches. The size and complexion of the class must determine the proper response.

The first is to meet the problems head on, dealing with them as one would in a scientific, professional paper. This requires concentrating on a few projects and developing them in depth. It also assumes either that students have a background in sampling and testing techniques or that they are willing to do a great deal of extra work. This approach is more difficult in a large class, but under the right conditions and with the right students, it can be rewarding.

Most of us, however, work most of the time under conditions that are not ideal and with students who are not expert at these procedures. These facts of life argue for an alternative approach. The alternative requires a flexible attitude, beginning with the recognition that the projects are not going to provide definitive results or break new scientific sod. Such was not the intention for the projects anyway. The efforts can nonetheless uncover interesting trends and provide significant insights, without meeting all the requirements that might be set for a Ph.D. dissertation.

The projects are, above all, a learning tool. They are meant to involve the students, give them experience in the field, and provide a basis for discussion. Being overly rigorous may actually detract from these goals. That is not an invitation to be sloppy and careless; it means the projects should be evaluated in terms of what they are intended to do. The results cannot be treated as definitive and must be interpreted with care, but they can provide a basis for discussion and be a means either to underscore key points or to draw out new ones. In most cases, the projects are best viewed as preliminary investigations. As such, they can be most valuable.

Perhaps what is more important, they can also be enjoyable. My experience has been that students respond very well to these challenges. Most seem to welcome the opportunity to take their education beyond the classroom and into the real world. As they do, they show remarkable initiative and imagination. Carrying out the projects may be as valuable as the results obtained. The students, in wrestling with designing questions and conducting surveys, gain a significant appreciation of both the issues and problems involved. For many, it may be their first real research experience, and while not many will win their wings, most will enjoy trying.

Several practical hints are worth passing along. When possible, it is useful to sample different groups. These can include groups of students, neighbors, or randomly selected individuals. It is not necessary to worry overmuch about being truly scientific, but it is worth trying to get a representative survey. How questions are designed is very important. Simple straightforward questions are the best. In most cases, however, it is also useful if people will just discuss the question in general terms. Impressions collected in this way can be most valuable. It goes without saying that tact is required in personal contacts. That is equally true of the price surveys and comparative-price projects. Merchants are often not humored by such efforts. There is nothing wrong, however, with simply going in and asking about prices as any customer would. This is probably the best approach to take.

Problems are not likely to be significant, except in the case of the comparison of prices in low-income and other areas suggested in Chapter 9. Not only are the methodological problems more significant in this case, but in many areas the issue has become hypersensitive. Thus, considerable discretion may be required; the instructor can decide what approach to take, according to local conditions.

The projects included in the text are merely illustrative. Individual instructors can think up their own projects according to local opportunities and the interests of the class. Students can also contribute their ideas. There is no shortage of possibilities. No projects were included for Chapters 2 and 12, but some opportunities exist and instructors may wish to devise their own.

The manner in which the projects are used depends on the individual instructor. I have found it useful for students to carry out the project, report it to the class, and lead the discussion that follows. In this way, it is possible to build the class session around the projects. This takes time and creates certain organizational problems, but it is worth the effort. With big classes, that procedure may not be practical. It might then be advisable to make the projects optional, have reports on only selected projects, or have the projects written up but not reported to the class. The projects could even be a basis for discussion without actually being carried out.

Our clarification has concentrated on projects that involve surveys or actually going out into the marketplace. Some projects concern other aspects, either library research or reviews of local laws and institutions. These present fewer methodological and practical problems, but are no less useful.

Suggested projects in some of the last chapters of the book mention using resource persons from the community in the class. There is an obvious danger here; those who have yawned their way through such talks are well aware of it. For that reason, prior contact is advisable. However, if such persons are carefully chosen and presented, they can make a valuable contribution to the class. There are increasing numbers of competent, well-trained, and dedicated people serving in the consumer area. Their experiences and perspectives can be most useful. In most cases, they are only too willing to have the opportunity to air their views.

It may be that once the project approach itself has been accepted, the details are not particularly important. Most instructors can work them out for themselves according to the specific conditions. The idea of using the market as a laboratory is important, however. It expands the scope of the course and provides a unique opportunity to integrate classroom material with experience. Some instructors might want to cooperate with a local consumer protection group. Others might want to develop a unified theme throughout the semester. All will find as I have found, that projects can give the course personality and can focus classroom activities.

Index